On This Day in History

LEONARD AND THELMA SPINRAD

REVISED BY

ANISTATIA R MILLER & JARED M. BROWN

PRENTICE HALL PRESS

Printed in the United States of America

10 9 8 7 6 5 4 3 2 1

ISBN 0-7352-0064-5

 PRENTICE HALL PRESS

A Simon & Schuster Company

On the World Wide Web at http://www.phdirect.com

Prentice Hall International (UK) Limited, *London*
Prentice Hall of Australia Pty. Limited, *Sydney*
Prentice Hall Canada, Inc., *Toronto*
Prentice Hall Hispanoamericana, S.A., *Mexico*
Prentice Hall of India Private Limited, *New Delhi*
Prentice Hall of Japan, Inc., *Tokyo*
Simon & Schuster Asia Pte. Ltd., *Singapore*
Editora Prentice Hall do Brasil, Ltda., *Rio de Janeiro*

Introduction

Every successful article, essay, and speech seems to begin with a hook: initial words that catch and reel in the audience's attention. Taking note of a timely anniversary, notable historical event, pertinent holiday, or an eloquent quote spoken on a particular day is always an effective way to attract an audience to the main message. Why? Because the pages of history are filled with points to ponder. Events which lead to larger questions, and can provide great insights into society, human nature, and the human condition.

From an historical viewpoint, every single day of the year is special, marking the anniversaries of history's grand and subtle turning points. This volume is a compendium of more than 1,725 important national and international incidents, anniversaries, holidays, and other observances.

These catalogued moments range from the celebratory to the solemn, from the momentous to the humorous. On June 8, for example, architect Frank Lloyd Wright was born; former U.S. president Dwight D. Eisenhower addressed the National Governors' Conference, pressing for better state government as an antidote for bigger national government; U.S. forces were authorized to go into combat in South Vietnam; the suction vacuum cleaner was patented; and the mail didn't get through. This was the day the U.S. Postal Service made its first-and last-attempt at "missile mail." On June 8, 1959, a guided missile was launched from the U.S.S. *Barbero* naval submarine. And faster than a speeding bullet, it veered off course taking its payload of 3,000 stamped letters straight to the ocean floor.

On December Seventeenth, the Wright Brothers made their first flight, and the U.S. Air Force discontinued Project Blue Book, concluding that there was no evidence of UFOs. Two great communicators, Arthur Fiedler, conductor of the Boston Pops, and *New York Times* columnist William Safire were born. And the NBA's most lopsided game finished when Cleveland beat Miami 148 to 80.

The accompanying background material is equally engaging. For example: "What is a momentous occasion? It is an event which is a landmark at that moment in time. For example, it was on this day in 1987, that the Dow Jones industrial average closed above 2,000 points for the first time. Since then the stock market has seen rises more than fourfold above that amount, making it seem tiny in retrospect."

But history is much more than a simple series of isolated incidents. We've cross-referenced many of these events with corresponding relevant dates so that you may find related and supporting material found on other days. July 16th, for example, was the day the Nixon tapes were revealed. The entry also directs you to see the data listed under January 4, 1974: the day President Nixon refused the U.S. Senate Watergate Committee's subpoenas. January 4th is cross-referenced to June Seventeenth, 1972-the day of the Watergate break-in. That entry, in turn, refers you to February 7, 1973: the day the U.S. Senate voted to form the Watergate Investigative Committee.

Broader, less time-specific subjects, often relate to particular months. *On This Day in History* also contains an overview for each month of the year which selectively sums up the period's most momentous events, binding them into a cohesive chain.

Don't forget. Looking up a particular day doesn't rule out tomorrow or another day as an inspirational source. Today is only the eve of the next day; and a fortnight is only two weeks away. But don't stop there. Check the local newspapers for the past five years. Surf the Internet for a particular subject. And you'll never run out of timely information if you supplement your reading with events that originated in your own back yard. After all, these entries are finite-limited by this book's publication date. But history never stops happening. New, noteworthy events occur daily, providing even more inspiration. If you keep your eyes open for late-breaking news, and page through this volume, you'll never be lacking timely information again.

January

Springing forward seems to be the theme of this first month of the year, even though spring is still a few months away. Caesar crossed the Rubicon River in January; and Queen Victoria admitted she wasn't amused. Oscar Wilde declared nothing but his genius; and the U.S. government declared a war on the "demon alcohol" by passing the Eighteenth Amendment.

1st.

New Year's Day.

1735 Birthdays of three American Revolutionary heroes: silversmith Paul Revere (1735), flag maker Betsy Ross (1752), General "Mad" Anthony Wayne, (1745).

1808 The U.S. Congress officially prohibited African slave trade.

1831 *The Liberator* was first published.

1863 President Lincoln issued the Emancipation Proclamation.

1898 Brooklyn merged with Manhattan.

1905 The Trans-Siberian Railway started its maiden voyage.

1909 Barry Goldwater was born.

1935 The colonies of Cyrenaica, Tripoli, and Eezaan united to form the country of Libya.

1942 Twenty-six nations signed the United Nations Declaration. (See January 9th and October 24th entries.)

Some notable American patriots were born on New Year's Day. Paul Revere, the Bostonian silversmith who rallied American colonists to arms against the arriving British troops; Betsy Ross, maker of the new nation's banner; and General "Mad" Anthony Wayne, who led the charge on many British garrisons, were all born on this day. An outspoken spokesperson for Republican conservatism, Arizona state senator Barry Goldwater, was also a New Year's child.

New Year's is a day of both new beginnings and a day of renewed commitment to beliefs. Some great Americans have pronounced their views on this day that no man can own another. In 1863, President Lincoln issued his Emancipation Proclamation. It reinforced Congress' prohibition of African slave trade which occurred on the same day in 1808. In the first issue of his anti-slavery periodical, *The Liberator*, published on this day in 1832, William Lloyd Garrison proclaimed: "I am in earnest. I will not equivocate; I will not excuse; I will not retreat a single inch; and I will be heard."

New Year's Day offers an opportunity to cast aside differences and resolve to renew alliances. On this day in 1898, the boroughs of Brooklyn and Manhattan merged to create Greater New York. The Trans-Siberian Railway started on its maiden voyage on this day in 1905, joining a continent. The route united far away Vladivostok, Manchuria, with the world's culture capital—Paris, France. And in 1935, the North African colonies of Cyrenaica, Tripoli, and Eezaan united to form the country of Libya. In 1942, this feeling of unity was felt worldwide when twenty-six nations signed the United Nations Declaration in Washington, D.C.

2nd.

1492   The Spanish army took the city of Granada from the Moors.

1900   Queen Victoria declared, "We are not amused." (See January 22nd, February 10th, May 24th, and June 20th entries.)

1968   The first successful human heart transplant operation was performed.

1990   The Dow Jones Industrial Average rose above the 2,800 mark. (See January 8th and November 14th entries.)

Many other figures throughout history could, no doubt, agree with the attitude voiced by Queen Victoria on this second day of the year in 1900, when she regally declared, "We are not amused." Certainly the Moors would have agreed with her in 1492, when on this date, the Spanish army took their beloved city of Granada. Looking back at those times, the present seems infinitely simpler. Everything and nothing is shocking or unexpected these days. The modern world's collective attitude could probably be summed up by saying: "We are not amazed." The world may now be characterized by escalating prices, but it's also elevated by great accomplishments. Dr. Christian Barnard achieved the unthinkable on this date in 1968. He performed the first successful human heart transplant operation, capturing the world's imagination and opening a whole new medical frontier. And on the business front, this was the day, in 1990, when the Dow Jones Industrial Average topped the 2,800 mark for the first time in its history.

3rd.

Congress usually convenes on or about this date.

106 BC Cicero was born.

1521 Martin Luther was excommunicated. (See October 31st and November 10th entries.)

1833 The British seized control of the Falkland Islands.

1882 Oscar Wilde told U.S. customs officials: "I have nothing to declare but my genius."

1938 The March of Dimes was organized.

1959 Alaska was given statehood.

1961 The United States severed relations with Cuba. (See January 7th entry.)

It may be coincidental that Cicero's birthday occurs around the time when the U.S. Congress convenes in Washington D.C. Today's Senate or House of Representatives may not be oversupplied with golden voices like Cicero's, but it is safe to say that the nation has more voices, more issues, and probably more listeners. At least modern-day radicals, dissidents, and protesters can expect to be received more gently than Martin Luther, who on this day in 1521, was excommunicated by the Roman Catholic Church for speaking his mind.

When Alaska was given statehood on this day in 1959, it was the first time the U.S. admitted a territory outside of the forty-eight contiguous states. This is also the day when, in 1833, the British seized control of the Falkland Islands off the southern-most tip of South America. There is no telling what borders will change or who will lay claim to a given possession in the not-so-distant future. But no matter where the border lies, it's advisable to avoid Oscar Wilde's state of mind when, on this very day in 1882, he said to U.S. Customs officials upon his arrival in New York, "I have nothing to declare but my genius."

There comes a time when people who have much in common disagree so violently they sever all ties to each other. This was the case in 1521, when Martin Luther, a man devoted to the purity of religious faith, was excommunicated by the Roman Catholic Church, the flagship of Christianity. Luther strongly protested a certain laxness that had become apparent amongst the clergy and the faithful, while the Church strongly objected to his criticisms. Also on this day, in 1961, the United States severed its relations with Cuba. American troops had fought for the island nation's freedom during the Spanish-American War, but the U.S., acting on strong anti-Communist feelings, sanctioned Castro's anti-imperialist government by refusing to trade or communicate—even though the island nation had officially recognized its new leader and government two years earlier.

The March of Dimes, an organization dedicated to fighting polio, a crippling disease that has affected millions worldwide, was organized on this date in 1938. An out-growth of President Franklin Delano Roosevelt's Warm Springs Foundation, the March of Dimes asks everyone to contribute what they can—a nickel, a dime, or a dollar—toward research, prevention, and treatment.

4th.

1642	Sir Isaac Newton was born.
1813	Shorthand inventor Sir Isaac Pitman was born.
1885	First successful appendectomy was performed.
1974	President Nixon rejected the Senate Watergate Committee's subpoenas. (See June 17th entry.)

It's Sir Isaac Newton's birthday. Born in 1642, in Woolsthorpe, England, Newton grew up to have an apple fall on his head. This simple event inspired him. He discovered the law of gravity—simply, what goes up must come down. In 1885, Dr. William West Grant of Davenport, Iowa, proved on this day that what must come out can come out. In 1885, he performed the first successful appendectomy, and proved for the first time that man could live without an appendix. This proof that a slightly abbreviated digestive system was still fully functional might have pleased one man born on this day in 1813, Sir Isaac Pitman, inventor of the Pitman shorthand system.

When First Lady Nancy Reagan began her famous "Just Say No!" campaign, she certainly did not have in mind an event which took place in the Capitol years earlier. It was on this day, in 1974, that President Richard M. Nixon said no to the U.S. Senate Watergate subcommittee's subpoenas. The subcommittee had requested copies of the President's White House tapes and documents so they could review his actions prior to the Watergate break-in.

5th.

Twelfth Night.

1759 Voltaire said, "Opinion has caused more trouble on this little earth than plagues or earthquakes."

1895 Wilhelm Roentgen discovered the x-ray. (See March 27th entry.)

1914 Henry Ford announced a $5 minimum wage for an eight-hour workday.

1943 George Washington Carver died. (George Washington Carver Day)

1964 Pope Paul VI and Patriarch Athengoras of Jerusalem met in the Holy Land.

Today marks Twelfth Night—the end of the Christmas season. It is easy to feel that in this era of shop-till-you-drop consumerism, Twelfth Night doesn't come soon enough. But today brings inspiration of its own. With its roots deep in Western European history, Twelfth Night is traditionally celebrated with festive humor, lighthearted jests, and good cheer.

George Washington Carver Day commemorates the death, in 1943, of a onetime slave who became a great inventor. Carver proved that the American dream isn't—or maybe is—peanuts. He gave the world a hundred and one uses for the humble goober, proving that even simple or common things can provide solutions to greater problems.

Automobile mogul Henry Ford started a trend on this day in 1914. He announced the establishment of two relatively revolutionary concepts for their time: an eight-hour workday and a $5-a-day minimum wage. As with many new ideas, most people thought he was crazy, heretical, or subversive. Though he proved them wrong in the end, words can become the toughest challenges for anyone with new ideas to overcome. As Voltaire said on this very day in 1759, "Opinion has caused more trouble on this little earth than plagues or earthquakes." However, one meeting which took place on this date in 1964, illustrates that no difference of opinion needs to permanently sever relations between people who share a common goal. This was the day when, for the first time in five centuries, the Roman Catholic Church met with the Eastern Orthodoxy. Pope Paul VI and Patriarch Athengoras of Jerusalem met in the Holy Land, ending the long-held belief that simply because they celebrated their Christianity in different ways, they had nothing in common.

6th.

Three Kings Day (Feast of the Epiphany).

Greek Cross Day.

1412   Joan of Arc was born.

1854   Sherlock Holmes was allegedly born.

1941   President Franklin D. Roosevelt made his "Four Freedoms" speech.

1942   Pan Am Airlines completed the first around-the-world commercial flight.

Three Kings Day—also known as the Feast of the Epiphany—is a gift-giving holiday in many parts of the world. Many residents of Tarpon Springs, Florida, and New York City celebrate today as Greek Cross Day. Devoutly religious men jump into the waters to retrieve Orthodox crosses in an ancient and always exciting combination of piety meets Polar Bear Club.

There's more to life than living in the present. To live to the fullest, and to achieve greatness, it is necessary to have vision. They don't have to be as grand as Joan of Arc's, but today is Joan of Arc's birthday. The Maid of Orleans' visions changed the fate of an entire nation and its leader. Today's visions are often tomorrow's realities. When President Franklin D. Roosevelt addressed the U.S. Congress on this day in 1941, he voiced his vision of "a world founded upon four essential freedoms: freedom of speech and expression, freedom of every person to worship God in his own way, freedom from want, [and] freedom from fear."

The freedom to travel anywhere in the world expanded its horizons on this date in 1942. That's when a Pan Am passenger plane completed the first around-the-world commercial flight.

This is the birthday of one of the most famous men who never lived. Here's an elementary clue my dear Watson: throughout the world, people have enjoyed his exploits, his brilliance, and his talent at deducing solutions. Yes, Sherlock Holmes was allegedly born on this day in 1854, according to his creator Sir Arthur Conan Doyle who fashioned the personality of the world's first consulting detective from one of his favorite teachers in medical school.

7th.

1782   The first commercial American bank, the Bank of North America, opened.

1830   The Baltimore & Ohio Railroad Company began rail service.

1913   A cracking process to obtain gasoline from crude oil was patented.

1953   President Harry S Truman announced that the U.S. had developed a hydrogen bomb.

1959   The United States recognized Fidel Castro's Cuban government.

1968   *Surveyor VII* landed on the moon, 1968.

1978   President Jimmy Carter said he favored a referendum on the future of Palestinians living in the Gaza Strip and West Bank. (See March 3rd entry.)

This is the anniversary of a few newfangled ideas. In 1830, The Baltimore & Ohio Railroad Company started operating out of Baltimore, Maryland. Believe it or not, the first American train was drawn by a team of horses. But nothing can keep a good idea down, and before long the country was linked by railroad tracks. In 1968, another transportation milestone was reached when the manned spaceship *Surveyor VII* landed on the moon.

Doing business strictly in cash is difficult and dangerous, especially if you want to expand your interests beyond your local area. When American businessmen decided to open an institution that could help them trade and negotiate with the rest of the world, they took a giant step toward national economic independence. The first commercial American bank, the Bank of North America, opened in Philadelphia, Pennsylvania, on this day in 1782.

The paths to many different forms of freedom can be equally explosive. It was on this date, in 1913, that William M. Burton of Chicago, Illinois, was given a patent for a cracking process that enabled him to obtain gasoline from crude oil. From one end of the globe to the other, his idea changed the way the world moves. Today, the world may not always appreciate the ultimate consequences of Mr. Burton's discovery, but it wasn't his concept that was the problem. It's the way in which it was used by others. For the same reasons, President Harry S Truman might have heeded sounder advice before he announced the U.S. development of a hydrogen bomb on this same date in 1953, had he been privy to the future consequences of building a better bomb.

The fruits of the actions taken did not bear what their authors had anticipated. It was on this date in 1959 that the United States recognized Fidel Castro's government in Cuba. And it was on this very day, in 1978, that President Jimmy Carter announced that he favored a referendum on the future of Palestinians living in the Israeli-held Gaza Strip and West Bank.

8th.

1815 Battle of New Orleans took place.

1935 Elvis Presley was born.

1942 Stephen Hawking was born.

1947 David Bowie was born.

1964 President Lyndon B. Johnson declared an "unconditional war on poverty in America."

1982 American Telephone and Telegraph (AT&T) was divested.

1987 The Dow Jones industrial average closed above 2,000 for the first time, ending the day at 2,002.25. (See January 2nd and November 14th entries.)

This day is not wisely celebrated as Battle of New Orleans Day. Some of us might not even know that Andrew Jackson defeated the British army, on this day in 1815, on what is now unquestionably American soil. The War of 1812 was already over. But this battle was fought because neither side got the news in time.

Perhaps it's part of human nature that life is too often viewed as a battleground. Even so, there are times when the cause is just, and it should be an all-out combat zone. In 1964, during the Vietnam War, President Lyndon B. Johnson declared on this day an "unconditional war on poverty in America."

When you look to the stars, what do you see? Today is a good day to ponder this. Two people born on January 8th set their sights skyward and came away with their fortunes;

but what's amazing is how different their farsighted perceptions were. One was Stephen Hawking, the physicist and author who managed to explain astrophysical concepts to the common man in his text *A Brief History of Time*. The other is rock musician David Bowie, whose songs about space travel and alien life hold strong parallels to the alienation and loneliness felt by each of us at one time or another. These men also share their birthday with a star. Elvis Presley, born in 1935. Presley faced controversy of his own when his career began. However, his wasn't up in the stars; it was below the belt. His on-stage gyrations were considered so obscene at the time that when he debuted on the *Ed Sullivan Show*, the camera showed him from the waist up.

The final bell tolled for an American monopoly on this day in 1982, when AT&T settled the U.S. Justice Department's anti-trust lawsuit against it by breaking up its conglomerate, divesting itself of twenty-two regional Bell System companies.

9th.

1522   Adrian of Utrecht became Pope Adrian VI.

1770   William Pitt, the elder, proclaimed: "Where law ends, tyranny begins—Unlimited power is apt to corrupt the minds of those who possess it."

1913   President Richard M. Nixon was born.

1945   American forces invaded the Philippine island of Luzon. (See October 20th entry.)

1951   United Nations headquarters opened. (See January 1st and October 24th entries.)

1972   Howard Hughes held a telephone news conference. (See March 13th entry.)

It is surprising how time can sometimes jump a century or two, and past words or events can gain new impact. Today is such a day. In 1951, the United Nations headquarters opened in New York City. And in 1913, President Richard M. Nixon was born. But before these two events changed the way we envision world politics and world leadership, in 1770, William Pitt, the elder, told the British House of Lords: "Where law ends, tyranny begins" and "Unlimited power is apt to corrupt the minds of those who possess it."

History can be fickle. Normally it singles out great achievers for notoriety over time. But sometimes it simply takes being one of a kind. This was the case with Adrian of Utrecht, who became Pope Adrian VI in 1522. This is the anniversary of the consecration of the only Dutch pontiff in history. Adrian VI was also the last non-Italian pope for over four hundred years.

Someone once said it's just human nature that promises are made to be broken. But today marks the anniversary of a promise fulfilled. U.S. Army General Douglas MacArthur had promised the Philippine people he would return to rescue them from the oppression of Japanese occupation. In October 1944, he stepped on the shore of Leyte just as he had promised. But it was on this date, in 1945, that he fulfilled his vow as American forces invaded the main island of Luzon, rescuing the country's capital.

The truth sometimes comes from unexpected sources. And when the truth came from the voice of eccentric billionaire recluse, Howard Hughes, the whole world listened. On this date in 1972, Hughes held a telephone news conference—the first he had granted in fourteen years. He officially denounced the fraudulent biography of his life in that interview. Its author, Clifford Irving, had made a fortune with the book, which he claimed to have written with Hughes. But Hughes branded the book and its author as fakes.

10th.

1738   Ethan Allen was born.

1901   The Texas oil boom started.

1946   The first manmade contact with the moon was established.

1978   Two Soviet cosmonauts were launched into space to dock with the *Salyut 6* research station.

1984   The U.S. and the Vatican re-established full diplomatic relations.

Today is American Revolutionary War commander Ethan Allen's birthday. Born on this day in 1738, Allen regarded himself primarily as an instrument of a supreme Being or will; and secondarily as a servant of the Continental Congress. He knew his priorities when he declared, "In the name of the great Jehovah and the Continental Congress. . . ." when he demanded the British surrender of Fort Ticonderoga.

We progress; we invest; we change. A valuable resource is simply one which someone has found a good use for. And on this day in 1901, oil was discovered in Beaumont, Texas. It ushered in an era of American prosperity as it introduced the world to a new energy source.

Each and every one of us should try to keep our lines of communication open. Regular, consistent interaction with friends, associates, and family members provides us with new insights. Communication cements all kinds of relationships. It's a good theme for today, since this is the anniversary of some monumental connections. In 1946, the first manmade contact with our nearest neighbor—the moon—was established when radar signals were bounced off the lunar surface. In 1978, two Soviet cosmonauts were launched into space to dock with the *Salyut 6* research station, creating an essential link between man and one of his creations. Even when links are broken, it doesn't mean they can't be mended. On this day in 1984, the U.S. and the Vatican re-established full diplomatic relations after 117 years of silence.

11th.

49 BC Caesar crossed the Rubicon River.

1569 Great Britain held its first lottery.

1755 Alexander Hamilton was born. (See July 11th and February 6th entries.)

1923 France and Belgium occupied the Ruhr Valley.

1935 Amelia Earhart became the first woman to fly solo across the Pacific. (She completed the flight on January 12th.)

1986 L. Douglas Wilder became Lieutenant Governor of Virginia. (See November 7th entry.)

A great personal life decision is sometimes described as "crossing the Rubicon." Today is the anniversary of the event which spawned the phrase: Roman emperor Julius Caesar's crossing of the Rubicon River. In 49 BC, Caesar committed himself irrevocably to war against Pompeii and the Roman Senate when he moved his troops into an offensive position from which there was no easy retreat. "The die is cast," he said.

Human destiny is at least in part what we ourselves make it. Amelia Earhart set out to do what no woman had ever done before on this day in 1935. She set out to fly across the Pacific Ocean—from Honolulu, Hawaii, to Oakland, California. She accomplished both her goal and her destiny one day later.

Take a good look at the face on a ten dollar bill today because it's Alexander Hamilton's birthday. His serves as a reminder that none of us really knows what lies ahead. Born on this day in 1755, this American Revolutionary War hero suffered a fate familiar to many of us. He was mortally wounded in a duel he fought against Aaron Burr.

Events have consequences that cannot be foreseen. Today is no exception. In 49 BC, Julius Caesar crossed the Rubicon River. In 1935, Amelia Earhart took a chance and became the first woman to fly from Hawaii to California. However, the consequences of the third event which took place on this day had broader repercussions than Caesar's conquest or Earhart's flight. In 1569 Great Britain held the world's first lottery in London's St. Paul's Cathedral.

Failing to keep a promise can have some drastic repercussions. Residents of a rural part of Germany discovered this simple truth firsthand in 1923, when France and Belgium occupied the Ruhr Valley after the German government failed to keep up its First World War reparation payments.

L. Douglas Wilder became Lieutenant Governor of Virginia on this day in 1986. What made this such a momentous occasion was that Wilder was the first African-American to become elected and sworn in as a Southern state official since the Civil War. Three years later, he became the nation's first elected African-American governor.

12th.

1737 John Hancock was born in Braintree, MA.

1773 First U.S. museum was established.

1876 Jack London was born in San Francisco, California.

1932 Mrs. Hattie Caraway became the first elected female U.S. senator. (Also see the January 11th Amelia Earhart entry.)

1990 Astronauts aboard the space shuttle *Columbia* retrieved an 11-ton floating science lab.

1994 President Bill Clinton signed an agreement to disarm the world's third largest nuclear arsenal.

There are some landmark anniversaries for American women worth mentioning today. In 1935, Amelia Earhart single-handedly conquered the Pacific Ocean by flying from Honolulu, Hawaii, to Oakland, California. And in 1932, Mrs. Hattie Caraway became the first woman elected to the U.S. Senate.

The nation's first public museum dedicated to the preservation of knowledge was founded in Charleston, South Carolina, on this day in 1773. The Charleston Museum was a pioneer effort in the great tradition of public service and education.

Signing one's "John Hancock" on an important document wouldn't mean much if, in 1737, John Hancock hadn't been born. He grew to become the first signer of the nation's Declaration of Independence. Unwavering dedication to his beliefs spurred him to make a big statement: he signed his name legibly so everyone could see that he stood by his convictions no matter what the cost.

It's John Griffith Chaney's birthday. He was born in San Francisco in 1876 to a roving astrologer and his spiritualist wife. John's life reads like the plot of a novel. He quit school at the age of fourteen and explored the San Francisco Bay area in a sloop. He rode the rails as a hobo and was even jailed for vagrancy. At the age of nineteen, he crammed a four-year high school course into one year and entered the University of California at Berkeley. After one year, he went on the road to seek his fortune in the 1897 Klondike gold rush. However, he didn't find his fortune until he began writing. But when he did, we all became richer for his efforts. We know him by his pen name—Jack London and his romantic adventure tales—like *Call of the Wild*, *White Fang*, and *To Build a Fire*—revolve around the elemental struggle for survival.

The world as we know it was saved not once, but twice, on this date in history. In 1990, American astronauts aboard the space shuttle *Columbia* retrieved an 11-ton floating science lab. It was a rescue mission that kept the faltering satellite from plunging to earth. Four years later, in 1994, President Bill Clinton settled an agreement to disarm the world's third largest nuclear arsenal in the Ukraine, saving the world from potential manmade decimation. The most imminent threats to mankind seem to be those produced by man. To quote a classic Pogo cartoon, "We have met the enemy and he is us."

13th.

1733 James Oglethorpe and 130 colonists arrived at Charleston, South Carolina.

1864 Stephen Foster died. (Stephen Foster Memorial Day)

1898 Émile Zola's article, "*J'accuse*," was published.

1966 Robert C. Weaver became the first African-American cabinet member.

1996 Michael Jordan became one of thirteen NBA players to accumulate at least 23,000 career points. (See February 17th and March 9th entries.)

To say that ideas are powerful is an understatement. Unlike chemical reactions or bombs, ideas that take root are capable of unlimited growth. Today, on this very day in 1898, the Parisian writer Émile Zola published an article entitled "*J'accuse*" (I accuse). It was written to defend Alfred Dreyfus, a French soldier who was being railroaded on treason charges. Zola's ideas aroused the emotions of France and the world. Before the case was over, not only was Captain Dreyfus vindicated, but the French government and military establishment were rocked to their heels and their attitudes drastically changed.

A gentle man died on this day in 1864 at Manhattan's Bellevue Hospital. He rocked no governments; roused no great pangs of conscience. Born in 1826 in Lawrenceville, Pennsylvania, Foster died at the age of thirty-eight—penniless. He simply wrote songs: musical images of the American South. Times change, and some of his lyrics are no longer considered politically correct. Yet he is most deservedly commemorated. This is Stephen Foster Memorial Day which is dedicated to the memory of the composer who wrote about the Swanee River; about the old folks at home; and about Jeannie with the light brown hair.

This seems to be a landmark day for successful beginnings. In 1733, James Oglethorpe and 130 colonists arrived at Charleston, South Carolina, on their way to settling what became the state of Georgia. But overcoming oppressive odds through courage and conviction is not limited to just this event. In 1966, Robert C. Weaver was appointed to the U.S. cabinet. President Lyndon Baynes Johnson made Weaver the Secretary of Housing and Urban Development. He was the first African-American to attain an executive-branch post.

On this day in 1996, in a showdown with the highly-touted Philadelphia 76ers rookie basketball player Jerry Stackhouse, Michael Jordan scored a game-high 48 points, making him one of thirteen NBA players in basketball history to accumulate at least 23,000 career points.

14th.

1639 Fundamental Orders of Connecticut were adopted.

1741 Benedict Arnold was born.

1794 The first successful, modern-day, Cesarean section was performed.

1875 Albert Schweitzer was born.

1914 Henry Ford started his first manufacturing assembly line.

1980 Iran's Revolutionary Council expelled all American news correspondents.

1994 U.S. President Bill Clinton and Russian President Boris Yeltsin signed the Kremlin accords.

Today is American traitor Benedict Arnold's birthday. Born in 1741, Arnold was a brave American Revolutionary soldier who decided to turn coat. But today is also the birthday of a man who symbolizes the good in human nature—service to one's fellow man, dedication, and sacrifice. In 1875, medical missionary, musician, and philosopher Dr. Albert Schweitzer was born in Kayersberg, Upper Alsace. The memory of these two men stands to remind us that human beings are not cast in a single mold. But we try as a society to reward good, and prevent evil. And in 1639, Americans developed a means of doing just that. The early settlers wrote a constitution entitled the Fundamental Orders of Connecticut. This document established a government by laws rather than by men.

Dr. Jesse Bennett of Edom, Virginia, performed the first successful modern-day Cesarean section on this day in 1794. What made this an even more monumental occasion was that he conducted this delicate surgery on his wife, bringing their new infant child into the world.

Henry Ford started his first manufacturing assembly line on this day in 1914. His concept of dividing labor into specialized activities executed by qualified people was not entirely new or original. But Ford was the first to widely apply the concept to the large-scale manufacturing process.

As a wise man once said: Might does not always make right. On this day in 1980, the Irani Revolutionary Council expelled all American news correspondents from the country. The Shiite Muslim government felt they had the might of religion on their side as they proclaimed a new national order that excluded any other country. But their only reward for their actions was the world's disapproval. On this same day in 1994, President Bill Clinton and President Boris Yeltsin signed Kremlin accords to stop aiming missiles at any nation. After nearly half a century of imposing might, two of the world's largest nations decided peaceful coexistence was truly right.

15th.

1870   The Democratic party was first represented as a donkey, in a *Harper's Weekly* cartoon by Thomas Nast. (See November 7th entry.)

1929   Reverend Dr. Martin Luther King, Jr. was born. (Martin Luther King, Jr. Day is celebrated on the Monday closest to this date.)

1929   Kellogg-Briand Pact was ratified by the U.S. Senate.

1943   The Pentagon, headquarters of the U.S. Department of Defense, was completed.

1967   The first Super Bowl was played as the Green Bay Packers of the National Football League defeated the Kansas City Chiefs of the American Football League.

1997   The crews of the U.S. space shuttle *Atlantis* and the Russian space station *Mir* celebrated together after succeeding in connecting their space crafts in orbit. (See June 29th entry.)

Man is a creature of hope. Back in 1929, the U.S. Senate ratified the Kellogg-Briand agreement for the peaceful settlement of international disputes. It was a general expression of hope following World War I—the war to end all wars. We know how well that worked! Ten years later the world was at war once again. However, on this same day in the same year, a man who dedicated his life to peace and equality, Dr. Martin Luther King, Jr., was born in Atlanta, Georgia.

We are creatures of competition. To struggle successfully and emerge victorious is a grand part of our human heritage. It was on this day in 1967, that America's greatest annual competition began when the National Football League's Green Bay Packers defeated the American Football League's Kansas City Chiefs. Unlike horse races, auto races, and Olympic events, however, there is only a winner and a loser in the Superbowl. There is no second place, despite the fact that both teams had to best the rest of the league to earn the right to be there, and both deserve the champion's laurels. In this respect, the grid iron has often been compared to the battlefield. It's an appropriate coincidence that this is also the anniversary of the completion of the United States' operational center for armed struggle. In 1943, construction was completed on the Pentagon, headquarters of the U.S. Department of Defense.

16th.

1853   André Michelin was born. (See December 29th entry.)

1883   The Pendleton Act went into effect.

1920   The Eighteenth Amendment to the U.S. Constitution went into effect. (See December 5th entry.)

1969   Soviet cosmonauts achieved the first link between two manned spacecraft while in orbit.

1975   The Commerce Department declared that the nation was in the worst recession since the Second World War.

1975   Former CIA head Richard Helms reported that the agency was involved in domestic spying.

1991   The Persian Gulf War began.

Experimentation, we are told, is the road to progress. Today we mark the anniversary of what was called a "noble experiment." It didn't work, but we like to think that it taught us something. The experiment was Prohibition. In 1920, the Eighteenth Amendment, which prohibited the importation and sale of alcohol, went into effect. It was abandoned thirteen years later when the Twenty-first Amendment made liquor legal again.

We thought we had solved the problem of governmental corruption by establishing a merit system of public employment. On this day in 1883, the Pendleton Act—which dictated the selection process employed by U.S. Civil Service—was made into law.

Our travels became much more comfortable than those of our forefathers who, for centuries, rode on roughshod cushionless, wood- or metal-rim wheels because of a person who was born in 1853. The original Michelin baby was born on this day. André Michelin grew up to become the French industrialist who first mass-produced rubber tires for automobiles.

Getting together for a common cause can sometimes be a complex maneuver. If you were one of the Soviet cosmonauts who achieved the first link between two manned spacecraft while orbiting around the earth on this date in 1969, you'd understand all too well how precarious a lofty goal can be. Luckily, most of us are willing to go to great lengths to communicate with each other to achieve these and less complex goals. The outcome is always better if we do. Otherwise, we could end up like the Iraqi army did on this day in 1991: after a five-month standoff with allied U.N. forces in Kuwait, the Persian Gulf War began with the bombing of military and industrial targets.

It may always be darkest before the dawn, but on this day in 1975, no one was sure if we'd ever see the light of day again. The Commerce Department declared that the nation was in the worst recession since the Second World War. And to add insult to injury, former CIA head Richard Helms reported to the U.S. Congress that the agency had been involved in domestic spying since the late 1950s because of an upsurge in radicalism.

17th.

46 AD St. Anthony the Abbot, died.

1706 Benjamin Franklin was born.

1871 Andrew Hallidie patented the cable car.

Benjamin Franklin, was born on this day in 1706 in Boston, Massachusetts. This American patriot is remembered as a writer, an inventor, a leader, a diplomat, and a publisher. He wrote in his publication, *Poor Richard's Almanac*, that: "A word to the wise is enough and many words won't fill a bushel."

Today is the feast day of St. Anthony the Abbot, the patron saint of animals. From horses and geese to cats and dogs, animals are formally blessed in churches on this day, in many parts of the world.

Life is often described as a battle: man against nature, man against beast, man against man. One story that began on this day, in 1871, can be viewed in this light. Andrew Hallidie patented the cable car. In 1869, this 33-year-old wire manufacturer watched a horse-drawn streetcar struggle up a steep hill in the rain. Determined to improve public transport in San Francisco, he finally installed the cable-car system two years later. The public laughed it off as "Hallidie's Folly." San Francisco has buses, subways, and cars now, but every time someone suggests discontinuing the cable cars, San Franciscans insist on keeping them.

18th.

1778   Captain James Cook discovered the Sandwich Islands.

1782   Daniel Webster was born.

1912   Captain Robert Scott reached the South Pole. (See December 14th entry.)

Today is Daniel Webster's birthday. Born in 1872, Webster was America's most awesome public orator. You may recall Stephen Vincent Benet's story, "The Devil and Daniel Webster," in which this eloquent speaker argued the case for a man's soul and won.

Being second best somehow has never meant quite what it should. This thought comes to mind today because on this date in 1912, a great explorer came in second and, was subsequently forgotten. This was the day when British explorer Captain Robert Scott reached the South Pole. It was a heroic feat, made even more memorable because Scott and his party died shortly after reaching their goal. But Scott's glory was greatly dimmed, because Roald Amundsen had reached the pole a month earlier—and he survived.

Polynesians had been inhabiting the Hawaiian islands since 400 AD. They had sailed from the Marquesa Islands and Tahiti to find a new paradise. But today's anniversary commemorates another discovery of these inhabited islands. In 1778, British explorer Captain James Cook landed on the Hawaiian Islands and renamed them after his mentor. He called them the Sandwich Islands—after the Earl of Sandwich. It got pretty confusing after that. The British called the island group one thing, while its royal kings referred to their land by another. But it was the Americans who later invaded Hawaii, staged a coup, and finally put an end to its sovereignty.

19th.

1736   James Watt was born.

1807   Robert E. Lee was born. (See April 9th entry.)

1825   Tin canning process for food was patented.

1839   Paul Cézanne was born.

1918   The Bolsheviks dissolved the Russian Constitutional Assembly. (See November 7th entry.)

1966   Indira Gandhi became prime minister of India. (See November 19th and June 6th entries.)

1983   The American Psychiatric Association urged a tightening of the rules for the use of the insanity plea in criminal trials.

Most of us are faced with an important decision at some point in our lives. But few of us ever have the kind of choices that were extended to Robert E. Lee, who was born on this day in 1807. He was offered the command of the Union Army. But he decided instead to become the Commander of the Confederate Army. People can find themselves in lost causes, but the nobility of the human spirit can somehow survive and triumph over defeat.

Some people and events stand as milestones in the chronicles of human progress. One such person is James Watt, who was born on this day in 1736. He saw how steam could be harnessed; and he actualized his thoughts by designing a steam engine. Since his time many other types of engines have been produced; but Watt inaugurated our machine-oriented age. Though his invention industrialized the industrialized world, it was not an overnight sensation. It had to prove itself more viable than other contemporary power sources like watermills, horses, and oxen.

Ezra Daggett and Thomas Kinsett. Their names are not household words; but their invention is in every household. In 1825, on this day, the Kinsetts of New York City patented a process for canning food in tin containers. They can be said to have pioneered the age of convenience for housewives and armies alike.

Some people are not affected by criticism. And Paul Cézanne, who was born on this day in 1839, was one of them. From the day he began to paint, he was severely criticized for the content and execution of his works. But he didn't give in to convention. He continued to search for bold expression rather than realistic representation. At the 1899 Salon des Independents in Paris, he finally achieved the acclaim he deserved. And as the century turned, Cézanne was considered to be the strongest influence on twentieth-century Cubist painters like Picasso and Georges Braque.

Though our society attempts to help rather than punish those who are found to be mentally impaired, in many cases there can be no simple litmus test to determine a person's sanity. On this day in 1983, the American Psychiatric Association urged a tightening of the rules for the use of the insanity plea in criminal trials.

20th.

1937 Presidential Inauguration Day.

1892 The first basketball game was played.

1896 George Burns was born.

Anyone who rises to communicate on this day does so in the shadow or the glory of some of the most noble phrases ever uttered, phrases spoken by men as they were inaugurated President of the United States. Since 1937, January 20th has been Presidential Inauguration Day. Franklin D. Roosevelt saw "one third of a nation ill-housed, ill-clad, ill-nourished"; John F. Kennedy urged his fellow Americans to "ask not what your country can do for you; ask what you can do for your country"; Harry S Truman observed that "the supreme need of our time is for men to learn to live together in peace and harmony"; and Dwight D. Eisenhower said that "whatever America hopes to bring to pass in the world must first come to pass in the heart of America."

In a Springfield, Massachusetts meeting hall, on this day in 1892, a YMCA worker named James Naismith introduced a great medium for international communication. It wasn't intended that way. Basketball was simply a game. But Naismith's game did not merely catch on. It took the world by storm. It is played everywhere—from alleys and schoolyards around the world to stadiums and Olympic courts.

Few people have ever lived for an entire century, but entertainer George Burns did. Born on this day in 1896, this native New Yorker kept audiences laughing for almost one hundred years. Even when asked about getting old, he managed to keep his sense of humor: "Well, my smoke rings aren't as big or as round as they used to be. In my Martinis I'm down from two olives to one."

21st.

1824   Stonewall Jackson was born.

1908   New York City prohibited women from smoking in public.

1950   Alger Hiss was convicted of perjury.

1954   First atomic-powered submarine was launched.

1976   The supersonic Concorde was put into service. (See November 22nd entry.)

Adversity is a school of hard knocks; but its alumni often shine. Today marks the birth, in 1824, of a man who symbolizes the integrity of stubborn courage. Thomas Jackson is better known as "Stonewall" Jackson. He was not merely a great Confederate Army leader during the Civil War; he personified strength and steadfastness. When the times call upon anyone to stand fast for fundamental beliefs, it is only fitting to recall the man who, in Robert E. Lee's famous phrase, stood like a stone wall. Occasionally the act of one individual dwarfs an historical event with the passing of time. Such was the case of a trial which ended on this day in 1950. A confessed Communist, Whittaker Chambers, accused former State Department official, Alger Hiss, of being a Communist agent. Hiss was convicted of perjury, but the trial brought a young California Congressman to even greater worldwide attention. Even though the trial was a cause celebre at the time, it also launched Richard M. Nixon's career.

The first atomic-powered submarine, the *U.S.S. Nautilus*, was launched on this day in 1954 at Groton, Connecticut. Atomic power—and we along with it— seem to have been getting into deep water ever since. However, not all modern-day inventions have conjured such doomsday premonitions or harbored potentially fatal consequences. On this same day in 1976, the supersonic Concorde passenger jet was put into service in England and France. It took construction of a second one before service was expanded to include New York City. Even though they fly faster, have proven themselves to be safer, and have lasted longer than more conventional passenger jet craft, there were never any other supercraft of this kind put into commercial service.

New York City prohibited women from smoking in public on this day in 1908. The lighting and inhaling of tobacco may not be socially correct in today's world, but the point made by early city forefathers was even less in keeping with our present belief that women should have equal rights to obey or disregard any proprieties they wish—even smoking.

22nd.

1901 Great Britain's Queen Victoria died. (See January 2nd, February 10th, May 24th, and June 20th entries.)

1905 The "Bloody Sunday" massacre occurred in St. Petersburg, Russia.

1879 Zulu warriors won the battle of Isandlwana in South Africa.

Not too many people give their name to a whole era, but Great Britain's Queen Victoria did. In a literal sense, the Victorian era ended on this day in 1901, when, after ruling the empire for six decades, Victoria Regina died. She personified a way of life, and the spirit of a civilization that believed in virtues like responsibility, dignity, and human obligation which we still call Victorian values.

A major turning point in history occurred on this date in 1905. The Russian Czar's soldiers fired on a group of peaceful demonstrators in front of the St. Petersburg palace. They were gathered to plead for better living and working conditions. Not only were many killed; thousands more were arrested and sent to prison or to Siberian labor camps. If the Czar's forces been less repressive and their actions less bloody at this event, there might not have been a Bolshevik revolution.

On this day in 1879, King Cetewayo and 20,000 Zulu warriors overwhelmed a well-trained British military regiment led by Lord Chelmsford at Isandlwana, South Africa. Only forty British soldiers managed to escape. In their push to expand the British empire from "Cairo to the Cape," military and political leaders were unprepared for the strategic brilliance of guerrilla warfare that the spear-and-shield-bearing Zulu warriors employed. The commissioned British troops were also not prepared to fight the courageous spirit and patriotic pride which King Cetewayo had instilled in his people. It took another twenty years before the British adopted the same strategy—but they never nurtured the same spirit.

23rd.

1542   King Henry VIII took the title of King of Ireland.

1849   Dr. Elizabeth Blackwell received the first M.D. awarded to an American woman.

1918   The Soviet government officially severed relations with the church.

1937   Soviet leaders confessed to an anti-Stalinist conspiracy.

1950   The Knesset proclaimed Jerusalem as Israel's capital.

1964   Poll tax was barred in U.S. Federal elections.

Today is a very significant anniversary for women, and for rest of us who would be nothing without women. In 1849, Dr. Elizabeth Blackwell—a native of Bristol, England—became the first female American doctor to receive her medical degree at the Medical Institution of Geneva, New York.

Today is a good day to remember that no individual or group should control the thoughts of another. On this date in 1937, a group of seventeen Soviet Russian leaders confessed in court to an anti-Stalinist conspiracy allegedly led by Leon Trotsky who had been living in exile for years. Why and how they came to confess brought psychological warfare—"brain washing"—to the world's attention.

Voting is a right, not just a privilege. And in 1964 on this date, the American government stamped its agreement to this belief. The Twenty-fourth Amendment to the U.S. Constitution went into effect, barring the poll tax that many local election boards charged voters who wished to cast their ballot in a Federal election.

While it's obvious that the future is uncertain, it is sometimes more difficult to perceive that the present is also tenuous, and even the past questionable, as history is nearly always recorded by the victors. On this day in 1542, England's King Henry VIII took the additional title "King of Ireland." In 1950, The Knesset—Israel's parliament—proclaimed Jerusalem as that nation's capital. Neither pronouncement was readily embraced by all. The dissenters did not quietly voice their objections, and battle lines were drawn. King Henry's proclamation was overturned, the Knesset has held fast.

The segregation of church and state has long been a political issue in many parts of the world. Should government offer support to religious concerns, or should it pay in tribute to Caesar that which is Caesar's? On this day in 1918, the Soviet government officially severed long-standing close relations between the Russian government and the Orthodox Church. All church property including land, houses of worship, relics, and icons were seized by state officials. In return, the church was guaranteed freedom of religious worship in the Soviet constitution, and freedom to be subjected to anti-religious propaganda.

24th.

41 AD   Roman Emperor Caligula was murdered.

1848   John W. Marshall discovered gold at Sutter's Mill, California.

1899   Edward John Phelps said, "The man who makes no mistakes does not usually make anything else."

1935   Canned beer first went on sale in the U.S.

1985   The space shuttle *Discovery* was launched in the NASA program's first secret military flight.

Being declared a leader does not mean people will automatically obey orders or follow your cause. Effective leaders inspire their peers and followers through sound judgment and good example. It was a lesson that one leader did not learn in his lifetime and, subsequently, few people mourned his death. On this day in 41 AD, the Roman emperor Gaius was murdered by two of his own Praetorian guards. Gaius' nickname was Caligula—or Little Boot—because he was fond of dressing up in soldier's uniforms, though in the end, he led no one. Not content to be emperor, the twenty-eight-year-old Caligula had just declared himself a god, but his generals, troops, and subjects did not agree. They had been terrorized by Caligula's cruelty and depravity throughout his brief, four-year reign.

The lure of gold is a potent force. It enticed European explorers to brave the unknown on both American continents, Africa, and Australia. Today, the prospect of gold attracts nations to claim portions of land near the north and south poles. A landmark gold discovery was made on this day in 1848. John W. Marshall found gold in a millrace of the American River at Sutter's Mill, California. When word got out, thousands of people headed west to seek their fortunes. The '49er gold rush opened the rest of the American wilderness from the Montana mountains to the Mexican deserts. It set the groundwork for the arrival of what we now laughingly call civilization. A few decades later, the Yukon's gold lured men and women to battle the frigid, northwest wilderness.

The basis of growth and progress is the need to dare and to do without fear of making a mistake. In 1899, lawyer-diplomat Edward John Phelps made a speech on this day in which he said, "The man who makes no mistakes does not usually make anything."

A great, modern-day convenience first went on sale in Richmond, Virginia, on this date in 1935. It changed the way men relax. This invention meant more wives were saved from abandonment in the evenings by errant spouses. Children were no longer sent off to the local saloon to fill their father's pail. Why? Because canned beer first went on sale in the U.S.

Not all discoveries become public knowledge as quickly as John Marshall's gold strike at Sutter's Mill, California, did on this day in 1848. In fact, on this very day in 1985, the space shuttle *Discovery*'s mission—the NASA space program's first secret military flight—was launched.

25th.

1759   Robert Burns was born.

1890   Nellie Bly completed her trip around the world.

1915   Transcontinental U.S. telephone service began. (See March 3rd and March 7th entries.)

1959   Pope John XXIII called an ecumenical council.

1959   American Airlines flew the first scheduled transcontinental Boeing 707 jet flight.

This was a red-letter day for Elizabeth Cochrane, who wrote for *The New York World* under the pen name of Nelly Bly. In 1890, she completed her amazing trip around the world in seventy-two days, six hours, and eleven minutes. On this same day in 1915, Alexander Graham Bell spanned the North American continent without leaving home. He made the first transcontinental phone call from New York to San Francisco. Another giant step toward bringing the world closer together took place on this day in 1959. Pope

John XXIII called for the assembly of the Second Ecumenical Council to explore international unity.

In the past three decades, bi-coastal has defined a lifestyle for many ambitious business executives—as well as modern dual-income couples. A quick power breakfast in Beverly Hills or a hard-driving dinner negotiation in Manhattan is a simple red-eye flight away. It all started on this day in 1959, when American Airlines flew the first scheduled transcontinental Boeing 707 jet flight from California to New York, changing life in the corporate world forever.

Robert Burns loved the simple things in life, and showed the world the nobility of the common man. His words are the spirit of Auld Lang Syne. Today is poet Robert Burns' birthday. Born in 1759, this native son of Scotland lived only 37 years, but his words have become immortal, finding a place in the hearts of every generation that followed.

26th.

1778 Australia was settled by the British. (Australia Day)

1784 Benjamin Franklin wrote to his daughter.

1830 Daniel Webster replied to Senator Hayne.

1875 The electric dentist's drill was patented.

1875 Douglas MacArthur was born.

If the American Revolutionary War had not been raging at the same time, Australia's first settlers—who were all convicts—would have been sent to America, a land settled by people seeking religious and political freedom. Even though these convicts were deemed bad by British law, the goodness in these men emerged. They worked together to overcome a harsh environment and inspired many other strong spirits to join them. Today is Australia Day, which commemorates the country's settlement by British convicts in 1778.

The U.S. Senate was the scene of an impartial debate on this day in 1830. At one point in the argument over states' rights and nullification, the eloquent statesman Daniel Webster summarized the cornerstone of our nation's doctrines in a reply to Senator Hayne: "Liberty and Union, now and for ever, one and inseparable."

Would it bother you if someone called you a turkey? It wouldn't have bothered Benjamin Franklin, who was very disappointed in 1784. On this day, he wrote to his daughter to say that he was unhappy about a sensitive government decision: The bald eagle had been chosen as America's national bird. He thought that the wild turkey—a noble, intelligent bird in Franklin's mind—should be the national symbol. Needless to say, he didn't win.

Sometimes, getting to the root of an invention can be like pulling teeth. However, in 1875, a patent was granted to George F. Green of Kalamazoo, Michigan, for a machine that greatly reduced the necessity of dental extractions. The electric dentist's drill was patented.

Some say that people are very much a product of their surroundings. Was this the case with General Douglas MacArthur? Born on this day in 1875 at a U.S. Army barracks in Little Rock, Arkansas, MacArthur grew up with the sights and sounds of military life from the moment he opened his eyes. He grew to become the nation's greatest military leader during the Second World War.

27th.

1756   Wolfgang Amadeus Mozart was born.

1832   Charles Lutwidge Dodgson was born. (See July 4th entry.)

1850   Samuel Gompers was born.

1880   The electric light bulb was patented.

1888   The National Geographic Society was incorporated.

1951   An Air Force plane dropped a one-kiloton atom bomb.

1964   France officially recognized the People's Republic of China.

1967   Three U.S. astronauts were killed in a fire aboard their Gemini spacecraft.

1973   The U.S. military draft ended when the Vietnam peace accords were signed in Paris.

An illuminating event took place on this anniversary. You could say it was the original bright idea when a light bulb went on, not in someone's head, but on someone's workbench. On this date in 1880, Thomas A. Edison received a patent for his incandescent electric light bulb. It has been easier to shed light in dark places ever since, thanks to Edison's invention; and people have also been seeking to turn off the lights since then. It took Edison roughly 1,500 attempts before he found the right substance to use as a filament. Why did he keep trying? Aside from the fact that he felt each failure was another lesson in how not to build a light bulb, he was afraid of the dark.

Today, we celebrate the life of a musical prodigy who composed lyrical works about a magic flute, mistaken identity, and a gentleman named Figaro. Born on this date in Austria in 1756, Wolfgang Amadeus Mozart went on to write 626 musical compositions—including operas, symphonies, sonatas, and concerti—during his short, thirty-five-year life span.

How much—if anything—do these names mean to you: Virgil Grissom, Edward White, and Roger Chaffee? You may remember them as the three astronauts who were killed in an Apollo rocket fire at Cape Kennedy, Florida. It happened on this day in 1967. We need to be mindful that while we have our eyes on the skies, trouble may be right at our feet. These astronauts did not die in outer space; their tragic accident occurred right on the ground.

Charles Lutwidge Dodgson was born on this day in Daresby, England, in 1832. An ingenious mathematician and logician who studied at Oxford University, Dodgson achieved his greatest fame when he wrote under the pen name of Lewis Carroll. His two famous novels, *Alice in Wonderland* and *Through the Looking Glass & What Alice Found There*, were written to entertain a pretty ten-year-old whose name was coincidentally Alice Pleasance Liddell. His fantastic nonsense has entertained many generations of children and adults ever since. As Dodgson himself wrote: 'The time has come,' the Walrus said, / 'To talk of many things: / Of shoes and ships and sealing wax / Of cabbages and kings / And why the sea is boiling hot / And whether pigs have wings.'

In the early part of this century, American laborers needed strong representation to attain a humane quality of life in the newly industrialized society. Decent wages, reasonable working hours, and fair treatment were not always easy to come by. When Samuel Gompers was born in London, England, on this day in 1850, child labor, low wages, and fourteen-hour workdays were still common practices in factories. At the end of his nearly forty-year career, Gompers changed that tide in labor. When he emigrated with his family to the U.S. in 1863, he followed his father's trade and became a cigar-maker. He gained his worldwide reputation by leading the national cigar-makers union away from the Knights of Labor to form the American Federation of Labor—the AF of L—and by promoting voluntarism. Gompers believed that unions should use strikes and boycotts to achieve their aims. He also encouraged them to apply written trade agreements and to establish national jurisdiction over the numerous local unions that existed.

On this date, in 1888, the doors to a whole new world opened for many generations of Americans—young and old alike. They led to faraway lands and peoples; introduced us to rarely-seen portions of the natural world; and showed us glimpses of our past and future through the eyes of great scientists, explorers, and photographers. Thanks to a suggestion made by the telephone's inventor Alexander Graham Bell, these worlds were not just documented in words. There were pictures, pictures, and more pictures. This is the anniversary of The National Geographic Society's incorporation in Washington, D.C., with Bell's son-in-law as its editor-in-chief.

Many decisive events of war and peace have occurred on this particular day in history. In 1951, a U.S. Air Force plane dropped a one-kiloton atom bomb on Frenchman Flats, Nevada, ushering in a new phase in the nuclear arms race. On a more peaceful note, in 1964, France officially recognized the People's Republic of China; and in 1973, the U.S. military draft was discontinued when the Vietnam peace accords were signed in Paris. Since this day also seems to tie in with things that are French, a quote from Victor Hugo seems appropriate: "There is one thing stronger than all the armies in the world, and that is an idea whose time has come."

28th.

1547 Edward VI became King of England.

1852 Wendell Phillips said, "There is nothing stronger than human prejudice."

1878 *The Yale News* was first published.

1916 Louis D. Brandeis was nominated to U.S. Supreme Court. (See November 13th entry.)

If we care to measure our nation's progress, today's landmark anniversary provides a convenient yardstick. On this date in 1916, Louis D. Brandeis became the first Jewish-American to be nominated to the U.S. Supreme Court. In his time, his nomination aroused a tremendous public furor. His ethnic origins and his liberal views made him repugnant to many Americans. Today, there seems to be nothing particularly remarkable about that appointment. Brandeis' name lives on not only in his historic opinions and dissents, but in the title of a great American university. Prejudice was also the subject of a speech made on this date in 1852. This was the day when New England orator and abolitionist leader Wendell Phillips said, "There is nothing stronger than human prejudice."

It is often said that children are our investment in our future. And today is the anniversary of two events where this saying rang true. In 1547, the nine-year-old Prince of Wales, Edward VI, succeeded his father Henry VIII as king of England. And on a more academic note, in 1878, the *Yale News*—the first daily college newspaper—was initially published in New Haven, Connecticut.

29th.

1843   President William McKinley was born.

1874   John D. Rockefeller, Jr. was born.

1877   The U.S. Congress established a commission to decide the Hayes-Tilden election.

Remember the good old days? They weren't always better than the present. On this date in 1877, the tangle of charges and confusion over the 1876 Presidential election was so thick that the U.S. Congress established a special Electoral Commission to decide whether Samuel Tilden or Rutherford B. Hayes had been elected. Old-style politics was not always best even in the good old days. Not too long ago, a politician criticized a particular concept of public policy as "creeping McKinleyism." That was possibly the only modern reference to the turn-of-the-century U.S. President who was born on this date in 1843. President William McKinley symbolized a totally passé style of laissez-faire conservatism. But he is best remembered because he was assassinated. Teddy Roosevelt became President after McKinley's death. Roosevelt reputedly ushered in modern American politics.

John D. Rockefeller, Jr., one of America's greatest philanthropists was born on this day, in 1874. Heir to the Standard Oil Company fortune, this only son of founder John D. Rockefeller, Sr., built New York City's famous Rockefeller Center and was instrumental in the selection of the city as the site for the United Nations' world headquarters. He also donated to the construction of the Lincoln Center for the Performing Arts; the restoration of colonial Williamsburg, Virginia; Manhattan's Museum of Modern Art; and the establishment of the United Services Organization which is better known as the U.S.O. As the world's richest man, Andrew Carnegie, once said: "A man who dies rich, dies in disgrace." John D. Rockefeller, Jr. never gave away his entire fortune, but he did contribute $250 million to the arts, education, and charitable aid.

30th.

1781 The Articles of Confederation were adopted by Maryland. (See November 15th entry.)

1835 Richard Lawrence tried to assassinate President Andrew Jackson.

1882 Franklin D. Roosevelt was born.

1889 Crown Prince Rudolf of Austria and Baroness Marie Vetsera committed suicide at Mayerling, Austria.

1933 Adolf Hitler became Chancellor of Germany.

1948 Mohandas K. Gandhi was assassinated.

1972 British soldiers shot and killed thirteen civil rights marchers.

Turn on the evening news or pick up a newspaper, and the leading stories are, more often than not, bad news. Why? Because violence and tragedy grab our attention in a way that good news just can't. This, you might say, was an attention grabbing day in history. In 1835, a demented painter named Richard Lawrence tried to assassinate President Andrew Jackson. In 1889, Crown Prince Rudolf of Austria, heir to the Austro-Hungarian empire, and Baroness Marie Vetsera committed suicide at Mayerling, Austria, triggering a major revolution in eastern Europe. In 1972, British soldiers shot and killed thirteen Roman Catholic civil rights marchers in Londonderry, Northern Ireland, in an incident that is still referred to as "Bloody Sunday" in the Emerald Isle. In 1933, Adolf Hitler became the Chancellor of Germany. That election launched his nation and the world into a full-scale war. But today also commemorates an ironic anniversary that reminds us that life is not always what we make it; sometimes life is what other people make for us. In 1948, the modern world's greatest symbol of peaceful resistance, Mahatma Gandhi, was assassinated in New Delhi, India.

One of history's true giants is a man who though stricken with polio, in tremendous pain, and unable to walk unaided, never appeared in public in a wheelchair. He knew that the people would not understand that he was more than capable. He brought a nation together; guided its people out of dark economic times; and proved that even in the light of a great physical handicap, any individual can conquer any obstacle. On this day in 1882, Franklin Delano Roosevelt was born in Hyde Park, New York.

Americans everywhere should revere the number thirteen: It represents the number of colonies that fought to be a united nation of states; it marks the number of states that ratified the Articles of Confederation that united them; and the American flag's original thirteen stars symbolized the courage and commitment that established our nation. Thirteen is an important number today because it was on this day in 1781, the Articles of Confederation were adopted by Maryland. It was the last of the original thirteen states to do so.

31st.

1709 Alexander Selkirk was rescued.

1919 Jackie Robinson was born.

1990 McDonald's opened its first fast-food restaurant in the Soviet Union.

Somehow, we seem to prefer to deal with facts in sensationalized fictional—almost mythological—terms. And truth, they say, is stranger than fiction. On this date, a true story—which nobody really remembers—provided the basis for a novel that everyone knows. In 1709, a British sailor named Alexander Selkirk was rescued after being marooned for four years on a Pacific island. You may not recognize Selkirk's name, but you might have heard the story of Robinson Crusoe and his adventures which was written by Daniel Defoe.

Occasionally one person becomes the living embodiment of an idea; the symbol of a widely held belief. When that happens, the symbol oftentimes works alone. That's the way it was with Jackie Robinson, a great baseball player who was born on this date in 1919. Robinson played for the Brooklyn Dodgers. He broke all-time records throughout his long career. He was also the first African-American major league baseball player. Robinson courageously fought to integrate the all-American sport. And in the end, his dedication helped open the doors for other African-American athletes like Ernie Banks of the Chicago Cubs.

An American institution took the Soviet Union by storm on this date in 1990. McDonald's opened its first fast-food restaurant in Moscow's Red Square: the world famous golden arches lit up in the world-famous anti-capitalist capitol.

February

There are many reasons why February should be a month close to our hearts. First of all, this is American Heart Month—a time to think of our health by exercising and eating smart. St. Valentine's Day is a time for romance; a time to tell those who are close to our hearts that we love them. But February is also American History and Black History Month. For love of our heritage and the brotherhood of man, we have designated this month as a time to remember our past. And Groundhog Day is set aside for those of us who only wish to consider the immediate present.

1st.

1790 U.S. Supreme Court convened for the first time.

1892 "The 400" social elite were named.

1993 Israelis said they would repatriate about 100 Palestinians.

The separation of powers, the system of checks and balances designed by the Founding Fathers, is part of this country's glory. And today was—and is—a red letter day for the government's judicial branch even though we somehow overlook the event that occurred in New York City on this date, in 1790: the U.S. Supreme Court convened for the first time.

In 1892, Mrs. William B. Astor gave a society ball on this day in New York City. Ward McAllister drew up her invitation list which was titled by the number of eligible guests. They were called "the 400." Ever since then, the term "the 400" has been synonymous with the social elite.

There are times when even the best intentions get rejected because past actions have built an impenetrable wall of distrust. Today is the anniversary of such an occasion. In 1993, the Israeli government said they would repatriate about 100 Palestinians who had been deported to Lebanon. Rather than embracing this singular act of kindness, the deportees rejected the plan.

2nd.

Groundhog Day.

Candlemas Day.

1848 The U.S. paid Mexico $15 million for southwestern lands.

1870 The "Cardiff Giant" was exposed as a hoax.

1876 The National Baseball League was formed.

1895 George Halas was born.

1990 South Africa lifted the ban on the African National Congress.

Today is Groundhog Day. Legend says that if a groundhog—or prairie dog—comes out today and sees his shadow, then six more weeks of winter follow. Of course, if he doesn't see that shadow, winter is supposed to last longer. In some parts of the world, people watch badgers or bears for similar omens. The origins of all these rites stem from a medieval British superstition observed as Candlemas Day. "If Candlemas Day be fair and bright, / Come winter, have another flight. / If Candlemas brings clouds and rain, / go wit and come not again."

Back in 1869, a gigantic, petrified human figure was discovered on a farm in Cardiff, New York. It created a sensation, for about a year. But on this day, the Cardiff Giant was exposed as a hoax.

This was a red-letter day for organized sports. In 1876, eight American baseball teams—Chicago, Boston, Cincinnati, Louisville, New York, Philadelphia, St. Louis, and Hartford—formed the National Baseball League. Additionally, in 1895, George Halas—the future co-founder of the National Football League—was born in Chicago.

While willpower and determination have shaped much of the world, some of the most momentous events seem to have been based on one person or government's decision not to stand in the way of destiny. This is the anniversary of two such events. In 1848, Mexico accepted $15 million from the U.S. for lands that eventually became the states of Arizona, California, New Mexico, and Texas. And in 1990, South African President F.W. de Klerk lifted the ban on the African National Congress, and promised to release political prisoner Nelson Mandela.

3rd.

1830 The revolution against the Ottoman occupation of Greece ended. (See March 25th entry.)

1865 President Lincoln attended a peace conference.

1943 Four U.S. chaplains died. (Four Chaplains Day)

1973 Fighting in the Vietnam War came to a virtual halt.

Not too many people are aware that today has a very special name. It is Four Chaplains Day. It marks the heroic deaths of a Catholic priest, a Jewish rabbi, and two Protestant ministers. They gave their life jackets to other crew members on board the sinking troop transport *Dorchester* and went down with the ship in the North Atlantic during the Second World War. In 1943, Father John Washington, Rabbi Alexander Goode, Reverend George Fox, and Reverend Clark Poling became men to be remembered.

Working together is not always easy. On this date in 1865, President Abraham Lincoln and Confederate Vice President Alexander H. Stephens met aboard a ship anchored at Hampton Roads, Virginia, in an attempt to end the Civil War. The meeting failed because the Confederacy demanded independence. Barely two months later—after more killing and more suffering—Confederate independence was lost anyway. They say talk is cheap; but in this case a lack of it cost thousands of men their lives. It's always wiser to communicate than to remain silent. It is true, however, that actions speak louder than words. That was definitely the case when, on this same day in 1973, fighting in the Vietnam War came to a virtual halt. The formal cease-fire had gone into effect.

4th.

1789   George Washington was elected U.S. president. (See February 22nd entry.)

1861   The Confederate States of America were organized.

1887   The Interstate Commerce Commission was established.

1970   President Nixon ordered all federal agencies to stop polluting the air and water.

As Americans, we seem to have a particular fondness for people who fight hard and gallantly, even if it's for a lost cause. One great example is the Confederate States of America which were organized on this date in 1861. It took a long time to bind up the wounds of the Civil War which pitted the Union in the North with the Confederacy in the South. But out of the ashes of that war and subsequent reconstruction rose great men and heroic acts on both sides.

Isn't it amazing how times change? Sometimes, the federal government reflects those changes by issuing resolves that appeal to the demands of the people. Today is the anniversary of two examples. In 1887, the Interstate Commerce Commission was established to regulate the transport of passengers and goods across state lines by land and water. America was on the move, and the government wanted to ensure the safe passage of people and cargo throughout the growing nation. But as we later learned, progress has its weak points. Gasoline emissions, industrial growth, and overpopulation took their toll on the nation's roads and waterways. In 1970, President Richard M. Nixon ordered all federal agencies to stop polluting the air and water by 1973.

5th.

1631 Roger Williams arrived in America.

1897 Indiana House of Representatives declared pi to be 3.2.

1900 Adlai E. Stevenson, Jr. was born.

1986 Corazon Aquino and Ferdinand Marcos both appeared on the national television program, *Nightline*.

1994 White separatist Byron De La Beckwith was convicted of murder in Jackson, Mississippi, for the 1963 death of civil rights leader Medgar Evers.

More than 300 years ago, on this date, Roger Williams arrived in the American colonies. In 1631, this young British minister had no idea he was to become our first great dissenter. As the founder of American religious tolerance, Williams established religious freedom as the law in Rhode Island.

Today is Adlai Stevenson, Jr.'s birthday. Some people questioned his qualifications as a presidential candidate; others commended his talent as an international diplomat; but all agree on his eloquence. Among the many memorable things he said was this: "Eggheads of the world unite. You have nothing to lose but your yolks."

On this day in 1897, the Indiana House of Representatives unanimously passed a measure redefining the area of a circle. It declared the value of pi to be 3.2. (The bill died in the Indiana Senate.)

Most of the time the media simply report the news. But occasionally, and perhaps more often than we realize, they make the news. It was on this day in 1986, that Corazon Aquino and Ferdinand Marcos both appeared on the national television program, *Nightline*. The debate between a dictator and the woman who would eventually unseat him halfway around the world, marked the beginning of a shift of international support away from the established regime.

The wheels of justice may creak too slowly for some of us. But most people agree that as long as those wheels do turn the system still works. This was the case on this day in 1994 when white separatist Byron De La Beckwith was convicted for a murder he committed three decades earlier in Jackson, Mississippi. For thirty-one years, police officials failed to arrest or convict the assailant of civil rights leader Medgar Evers. However, justice did prevail over a wrongdoing in the end.

6th.

1693   College of William and Mary was chartered. (See December 5th entry.)

1756   Aaron Burr was born. (See January 11th and July 11th entries.)

1895   George Herman (Babe Ruth) was born.

1933   The Twentieth Amendment to the U.S. Constitution went into effect.

1959   The U.S. successfully test-fired a Titan missile.

1971   The *Apollo 14* astronauts prepared to head back to earth.

1983   Chief Justice Warren Burger asked Congress to ease the Supreme Court's work-load.

1985   Australian Prime Minister Robert Hawke canceled an agreement with U.S. President Ronald Reagan.

If there is a single most notable aspect of our nation's growth, it is probably wrapped up in one word—education. This point is timely today because, on this date in 1693, the country's first college charter was granted, at Williamsburg, Virginia. The institution which opened under that charter is the College of William and Mary. Years later, it became the founding home of Phi Beta Kappa, the national collegiate honor fraternity.

The Amendment to the U.S. Constitution with the most picturesque name became part of the law on this day in 1933. It is popularly known as the Lame Duck Amendment. You all know what a lame duck is—a politician who has been defeated for reelection but is still in office. Before the Twentieth Amendment was enacted, politicians were elected in November and not sworn in until the following March. In the interim, lame ducks continued to run the government. The schedule was first adopted in the eighteenth century, when communication was slow and changes took time. Today, lame ducks only have two months before they are replaced by newly elected officials.

Today is the birthday of one of America's greatest heroes. He was cheered longer and louder than virtually anybody of his time. He never ran for office or starred on Broadway or discovered a cure for a disease. His name was George Herman Ruth, the American baseball player who was the epitome of irreverent, boisterous, happy-go-lucky, party-hearty masculine America. It is worth remembering, on Babe Ruth's birthday, that America loves its rough diamonds—people who do whatever it is they do best.

Working overtime is not limited to civilians. Some of our highest-ranking public officials have felt the crunch of a heavy workload. It was on this date, in 1983, that Chief Justice Warren Burger asked Congress to create a court made up of federal judges to ease the Supreme Court's workload.

The ways in which we measure progress successively change with each generation. Three events that occurred on this date in history prove this point. In 1959, the U.S. successfully test-fired a Titan intercontinental ballistic missile from Cape Canaveral, Florida. It was believed that advancements in defense technology would ensure the world's safety. A little over a decade later, in 1971, the *Apollo 14* astronauts prepared to head back to earth after spending thirty-three hours on the moon. Many people postulated that space technology would secure not only the ground we live on, but the skies above us. But by 1985, security took on a whole new meaning when Australian Prime Minister Robert Hawke canceled an agreement with President Ronald Reagan allowing Americans to monitor MX missile tests from Australian military bases. The land down under became the world's first antinuclear nation.

Today, on the birthday of Aaron Burr, the third vice-president of the United States, history remembers him simply as the man who mortally wounded Alexander Hamilton in an infamous duel. Only recently has it been suggested that Alexander Hamilton—who founded the *New York Post* newspaper—may have done more damage to Burr with a pen in the final days between the duel and his death, than Burr's bullet had done to him. It's doubtful that we'll ever know how or why the man who served as Vice President under Thomas Jefferson was charged three years after the duel with treason for allegedly trying to break up the union, and later convicted of a misdemeanor: attempting to invade Spanish territories to make himself emperor of Mexico.

1804   John Deere was born.

1812   Charles Dickens was born.

1882   John L. Sullivan won the last bare-knuckle heavyweight boxing championship.

1885   Sinclair Lewis was born.

1906   China's last emperor was born.

1973   The U.S. Senate voted to form an investigative committee to look into the Watergate break-in. (See January 4th and June 17th entries.)

Back in 1882, the Boston Strong Boy, John L. Sullivan, won the heavyweight championship of the world in Mississippi City, Mississippi. On this date, Sullivan knocked out Paddy Ryan in the ninth round with his bare-knuckled fists. After this fight, boxers had to wear gloves.

Today is a double birthday celebration. Two honored writers who were both adept at creating characters that personified attitudes of their times were born on this day. One was Charles Dickens, who chronicled the social conditions of Victorian England; the other was Sinclair Lewis, who penned a graphic portrait of 1920s and 1930s America. They created immortal characters like Fagan, Scrooge, Babbit, and Elmer Gantry. Dickens and Lewis had one particular quality in common; when they saw injustice, they tried to do something about it.

Some men make their name by being the first to do something. Others make their name by doing what they do best. Today is the birthday of a man who was one of the latter. In 1804, John Deere was born in Rutland, Vermont. He and his partner, Major Leonard Andrews, weren't the first men to successfully develop and manufacture a steel plow, but they did produce a better farm tool than their competitors. When Deere went out on his own, he continued making farm implements with that same philosophy in mind.

China's last Son of Heaven was born on this day in 1906. When he was two years old, P'u-i [pronounced poo-yee] was taken to Beijing's Forbidden City and was crowned emperor. A regency government ruled in his place as the young monarch grew up in the palace—isolated from his family and his empire. Four years later, his regents abdicated his throne to the Republican Revolution; he didn't know he had lost a 2000-year-old empire. When P'u-i was eighteen, he wanted to move to England or America and the new government wanted him out of the palace. But only the Japanese offered him assistance. He repaid them for their help by becoming Emperor K'ang-tee of the puppet Japanese nation Manchukuo—his ancestral home of Manchuria. After the Second World War, he was captured and returned to China where he was re-educated as a citizen of the People's Republic of China.

8th.

1828   Jules Verne was born.

1922   President Warren G. Harding had a radio installed in the White House. (See November 2nd entry.)

1925   Jack Lemmon was born.

1974   Three astronauts aboard the *Skylab 3* returned to earth.

1986   Five-foot-seven-inch Spud Webb of the Atlanta Hawks won the NBA Slam Dunk Competition.

1997   President Clinton announced he was releasing the first of a $200 million program of grants to provide schools with computers and Internet training. (See February 14th entry.)

It's often been said that fact can be stranger than fiction. Maybe today it would be more accurate to say that fact is catching up with fiction. Jules Verne, who was born in 1828 on this day, was the king of science fiction in his time. He practically invented the form. He wrote about traveling around the world in eighty days and navigating the bottom of the sea. He wrote about voyaging to the moon, and exploring the center of the earth.

This is the anniversary of a world's—or rather a solar system's—record. The three astronauts manning the *Skylab 3* space mission safely returned to earth after spending eighty-four days in orbit on this day in 1974.

Three cheers for every man! Why is this particularly relevant today? Because on this day in 1925, an actor who played your "Average Joe" was born. Jack Lemmon has portrayed ambitious junior executives, wage-earners working for the "company store," neurotic-but-lovable divorcés, and even a soft-hearted curmudgeon or two. But no matter what role he plays, he always makes the entire audience feel as if he's one of the gang. In 1986, a man of average height reached for the sky and landed with the National Basketball Association's coveted Slam Dunk Competition award. Standing at a tall five-feet-seven-inches, Atlanta Hawk's basketball player Spud Webb proved that any one with the spirit and the will can win, even when he or she looks just like everyone else in a crowd.

9th.

1718 French colonists arrived in Louisiana.

1773 William Henry Harrison was born. (See April 4th entry.)

1870 National Weather Service was established.

Today is the National Weather Service's anniversary. In 1870, this branch of the U.S. Army was officially established to gather and report on the nation's atmospheric conditions. Today, this line of research includes flying into hurricanes to determine wind speed and chasing thunderstorms to research the effect of lightning bolts.

Today is the birthday of the undisputed record holder for the shortest U.S. Presidential term ever served. In 1773, William Henry Harrison was born. On March 4, 1841, Harrison was inaugurated. Within a few days, he caught a cold. And exactly one month later, President Harrison was dead.

Today is New Orleans' birthday—or rather l'Anniversaire d'Orleans Nouveau. In 1718, Jean-Baptiste Le Moyne and a small group of French colonists arrived at the mouth of the great Mississippi to establish a settlement in the Louisiana bayou country. French-Africans from Haiti—Creoles—soon joined them to work on the plantations. Fifty years later, a band of French-speaking Acadians who were expelled from Nova Scotia—Cajuns—made their home in this thriving port city.

10th.

1763   France ceded Canada to England.

1840   Queen Victoria married Prince Albert. (See January 2nd, January 22nd, May 24th, and June 20th entries.)

1893   Jimmy Durante was born.

1927   Leontyne Price was born.

1933   The first singing telegram was sung.

1936   The Gestapo was given a free hand in Germany.

1942   The luxury liner *Normandie* capsized at pier in New York Harbor.

There is an old newspaper saying that if a dog bites a man, it's not news. But if a man bites a dog, that's news. Today's anniversary made news in much the same way. In 1942, the former French luxury liner, the *Normandie*, drowned—not sank—in New York Harbor. The U.S. Navy was converting the *Normandie* into a troopship. It had caught fire the day before, and the firefighters had poured tons of water into its hull. The next day, the waterlogged ship overturned and capsized, like a beached whale.

Today is the singing telegram's anniversary. Surprisingly, there are adults who have never even heard a singing telegram. In 1933, the singing telegram service made it possible for customers to have singing messengers deliver their greetings. You could have someone sing "Happy Birthday" to a friend in an another city. It was a cute idea that was even revived in the 1970s and has survived to the present.

There are many burning issues in books, thank goodness this one isn't slated to be a burned issue itself. Had it been around in Nazi Germany, it might have had an ignominious end atop a pyre of disapproved reading material. In 1936, on this date, the German Geheimstaatspolizei—or Gestapo—was given its power. Their actions were so atrocious that their name is still synonymous with evil and repression.

Canada officially became a British territory on this day in 1763. France ceded the last of its northern holdings in the New World, and New France became Quebec. Fifty years earlier they had lost Nova Scotia and Newfoundland in the Queen Anne's War. They had attempted to expand their holdings into the Ohio and Mississippi River Valleys, triggering the French and Indian War. They lost everything in the push to have it all.

Every working wife and every aspiring house-husband should celebrate today's anniversary. In 1840, Great Britain's Queen Victoria married Prince Albert of Saxe-Coburg-Gotha at London's St. James Palace. Their royal wedding was followed by an equally regal wedding breakfast at Buckingham Palace. But that's when the fairy tale transformed into a more modern reality. Despite the new husband's desire to see the world with his new bride, the young couple's honeymoon was only two days long. As head of the vast British empire, Victoria felt she couldn't spend any more time away from her job.

This is not only the anniversary of the first singing telegram, it's the birthday of two great American singers. Both Jimmy Durante and Leontyne Price were born on this day. In 1927, internationally-acclaimed opera star Leontyne Price was born in Laurel, Mississippi. And in 1893, Jimmy Durante was born in New York City. He may not have sung his way to the world's great operatic stages like Price did, but he did sing his way from vaudeville theaters to motion pictures and then to television. However, he never tried drama. John Barrymore reportedly suggested it once. "You should play Hamlet," he said. Durante replied, "To Hell with them small towns! I'll take New York!"

11th.

1254   The British Parliament first convened.

1531   King Henry VIII was recognized as the supreme head of the Church of England. (See November 17th entry.)

1812   The gerrymander was born.

1847   Thomas Alva Edison was born. (National Science Youth Day)

1929   Italy signed the Lateran Treaty with the Vatican.

1975   Margaret Thatcher became the first female head of the British Conservative Party.

1984   The space shuttle *Challenger* returned to earth.

1989   Barbara Harris became the first consecrated female Episcopal bishop.

This is the British Parliament's birthday. In 1254, Earl Richard of Cornwall summoned two elected knights from every shire and all of the king's barons to meet at Westminster Abbey while his brother King Henry III was fighting in France. They met to confer on the matter of raising more money for military defense. Before this epic meeting, the king consulted only with his royal advisors and key members of the clergy. The establishment of this parliamentary assembly assured the barons and elected representatives a significant voice in government. Sadly, when King Henry returned four years later, he tried to dissolve the parliament. But the barons prevailed.

If mother—as the saying goes—was the necessity of invention, then today could be a Mother's Day of sorts. This was the day a man who lived by his own scientific inventions, inspired by the natural curiosity he had developed in his youth, was born. Thomas Alva Edison was born on this day in 1847 in Milan, Ohio. And for some years, the occasion of his birth was observed as National Science Youth Day.

Back on this date in 1812, the Governor of Massachusetts, Elbridge Gerry, signed a bill setting his state's district lines. A cartoonist looked at the new oddly placed borders and drew a caricature of the redistricting. To him, it looked like a salamander. Combining Governor Gerry's name with the map's shape, the cartoonist came up with a new word: gerrymandering. It means distorting a natural contour to suit your own ends. And you can, so to speak, gerrymander an issue as well as a state. You can take a situation and create your own borderlines. That is particularly easy when you have a complicated subject. But in the end, these Jerry-rigged subjective perceptions might not hold up to others' scrutiny.

This is a double landmark day for the Episcopal Church. First, in 1531, King Henry VIII was officially recognized as the Church of England's supreme head. The dispute between the king and the Vatican escalated with this radical act. But certainly even the non-conforming Henry would have been alarmed when Barbara Harris became the first consecrated female bishop in the Episcopal Church over four and a half centuries later. In 1989, the ceremony—held in Boston, Massachusetts—signaled the end of the long-held tradition that only male clergy could rise through the Church's ranks.

In Great Britain, the separation of Church and State had been disputed for nearly five centuries until King Henry VIII declared himself as the Church of England's supreme head on this day in 1531. But reform—both spiritual and political—has occurred more than once on this day. In 1975, Margaret Thatcher became the first female head of the British Conservative Party. And fourteen years later, in 1989, Barbara Harris was consecrated as the first female bishop of the Episcopal Church in Boston, Massachusetts.

The Vatican gained its independence on this day in 1929. The seat of the Roman Catholic Church—situated in the center of Italy's capital—was not a separate entity even though its interests spread far beyond the borders of its host nation. But when the

Italian government signed the Lateran Treaty, Vatican City gained sovereignty. It was a fortuitous event. In less than a decade, Italy's fascist government expanded its interests and influence in a very different direction.

It wasn't the first time an astronaut walked in space, but on this date in 1984, the space shuttle *Challenger* returned to earth after an eight-day mission that featured the first untethered space walk.

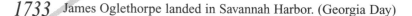

1733 James Oglethorpe landed in Savannah Harbor. (Georgia Day)

1746 Tadeusz Kosciuszko was born. (Kosciuszko Day)

1809 Abraham Lincoln was born. (Celebrated on the closest Monday to February 22nd as President's Day; see February 22nd; April 14th, and April 15th entries.)

1809 Charles Darwin was born.

1880 John L. Lewis was born.

1893 General Omar N. Bradley was born.

This is a special day for many Americans, no matter who they are or where they live. In 1809, Honest Abe Lincoln was born in Kentucky. If you hail from Atlanta or Savannah you know that in 1733 James Oglethorpe and a group of colonists landed in Savannah Harbor. If you are of Polish descent, you probably know that in 1746, the American patriot and war hero Tadeusz Kosciuszko was born. But not many people know that in 1880, John L. Lewis—the founder of the United Mineworkers Union—was also born.

For many Americans, there is a special warmth about this day because it is Omar N. Bradley's birthday. Born in 1893, this native Missourian was known during the Second World War as the G.I.'s general. Bradley was one of the nation's most loved and longest-lived top generals. He was also a plain and gentle man. If we are looking for the model of a dedicated public servant, we don't have to look beyond Omar Bradley. He made an interesting observation in a 1948 Armistice Day speech: "Humanity is in danger of being trapped in this world by its moral adolescents."

Because of one man who was born on this day, the world saw itself in a very different light. In 1809, Charles Darwin was born in Shrewsbury, Shropshire. When he was thirty years old, Darwin sailed aboard the *H.M.S. Beagle* to South America to record the unique plant and animal life of the west coast and its surrounding islands. His observations were documented in a book entitled, *On the Origins of the Species by Means of Natural Selection.* Suddenly, the whole world was praising and criticizing his alleged theory that only the fittest survive. But what Darwin really discovered was that only those who are able to adapt to their environment endure and progress.

13th.

The Feast of St. Agabus.

1633 Galileo was detained by the Italian Inquisition in Rome. (See February 15th entry.)

1635 The Boston Latin School was founded.

1795 The first state university opened in Chapel Hill, North Carolina. (See February 6th entry.)

1892 Grant Wood was born.

1919 Tennessee Ernie Ford was born.

1920 League of Nations recognized Switzerland's neutrality.

This is the feast day dedicated to St. Agabus—the patron saint of fortune tellers. But it doesn't need a Tarot deck or a crystal ball to see that today is also an important day for American education. In 1635, the nation's oldest secondary school, the Boston Latin School, opened. America has been dedicated to free public education ever since. And in 1795, the nation's first state institution of higher education, the University of North Carolina at Chapel Hill, also opened.

Rural America was honored by two men born on this day. In 1892, Grant Wood was born in Anamosa, Iowa. Wood's painting—*American Gothic*—is still the world's most recognized portrait of farm life. His vision of the men and women who tilled the soil to feed a nation continues to tell the story of their hardship and their tenacious, hard-working spirit today. In 1919, Tennessee Ernie Ford was born in Bristol, Tennessee. This homegrown country singer painted an innocent, romantic portrait of American rural life with his voice and his guitar. Ford used to finish his shows with a few words that capture his view of the world: "Bless your little pea-pickin' hearts."

Remaining neutral on any issue, in any field of endeavor is difficult. In the area of international politics, neutrality is nearly impossible to achieve. But on this date in 1920, Switzerland accomplished just that when the League of Nations officially recognized the alpine nation's neutral position in the political arena. By maintaining their nonpartisan stance, Switzerland has been host to numerous peace conferences; and home to many service organizations dedicated to aiding war and disaster victims throughout the world.

14th.

Valentine's Day.

1766   Thomas Malthus was born.

1894   Jack Benny was born.

1946   The first all-electronic computer was introduced. (See June 23rd entry.)

1989   The Ayatollah Khomeini called for the assassination of Salman Rushdie.

Today is Valentine's Day, the celebration dedicated to lovers young and old, greeting-card companies, and the people who sell those heart-shaped candy boxes. It is interesting to note that Valentine's Day is also Thomas Malthus' birthday. Born in Surrey, England in 1766, Malthus argued in his Essay on Population that populations grow geometrically, while the crops and livestock to feed them grow arithmetically. Because that supply-and-demand ratio never balances, Malthus firmly believed people should marry later in life. According to him, "moral restraint" was the best way to prevent a worldwide famine.

It is said that the pen is mightier than the sword. Today's anniversary clearly demonstrates the strength of words and ideas. But it is also an example of how much trouble words can create for their author. In 1989, Iran's Ayatollah Khomeini called for Salman Rushdie's assassination. The conservative Muslim leader claimed that certain passages of the author's novel—*The Satanic Verses*—ridiculed Islam's essential doctrines. Like a page out of medieval history, Rushdie was marked as a heretic by a religious leader for publishing his thoughts.

This is Jack Benny's birthday. In 1894, little did the residents of Waukegan, Illinois, know that one of their native sons would grow to become best known for his lack of musical talent. Hiding flaws and shortcomings may help us to overcome our insecurities, but they also humanize us, give us character, and make us approachable. It certainly worked for Jack.

This is the computer's birthday. The world's first all-electronic computer was unveiled at the University of Pennsylvania's Moore School of Electrical Engineering in 1946. The Electronic Numerical Integrator And Computer—ENIAC for short—weighed thirty tons, stood ten feet tall (about the size of a motor home), and could calculate a ballistic trajectory in thirty seconds. It took only nine years for mathematician Alan M. Turing's idea—which he had conceived while taking a walk in a scenic rural English cow pasture—to become a reality.

15th.

1564 Galileo Galilei was born. (See February 13th and 19th entries.)

1820 Susan B. Anthony was born. (See December 13th entry.)

1898 The U.S. battleship *Maine* was bombed.

1964 Cassius Clay became the world's heavyweight boxing champion.

1971 Great Britain and Ireland switched to decimal-based currency.

If you stayed awake in your American history classes, you ought to recall the slogan, "Remember the *Maine*!" But who remembers that these words refer to the bombing of the U.S. battleship *Maine* in Cuba's Havana Harbor? When it happened on this date, in 1898, how many people were convinced that the Spanish were at fault? Newspaper tycoon William Randolph Hearst had been campaigning for a war. It was this incident that actually triggered the Spanish-American War, though it is not known to this day if the explosion was deliberate.

The story of Galileo Galilei is as important to remember on his birthday as it was 400 years ago. In 1564, Galileo was born in Pisa, Italy. When he created a telescope so he could observe the heavens, the public loaded him down with honors. But when he publicly supported Copernicus' theory that the earth revolved around the sun, he was detained by the Italian Inquisition for the crime of heresy. At the time, the Church still taught that the earth was the center of the known universe.

We like to think today that we are much more tolerant than our forefathers. But are we? He flew like a butterfly and stung like bee; today's the day Cassius Clay became Muhammed Ali. In 1964, the Olympic gold medalist boxer won the first of his world title fights against Sonny Liston. This bout didn't have a colorful name like the Rumble in the Jungle or the Thrilla in Manila. But Cassius Clay did shock the world when he made the announcement he had joined the Nation of Islam and changed his name to Muhammed Ali.

Two landmark events occurred on this day that frustrated both bankers and consumers for a number of years. This is the anniversary of Great Britain and Ireland's shift to a decimal-based currency system. In 1971, shillings, bobs, and crowns were replaced by 5, 10, and 50 pence coins. The familiar haypence and sixpence denominations disappeared; a 41 pence chocolate bar sounded so much more expensive than a 7 shilling/6 pence one. But, to coin a phrase, consumers learned to live with the change.

In 1820, no one knew that a young girl's birthday would stir up the American currency system over a century later. That was when suffragist Susan B. Anthony was born in Adams, Massachusetts. When the U.S. Treasury issued the quarter-sized Susan B. Anthony dollar in 1979, American consumers got confused. People accidentally put the new dollars into quarter slots in the midst of an economic recession. So the first American coin to feature a woman's portrait was discontinued.

16th.

1862 Ulysses S. Grant demanded the Confederate forces' unconditional surrender.

1903 Edgar Bergen was born.

1923 King Tutankamen's burial chamber was opened. (See November 4th and June 26th entries.)

1959 Fidel Castro became Cuba's premier.

1986 Mario Soares became the head of Portugal.

Some phrases are far more dramatic and meaningful than others. General Ulysses S. Grant, on this date in 1862, laid down his terms for unconditional surrender to the besieged Confederate forces at Fort Donelson, Tennessee. This phrase, unconditional surrender, is a yardstick by which the totality of victory is still measured. Unfortunately, more amiable words were not conveyed by both sides as might have been the case at the Union Club in New York. Both General Ulysses S. Grant and the Confederate Army's General Robert E. Lee were members of this exclusive gentlemen's club which still exists today.

Edgar Bergen was born on this day in 1903 in Chicago. He was a star entertainer, but he also did something few entertainers do. Bergen contributed to the English language. When we refer to a Charlie McCarthy or a Mortimer Snerd, we are using names that Bergen gave to two of the ventriloquist's dummies he used in his act. McCarthy and Snerd's names became synonymous with the terms wise-cracking and simple-minded. As we face the rest of the world, one of our primary goals is not to be either a Charlie McCarthy or a Mortimer Snerd; and the second is not to be too wooden.

Change hallmarks this particular day in history. In 1959, Fidel Castro became Cuba's premier after ousting the pro-capitalist Batista regime. In its desire for independence, Cuba chose to live under communist rule, rather than allow foreign investors free reign over their land and valuable sugar resources. But when they shunned these capitalists, they shunned their capitalist government, too. And the rest is a chilly history for a tropical nation. Also on this date, Mario Soares became the first civilian head of Portugal, in 1986. After sixty years of military rule, the nation consciously chose to try a new form of government.

17th.

1621 Miles Standish became a military captain.

1801 Thomas Jefferson was elected U.S. president. (See April 13th entry.)

1947 The Voice of America began radio broadcasts.

1963 Michael Jordan was born. (See January 13 and March 9 entries.)

1973 American envoy Henry Kissinger and Chairman Mao Zhedong met.

Back in 1621, news was made this day by a gentleman named Miles Standish. Now you all know who Miles Standish was—or do you? Most of you might assume this was the day he sent John Alden to propose to Priscilla Mullen on his behalf. If Standish is known at all today, it is because Henry Wadsworth Longfellow wrote a poem entitled "The Courtship of Miles Standish." (Incidentally, he did end up marrying, not once but twice.) But this isn't the anniversary of that fateful—and fictional—day. This was the day he was made the military captain of the Massachusetts Pilgrim colony.

Thomas Jefferson was elected the third U.S. president on this day in 1801. This may not be an earth-shaking revelation. The real surprise is that this election ended in a tied vote between Jefferson and Aaron Burr. The final decision was made by the House of Representatives on the thirty-sixth ballot.

Communications between the U.S. and Communist nations radically changed during the twentieth century—especially on this day. In 1947, the first "The Voice of America" broadcast took place. Officially condemned by Josef Stalin as capitalist propaganda, these radio programs offered news-hungry Iron Curtain nations glimpses of the outside world after U.S.-Soviet relations had ceased. On this same day in 1973, American envoy Henry Kissinger and Chairman Mao Zhedong met for the first time in Beijing, China. It began an era of détente between The People's Republic of China and the U.S.

18th.

1861 Jefferson Davis said, "All we ask is to be let alone." (See June 3rd entry.)

1885 *The Adventures of Huckleberry Finn* was published.

1930 The first cow flew.

1930 Pluto was discovered.

There are any number of earth-shaking events which we file away in our memories. Today marks an anniversary that may very possibly have escaped everyone's attention. On this date in 1930, a cow didn't jump over the moon, but it flew—or more exactly— a cow flew in an airplane over the Midwest, and was milked en route.

When Jefferson Davis was inaugurated as the president of the Confederate States of America on this date in 1861, he made a profound statement that is still as worthy of sympathy today as it was then. "All we ask," he pleaded, "is to be let alone."

The spirit of adventure seems to prevail on this day throughout history. Mark Twain's novel, *The Adventures of Huckleberry Finn*, was first published on this day in 1885. Youthful adventure was certainly in the minds of the men who, in 1930, helped the first cow fly—in an airplane, of course.

Astronomer Clyde Tombaugh didn't see that flying cow while peering through the Lowell Observatory telescope in Flagstaff, Arizona. But he did discover the planet Pluto on exactly the same day. According to many modern astrologers, the dark planet at the farthest end of our solar system represents the dark underworld—nature's more nefarious side. Others believe that the planet Pluto represents our irrepressible desire to explore, and the vast potential—even in our modern times—for new discovery.

19th.

1473 Copernicus was born. (See also Galileo, February 15th.)

1717 David Garrick was born.

1878 Thomas Edison received a patent for his phonograph. (See February 11th, August 31st, September 3rd, October 6th, and October 21st entries.)

1881 Kansas became the first state to prohibit all alcoholic beverages. (See October 28th entry.)

1945 Thirty-thousand U.S. Marines landed on the Japanese island of Iwo Jima. (See February 23rd entry.)

1984 Phil and Steve Mahre took the gold and silver medals in the slalom, becoming the first brothers to win in same event at the Olympics. (See February 24th entry.)

1986 The U.S.S.R. launched the *Mir* space station into earth's orbit. (See June 29th entry.)

1989 Broadway's biggest flop, *Legs Diamond,* closed. (See March 24th, April 7th, May 23rd, December 20th, and December 30th entries.)

Did you ever stop to think about what today's world would look like to a man who lived over 500 years ago? Well, Copernicus—who was born on this date in 1473—would not be surprised in the least. If Copernicus hadn't proposed that the earth revolved around the sun, we might still be shortsighted, earthbound creatures today. Galileo might never have invented a telescope. Jules Verne and Arthur C. Clarke might not have written about space travel or moon walks. For Copernicus, the sky was the limit.

The acting profession has a landmark anniversary today. In 1717, the British actor David Garrick was born. He was not only one of the London stage's greatest actors; he made the theater a center of culture. He was so revered by the public that he was buried in Westminster Abbey.

Friendly competition. It's more than just playing fair—playing fair is part of any competition. Friendly competitors may want to win, but they will also go out of their way to spur their opponents to achieve their personal best. Take for example the case of twin brothers Phil and Steve Mahre, who one this day in 1984, took the gold and silver medals in the men's slalom at the Winter Olympics. Steve went first. At the finish line he radioed crucial course information up to Phil. It was the first time two brothers won in the same Olympic event at the same time.

20th.

1437   King James I of Scotland was murdered.

1792   The U.S. Postal Service was created.

1902   Ansel Adams was born.

1927   Sidney Poitier was born.

1938   Anthony Eden resigned as Great Britain's Foreign Secretary.

1941   Buffy Sainte-Marie was born.

1946   Council of Economic Advisers was established.

1962   Astronaut John Glenn orbited the earth. (John Glenn Day) (See July 18th entry.)

1967   Kurt Cobain was born.

1971   Radio and television stations nationwide left the air for a national emergency.

Not many people can say there is a national day named after them, but today is such a day. Today is John Glenn Day, which was proclaimed after John Glenn became the first U. S. astronaut to orbit the earth in 1962.

Politics rarely leave room for idealism; but on this day, one politician did put his ideals first. In 1938, Great Britain's Foreign Secretary Anthony Eden resigned in protest of Prime Minister Neville Chamberlain's appeasement policy toward Nazi Germany. It was a gallant gesture. And Eden's public display of conscience may have inspired the entire nation in the hard days that followed.

When considering the proliferation of government agencies, just remember that a camel is a horse designed by a committee. In 1946—on this very day—the Council of Economic Advisers to the President of the United States was established. Obviously, that's why we have not had any economic problems since then.

Poor leadership is sometimes rewarded with an equally miserable end. This was certainly the case on this day. In 1437, Scotland's King James I had ruled with more than an iron fist throughout his thirteen-year reign. He treated his nobles harshly; and he approved some very unpopular laws. He forbade drinking after 9 P.M.; he banned his subjects from playing football; he ordered his people to wear clothes appropriate to their social status; and he imprisoned any unemployed person who failed to seek a new job. His reforms didn't garner praise or support. While King James was visiting a priory at Perth, his cousin Sir Robert Stewart, Sir Robert Graham, and eight soldiers murdered the unpopular monarch.

Communication has taken some interesting turns on this day in history. In 1792, George Washington signed an act that created the U.S. Postal Service. This federal service and subsequent agencies like the Federal Communications Commission assured that information would flow smoothly from coast to coast. One agency—the National Emergency Broadcast Service—was organized to keep the public informed in the event of a major crisis. Everything seemed to go well until this date in 1971. On that day, radio and television stations nationwide were erroneously given a presidential order to leave the air for a national emergency and a momentary panic seized the nation.

Four socially-conscious men and women celebrate their birthdays today. In 1902, naturalist/photographer Ansel Adams was born. His portraits of America's natural majestic wonders served as proof that we must take greater care of our unique and beautiful untamed environment. In 1927, actor Sidney Poitier was born. Throughout his career, Poitier has stressed the individual's right to dignity and respect. In 1941, Buffy Sainte-Marie was born. Pride in aboriginal heritage and personal self-esteem have been recurring themes in this singer/songwriter's work. Lack of social recognition and economic opportunities for today's youth was the focus of singer/songwriter Kurt Cobain's work.

Born in 1967, Cobain was the voice of Generation X who was tragically silenced by his own anger and despair. Like the other men and women born on this day, he spoke from his heart and demanded his moment to be heard.

21st.

1795 Freedom of worship was established in France.

1838 Samuel F.P. Morse gave the first public demonstration of his telegraph. (See April 27th and May 24th entries.)

1866 Lucy Hobbs became the first female American dentist.

1878 The world's first telephone directory was published.

1954 U.S. Army accused Senator Joe McCarthy of browbeating. (See December 2nd entry.)

1972 President Nixon visited Communist China.

1989 Playwright Vaclav Havel was convicted. (See December 29th entry.)

Today is the historic anniversary of Lucy Hobbs' graduation. In 1866, she became America's first female dentist when she received her degree from the Ohio College of Dental Surgery in Cincinnati. This made possible that most unusual of all events—a woman asking a man to open his mouth.

Today is the anniversary of one of the U.S. Army's most historic declarations of war. It was a war of ideas, not bullets. That's Congress' department. But on this date, in 1954, the Army accused Senator Joseph R. McCarthy of browbeating Army personnel during his Communist witch hunts. This Army accusation led to the Senate hearings which eventually led to McCarthy's censure.

It isn't always what is done, but who does it that counts. This point was made clear when on this date in 1972, President Richard M. Nixon, an ardent anti-communist, traveled on a friendship mission to the Peoples' Republic of China. Because of his reputation, only he could have persuaded American anti-communists to sit still for this U.S. policy change.

Freedom celebrates many anniversaries on this day. In 1795, the religious persecution of the Huguenots and other Protestant sects ended in France when the government established freedom of worship as part of the nation's essential doctrines. Could it happen now? In 1989, freedom of speech and thought was denied to playwright Vaclav Havel who was convicted on this day for his role in an officially-banned rally. Havel was sentenced in a Prague courtroom to a nine-month jail term for speaking out against a repressive government. When he later became President of the Czech Republic, one of the first freedoms he established for the newly organized nation was the right for each citizen to voice his or her own opinion.

Samuel F.P. Morse gave the first public demonstration of his telegraph on this day in 1838. This revolutionary device quickly transformed the way people sent and received information. Another new invention, the telephone, made even quicker communication possible. Exactly fifty years after this artist and inventor from Charlestown, Massachusetts, demonstrated his telegram, the world's first telephone directory was published by the New Haven Telephone Company.

22nd.

1630   Popcorn was introduced.

1732   George Washington was born. (Celebrated on the closest Monday to this date as Presidents' Day. See February 12th entry.)

1862   Jefferson Davis was inaugurated as Confederate President.

1889   The Dakota Territory was divided into North and South Dakota.

1924   Calvin Coolidge delivered the first presidential radio broadcast from the White House.

1973   The U.S. and the Peoples' Republic of China agreed to establish liaison offices.

Today is George Washington's birthday. And although we now celebrate Washington's and Lincoln's birthdays together on President's Day, it doesn't really matter because Washington was not really born on February 22, 1732, anyway. When he was born,

America was still on the old Julian calendar. February 22nd was actually February 11th; we added on 11 days when we adopted the Gregorian calendar. But this was neither arbitrary nor disrespectful. After many years of celebrating his birthday on February 11, Washington himself finally changed it to the day we all know.

America has a collection of folkways and family recipes that, put together, have made up our particular way of life. One recipe was given to the rest of us by Native Americans on this date in 1630. That was when the locals introduced the Pilgrims to popcorn. Things have been popping ever since.

As this day in history demonstrates, separation can have both positive and negative effects. In 1862, Jefferson Davis was inaugurated as President of the Confederate States of America. Although the Civil War had already begun, Davis' inauguration symbolized the official split between the northern and southern states. But on this same date in 1889, the vast Dakota Territory was divided into North Dakota and South Dakota, creating a more reasonable way to govern this large section of western America.

Today's anniversaries remind us to keep our lines of communication open. In 1924, Calvin Coolidge delivered the first presidential radio address from his White House office. With the advent of radio, relationships between the nation's chief executive and the public became more personal. In 1973, international communication between the U.S. and the People's Republic of China was established. Both countries agreed to set up liaison offices in Washington D.C. and Beijing, China.

23rd.

1685   George Friedrich Handel was born. (See September 14th entry.)

1836   The Siege of the Alamo began.

1886   Electrolytic process for manufacture of aluminum was invented.

1905   The Rotary Club was established.

1945   The American flag was raised on the island of Iwo Jima, Japan.

1982   Canada, Japan, and the European Common Market nations joined the U.S. in economic and diplomatic sanctions against Poland and the Soviet Union.

This is literally a flag-waving day in history. In 1945, the Marines raised the American flag on the Japanese island of Iwo Jima. A famous photograph—taken by Associated Press photographer Joe Rosenthal at the height of the fighting was the inspiration for the Iwo Jima monument outside the Arlington National Cemetery near Washington D.C. It represents a spirit of valor which continues to inspire all of us today. Valor is a tradition not at all unique to America; nor is it a unique American custom handed down from one generation to another. But today also marks the anniversary of the siege of San Antonio, Texas. In 1836, the city was defended against the Mexican Army by a small band of determined men who were posted in a mission called the Alamo. The gallantry of those men, including frontiersmen Jim Bowie and Davy Crockett, is well remembered throughout the world.

Sometimes a thing is so commonplace and ordinary today that we pay very little attention to its anniversary. In 1886, Charles M. Hall invented the electrolytic aluminum manufacturing process. If you stop to think of it, his invention made modern aviation possible, and cooking a lot easier. Hall made a fortune from his invention, but he is one of a vast army of relatively unsung Americans—though infinitely better rewarded than most of them—who have made this world better for their presence.

One way that people attempt to resolve a common cause is by gathering regularly to discuss shared problems or to voice mutual concerns. Today marks the anniversary of the Rotary Club. In 1905, Chicago attorney Paul P. Harris and three of his friends organized a club that is now an international institution. The Object of Rotary, as the club's stated goal is titled, is "to encourage and foster the ideal of service as a basis of worthy enterprise." The Object goes on to state four means to attain this goal: "through the development of acquaintance as an opportunity for service; the promotion of high ethical standards in business and professions; through service in one's personal, business and community life; and the advancement of international understanding, goodwill and peace."

Friendship is a powerful asset. When you have friends, you have support for your cause—especially if that cause is freedom. It was on this day in 1982 that a number of caring friendly nations stood together to oppose the use of aggression by one nation against another. The Soviet Union had imposed martial law in Poland to suppress that country's growing opposition to outside rule. In support of Poland's fight for freedom, the U.S., Canada, Japan, and the ten nations that made up the European Common Market mutually agreed to impose economic and diplomatic sanctions, cutting off the aggressor's supply connections. The action weakened the Soviets' effort. In the end, Poland won its freedom.

24th.

1803 The U.S. Supreme Court ruled that one Act of Congress was unconstitutional.

1874 Honus Wagner was born.

1980 The U.S. hockey team defeated Finland, four goals to two, to clinch the gold medal at the Winter Olympic Games in Lake Placid, New York. (See February 19th entry.)

1996 Cuba downed two small American planes it claimed were violating Cuban airspace. (See April 17th entry.)

One of the glories of our American heritage is our Constitution—the supreme law of the land. But it wasn't always that way. We owe a great deal to a court decision which marks its anniversary today. In 1803, the U.S. Supreme Court voided an Act of Congress in the case of Marbury v. Madison. It was the first time a law passed by Congress was deemed unconstitutional. This case not only established that the U.S. Constitution held primary jurisdiction, it also crystallized the Supreme Court's power to ultimately rule on questions of constitutionality.

In professional baseball's early days, there were some very accomplished players who were also popular heroes. Some players were legendary, like the Five Immortals. But there was one who, long after his playing days were over, was a still familiar ballpark figure. Honus Wagner started playing professionally in 1895. He was the Five Immortals' infielder who was first named to the Baseball Hall of Fame. Born on this date in 1874, Wagner was also an active baseball coach until the Second World War.

25th.

1570 Great Britain's Queen Elizabeth I was excommunicated.

1873 Enrico Caruso was born.

1913 The Sixteenth Amendment to the U.S. Constitution went into effect.

1943 George Harrison was born.

Today is an anniversary which prompts no great celebration, but is very much worth noting. In 1913, the Sixteenth Amendment to the U.S. Constitution went into effect. This act authorized the income tax. The helping hand of government has been known on occasion to help itself. We all have Uncle Sam as a partner. None of us works alone.

Two men were born on this date whose careers invite an interesting comparison. In 1873, Italian opera tenor Enrico Caruso was born; and in 1943, George Harrison of the British pop band, "The Beatles," was born. Caruso and Harrison moved in different musical circles, but they both maintained a strong integrity about doing their jobs their own way. They believed in what they were doing. And both men became cultural heroes. When they began, neither could have imagined the success they would achieve, but they kept at it anyway. As the line from a popular musical reminds us: "Sing for your supper and you'll get breakfast." These men sang and were rewarded with so much more.

Two grave historic injustices occurred on this day. In 1570, Pope Pius V issued a bill of excommunication against Great Britain's Queen Elizabeth I who had beheaded the devout Catholic Mary Queen of Scots. In his zeal to right Great Britain's perceived wrongs against the Church, the pontiff not only condemned the young queen's soul; he also declared her deposed from her earthly throne. He then proclaimed that her own subjects were free to murder her without earthly or heavenly condemnation. No matter what someone does against another, an eye for an eye does not resolve the problem.

26th.

1815 Napoleon escaped from the island of Elba.

1846 Buffalo Bill was born.

1928 Fats Domino was born.

1932 Johnny Cash was born.

1943 Brian Jones was born.

1993 A bomb exploded in the World Trade Center.

On this very day in 1815, Napoleon Bonaparte escaped from the island of Elba. He had been exiled after his reign as self-proclaimed Emperor of France. In the one hundred days following his escape, countless lives were lost. It ended with the Battle of Waterloo, and Napoleon was exiled once again, but this time to the island of St. Helena.

Today is Buffalo Bill Day, which "ain't what it used to be." In his time, Buffalo Bill—or Colonel William F. Cody—was the symbol of the American wild west. It didn't matter that a lot of what he presented was purely show business. Buffalo Bill's Wild West Show gave the whole world a thrilling view of the American frontier. Cody was born on this day in 1846. With some help from his press agent Ned Buntline—who dubbed him Buffalo Bill—this Pony Express rider and frontier scout romanticized the adventurous wild west. The legends did have some negative effects for three or four generations, but let the record be set straight. Bill himself respected the aboriginal people he encountered on the plains. And in later years, he fairly employed a number of great men like Sitting Bull. Buffalo Bill may have killed some 4,280 buffaloes in his lifetime, but he didn't massacre this uniquely American animal wholesale. Like the Native Americans whom he often accompanied on these hunts, he killed only enough for food and clothing for the hunters' families.

Modern music has three distinctly different birthdays to celebrate today. In 1928, jazz composer and pianist Fats Domino was born. His inspired songs like "Blueberry Hill" influenced a generation of exuberant, hopeful youth. In 1932, country and western legend Johnny Cash was born. This hard-edged, rough diamond wrote songs dedicated to American rural life, where young men and women only tentatively walk the line and demand the freedom of the open spaces. In 1943, British pop guitarist Brian Jones was born. A member of the not-so-clean-cut rock band—The Rolling Stones—Jones and the rest of the group exemplified youthful rebellion against a conformist social standard. Art may reflect life, but new music is often the collective voice of younger generations.

America lost a part of its innocence when a 1,200-pound bomb exploded in the World Trade Center on this day in 1993. It was the first major act of terrorism on American soil, and it caused a shockwave of heightened security consciousness across the country. No one had ever considered that this sort of cowardly violence would ever reach this continent. The perpetrators were quickly apprehended. As President Clinton said, "Once again we have shown that terrorism will not pay." Attorney General Janet Reno stated, "The message we wish to send is that no ocean is too wide, no distance too far, no time period too long and no effort too great to make those who kill or injure Americans immune from the U.S. justice system." But the damage was done. Six people lost their lives, a thousand were injured, and security measures were permanently increased at airports and other likely targets.

27th.

1807 Henry Wadsworth Longfellow was born.

1902 John Steinbeck was born.

1922 The U.S. Supreme Court unanimously guaranteed women's suffrage.

1933 The Reichstag building burned in Germany.

1939 The U.S. Supreme Court outlawed sit-down strikes.

1973 The American Indian Movement began the occupation of Wounded Knee. (See May 8th and December 29th entries.)

1973 The United States accused North Vietnam delaying the release of American POWs.

All the world, Shakespeare wrote, is a stage. But some world events are themselves staged. And today's anniversary sadly reminds us of this truth. In 1933, the Reichstag parliamentary building—the seat of Germany's fragile democracy—burned in Berlin. Adolf Hitler had been elected Chancellor of Germany, but the nation was politically divided. The Nazi party did not have majority rule and it used this incident to incite a public outcry. The party promptly denounced the fire as a Communist plot. Ultimately that public handed dictatorial powers to Hitler. History's verdict is that the fire was probably set by the Nazis themselves.

When we look at America today, we see not only what is before our eyes but also the mythological images that are part of our legacy. Henry Wadsworth Longfellow—who was born on this day in 1807 in Portland, Maine—contributed a great deal to our treasury of American mythology. The legends of Hiawatha and Evangeline as well as the epic tales of the "Wreck of the Hesperus," "Miles Standish's Courtship," and "Paul Revere's Ride" are only a few of the word images Longfellow painted.

John Steinbeck was born on this day in 1902. And like Henry Wadsworth Longfellow who was also born on this day, Steinbeck contributed to America's mythological legacy. He chronicled the strength of the human spirit during the Great Depression in his novel, *The Grapes of Wrath*. And he documented the wisdom of the average American in his travelogue, *Travels with Charlie*.

The U.S. Supreme Court marks two important anniversaries today. In 1922, this august body unanimously guaranteed women's right to vote. After years of civil disobedience—including sit-down strikes and hunger strikes the suffragists won their battle to be heard. But in 1939, the U.S. Supreme Court outlawed sit-down strikes. The civil unrest spurred by the nation's great economic depression had forced the government's hand for too long. To stop the seemingly endless stream of sit-down strikes organized by unemployed workers and union laborers, the court limited their right to protest.

The issue of human rights marks the anniversaries of two controversial events that occurred on this day in 1973. Angered by the government's disregard for the rights of Native Americans, the American Indian Movement began the occupation of the Ogalalla Sioux settlement at Wounded Knee, South Dakota. The three-month-long siege took place on the site of an 1890 massacre where American cavalrymen killed hundreds of aboriginal men, women, and children. In the meantime, the government was protesting the violation of the Paris Peace Accords. The United States accused North Vietnam of intentionally delaying the release of American POWs and denying those prisoners their rights under the conventions of war.

28th.

Bachelors' Day (in non-leap years).

1854 The Republican party was founded.

1882 Geraldine Farrar was born.

1901 Linus Pauling was born.

1915 Zero Mostel was born.

1940 Mario Andretti was born.

You probably don't know that today is designated as Bachelors' Day. At least that's the case three years out of every four. In leap years, bachelors are traditionally given their day on the twenty-ninth of February. It's based on an old Leap Day tradition in which a lady could propose marriage to a man. Later, it was changed to every year. Period. Luckily, we no longer have to adhere to such preposterous proprieties. Men have been liberated from the grave responsibility of being the one to initiate nuptials. And women have been liberated from the anxiety of waiting for this day to arrive each year.

Americans never seem to make much of American opera star Geraldine Farrar's birthday. Born on this date in 1882, Farrar grew up amid the prejudice against American opera singers—even in their own country. American singers before and after her often changed their names to sound Italian in order to be accepted on the operatic stage, but Geraldine Farrar paved the way for the end of this senseless bias. As she matured, she brought glamour and some public acceptance in America to the profession.

Three famous men born on this day devoted their lives to us in very different ways. First was Linus Pauling, the renowned scientist, humanitarian, and advocate of vitamin C. Born in 1901, he spent much of his life helping us live longer by searching for cures to cancer and heart disease. Champion race car driver Mario Andretti kept us on the edge of our seats throughout his career, making life a little more exciting. The third man, actor Zero Mostel, is perhaps best known for his starring role as Tevye in the Broadway musical *Fiddler on the Roof.* As we consider what each of us can offer the world, think of what Tevye said: "To life!"

A new political party was organized on this day in 1854. Their common cause was simply the total abolition of slavery; their candidate for the 1856 presidential election was John Fremont. Their rallying cry was "Free Soil, Free Labor, Free Speech, Free Men, Fremont!" And they lost. But they didn't give up and their next candidate won. His name was Abraham Lincoln, and that group which stood so firmly for freedom and equality was—and still is—the Republican party.

29th.

Leap Day. (See Bachelors Day, February 28th entry.)

1960 The first Playboy Club opened.

1968 President's National Advisory Commission on Civil Disorders warned of racism.

We only get a February 29th once every four years, so we better make the most of it. People who are born on Leap Day have the privilege of growing old four times slower than the rest of us do. The flip side of that coin is that they only have birthdays once every four years. Just like many turns of fate, a good stroke of luck can have its drawbacks.

One of the world's most famous bachelors marked the celebration of Leap Day by opening an establishment dedicated to bachelors worldwide. It seems appropriate since historically, Leap Day was also known as Bachelors' Day. In 1960, Hugh Hefner, the publisher of *Playboy Magazine*, opened the Playboy Club on Chicago's Gold Coast. Though you may know this living symbol of male sophistication and bachelorhood opened a private membership club, you might not know that it gave many famous African-American entertainers their first shot at stardom. The Playboy Club also provided a new forum for a few controversial comedians who went on to become pop icons such as Lenny Bruce and George Carlin.

In 1968, this was the day when the President's National Advisory Commission on Civil Disorders issued a report about the racial and social problems that were plaguing the nation. It said: "Our nation is moving toward two societies, one black and one white—separate and unequal."

March

Some people say that if March comes in like a lion, it will go out like a lamb. Of course with the unpredictability of weather it seems that this forecast is more often the exception than the rule. However, as one of the most common American colloquialisms reminds us: If you don't like the weather, just wait a minute. It will change.

1st.

1692   The Salem Witch Trials began. (See May 27th entry.)

1781   The Continental Congress adopted the Articles of Confederation. (See January 30th and November 15th entries.)

1790   The first U.S. census was authorized.

1872   Congress authorized the creation of Yellowstone National Park. (See March 28th, May 11th, August 25th, and September 25th entries.)

1954   Ron Howard was born.

1961   The U.S. Peace Corps was established.

Did you ever stop to think how much we depend on numbers? Think about it today, because it is the anniversary of the day the first U.S. census was authorized. Since that first day in 1790, we have been counting heads—to determine Congressional districts, to allocate government money, to figure out unemployment rates, and so forth. Numbers are part of life, from baseball terms like three strikes you're out; to payment terms such as net thirty days.

President John F. Kennedy's most notable monument for many years was a noble idea. The Peace Corps was born on this date in 1961. Years later, when Jimmy Carter went to the White House, one of the things that endeared him to voters was that his mother, who was in her sixties, had been a Peace Corps volunteer in India. The Peace Corps, unlike other American aid organizations, supplies needy nations with shared knowledge, not handouts. Skilled, experienced people traveled to third-world nations and to this country's depressed areas to impart their know-how; to work side-by-side with inhabitants, to help them help themselves.

Today is Ron Howard's birthday. You may remember him as little Opie Taylor, Sheriff Andy's son, on the *Andy Griffith Show* or as the happy-go-lucky teenager, Richie Cunningham, on *Happy Days*. We watched him grow up on television, becoming a part of the family. Since those days, Ron Howard's gotten married and raised his own family just like the rest of us. But the images of the childhood and adolescence he created on screen linger in our minds.

2nd.

1836 Texas declared its independence from Mexico.

1877 Hayes-Tilden election was decided by a special Congressional commission. (See January 29th entry.)

1904 Dr. Seuss was born.

1973 Vietnam peace treaty was signed in Paris.

What would today's journalists say if a presidential election took place, and four months later, nobody had been able to decide who was elected? What would they say if a special commission made the decision about which votes counted and which votes didn't? That is a somewhat oversimplified account of exactly what happened in 1876 and 1877. It concluded on this day when a special electoral commission declared Rutherford B. Hayes as the elected U.S. President over Samuel J. Tilden.

On this day in 1973, the United States, the Viet Cong, and the North and South Vietnamese signed a peace treaty in Paris, France, ending the Vietnam War. It cost many lives; divided Americans into two opposing camps; prompted riots in the nation's cities; affected national and local elections; and—to a frightening extent—disaffected a substantial portion of an entire generation. But had those negotiations failed, countless more Americans might have been killed.

Was it mere coincidence that on Sam Houston's forty-third birthday, Texas declared its independence from Mexico? The Lone Star Republic had Sam Houston as President; and ultimately when the republic became the Lone Star State, Houston spent fourteen years as the state's senator. He only retired when secession from the union became a popular vote.

The wisest leaders know not only when to stand firm, but also when to move with the times. Take our own times, for example. One birthday is special for me and for you, and before I am done you'll know who it is, too. He was born Theodor in the year 1904. Born, they say, on this very day. He grew up and drew pictures—pictures galore! He drew Horton and Grinch and the Cat in the Hat, too. He drew Gerald McBoing Boing, the Lorax, and a Who. He's called Dr. Seuss—Theodor Geisel to boot. Everyone loves him, even owls give a hoot. He reminds us to care in the simplest way. About everything, everyone, every day.

3rd.

1791   The District of Columbia was organized.

1847   Alexander Graham Bell was born. (See January 25th and March 7th entries.)

1849   Congress established the Home Department.

1861   Czar Alexander II abolished serfdom.

1931   "The Star Spangled Banner" became the U.S. national anthem.

1969   *Apollo 9* was launched to test the lunar landing module.

The history books are filled with laws that Congress should have acted on quickly but didn't because we the people didn't want it yet. In fact, Congress sometimes lags considerably behind public sentiment and public practice. Today's anniversary is a case in point. "The Star Spangled Banner" was written by Frances Scott Key in 1814. And we were using Key's song as our national anthem shortly after it was published. However, on this date in 1931, Congress officially made it our national anthem. It only took Congress 117 years to catch up to the times.

The man responsible for the swift delivery of more good news, bad news, and gossip than anyone wants to hear was born today in 1847. When Alexander Graham Bell was a young man he left his home in Edinburgh, Scotland, to teach what he called "visible speech"—a sort of sign language—to the hearing impaired in Boston, Massachusetts. In the course of his work, he experimented with a device that transmitted sound electronically. His tests finally succeeded when he called out to his assistant: "Mr. Watson, come here. I want you." His voice came through a small horn connected to a wire stretched from another part of the house. Bell's telephone eventually knit sprawling cities and the whole world together. It spawned new businesses. It created a new household necessity.

Nations like buildings must be constructed brick by brick, step by step to ensure a solid foundation and a secure structure. One might think that our nation's capital—including all of its governing departments—were established all at once. But in truth, it took many decades to create what we now take for granted, and today marks the establishment of two key elements. In 1791, the District of Columbia was organized, establishing a nonpartisan home for our federal government. And in 1849, the U.S. Congress established the Home Department which is now known as the Department of the Interior.

On this day in 1969, some wise men at NASA launched the *Apollo 9* space mission to test the soundness of the lunar landing module before having astronauts use it on the moon. Bravery must always be tempered by the wisdom of experience, otherwise brave acts become foolhardy ventures.

While the Civil War between the northern and southern states over the abolition of slavery was still being waged, Czar Alexander II of Russia issued a manifesto which officially abolished serfdom. On this day in 1861, Alexander decreed that no individual could force another to work in exchange for life and little else. The feudal system that had long been synonymous with peasant life was finally dissolved. No longer enslaved by landowners and nobles, an individual was free to work wherever and for whomever he chose; and had the right to be paid for labor.

4th.

1789   The U.S. Constitution went into effect.

1888   Knute Rockne was born. (See November 1st entry.)

1937   Presidential Inauguration Day, until 1937. (See January 20th entry.)

Up until President Franklin Delano Roosevelt's second term, this was Inauguration Day in the United States. On this day in 1801, Thomas Jefferson became the first president to be sworn in at the nation's capital. In 1861, Abraham Lincoln stood on the same spot and said: "This country, with its institutions, belongs to the people who inhabit it. Whenever they shall grow weary of the existing government, they can exercise their constitutional right of amending it, or their revolutionary right to dismember or overthrow it." In 1933, FDR stood before the nation and proclaimed: "The only thing we have to fear is fear itself" and called for "action, and action now." If there is one paramount thread in inaugural addresses, it is that the people ultimately decide their own destiny.

Today marks the anniversary of the U.S. Constitution's official enactment. In 1789, the entire nation banded together under this important statement of rights and responsibilities. It has been challenged; it has been amended; but it remains the organic, yet supreme law of the land.

Today is the birthday of an immigrant who, for many, epitomizes middle America. He was born in Voss, Norway, on this date in 1888. He came to this country with his family when he was five years old. He went to college and became a chemistry instructor, as well as assistant coach of the football team. His name was Knute Rockne. If anyone can be said to have revolutionized American football and put it on the map, it was this man, Notre Dame's Gipper.

5th.

The Feast of St. Pirans.

1770 The Boston Massacre took place.

1908 Rex Harrison was born.

1946 Winston Churchill delivered his "Iron Curtain" speech.

Today is the feast day dedicated to St. Pirans, patron saint of miners. With his protection, men and even some woman entered dark tunnels dug deep into the earth in search of coal, silver, and gold. In many ways, he is a saint to be invoked by anyone who seeks to disclose a hidden treasure.

Massacre—like so many other words in our language—is a relative term. It can refer to the cold-bloodedness as well as the volume of slaughter. It is a reminder that mere numbers are not the measure of impact. This is the date when, in 1770, British troops fired into an unruly crowd in an incident known as the Boston Massacre. In light of later worldwide developments, it is interesting to know that just five men died in that massacre. At the battle of Lexington—when the American Revolution started—eight men were killed and ten were wounded. By comparison, millions were killed on the battlefield, in concentration camps, and in besieged cities durig the Second World War.

Probably no phrase has been a more eloquent summary of an attitude than an expression Winston Churchill coined on this day. In 1946, Churchill delivered a speech in Fulton, Missouri, in which he said: "From Stettin in the Baltic to Trieste in the Adriatic, an iron curtain has descended across the Continent." For nearly five decades, the Iron Curtain separated two hostile ideologies. The rift didn't start with Churchill's speech, but his words crystallized the realization that an international breach was forming.

British actor Rex Harrison was truly a man's man. Born on this day in 1908, this Lancashire native grew to become a legendary film and stage presence, playing everyone from the King of Siam to eccentric murderers. But as the idiosyncratic Professor Henry Higgins in the musical *My Fair Lady*, Harrison posed a question still asked today. Why can't a woman be more like a man?

6th.

Alamo Day. (See February 23rd entry.)

1475   Michelangelo was born.

1857   The U.S. Supreme Court ruled that the slave Dred Scott could not sue for his freedom in a federal court.

1936   The Spitfire MK1 took to the air.

1946   France recognized Vietnam as a free state within the French Indochina Federation.

1967   Svetlana Alliluyeva announced her intention to defect from the U.S.S.R.

Some people leave their mark on the world in the shape of ideas; some leave a legacy of deeds; and others seem to leave no mark at all. But fewer people still have ever donated their genius. Today we celebrate Michelangelo's birthday. In 1475, this visionary artist was born in Caprese, Italy. When he died he left behind the glorious ceiling and altar of the Vatican's Sistine Chapel; and the immortal statues of David and the Pieta as his heirlooms. He championed a new realism at a time when we were uncertain how to define human proportions—both physically and spiritually. He made us see the beauty of who and what we really are in relation to the universe that surrounds us.

Freedom must never be taken for granted. Many people have paid a high price for freedom on this day. In 1946, France recognized Vietnam as a free state within the French Indochina Federation. But in 1857, the slave Dred Scott was denied his freedom when the U.S. Supreme Court ruled that he could not sue for his freedom in a federal court. In 1967, Svetlana Alliluyeva announced her intention to defect from the U.S.S.R. Even though she was the daughter of Soviet dictator Josef Stalin, she was willing to give up her home to gain the freedom she desired.

During the Second World War, England and Germany had unique icons that symbolized their respective might as nations—airplanes. Germany had designed the Messerschmitt which was considered to be the world's fastest fighter plane. But it was on this date in 1936 that a British prototype took to the air—the Supermarine Spitfire. Designed by Reginald Mitchell, the Spitfire was the pride of England's R.A.F. fleet well into the 1950s. It was also a source of jealousy for German pilots throughout the war. You see, the Messerschmitt had been designed to hold the perfect German. Though Hitler was little more than five feet tall—shorter than the average build of the Luftwaffe airmen— no one in his ranks wished to tell him he wasn't the perfect German. Their plane was fast, but very cramped.

7th.

1849   Luther Burbank was born. (Burbank Day)

1854   The sewing machine that could stitch buttonholes was patented.

1876   The telephone was patented. (See January 25th and March 3rd entries.)

1936   Germany violated the Treaty of Versailles.

1945   The Remagen Bridge was captured.

Today is Burbank Day. You may know that Burbank is a famous city in California. However, you might not know that the Burbank Day that city celebrates each year commemorates Luther Burbank's birthday, unless you are a horticulturist. Burbank developed over two hundred varieties of fruits and vegetables, as well as hundreds of hybrid flowers at his California laboratory. The world became a more colorful and delectable place thanks to this man's efforts.

It has been said that every deed is just another stepping stone on an eternal road. No action—however isolated it may appear in the present—ever stands alone. Today marks two anniversaries that prove this point. In 1936, Germany violated the Treaty of Versailles by occupying the Rhineland. One single act led that nation on the rocky road to war. Nine years later, in 1945, the U.S. Ninth Armored Division captured Germany's Remagen Bridge. That maneuver changed the course of the Second World War in favor of the Allied powers.

When it comes to patent, buttons ring a bell on this day. In 1854, Charles Miller of St. Louis, Missouri, was granted a patent. He had invented a sewing machine that could stitch buttonholes. And in 1876, Alexander Graham Bell was granted a patent for his telephone.

8th.

1765 The British House of Lords passed the Stamp Act. (See March 18th and March 22nd entries.)

1841 Oliver Wendell Holmes, Jr. was born.

1950 The U.S.S.R. declared that they had built an atomic bomb.

1962 Arnold Schuster was killed in Brooklyn.

1979 President Jimmy Carter went on a Middle East peace mission. (See January 7th entry.)

It is Oliver Wendell Holmes, Jr.'s birthday. Born on this date in 1841, Holmes was the son of a New England doctor who was also a famous literary figure. Oliver Junior chose to walk a different path. He became an attorney. As a U.S. Supreme Court Justice, Holmes was famous for the brilliance of his dissents and for the power of his judgments. Like his noted father, he was a prolific writer. Like his father, he was long-lived. He served on the Supreme Court for over three decades. He resigned when he was well past ninety. In 1919, Holmes wrote a phrase that is as true today as it was then: "The best test of truth is the power of the thought to get itself accepted in the competition of the market."

Not too many people today recognize the name of Arnold Schuster. But on this date in 1952, this law-abiding citizen recognized the legendary bank robber Willie Sutton; told the police; and was later shot and killed in Brooklyn, New York. Shuster's murder was never solved, and it discouraged many other law-abiding citizens from turning criminals in to the police.

As a nation, Americans don't take declarations of any kind lightly. When Great Britain's House of Lords imposed the Stamp Act on this day in 1765, Americans spoke out by boycotting all imported British goods including sugar and tea. This first direct tax placed on the fledgling colonies was supposed to pay for military defense during the French and Indian War. But Americans cried out that taxation without representation was tyranny. In 1950, the U.S.S.R. declared that they had built an atomic bomb, and once again, Americans did not take the declaration lightly. The U.S. military built more atomic weapons to balance the power between these two mighty nations.

Sometimes, the actions of one individual can inspire many to find a reasonable resolution to their problems. On this day in 1979, President Jimmy Carter began a Middle East peace mission. This simple act of diplomacy eventually led to the signing of the first Egyptian-Israeli peace treaty, ending the long-running conflict between the two nations.

9th.

1401	Amerigo Vespucci was born.
1790	Benjamin Franklin wrote his creed.
1796	Napoleon Bonaparte married Josephine de Beauharnais. (See June 24th entry.)
1822	Artificial teeth were patented.
1860	Japanese ambassador Niimi Buzennokami arrived in San Francisco, California.
1862	The first battle of the ironclads took place.
1943	Bobby Fischer was born. (See September 1st entry.)
1975	Alaskan pipeline construction began.

This is Amerigo Vespucci's birthday. In 1401, the man after whom America is named was born in Florence, Italy. No one understands why America was given the Christian name of the navigator and mapmaker who placed the continent on a navigational chart, whereas Colombia was named after the surname of the discoverer of the New World. It is hard to imagine the United States of Vespucci.

On this day in 1790, Benjamin Franklin took pen in hand and wrote a letter to the Reverend Ezra Stiles, who had asked about Dr. Franklin's religious beliefs. "I believe in one God," wrote Franklin, "Creator of the Universe. That he governs it by his Providence. That he ought to be worshipped. That the most acceptable Service we render to him is doing good to his other children."

The old saying goes "his bark is worse than his bite." On this day, our bite got a little better. In 1822, Charles Graham of New York City was granted a patent for artificial teeth.

Making connections isn't always a simple task, but sometimes persistence pays, as today's anniversaries will attest. In 1860, Japanese ambassador Niimi Buzennokami arrived in San Francisco, California. After centuries of isolation and years of delicate negotiation, Japan finally established diplomatic relations with its eastern neighbor, the United States. And in 1975, the Alaskan pipeline was begun, connecting the contiguous United States to its northern sister-state's most valuable resource—oil.

Today marks a few meetings of great minds. On this date in 1796, Napoleon Bonaparte married Josephine de Beauharnais. Their romance inspired an empire, though their reign didn't last. In 1943, another master strategist was born in Chicago. Chess player Bobby Fischer rose to prominence when he played board champion Boris Spassky for the world chess title. Hopefully, we can all be inspired by strategic meetings rather than following the example of the ironclads. When they met in 1862, the two pioneer warships—the *Monitor* and the *Merrimac*—fought a furious battle in the harbor near Hampton Roads, Virginia.

10th.

1862   The U.S. government issued its first paper money.

1946   Italian women voted for the first time.

1948   Jan Masaryk was defenestrated.

1949   Mildred Gillars was convicted of treason.

1975   Carla Hills became the Secretary of Housing and Urban Development.

You all know how difficult it is toting a pocketful of change around. Imagine what it was like when you had to lug your dollars around in the same fashion. This is the anniversary of a truly ingenious solution. In 1862, the U.S. government issued its first paper money. Instead of carrying bags of five, ten, and twenty dollar coins, the government made it easier to transport and conceal the very same amount.

History is filled with mysteries that can throw considerable light on larger matters when and if they are ever solved. For example, a question still mark hangs over this particular day. It goes back to 1948, when the late Jan Masaryk, son of Czechoslovakia's founder and a champion of democratic self-government fell from a window in Prague and died. Masaryk was his nation's anti-communist Foreign Minister. Many believe he was pushed; and his tragic death did make it easier for the Communists to consolidate their control.

The world's view of women has changed on this day a number of times in recent history. In 1946, Italian women were allowed to vote for the first time. Their influence was limited to local elections, but that first step was a major one. In 1949, Mildred Gillars was convicted of treason. During the Second World War, Gillars was known as Axis Sally. She applied a woman's touch to her Nazi propaganda broadcasts, reminding Allied soldiers that their sweethearts might not wait for them so they should give up the battle and go home. In 1975, the third woman to hold a U.S. cabinet position was appointed. Carla Hills became the Secretary of Housing and Urban Development.

11th.

1302 Romeo and Juliet's wedding day, according to Shakespeare. (See April 23rd entry.)

1779 U.S. Army Corps of Engineers first established. (See June 14th entry.)

1888 The Blizzard of 1888.

1922 Jack Kerouac was born.

1941 Lend-Lease Law was signed.

1942 General Douglas MacArthur left the Philippines for Australia, vowing: "I shall return." (See January 26th, April 11th, April 19th, and October 20th entries.)

1950 Bobby McFerrin was born.

1986 One million days since the traditional founding of Rome (April 21, 753 BC). (See April 21st entry.)

Everybody talks about the weather, but nobody does anything about it. Ask anyone what subject makes news more often than any other. Chances are the answer will be sports or crime. But the truth is that the weather makes news daily. It definitely was on everyone's mind back in 1888. On this day, a blizzard started in the north-eastern United States. The storm lasted for three days, piling up mountains of snow recorded as high as five feet with drifts towering over twenty feet tall in some areas. Four hundred people perished and damages were estimated at $20 million at the time. The people who lived through the Blizzard of 1888 talked about it for the rest of their lives.

This is the anniversary of the Lend-Lease Law. In 1941, President Franklin D. Roosevelt signed an act that authorized the shipping of war supplies to England and other nations fighting Nazi Germany during the Second World War without physically involving ourselves.

Perseverance. Determination. Commitment. These qualities are equally necessary in times of war and times of peace. We should not forget these three words lest we forget our present, mutual goal: perseverance, determination, and commitment. It was on this day in 1942, as Japanese forces continued to advance in the Pacific, that General Douglas MacArthur embodied these attributes as he left the Philippines for Australia, vowing: "I shall return."

Since today is singer and composer Bobby McFerrin's birthday, it's time to begin the day on a lighter note by quoting the lyrics of one of Mister McFerrin's most popular songs: "Don't worry, be happy."

American novelist and poet Jack Kerouac was born on this day in 1922. He epitomized the Beat Generation of New York and San Francisco during the 1950s. His work introduced beatniks to Zen Buddhism in *The Dharma Bums*. He revealed America as seen through his eyes in his classic novel—*On The Road*—which he wrote in less than a month. Surprisingly, English was this acclaimed author's second language. His parents were French-Canadian.

12th.

1832   Charles Boycott, the Irish estate manager who caused boycotts, was born.

1912   The Girl Scouts of America was founded. (See September 4th entry.)

1933   President Roosevelt gave his first fireside chat.

1938   Nazi Germany occupied Austria.

1984   British ice dancing team, Torvill and Dean, became the first skaters to receive nine perfect 6.0 scores in the world championships.

1986 Susan Butcher wins the 1158-mile Iditarod Trail Sled Dog Race.

1987 *Les Miserables* opened on Broadway. (See February 23rd, March 24th, April 7th, May 23rd, December 20th, and December 30th entries.)

1994 The Church of England (Anglican) ordained its first female priests. (See February 11th entry.)

When our country was very young, each president was seen by the people only in the few places he had occasion to personally visit. As the nation grew, the chief executive was still seen and heard by a relatively small handful of the electorate, but his picture and words were carried in the nation's newspapers. Then came Franklin D. Roosevelt. In 1933, he tried something new on this date; he broadcast a fireside chat on national radio and the entire nation heard his message from his own lips.

We often find ourselves wondering what would have happened if one deed in a chain of events had been different. And today's anniversary gives us a reason to ponder. In 1938, Adolf Hitler's Nazi Germany invaded Austria and set about what they called *Anschluss*—the incorporation of Austria into Germany. It shocked the world. But the world did nothing about it. And Hitler occupied more neighboring nations.

Some goals take a little more than a hundred percent effort. And today's anniversaries are both obvious examples of what can happen when you try just a little harder to succeed. On this day in 1984, the British ice dancing team, Torvill and Dean, become the first figure skaters to receive nine perfect scores of 6.0 in the world championships. And two years later, in 1986, Susan Butcher became the first woman to win the grueling 1,158-mile Iditarod Trail Sled Dog Race in the Alaskan wilderness.

What's in a name? Captain Charles Boycott, an Irish estate manager, was born on this day in 1832. You might think he would have been teased about his unusual name, except that it didn't have the meaning at that time that it does today—at least not until he had earned a reputation for unfairness that drove the peasant tenant-farmers in his charge to organize against him in an 1879 act of civil disobedience. Not everyone sets out to make a name for themselves and, no doubt, this is not what Charles Boycott had in mind.

13th.

1733   Joseph Priestley was born.

1781   Uranus was discovered.

1852   The first Uncle Sam cartoon was published.

1877   Ear mufflers were patented.

1881   Czar Alexander III was assassinated.

1884   World standard time was established.

1935   Tennessee outlawed the teaching of evolution. (See May 5th entry.)

1972   Clifford and Edith Irving pleaded guilty to conspiracy charges. (See January 9th entry.)

1974   The Arab nations agreed to end their five-month oil embargo. (See October 17 entry.)

1988   I. King Jordan became president of Gallaudet University in Washington, D.C.

1992   The House of Representatives unanimously voted to publicly identify 355 current Capitol Hill check bouncers.

Though time may seem to pass more slowly in some places than in others, clocks all over the world are synchronized. It isn't the same time everywhere, but we can look at our watches and calculate the time in Singapore or Moscow or Timbuktu. We've only been able to do that since 1884. That's when an international conference which was held on this date in Washington, D.C. established an international time standard. Using Greenwich, England (00°00' longitude) as the commencement point from which all time is measured as plus or minus Greenwich Mean Time, all the time in the world was adjusted at thirty minute and one hour intervals. For example, Maritime Standard Time is thirty minutes earlier than Eastern Standard Time; and Mountain Standard Time is one hour later than Central Standard Time.

Uncle Sam is America's most popular relative. He's been around a long time and today's his birthday. In 1802, the lanky Yankee in the star-spangled suit was born in the issue of *The New York Lantern*, a weekly newspaper. Frank Bellew drew the original character that replaced the nation's previous cartoon symbol—Brother Jonathan.

Nature played a key role in a couple of events that occurred on this date. In 1733, Joseph Priestley was born in Leeds, England. This Yorkshire chemist's discovery—oxygen—swept the world like a breath of fresh air. And in 1781, British astronomer Sir William Herschel discovered a huge planet residing just past the planet Saturn in our solar system. Uranus was the first of three planets to be sighted during the next two hundred years.

Isn't it ironic that on the same day the planet Uranus and oxygen were discovered, we would also mark the anniversary of our return to ignorance? In 1935, the state of Tennessee officially outlawed the teaching of evolution in schools. The fundamentalist fervor that triggered this action also fueled the famous John Scopes "monkey trial." Attorney Clarence Darrow bravely defended the young teacher who was accused and and eventually convicted of teaching a religious heresy.

The struggle to be heard hit a high watermark on this day in 1988, when I. King Jordan became president of Gallaudet University in Washington, D.C. Students of this liberal arts college for the hearing impaired demanded to be heard: They protested the school's tradition of hiring hearing-persons as presidents. Jordan became the school's first hearing-impaired president, succeeding Elisabeth Ann Zinser who was a hearing person.

Hasty actions can be the undoing of well-meaning schemes. On this day in 1881, Czar Alexander III was assassinated by radical terrorists who demanded a constitutional government in Russia. Ironically, the czar had just signed a bill to establish exactly what they wanted. When he died, so did the enactment of the agreement. In their haste to obtain certain freedoms, the conspirators destroyed their own dreams by not waiting for an official response.

Building public trust and confidence, including and beyond financial credit, is only the tip of the iceberg; maintaining that trust takes a lifetime of unfailing and honest work. When the U.S. House of Representatives unanimously voted, on this day in 1992, to publicly identify 355 current and former members who had overdrawn their accounts at the House bank, public confidence was dampened by an atmosphere of mistrust in elected officials.

Chester Greenwood of Farmington, Maine, was granted a patent on this day in 1877, for an invention that anyone who has been spared from cold ears on a frosty day can applaud. Inspired, no doubt, by a chilly New England winter, Mr. Greenwood invented a pair of ear mufflers.

Dependence on a single resource is a weakness that can enslave and destroy even the mighty. The United States learned that lesson on this day in 1974. The group of oil-producing Arab nations who had imposed a five-month embargo on sales to the U.S. ended their sanction. American dependence on outside oil resources crippled both industry and the economy. They tried to solve the problem by tapping into oil sources closer to home.

14th.

1743 America's first town meeting was held.

1794 Eli Whitney received a patent for the cotton gin. (See December 8th entry.)

1879 Albert Einstein was born.

1947 Philippine military and naval bases were leased to the U.S.

1950 New York hired a rainmaker.

Today is Albert Einstein's birthday. Born in 1879 in Ulm, Germany, Einstein's life story illustrates quite a few morals. For one thing, the man who is regarded as one of the world's great geniuses was not a particularly good student. He was not really a late bloomer, just an individualist who went at his own pace in his own way. He won the 1921 Nobel Prize in Physics for creating a tremendous revolution with his theory of relativity, which he once explained in simple terms, "When a man sits with a pretty girl for an hour, it seems like a minute. But let him sit on a hot stove for a minute and it's longer than any hour. That's relativity." He also escaped Nazi Germany and immigrated to the United States, where he spent the rest of his life championing the need for atomic research. Einstein even wrote to President Franklin Roosevelt to plead his cause. If there is any truth in the old adage that right makes might, Einstein's story seems to bear it out. This man of peace helped forge the key to the world's most terrible weapon. He was a German exile who became one of his adopted country's great assets.

Eli Whitney got a patent for his cotton gin on this day in 1794. The cotton gin patent, however, turned out to be only one of his great contributions. His cotton gin did reduce the need for hand labor which gave a tremendous boost to the South's development. But Whitney also fathered the idea of mass production; the use of interchangeable parts; and the concept of the assembly line. Very few Americans have contributed as much to the nation's economic development as Eli Whitney. The next time you go to your mechanic to have the car fixed, you might stop and think of how much more that repair bill might be if Whitney hadn't come up with the concept of interchangeable parts.

Throughout the United States, town meetings are regularly held to keep local populations informed about and involved in matters directly affecting their community. Today is the anniversary of America's first town meeting. In 1743, a group of concerned citizens met at Boston's Faneuil Hall to voice their opinions on key issues.

Terminating an agreement is not necessarily a sign of weakness nor the start of an argument. When military and naval bases in the Philippine Islands were leased to the U.S. for ninety-nine years on this day in 1947, the political climate in the Pacific Rim was still shaky. American military presence ensured that nation's security amid great political turmoil. As it is a former American territory, the U.S. government felt a strong allegiance to this large group of islands situated off the Chinese coast. During the 1970s, the agreement was amended several times to suit the needs of both nations. But in 1991, the U.S. terminated its lease and evacuated its bases. It wasn't that U.S. military defense had weakened, or that diplomatic relations between the nations had ceased. Simply, there was no longer any looming foreign threat to warrant that kind of presence.

Desperate times often trigger desperate actions. After months of suffering a severe drought followed by a dry winter, it looked as if there wouldn't be enough water to supply New York through the summer. A crisis was in the making. On this day in 1950, New York hired an old-fashioned rainmaker. Dr. Wallace Howard, director of New Hampshire's Mount Washington Observatory, tried every trick in the book to make it rain. And one month later, it snowed. The crisis was averted.

15th.

The Ides of March.

Buzzard Day in Hinckley, Ohio.

44 BC Julius Caesar was assassinated.

1937 The world's first blood bank was established.

It was William Shakespeare who warned us to beware the Ides of March. We used to think his advice was prophetic, because March 15th—the Ides of March—used to be the day when your Federal income taxes were due. We now have an extra month for that delightful exercise, when the government exacts it's fiscal pound of flesh. But there is enough in history to keep reminding us of the Ides of March. Julius Caesar was forewarned about the Ides of March. It was an accurate warning. He was stabbed to death on that very day in 44 BC by a group of Roman senators including his friend Brutus. Being killed is bad enough, but having it done by a friend is even worse.

Just remember the sage advice of baseball great Satchel Paige: "Don't look back; someone might be gaining on you." Nature's clock is more reliable than any manmade timekeeper. Today is one of those natural time markers. The town of Hinckley, Ohio, commemorates this day as Buzzard Day. Like the swallows that return to San Juan Capistrano, the buzzards are scheduled to return on this day to Hinckley. The town sets aside the first Sunday after this date as Buzzard Sunday. So let us remember, with an eye to the buzzards, that there is a time and place for everything.

Today marks the anniversary of a lifesaving bank. The deposits and withdrawals made at this bank have spelled the difference between life and death for many people. What's even more surprising is that no one is turned away at the door if they need to make a withdrawal, even if they've never made a deposit in their lives. Dr. Bernard Fantus established the world's first blood bank on this day in 1937, at Chicago's Cook County Hospital. Both blood and plasma could finally be safely collected, stored, and distributed to patients who did not have family with similar blood types—a breakthrough for surgical procedures and emergency treatment.

16th.

1534 England severed relations with the Roman Catholic Church. (See February 11th and February 25th entries.)

1751 James Madison was born.

1802 The U.S. Military Academy at West Point was established by law.

1910 Harry Houdini became the first man to fly an airplane in Australia.

1926 The first liquid-fuel rocket was flown. (See March 23rd entry.)

This is the anniversary of the day President Thomas Jefferson signed a law establishing a great educational institution. The U.S. Military Academy at West Point, New York was born in 1802 on this date. Throughout its history, it has been far more than a military institute. We sometimes forget that, at a time when higher education was offered only to rich Americans, West Point offered it to those who merited it—regardless of their economic station. The long gray line of cadets produced great generals; but it has also produced distinguished presidents, corporate heads, and academic leaders. Its motto stands as solid as its reputation: "duty, honor, country."

The first liquid-fueled rocket was flown on this date in 1926. Dr. Robert H. Goddard succeeded in his experiment in Auburn, Massachusetts. Ironically, few people noticed.

But if the U.S. was not interested in rocketry at the time, another country was. While the Second World War was raging, the young German scientist Wernher von Braun pushed the development of Goddard's idea and created rocket-powered weapons like buzz bombs and missiles. After the war, von Braun came to the U.S. and helped guide our historic space program. Goddard's idea finally flowered in his homeland after all.

On President James Madison's birthday, consider how much influence an individual can have on the creation of a nation. Born in Port Conway, Virginia, in 1751, Madison grew to become a key figure in the planning and ratification of the U.S. Constitution. In collaboration with Alexander Hamilton and John Jay, Madison also wrote twenty-nine out of eighty-five issues of the *Federalist Papers*, a published commentary on the drafting of the Constitution. And as a member of the House of Representatives, Madison was also the sponsor of the Constitution's first ten amendments. Later in life, Madison was elected president of the United States—chief executive of the nation's constitutionally based government.

On this date in 1910, master magician Harry Houdini became the first man to fly an airplane over the Australian continent. He also drove a car for the first time on that trip. After he left, he never did either again. Just because you've done something once, doesn't mean you have to do it again.

17th.

St. Patrick's Day.

1328 Scotland won its independence from England.

1776 British forces evacuated Boston, Massachusetts.

1834 Gottlieb Wilhelm Daimler was born.

1969 Golda Meir became Israeli Prime Minister. (See May 3rd entry.)

Few holidays are as enthusiastically celebrated as St. Patrick's Day. Ireland's patron saint died on this date in the city of Saul in the year 461 AD. Today, everybody in the U.S. participates in "the wearing of the green" in honor of the man who reputedly drove the snakes from Ireland and converted the Celts to Christianity. By happy coincidence, the Irish-American city of Boston, Massachusetts also celebrates the 1776 evacuation of the British from colonial shores. But no matter which event is more important, on this day we can all apply the motto that appeared on the American Revolutionary flag emblazoned with a writhing snake: "Don't Tread on Me."

Oppression can never stand up to courage fueled by a sincere desire for freedom. Scotland won its independence from British rule on this day. In 1328, a treaty was signed in Edinburgh, ending thirty-two years of war. The peace only lasted for five years, but British feudal superiority over Scotland did not survive because of the freedom-loving spirit of its people.

Today is the birthday of a man whose name symbolizes precision, quality, and elegance—even though you may not immediately recognize it. In 1834, Gottlieb Wilhelm Daimler was born in Württemberg, Germany. He studied engineering and became well known as an engine designer. In 1885, Daimler designed his first high-speed internal combustion engine; and his first engine-powered bicycle. The next year, he developed a horse-driven four-wheel carriage with a single-cylinder engine option. The following year, he created an engine-powered boat. And two years later, he produced a four-speed-drive, four-wheel, engine-powered carriage for the Sultan of Morocco. With this profit, he opened the Daimler Motor Company. In 1901, Daimler sold the first of his enhanced automobiles which he named after his financial backer's daughter—Mercedes—because he felt a German name wouldn't sell as well in France.

18th.

1766   Great Britain repealed the Stamp Act. (See March 8th entry.)

1837   Grover Cleveland was born.

1949   The North Atlantic Treaty Organization (NATO) was formed.

1965   Soviet cosmonaut Alexei Leonov became the first man to walk in space. (See July 17th and May 30th entries.)

Four years after the end of the Second World War, the western Allies, including the United States, Great Britain, and France, formed the North Atlantic Treaty Organization on this date in 1949. NATO was a noble experiment—an attempt to share a common defense responsibility among the member-nations' armed forces. To the amazement of many, and despite defections and dissensions, NATO lasted and stretched its sphere of influence far beyond the North Atlantic Rim.

Grover Cleveland was a unique President. He was elected for two non-consecutive terms, as the twenty-second and the twenty-fourth President of the United States. He was also the target of perhaps the most vicious political campaign in American history. During the 1884 election, Cleveland was called the "Rum, Romanism, and Rebellion" candidate in a speech given by a supporter of competitor James G. Blaine. As if that were not enough, Cleveland was accused of fathering an illegitimate child. He defused that issue by admitting the charge. If you think that politics plays rough today, bear in mind, the man born on this date in 1837 in Caldwell, New Jersey, went through the mill twice to get elected. He also proved that honesty and integrity will beat mudslinging every time.

Alexei Leonov became the first man to walk in space on this day in 1965. Flying aboard the *Voskhod 2* along with Paul Belyayev, this courageous cosmonaut let himself out of the capsule's air lock about 110 miles above the Crimea, took photographs, and commenced a free fall that lasted ten minutes before going back inside.

19th.

The swallows return to San Juan Capistrano, California.

1891 Earl Warren was born.

1920 U.S. Senate rejected American involvement in the League of Nations. (See June 28th entry.)

1995 Michael Jordan returned to play basketball. (See February 17 entry.)

One swallow does not a summer make, but today the swallows herald a pretty certain sign of spring in an area where spring is not that easy to differentiate from winter. This is the day when, according to tradition, the swallows come back to the San Juan Capistrano mission in California. It is celebrated in legend and song by people who have never been within a thousand miles of Capistrano, but it helps remind them and us that spring is just around the corner.

When Earl Warren was born on this date in 1891, his hometown of Los Angeles, California, was barely past its frontier days and the U.S. was—so to speak—still in short pants. But before he died, Chief Justice Earl Warren presided over two contrasting chapters in American history that helped this nation mature. One was the case of *Brown v. Board of Education of Topeka*, in 1954, in which the Supreme Court banned racial segregation as public policy, and reversed the previously accepted idea of separate but equal facilities for African-Americans and whites. Justice Warren's other historic role was as Chairman of the Warren Commission, which was established to investigate President John F. Kennedy's assassination, and decided that assassin Lee Harvey Oswald had acted alone. It was largely because of Warren's tremendous prestige and integrity that this decision remained relatively unquestioned for so many years.

On this day in 1920, the U.S. Senate rejected the Treaty of Versailles and kept our nation out of the League of Nations. Some historians have contended that if the U.S. had joined the League there might have been sufficient international agreement to prevent the Second World War. That point, of course, is moot. But today we mark the anniversary of the last time the U.S. saw fit to return to an isolationist policy. Soon thereafter, perhaps inevitably, it became impossible for the U.S. to maintain that posture.

20th.

1751 King George III succeeded to the throne of England.

1852 *Uncle Tom's Cabin* was published in book form. (See June 14th entry.)

1928 Mr. Rogers was born.

It has been a long time since the disposition of a king has determined history. The last king whose disposition affected us here in America was George III of England. He succeeded to the throne on this day in 1751. King George thought he could push the colonists around, and he found Prime Ministers who agreed with him. If he had not acted as he did, we might all be British today. Like the late New York mayor, Fiorello LaGuardia, it may be said of King George that when he made a mistake it was a beaut.

It's Fred Rogers' birthday. As Mister Rogers, he has taught generations of children the basics of life from social interaction and vocabulary to how to tie your shoes and play cat's cradle. Mister Rogers' PBC television show first aired in the early 1960s and continues to be broadcast daily.

21st.

The vernal equinox (the first day of Spring).

1960   Police in Sharpeville, South Africa, fired into a crowd of demonstrators.

1965   The Reverend Dr. Martin Luther King, Jr., led a civil rights march from Selma, Alabama. (See January 15th entry.)

It can be snowing or freezing but the calendar is very clear about it; today, give or take a few hours for a vagrant vernal equinox, is the beginning of Spring. It colors our outlook; it makes us generally a bit more optimistic; it has us looking for the first buds and blossoms. Maybe the calendar is smarter than we are. Maybe the idea of Spring in our hearts is simply good medicine after a long hard winter—or a short dull winter, for that matter.

On this day in 1965, the Reverend Dr. Martin Luther King, Jr., led a civil rights march from Selma to Montgomery, Alabama, demanding equal rights for African-American citizens. It was neither the first nor the last march, nor the most unusual instance of this remarkable man's leadership. This peaceful demonstration had a better outcome than another civil rights march held on this day in 1960. In Sharpeville, South Africa, police fired into a crowd of peaceful demonstrators, killing sixty-nine people and wounding hundreds of others.

22nd.

1621   First American non-aggression treaty was signed.

1765   The Parliament passed the Stamp Act. (See March 8th and March 18th entries.)

1882   The Edwards Law outlawed polygamy in the U.S.

1930   Stephen Sondheim was born.

1945   Arab League was formed.

1948   Andrew Lloyd Weber was born.

On this date in 1882, the guardians of public morality cheered the adoption of the Edwards Act which outlawed polygamy. Aimed at dissident Mormons who clung to that sect's earlier belief in multiple marriages, this act protected the values of nice people who did not talk about sex; and the virtue of women who didn't have very many rights. In our own times, we have adopted a different version of multiple wives—or husbands. To phrase it in computer terms, marriage is now conducted in serial mode instead of in parallel.

Do the words non-aggression treaty elicit thoughts of modern diplomacy? Their roots go back father than you might think. The first American non-aggression treaty was made on this date, in 1621. Governor John Carver of the Plymouth colony and Native American Chief Massasoit made the agreement. As such agreements go, it was a pretty good one. It lasted half a century.

The Arabs have been a great force in history more than once. From the days of the Crusades to the great Ottoman empire, Islam's believers have banded together to defend their faith. While Israel was developing into an independent, non-Islamic nation in 1945, Islamic nations in the Near and Middle East once again formally united on this day as the Arab League.

The musical theater world has great cause to celebrate on this day. In 1930, the writer and composer of *A Little Night Music*, Stephen Sondheim, was born. And in 1948, Andrew Lloyd Webber, the creator of *Cats* and *Phantom of the Opera*, was born.

23rd.

World Meteorological Day

1775 Patrick Henry uttered: "Give me liberty or give me death!"

1910 Akira Kurosawa was born.

1912 Wernher von Braun was born. (See March 16th entry.)

1942 The U.S. Army moved Japanese-Americans to interment camps.

1964 The Reverend Dr. Martin Luther King, Jr., said: "We must learn to live together as brothers or perish together as fools."

1978 The U.S. Senate raised the retirement age to seventy. (See April 6th entry.)

When the Reverend Dr. Martin Luther King, Jr., said on this day in 1964, that "We must learn to live together as brothers or perish together as fools," he was voicing the spirit which lies behind today's observance of United Nations' World Meteorological Day. Meteorologists and weather experts know that, regardless of national boundaries, we all share the same weather cycles.

On this day in 1775, at the Virginia convention, a fire-breathing lawyer named Patrick Henry rose and spoke the words that generations of Americans remember as the heart of our national heritage: "Is life so dear," asked Patrick Henry, "or peace so sweet as to be purchased at the price of chains and slavery? Forbid it, Almighty God! I know not what course others may take, but as for me, give me liberty or give me death!" Yet, in 1942, the U.S. Army moved Japanese-American citizens from their homes on the California, Oregon, and Washington coasts to internment camps high in the Sierra Mountains because people feared a potential conspiracy based on ethnic origins. As the Reverend Dr. Martin Luther King, Jr., said on this day in 1964: "We must learn to live together as brothers or perish together as fools."

Today is the birthday of an inspired filmmaker who, in turn, has inspired the film industry. In 1920, Akira Kurosawa was born in Tokyo, Japan. Besides being the first Japanese film director to receive international acclaim, Kurosawa's films have inspired some of the world's most famous American and Italian productions. The *Seven Samurai* inspired the western classic *The Magnificent Seven*. *Yojimbo* and *Sanjuro* spurred Sergio Leone to create The Man with No Name series starring Clint Eastwood, and another American production company to produce *Last Man Standing* with Bruce Willis. And Kurosawa's classic, *The Hidden Fortress*, served as the basis for the *Star Wars* trilogy.

24th.

1603 The crowns of England and Scotland were joined.

1882 Robert Koch announced discovery of the tubercle bacillus.

1902 Thomas E. Dewey was born.

1958 *Cat on a Hot Tin Roof* opened on Broadway.

If it were just because this was the day German physician Robert Koch announced the discovery of the bacillus that causes tuberculosis in 1882, it would be a significant anniversary. Dr. Koch's greatest discovery paved the way for saving many lives. But above all, it showed the need for applying scientific skills to isolate disease-bearing microorganisms.

Thomas E. Dewey was born on this day in 1902, in Owosso, Michigan. He was renowned as a criminal prosecutor, as the governor of New York State and as a two-time presidential candidate; but he will probably be best remembered in history for the 1948 election night when at least one great newspaper, *The Chicago Tribune*, was so sure of the outcome that it printed an edition declaring Dewey's victory over Harry S Truman. They were wrong.

You never know when opportunity will come knocking on your door and today's anniversary is a prime example. In 1603, Scotland's King James VI awoke to the surprising news that he was no longer King of Scotland; he was the king of both England and Scotland. Sixty hours after Queen Elizabeth I's death, Sir Robert Carey brought the message to James in Edinburgh. James was so excited that he knighted three hundred new Scottish and English lords on his way to attend his coronation in London as King James I.

Today is the anniversary of the Broadway premiere of Tennessee Williams' play, *Cat on a Hot Tin Roof* which took place in 1958. It's easy to follow in Big Daddy's footsteps and declare that there has been the smell of mendacity floating around for some time now.

25th.

1821   Greek patriots led an uprising against the Ottoman Empire. (See February 3rd entry.)

1871   Gutzon Borglum was born.

1911   The Triangle Shirt Waist Company fire occurred.

1982   The Canada Act was signed.

It is a sad fact of life that some things that need doing are not done until a shocking event awakens us. That concept comes to mind because today marks the anniversary of the Triangle Shirt Waist Company fire. In 1911, a fire in a crowded New York clothing factory resulted in the deaths of 147 people who had been working in disgraceful sweatshop conditions. The ensuing public outcry spurred a revision of both labor laws and building codes. But tragically, it took a disaster to bring reform.

Born in Bear Lake, Idaho, on this date in 1871, Gutzon Borglum's birthday inspires us to ponder why sometimes the work of men is well known while the men who did the work are forgotten. Probably every American would recognize a picture of the Mount Rushmore National Memorial—the huge carvings of George Washington, Thomas Jefferson, Theodore Roosevelt, and Abraham Lincoln protruding from a South Dakota mountainside. But few people know that this massive stone monument was created by the sculptor Gutzon Borglum. And even fewer people know that his vision included carving the bodies of all four presidents, not just their heads.

According to tradition, this is Greek Independence Day. In 1821, Greek patriots led an uprising against the Ottoman occupation of their nation. When Alexander Ypsilantis and other members of the Friendly Brotherhood crossed the Pruth River in Moldavia, they were defeated by a strong military defense force. But the incident triggered a number of anti-Ottoman revolts in the Peloponnese and on several islands. After nine long years of revolution, Greece won its freedom as a sovereign nation.

Canada had been a self-governing dominion of Great Britain since 1867, but on this day in 1982, Queen Elizabeth II signed the Canada Act which not only ratified the Canadian Constitution, it made that nation wholly independent. Canada's fight for freedom from British rule was won without bloodshed. It may have taken longer to accomplish than America's fight against tyranny, but peaceful settlements always take longer to negotiate.

26th.

1871 Prince Jonah Kuhio Kalanianaole was born. (Prince Kuhio Day.)

1885 Commercial motion picture film was first manufactured.

1953 Dr. Jonas P. Salk announced a polio vaccine.

What Prince served in the U.S. Congress? That's a question that might stump some of the experts, unless they know something about today, which happens to be Prince Kuhio Day. This is when the state of Hawaii commemorates Prince Jonah Kuhio Kalanianaole's birthday. This member of the Hawaiian royal family represented the early Territory of Hawaii as a delegate to the U.S. House of Representatives.

This is the anniversary of a communications miracle. On this day back in 1885, George Eastman manufactured the first commercial motion picture film. We all know how the ability to photograph moving pictures of great dramas and of current events created a media revolution. That's what can happen with a simple idea.

It was on this day in 1953, that Dr. Jonas P. Salk announced the development of the polio vaccine. Salk's vaccine had a stringent test ahead of it, but this was the day when a long-sought victory against the dreaded disease that caused infantile paralysis appeared likely. It strongly reminds us that for every serious problem there is the potential for a good solution.

27th.

1512 Spanish explorer Juan Ponce de Leon first sighted Florida. (See April 2nd and April 8th entries.)

1703 Czar Peter the Great founded the city of St. Petersburg.

1794 President George Washington signed an act to build a U.S. Navy.

1845 Wilhelm Roentgen was born. (See January 5th entry)

1884 The first long-distance telephone call was made between Boston and New York.

1886 Ludwig Mies van der Rohe was born.

1899 Guglielmo Marconi sent the first radio signals. (See April 25th and June 2nd entries.)

Today marks the anniversary of two media milestones. In 1899, Guglielmo Marconi sent signals through the air via radio waves across the English Channel. It is also the day the first long-distance telephone call was made. In 1884, people in Boston and New York first spoke to each other through a length of wire. Today's worldwide transmissions are descendants of these great events. Cellular phones and satellite modems make these early miracles seem somewhat quaint. And as for Marconi and Bell's innovations, a savvy twelve-year-old can buy a kit and build them both after school. They're really quite basic. But, as author Kahlil Gibran put it, "The obvious is that which is never seen until someone expresses it simply."

The United States was born as a seafaring nation, and its naval victories began with the American Revolution. But after the Revolution, we had no real navy. On this day in

1794, President George Washington—an old Army man himself—signed the Act of Congress designed to build a navy.

These are intrusive times. X-rays examine the interiors of our luggage, our mail, and ourselves. This may be an appropriate commentary on our times because today is Wilhelm Roentgen's birthday. Born in Lennep, Prussia, in 1845, Roentgen discovered what was originally called the Roentgen Ray. It opened a door through which modern physics has enlarged its view and understanding of the previously unseen.

Buildings are monuments to civilization. It is interesting to note that today's birthday occurred on the same day Czar Peter the Great founded the city of St. Petersburg. In 1703, the monarch personally planned and developed the lavish buildings and monuments of Russia's most beautiful city. Then, in 1886, Ludwig Mies van der Rohe was born in Aachen, Germany. This founding father of starkly majestic modern architecture lived and created by a simple yet profoundly inspirational rule: "God is in the details."

28th.

1797 The first washing machine patent was issued.

1930 The Turkish cities of Constantinople and Angora became known as Istanbul and Ankara.

1995 Fourteen wolves were set free in Yellowstone National Park.

We like to think of our times as the great age of convenience—from precooked foods to numerous labor-saving devices. But it has been a long time coming. For example, it was way back in 1797 on this date, that a U.S. patent was granted to Nathaniel Briggs of New Hampshire for a washing machine. It took more than a century before electricity and human ingenuity produced the labor-saving device we now depend upon.

Throughout history, cities and countries have disappeared with a stroke of the pen. They aren't destroyed. Their buildings don't disintegrate. They just change their names. You won't find Zanzibar on the map any more; you'll find Tanzania where it used to be. You may have misplaced Ceylon which was where Sri Lanka rests now. And it may be decades before Mynamar is simply Mynamar and no longer referred to as Mynamar, formerly Burma. Two of the world's most ancient cities changed their names on this date, in 1930. The cities were Constantinople and Angora; they are now Istanbul and Ankara.

Wolves hadn't roamed the Wyoming wilderness since the 1920s. Their bad reputation had been brought over by European settlers, who carried generations-old misconceptions with them. Explorers Lewis and Clark called the wolf the "shepherd of the buffalo." But when millions of buffalo were slaughtered to near extinction by the settlers, the wolves preyed on the settlers' cattle and sheep. Ranchers, farmers, and bounty hunters trapped or shot the wolf to near extinction in return. But on this day in 1995, fourteen western Canadian timber wolves were released into Yellowstone National Park to restore the balance of nature that had existed before the settlers tipped the scales. Their release signaled the defeat of a seven-year battle by the Wyoming and Montana legislatures to stop the reintroduction of the wolf.

29th.

1790 John Tyler was born.

1812 The first White House wedding took place.

1867 The British North America Act established the Dominion of Canada.

1961 Washington, D.C. residents won right to vote in the Presidential elections.

1973 The last U.S. prisoners of war and armed forces left Vietnam.

This is an anniversary many Americans remember. In 1973, the last American prisoners of war—POWs—and armed forces left Vietnam.

Until 1961, there was a whole class of law abiding, literate, tax-paying U.S. citizens, who were denied the right to vote in the Presidential elections. It wasn't caused by racial or religious prejudice. It was simply because they happened to live in the District of Columbia, rather than in a state. On this date, the Twenty-third Amendment to the U.S. Constitution finally granted the residents of the nation's capital the right to vote in a presidential election.

Today is John Tyler's birthday. You might not recognize his name as readily as the campaign phrase, "Tippecanoe and Tyler, too." That's our John Tyler. Born in 1790 in Greenway, Virginia, Tyler was the first vice president to wake up one day and find himself the President of the United States. President William Henry "Tippecanoe" Harrison had died one month after taking office and Vice President John Tyler moved into the

White House without much Congressional enthusiasm. We have had all too much experience since then with sudden accessions to the Presidency like Teddy Roosevelt, Harry S Truman, Lyndon B. Johnson, and Gerald R. Ford. So we should be grateful that the first time it became necessary, in 1840, Tyler was there to make it work.

Wedding bells rang for the first time in the White House on this day in 1812. Lucy Payne Washington married Supreme Court Justice Thomas Todd at the President's home. Lucy was First Lady Dolly Madison's sister, so it seemed only right that the presidential couple host her wedding to a member of the highest court in the land. But, truly, on that day their status as bride and groom outranked anyone else in attendance.

Freedom celebrates a victory without bloodshed on this day. In 1867, Great Britain's Parliament passed the British North American Act. The four Canadian provinces of Quebec, New Brunswick, Nova Scotia, and Ontario were granted the right to form an almost autonomous, but definitely separate dominion. They still owed their allegiance to the queen, and relied on London as the center of ultimate jurisdiction, but in all other respects, Canadians gained their right to independence.

30th.

1840 Beau Brummell died in poverty.

1858 The eraser-topped lead pencil was patented.

1867 Secretary of State William H. Seward completed the negotiations for the U.S. purchase of the Alaskan territory. (Seward's Day and Alaska Day)

One of the wisest or luckiest decisions ever made was sealed on this day. In 1867, U.S. Secretary of State William H. Seward completed negotiations for America's purchase of the Alaskan territory from Russia. The price was $7,200,000. Critics at the time called the deal Seward's Folly. We can only hope that we may commit similar follies in our own time.

A word to people who have trouble looking neat or fashionable. There is hope, ladies and gentlemen, that sartorial splendor and good fortune do not necessarily go hand in hand. On this day in 1840, Beau Brummell—whose name is synonymous with stylish elegance—died penniless in France.

What was the world's greatest invention? Some will say the wheel; some will nominate electricity. A lesser known contender is H.L. Lipman's invention which was patented on this date in 1858. This Philadelphia resident patented the concept of attaching an eraser to the end of a lead pencil. Any man who gives the world a chance to eradicate a mistake deserves to be recognized as a public benefactor.

31st.

1840 Ten-hour government work day was instituted.

1854 Treaty of Kanagawa opened Japan to U.S. trade.

1933 The U.S. Congress authorized the Civilian Conservation Corps.

1949 The province of Newfoundland entered into the confederation of Canada. (See July 1st entry.)

Anniversaries are a convenient way to illustrate how times have changed. In 1840, for example, President James Van Buren established a ten-hour work day for government employees, as a means of bettering their working conditions.

Today marks the anniversary of the signing of the Treaty of Kanagawa in 1854. You may not recognize the name, but you might recognize the event. It was the agreement that opened Japanese ports to U.S. ships—the beginning of Japanese-western trade. One cannot help wondering how different the world's history might have been if this treaty had never been signed, if Commodore Perry had stayed in the North Atlantic; and if the transistor and the silicon chip hadn't been invented.

A unique bill was authorized by the U.S. Congress on this day in 1933, which transformed our nation. The Civilian Conservation Corps was established by President Franklin Delano Roosevelt to provide vocational training and jobs for unemployed young Americans. That in itself made the program commendable; the Great Depression had deprived an entire generation of job opportunities. But the CCC—as it's better known—also built levies along the Mississippi River to protect its often-flooded valley; constructed campgrounds in our national parks; planted trees in previously logged forests; built badly needed fire lanes in heavily forested wilderness areas; and worked to conserve our already dwindling natural resources. Sadly, the program was abolished in 1942.

April

INTRODUCTION

April showers may bring May flowers, but most of us are too busy worrying about our taxes to stop and smell the daffodils, tulips, lilies, and hyacinths which are some of the most popular blossoms of spring.

1st.

April Fool's Day.

1789 The U.S. House of Representatives finally achieved a quorum and convened.

1863 First wartime U.S. conscription law was enacted.

Today is a difficult day on which to be taken seriously. It is the day when the aquarium receives a lot of phone calls for Mr. Fish, and the practical jokesters go to town. Salt and sugar get switched, quarters are occasionally glued to the sidewalk, and all sorts of improbable tales are told with a straight face in the hope of declaring listeners to be April Fools. The April Fool's Day tradition was very much alive in 1789. The newly-established U.S. House of Representatives was finally able to assemble a quorum and get down to business. It had taken them almost a month to get that far.

The United States was not fooling around on this day in 1863, when our first wartime conscription law went into effect. By then we had fought at least three wars—if you count the Mexican War. Conscription is, so to speak, a latter-day American phenomenon since the foundations of our nation were built by volunteer enlistees.

2nd.

1513 Ponce de Leon landed in Florida. (See March 27th and April 8th entries.)

1792 Congress authorized U.S. Mint.

1805 Hans Christian Andersen was born. (International Children's Book Day)

Today is International Children's Book Day, which is observed on Hans Christian Andersen's birthday. Did you ever stop to think that the most international of all story forms is the fairy tale? Andersen, who was born in Odense, Denmark, on this day in

1805, created an immortal world of literature as did the brothers Grimm, and Charles Perrault. Dealing with basic emotions and simple confrontations is what their tales have in common. Fairy tales appeal to children because they can clearly understand each message.

Believe it or not, there is a fairy tale in the making. On this date, in 1513, the Spanish explorer Ponce de Leon landed in what is now Florida, near the present-day city of St. Augustine. He was looking for the Fountain of Youth; it is an odd quirk that a place known for its number of retired residents should have been first explored in a search for eternal youth.

Somebody once said that the difference between a government and a mob is that a government makes its own hard money. From that point of view, today is a notable anniversary. On this date in 1792, Congress authorized the establishment of the U.S. Mint. Ever since then, we seem to have been engaged in a dispute between those who thought we were running out of money and those who thought we could always mint more.

3rd.

1783 Washington Irving was born.

1882 Jesse James was killed.

1936 Bruno Richard Hauptmann was executed.

1948 Marshall Plan was enacted.

1978 President Jimmy Carter decided not to produce the neutron bomb.

1982 British Prime Minister Margaret Thatcher ordered a naval task force to the Falkland Islands. (See June 14th entry.)

1984 President Ronald Reagan signed a policy directive designed to combat international terrorism.

Today is the anniversary of four decisions with far-reaching consequences. In 1948, Secretary of State George Catlett Marshall's $5 billion European Recovery Program—the Marshall Plan—was enacted by the U.S. Congress. Marshall had proposed the aid package aimed at rebuilding postwar Europe during a Harvard University speech one year earlier. In 1978, President Jimmy Carter decided not to produce the neutron bomb.

His decision canceled development of a weapon designed to destroy living beings while leaving buildings intact. But less peaceful decisions have also been made on this day. In 1982, Prime Minister Margaret Thatcher, ordered a naval task force to the Falkland Islands. The islands had been British territory since 1833, and Argentina's seizure of these South American islands was considered an act of aggression. And in 1984, President Ronald Reagan signed a policy directive designed to combat international terrorism. The act gave the U.S. power to launch preventive and retaliatory strikes against foreign terrorists.

Today is Washington Irving's birthday. Born in New York City in 1783, Irving created characters like Father Knickerbocker, Ichabod Crane, the Headless Horseman, and Rip Van Winkle. He told the story of Granada's glorious Alhambra. He taught America to laugh at itself.

There is an interesting contrast brought to mind by this day. It happens to be the anniversary of the outlaw Jesse James' death in 1882 in St. Joseph, Missouri; and Bruno Richard Hauptmann's execution in New Jersey in 1936. By all accounts, Jesse James was a professional thief and killer. Yet he was also an American folk hero of sorts. He was shot by Robert Ford, a member of his own gang. By contrast, Bruno Hauptmann was convicted of the kidnap and murder of aviator Charles A. Lindbergh's baby. He denied his guilt with his last living breath. In both cases the press had a Roman holiday.

4th.

1841   President William Henry Harrison died of pneumonia. (See February 9th entry.)

1859   Daniel Emmett gave a premiere performance of his song "Dixie."

1902   The Rhodes scholarships were established.

1949   NATO became official. (See March 18th entry.)

1968   Reverend Dr. Martin Luther King, Jr. was assassinated. (See January 15th entry.)

On this day in 1901, the founder of Rhodesia and empire builder, Cecil Rhodes, set aside $10 million in his will for the establishment of that most coveted of awards to American college graduates—the Rhodes scholarship. Since that day, Rhodes Scholars have come from every part of the country and every walk of life; and their studies in the great English universities have helped both nations to understand each other a little better.

There is a certain ironic twist to today's anniversary. In 1859, composer Daniel Emmett first introduced his song, "Dixie" in New York City. Even though he wrote about wishing to be down south in the land of cotton where old times there are not forgotten, he chose to sing for his dinner under the great northern lights of Broadway. Perhaps passions occasionally have to take a back seat to the possibility of fame and fortune.

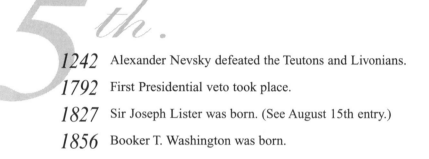

5th.

1242 Alexander Nevsky defeated the Teutons and Livonians.

1792 First Presidential veto took place.

1827 Sir Joseph Lister was born. (See August 15th entry.)

1856 Booker T. Washington was born.

On this day, in 1792, President George Washington, for the first time, used his power to veto a bill passed by Congress. He rejected a measure apportioning the number of representative districts. It was a Presidential precedent and Washington's successors have been far less reluctant to use their veto power. Our system of governmental checks and balances was designed to give all three branches some kind of governance over the other two. Whether this would have continued if the first President had not chosen to exercise the veto is something we will never know.

Today is Booker T. Washington's birthday. Born in 1856 in Franklin County, Virginia, Washington emerged from a childhood in slavery to become a pioneer of African-American education and the first head of the famous Tuskegee Institute. He worked to gain the rights for all African-Americans to receive an education. We now take that right for granted, but for many years it was outlawed in this country. His progressive spirit inspired many young people to reach far above public expectations or objections.

Today is the birthday of a pioneer of preventive medicine and the founder of antiseptic medicine. In 1827, Sir Joseph Lister was born in Essex, England. He grew up to become a surgeon at the Glasgow Royal Infirmary. Placing him in charge of a new surgical block in 1861, the hospital's managers hoped that the young doctor and the new facilities would decrease the incidence of "hospital disease" among postoperative patients. This fatal illness was killing nearly fifty percent of Lister's Male Accident Ward patients. Dr. Lister tried many methods to combat the outbreak, but it wasn't until August 12, 1865, that he found a cure. Using an antiseptic barrier to protect surgical wounds from airborne bacteria, Lister reduced patient mortality to less than fifteen percent within a year.

On this day in 1242, Teutonic and Livonian invaders were defeated by a relative handful of soldiers as they advanced on the Russian city of Novgorod. Led by the first non-Mongol czar, Alexander Nevsky, the brave yet ill-equipped Russian army stood on the shores of Lake Pepius awaiting their fate. The Battle of the Ice, as it was later called, was just that. As soldiers met in combat, the weight of men and horses weakened the ice on the frozen lake. Miraculously, the ice broke beneath the enemy, taking them to a chilling death. The city was saved. And according to history, the battle signaled the end of the Mongol rule of Russia.

6th.

1830   The First Church of Latter Day Saints (Mormons) was organized.

1909   The North Pole was first reached by modern man.

1909   The first African-American reached the North Pole.

1917   The U.S. entered the First World War. (See December 7th entry.)

1965   The U.S. launched the Early Bird communications satellite.

1978   President Jimmy Carter signed legislation extending the mandatory retirement age from sixty-five to seventy. (See March 23rd entry.)

1984   Space shuttle *Challenger* was launched to recover and repair a damaged satellite.

Religious intolerance and persecution wrote a new and unhappy chapter in the chronicles of American history because of the establishment of a new church. On this date, in 1830, the Church of Jesus Christ of the Latter Day Saints—more commonly known as the Mormon church—was founded by Joseph Smith in Seneca County, New York. Smith was murdered by an outraged mob a few years later. Driven from more than one community, the Mormons ultimately made a heroic transcontinental trek to Utah. Led by Brigham Young, the Mormons built a flourishing community in the Rocky Mountains and thrived.

On this date in 1909, Robert E. Peary and Matthew Henson reached the North Pole with a team of Inuit guides. It marks the first time modern man ever reached the world's northernmost compass point. There is only one aspect of this event that has been rather generally overlooked. Credit for this feat has traditionally gone to Peary alone. Matthew Henson, an African-American, was the other first explorer to stand at zero north latitude, side-by-side with Peary.

Today marks the anniversary of America's first military involvement in international affairs. In 1917, the United States entered the First World War when the U.S. Congress approved a declaration of war against Germany. It was our first full-scale expedition into armed conflict on continental European soil. Its aim was to protect the rights of our allies.

Today's key historical events show how much we have changed our view of progress. In 1965, the U.S. launched the Early Bird communications satellite. Progress was measured by a nation's ability to compete in the race for prominence in outer space. Two decades later, progress was measured by man's ability to responsibly maintain what he had established. In 1984, the space shuttle *Challenger* was launched to recover and repair a damaged satellite while in orbit.

It was on this date in 1978 that we extended our usefulness a few more years, putting off being put out to pasture. President Jimmy Carter signed legislation extending the mandatory retirement age for most private employees from sixty-five to seventy years of age.

7th.

1873   John McGraw was born.

1897   Walter Winchell was born.

1948   The United Nations World Health Organization was established. (World Health Day) (See November 12th entry.)

1949   *South Pacific* opened on Broadway.

1953   Swedish diplomat Dag Hammarskjöld was elected U.N. secretary-general. (See July 29th entry.)

This is World Health Day. In 1948, the United Nations established the World Health Organization to research and prevent disease and improve public health worldwide. Thanks to this organization, smallpox was completely eradicated and the fight continues to eliminate other fatal illnesses in every corner of the planet. The World Health Organization is uniquely privileged; it is concerned with a subject that transcends national borders and prejudices. Medical science does not usually consider its processes state secrets; it does not wage economic warfare; it does not hold human life to be merely a cheap and replaceable commodity.

The impact some people make is often felt beyond their own time. That was probably true of Walter Winchell who was born on this date in 1897. During the 1930s and 1940s, Winchell was one of America's most influential columnists and broadcasters. But as a lasting influence, he is remembered more as a maker of words than as a rumor peddler. We often hear words and phrases like "scram," or people being "that way." Those are idioms that Winchell not only popularized; he invented most of them. Some of his usages of the English language have faded. But in the end, it isn't what Winchell said; it was how he said it that was significant.

When John J. McGraw was born on this date in 1873, baseball was a fairly new game. McGraw helped to make baseball the national pastime. He spread its fame and charm worldwide. He was a fine player, and a great manager. McGraw not only developed championship teams and trained outstanding future managers; he led the New York Giants on several international tours. He wrote books about the game and created a whole standard of conduct for the playing field: taking a combative stance; arguing with umpires; and running his ball club with an iron hand that earned him the nickname "Little Napoleon."

Today is the anniversary of a controversial theatrical landmark. In 1949, the musical *South Pacific* opened on Broadway to a shocked audience. The successful team of Rodgers and Hammerstein had written a musical about the affects of racial prejudice! One song struck deep into hearts of theatergoers that night—"You've Got to Be Taught." It reminded people that prejudice often was taught at home.

8th.

1513   Ponce de Leon landed at St. Augustine, Florida. (See March 27th and April 2nd entries.)

1730   Consecration of first synagogue in New York.

1873   Oleomargarine was patented.

On this date in 1873, a patent was issued for the manufacturing process used to produce oleomargarine. Within a year, laws to protect dairy producers against competition from the butter substitute were enacted. But margarine persisted.

A Sephardic Jewish congregation first settled in New York City during the 1650s, but authorities wouldn't permit them to build a place of worship. On this day in 1730, the Spanish and Portuguese Synagogue was officially consecrated. Freedom of worship took a while in colonial America. Even after the enactment of the Bill of Rights, it was still an uphill fight. Maybe that is what makes this basic freedom one that people are still so willing to defend.

9th.

1105   Great Britain's King Henry I was reprimanded for his long hair.

1865   Robert E. Lee surrendered to Ulysses S. Grant. (See January 19th entry.)

1926   Hugh M. Hefner was born. (See February 29th entry.)

1965   The Houston Astrodome opened in Houston, Texas.

America's great leaders are generally remembered for their hours of triumph. Today we remember one who achieved greatness even in the hour of his defeat. Robert E. Lee surrendered his Confederate Army on this day in 1865. He handed over his sword at the Appomattox Court House in Virginia, to a fellow member of Manhattan's Union Club, General Ulysses S. Grant. But after this low point in his career, Lee proved to be a great peacetime leader. His living memorial—Washington and Lee University—still stands today in Virginia.

When future historians try to figure out when the great American sports explosion really took off, they can start with an event that took place on this day. In 1965, the Houston Astrodome—a huge, enclosed sports stadium—opened in Texas. Spectator sports became impervious to inclement weather, making big-time sports an unassailable year-round institution.

History often repeats itself, and an event that occurred on this day proves it. In 1105, King Henry I of England and his entire court were verbally reprimanded in church by Bishop Serlo of Seiz during the Easter service. He complained that the assembled wore their hair like women. It was fashionable for men in the English court to grow waist-length, flowing tresses. After the service, the king begrudgingly allowed the bishop to shear his locks. Fashion trends have split generations and social groups for as long as we can remember.

Today is Hugh M. Hefner's birthday. From the day he was born in 1926, Hefner exercised his imagination—inventing adventure games for his friends and drawing cartoons. We all know that he built the *Playboy Magazine* empire and a worldwide chain of private clubs. But did you know that Hef was also a champion of civil rights, equal opportunity employment, and numerous other causes that he contributed to through his Playboy Foundation? We often remember the more sensational stories about famous people rather than their finer points.

10th.

1790 The U.S. Patent law was approved.

1849 The safety pin was patented.

1866 American Society for the prevention of Cruelty to Animals (ASPCA) was chartered.

1945 Buchenwald concentration camp was liberated.

Today marks a few important anniversaries for those who have built better mousetraps. In 1790, the first U.S. patent law was approved to protect inventions against piracy. And in 1849, the safety pin was patented by Walter Hunt of New York, thanks to that law.

Some enlightened New Yorkers obtained an important charter on this date in 1866. They founded the American Society for Prevention of Cruelty to Animals. The mistreatment of animals, particularly cart horses and beasts of burden, was so commonplace that it wasn't generally regarded as cruel behavior at the time. More than a century later, the ASPCA is still championing the rights of abandoned pets; and the safety of wild animals that have been abused.

Cruelty is not peculiar to a particular era. Seventy-nine years to the day after the New York anti-cruelty movement began fighting for animal rights, the victorious Allies in the Second World War came upon the horror of the Nazi concentration camps. Today marks the anniversary of the liberation of the Buchenwald concentration camp in Germany. In

1945, the U.S. Army's Eightieth Division found piles of corpses, living skeletons, crematoria, gas chambers, and paraphernalia which made the tortures of the Inquisition look like kindergarten. On this day, civilization discovered that barbarism was not dead. But it was not the last time such atrocities against human beings were discovered.

11th.

1947 Jackie Robinson played his first major league baseball game for the Brooklyn Dodgers. (See January 31st entry.)

1951 President Harry S Truman removed General Douglas MacArthur from command. (See April 19th entry.)

1986 Washington state employees won a suit requiring the state to pay women as much as men for comparable work.

President Harry S Truman once said: "The buck stops here." On this day, in 1951, the buck stopped with a vengeance when President Truman removed General Douglas MacArthur from his command during the Korean War. The two men had disputed American involvement in that war from the very beginning. MacArthur came back to a hero's welcome. He spoke before a joint session of Congress and told the nation that old soldiers never die, they just fade away. But the power of the Presidency did not fade away.

Today we salute a landmark victory for women's rights. In 1986, Washington state employees won a lawsuit that hit the state below the belt. The decision required the Evergreen State to dig deep into its pockets and pay women as much as men for comparable work.

12th.

1606 Great Britain adopted the Union Jack.

1861 The American Civil War began.

1945 Franklin Delano Roosevelt died. (See January 30th entry.)

1955 The Salk vaccine was declared safe and effective. (See March 26th entry.)

1961 Yuri Gagarin became the first man to fly in space, orbit the earth, and make a safe landing.

1985 Senator Jake Garn became the first U.S. senator to fly in space.

1988 Harvard University was granted first animal life-form patent. (See June 16th entry.)

Fort Sumter stands in the harbor of Charleston, South Carolina, and on this day in 1861, it was the hub of history. The Confederate Army fired on this Union garrison, and the Civil War began.

Space travel played an important role in two events that occurred on this date. In 1961, Soviet cosmonaut Yuri Gagarin became the first man to fly into space, complete one full orbit around the earth, and make a safe landing. Twenty-four years later, in 1985, a U.S. Senator made space travel history. Senator Jake Garn of Utah became the first senator to fly into orbit as a passenger on the space shuttle *Discovery*.

This is the anniversary of a unique patent. It wasn't the design for building a better mousetrap. In fact, quite the opposite. In 1988, Harvard University was granted a patent for building a genetically-engineered mouse. The first animal life-form ever patented marked the beginning of a new scientific frontier—which society may or may not agree—increases man's understanding of nature.

Flags have served as visible identities of individuals, groups, and nations. Soldiers and civilians alike still swear allegiance to causes represented by banners. One very familiar flag created a debate over the cause it represented—the Union Jack. In 1603, King James VI of Scotland had become King James I of Scotland and England. He commissioned a new national flag that reflected this union and that would serve as a standard for his shipping and naval fleets. On this day in 1606, Great Britain adopted the Union Jack—a banner which combined the Scottish cross of St. Andrew with the British cross of St. George. It wasn't always the happiest of unions: Scotland feared British exploitation; and England feared a flood of Scottish immigration. But King James immediately managed to convince his people to swear an undying allegiance to a Scottish game which involves maneuvering a ball between flags on a course. Of course, that game is golf.

13th.

1598 King Henry IV of France signed the Edict of Nantes.

1742 Handel's *Messiah* premiered in Dublin, Ireland. (See September 14th entry.)

1743 Thomas Jefferson born. (See February 13th entry.)

1852 Frank W. Woolworth was born.

1870 The Metropolitan Museum of Art was founded.

1923 The Illinois state legislature voted to allow women to serve on juries.

1958 Van Cliburn won Moscow's Tchaikovsky International Piano Contest.

Today is Thomas Jefferson's birthday. Any time Americans meet freely to hear an uncensored comment by someone exercising the right to speak his or her mind, we are reaping the rewards of that joyous event which took place on this day in Shadwell, Virginia in 1743. Jefferson became the principal author of the Declaration of Independence. He also contributed essential concepts to the U.S. Constitution and the Bill of Rights. He bequeathed funds and his entire book collection to the establishment of the Library of Congress—our nation's depository for every copyrighted work. Those are just a few of the reasons why Jefferson's birthday is every American's celebration.

New York's Metropolitan Museum of Art is world famous for its magnificent collections. It was founded on this date in 1870, when America was considered an agrarian nation, and a cultural backwater. At the time, the idea that an American art museum would eventually be of equal stature to the Louvre in Paris or the Prado in Madrid seemed a bit ambitious. But on this same date in 1958, the international music world lost its long held and very similar feelings about American musicians. Texas-born pianist Van Cliburn won Moscow's Tchaikovsky International Piano Contest.

It's ironic that on the same day New York's Metropolitan Museum of Art was founded in 1870 and Texas-born pianist Van Cliburn won Moscow's Tchaikovsky International Piano Contest in 1958, we would also celebrate the birth of the man who created an American icon: the five-and-dime store. This is Frank W. Woolworth's birthday. Born in 1852, the creator of the dime store launched his empire with a shop in Rodman, New

York. Woolworth's concept was so successful that it soon became a nationwide chain. His dime stores not only sold inexpensive perfumes, toys, candies, record albums, and housewares, they offered patrons refreshing soda fountain specialties and snacks as well. Quite a few Americans have seen the Metropolitan's art treasures, and many have heard a live opera. But millions more Americans fondly remember their first childhood visits to Woolworth's, though the last Woolworth's closed its door in the late 1990s.

The cause for civil rights celebrates two notable anniversaries on this day. In 1598, King Henry IV of France signed the Edict of Nantes, granting civil rights to the Protestant Huguenots—a religious minority who had been persecuted by the Catholic majority for their beliefs. And in 1923, the Illinois state legislature voted to allow women to serve on juries. This august body decided that women were capable of responsibly deliberating a set of given facts and reaching a final decision without changing their minds.

14th.

1536 Wales became part of England.

1865 President Abraham Lincoln was shot. (See February 12th and April 15th entries.)

1890 The Pan-American Union was founded. (Pan American Day) (See November 18th entry.)

1910 President William Howard Taft threw the first ball to start the major league baseball season.

1912 The passenger liner *S.S. Titanic* hit a North Atlantic iceberg. (See April 15th entry.)

Today is Pan-American Day. In the context of recent times, it should be understood that this is a day designated to remind us that we are not the only Americans; that in South, Central, and North America there are many American nations. In 1890, these neighboring nations founded the Pan-American Union. We need to be reminded every now and then of the spirit of the Good Neighbor, as President Franklin D. Roosevelt put it; or the Alliance for Progress, as President John F. Kennedy saw it; or NAFTA—the North American Free Trade Agreement—as President Bill Clinton recognized it.

There are a number of real-life tragedies which have repeatedly been subjects of drama. Two such events occurred on this day. In 1865, President Lincoln went to Ford's Theatre to see a play. John Wilkes Booth, an actor from an illustrious theatrical family, went to the theatre that night, too. The rest, as they say, is history. Years later, in 1912, the *S.S. Titanic*—a gigantic luxury liner making its maiden voyage from England to New York—struck an iceberg in the North Atlantic. Out of the 2,200 people on board, 1,523 died.

President William Howard Taft started a tradition on this day in 1910. He threw the first ball onto the playing field to start the major league baseball season.

Wales became part of England on this day. In 1536, King Henry VIII gave his consent to an Act of Parliament that officially established the union between the neighboring nations. Even though they had lived in relative independence for over three centuries, Henry felt he had to gain further control over the Welsh clergy. And this act further restricted Welsh freedom. Twenty-four new shires had been created to parcel the nation. And newly-elected representatives for each of those districts were admitted to Parliament, but no Welsh-speaking citizen was allowed to be nominated under the new restrictions. So consequently, the citizens had no voice in government.

15th.

U.S. income tax filing day. (National Hostility Day)

1452 Leonardo da Vinci was born.

1865 President Abraham Lincoln died. (See February 12th and April 14th entries.)

1912 The passenger liner *S.S. Titanic* sank. (See April 14th entry.)

Some years ago, a gentleman with a penchant for designating special days and weeks announced that April 15 was to be known as National Hostility Day. It makes sense. After all, this is the day when you must file your Federal income tax return. Every year on this day, American post offices are packed with people filling out forms, writing in their checkbooks, buying stamps, and mailing their returns. Frowns and furrowed brows sometimes become sighs of relief as these citizens exit the building.

On this day in 1452, the village of Vinci in Italy's Tuscany was the site of a great event. Inventor, designer, painter, and sculptor Leonardo da Vinci was born. The world became a richer place as da Vinci's genius grew and took form.

16th.

1818   The Rush-Bagot agreement was ratified.

1867   Wilbur Wright was born. (See August 19th and December 17th entries.)

1889   Sir Charlie Chaplin was born.

1900   The first books of U.S. postage stamps were issued. (See May 6th and July 1st entries.)

1944   The city of Seattle, Washington, suffered a severe labor shortage.

1947   Bernard Baruch spoke of "a cold war."

1962   Walter Cronkite became anchorman of the *CBS Evening News* television broadcast. (See November 4th entry.)

1987   The Federal Communications Commission warned broadcasters it would impose a broader definition of indecency over the airwaves. (See June 19th entry.)

1990   The U.S. Supreme Court let stand a ban on school dances in Purdy, Missouri. (See February 1st entry.)

This is a perfect day to study contrasts. On this date in 1818, the U.S. Senate ratified the Rush-Bagot agreement between the United States and Canada which led to the creation of the world's largest demilitarized, unfortified national border. The agreement was the result of meetings between British minister to the U.S. Charles Bagot and Acting Secretary of State Richard Rush one year earlier. Despite their differences in the War of 1812, these two nations forged a peaceful settlement. If every now and then we feel beleaguered by the throws of international politics, we have the comfort of knowing our longest border is a friendly one. But on this same day in 1947, Presidential advisor Bernard M. Baruch made a speech to the South Carolina state legislature in which he said "Let us not be deceived—we are today in the midst of a cold war." Some have contended that this was not so much a diagnosis as a self-fulfilling prophecy.

Perhaps the greatest appeal for partnership ever appeared in a Seattle restaurant window on this day in 1944, a time when the city was in the midst of a severe labor shortage. The handwritten sign read: "Woman wanted to wash dishes. Will marry if necessary."

Humor aside, the foundations of a good marriage lay beneath it. It was an invitation to work together toward common goals.

When freedom of speech becomes freedom to offend, insult, and degrade, how can we respond? One attempt was made on this day in 1987. In response to a rapidly growing trend in "shock jocks", the Federal Communications Commission issued a warning to broadcasters that it would impose a broader definition of indecency over the airwaves. Shock jocks are radio commentators and disk jockeys who broadcast inflamatory programs designed to narrowly skirt the edges of the broadcast regulations on decency. The radio stations had encouraged this bad behavior because it attracted listeners, garnering more advertising dollars. But many of the listeners were not fans. They were offended and angry, yet they continued to tune in.

When motion pictures with sound began to mark the end of the era of silent films in the late 1920s, not everyone thought the new technology was an improvement. "Talkies are spoiling the oldest art in the world—the art of pantomime," said Charlie Chaplin in 1929. "They are ruining the great beauty of silence. They are defeating the meaning of the screen." He is remembered, especially on his birthday, as one of the great masters of the silent screen. More than simply lambasting talkies, Chaplin's words describe the art form he had studied all his life. Pantomime. Wordless communication. Born in 1889 to British music-hall performers Charles and Hannah Chaplin, Charlie made his stage debut at the age of five. His first film premiered in 1914. And he went on to make thirty-five movies that year. In 1919, he founded the United Artists production company along with film stars Douglas Fairbanks and Mary Pickford as well as film director D.W. Griffith. His success paved the way for the subsequent achievements of Buster Keaton, Harold Lloyd, Harry Langdon, and Stan Laurel. Chaplin was even knighted for his work. Yet he will always be best remembered as the happy little tramp he played with his trademark mustache, bowler, and cane in such films as *Modern Times*, and *The Kid*.

17th.

1194 Richard the Lionhearted returned to England.

1542 Giovanni da Verrazano discovered New York Harbor. (Verrazano Day)

1837 J. Pierpont Morgan was born.

1894 Nikita Khrushchev was born. (See September 12th and October 30th entries.)

1961 Bay of Pigs incident ended in Cuba. (See February 24th entry.)

A king was crowned for the second time on this day. In 1194, Richard the Lionhearted was reaffirmed as England's monarch, ending an epic journey that began with his victory over the Moslem leader Saladin during the Third Crusade. On his way home from Palestine, he was taken prisoner by Duke Leopold of Austria and Holy Roman Emperor Henry VI. Richard's abductors demanded a ransom of 100,000 marks for his release. To make matters worse, his brother John had seized the throne in his absence with the help of King Philip II of France. John did little to help his brother, but Richard's loyal followers prevailed. The final proof of Richard's greatness came when he forgave his ambitious brother after he regained his throne.

Coastal cities throughout history have sprung up around safe harbors. Harbors played important roles on this day in history. In 1524, Giovanni da Verrazano discovered New York Harbor. And in 1961, Cuba's Bay of Pigs was the scene of the defeat of a U.S.-supported invasion force of Cuban exiles by Fidel Castro's army.

An archetypal capitalist and an archetypal socialist were both born on this day. In 1837, J. Pierpont Morgan was born. He grew up to be the personification of American ruthless wealth and self-serving philanthropy. And in 1894, one of the cold war's leading protagonists, Soviet Premier Nikita Khrushchev, was born. Though polar opposites on the subject of economics, they shared a strong common bond of belief that they knew what was right.

18th.

1775   Paul Revere made his legendary ride. (Paul Revere Day) (See January 1st and April 19th entries.)

1858   A sixty-day-long rainfall began in Chicago.

1906   The San Francisco earthquake occurred.

1924   Simon & Schuster published the first crossword puzzle book.

1934   The first laundromat opened.

On this day in 1775, Paul Revere rode to Lexington and Concord, Massachusetts, conveying the message that the British were coming. Even though Henry Wadsworth Longfellow's epic poem centered on this patriotic silversmith's feats, the truth of the matter is that Revere didn't ride alone. He and William Dawes both rode to Lexington;

Revere was captured by the British on the way to Concord, and Dawes was not. Perhaps Longfellow decided that there weren't enough words that rhyme with Dawes.

Solutions often create more problems which require more solutions. Today we salute the opening of the first laundromat. In 1934, the great American pastime of literally washing your dirty linen in public started in Fort Worth, Texas. Luckily, in 1924, Simon & Schuster published the first crossword puzzle book, which meant you could at least do something more thought-provoking while your clothes got clean than watch them tumble dry.

This is the anniversary of the 1906 San Francisco earthquake. The tremor's center was actually located in the small town of Olema, California, north of the city. Olema grew another forty feet north to south as the earth shifted. But the greatest damage occurred in the bayside metropolis where the quake and subsequent fires razed the city. All seemed lost on this day in 1906, but it is heartening to note that only a few years later, San Francisco was the site of a great World's Fair.

This day marks the anniversary of a rainfall of biblical proportions. The spring rains started in Chicago, Illinois, on this date in 1858. A few days later, citizens began to worry when it didn't stop. It poured for forty days and forty nights. Fifty days went by without a break. Sixty days and sixty nights later, the rains that had drenched both body and spirit stopped.

19th.

1775   The American Revolutionary War started. (Celebrated as Patriot's Day and Boston Marathon Day on the third Monday of the month.)

1951   General Douglas MacArthur gave his farewell speech. (See April 11th entry.)

1956   Grace Kelly married Prince Rainier of Monaco.

1982   Astronauts Sally Ride and Guion Bluford, Jr. became the first woman and first African-American selected for the NASA program. (See June 24th and August 30th entries.)

Today is the anniversary of "the shot heard round the world." In 1775, British troops were met in the village square at Lexington by Captain John Parker and a prepared group of armed farmers. They were ready to fight because they had been warned by Paul Revere and William Dawes the night before that the British had landed. Historians now believe that the British did not mean at all to start a war, and that the start of shooting was not only unpremeditated but almost accidental. But men were killed, and the British moved on from Lexington to the Battle of Concord where, as Ralph Waldo Emerson wrote, "once the embattled farmers stood, And fired the shot heard round the world." Patriot's Day is also the anniversary of another test of strength: the annual running of the Boston Marathon.

Today an old soldier bid his farewell. On this date in 1951, General Douglas MacArthur addressed a joint session of the U.S. Congress. Removed from his command by President Harry S Truman, MacArthur's military career ended with a few memorable words. He recalled the song about old soldiers that never die, saying: "like the old soldier of that ballad, I now close my military career and just fade away." MacArthur was a brilliant leader for whom there was no middle ground. During his career, he aroused strong feelings both for and against him. His accomplishments were tremendous, but were often followed by controversy.

We often equate love with storybook romances. On rare occasions, fairy tales do happen in real life. Today marks one of those once in a lifetime incidents. In 1956, a glamorous Hollywood actress married a royal prince. When Grace Kelly was joined in holy wedlock with Prince Rainier of Monaco, the whole world watched a story-book ending come true.

20th.

1657 Asser Levy and Jacob Barimson were granted full citizenship.

1889 Adolf Hitler was born.

1976 The Supreme Court ruled that federal courts could order low-cost housing for minorities in white urban suburbs.

History is filled with ironies, and a few events that occurred on this day prove my point. In 1657, Asser Levy and Jacob Barimson were granted full citizenship in the city of New Amsterdam, which was later renamed New York. This nation was first settled by those seeking religious freedom, though with each new group of immigrants, the battle was renewed. And on this day, settlers of Judaic origin won their contest. Coincidentally, on this same day in 1889, freedom's most notorious enemy, Adolf Hitler, was born in Branau, Austria. Fascism's rise and fall taught us that we must protect freedoms in the same way the U.S. Supreme Court did in 1976. They ruled that federal courts could order low-cost housing for minorities in white urban suburbs to ease racial segregation on this day.

21st.

753 BC Rome was founded.

1836 Sam Houston's army defeated the Mexican forces at San Jacinto, Texas. (San Jacinto Day)

1838 John Muir was born. (See September 25th entry.)

1895 Woodville Latham demonstrated motion picture projection. (See March 26th entry.)

1926 Elizabeth Alexandra Mary Windsor was born. (See June 2nd entry.)

In 1836, Sam Houston's forces defeated the Mexican army at San Jacinto, Texas. This decisive battle occurred less than two months after the fall of the Alamo and turned the tides for Texas in its war for independence. Only Texans seem to remember San Jacinto Day. The rest of us remember the Alamo. Victory can be sweet, but heroism and personal sacrifice are memorable.

When moving pictures were invented, they were a private sort of entertainment. You watched images move by peeping into a box where a huge wheel flipped one card after another. They were called peep shows back then. Woodville Latham changed all that when he demonstrated a process of projecting moving pictures onto a screen. On this day in 1895, he showed an amazed New York audience the first projected motion pictures. Ten years earlier, George Eastman had invented motion picture film, but it took Latham's invention to complete the chain of events. A whole new era of mass entertainment was born that day.

Rome may not have been built in a day, and it might not have been founded by twin brothers raised by a nurturing wolf. But on this day in 753 BC one of the ancient world's greatest cities was founded on a site surrounded by seven hills. Rome was the hub of an empire that stretched as far as Constantinople to the east and Ireland to the west. Roman forces conquered Egypt and Palestine. The Roman senate created roads, waterways, and monuments across Europe. In later centuries, Rome also became the seat of Christianity. All roads led to Rome, until their governmental system became so complex they were no longer able to control their empire.

John Muir's birthday gives us cause to celebrate our nation's natural wonders. In 1838, this naturalist and author was born in Dunbar, Scotland. When he was eleven years old, his family emigrated to Portage, Wisconsin, where he studied engineering. In 1867, an industrial accident nearly cost Muir his eyesight. Temporarily blinded, he vowed to devote his life to witnessing God's work in nature if only his sight would return. It did, and he did. Muir walked through woods and fields from Wisconsin to the Gulf of Mexico observing the solemn beauty of the forests and hills. The next year, he walked through California's majestic glaciers and forests in Yosemite Valley. He walked north through Humboldt County's giant sequoia forest; and south through the exotic Joshua tree desert. After a decade of walking, Muir fulfilled his destiny when he urged the federal government to adopt a national forest conservation policy. And in 1903, he shared his vision with President Theodore Roosevelt as they camped together in Yosemite National Park. The Muir Woods National Monument—a redwood forest with trees that are nearly 2,000 years old—was dedicated by a grateful nation in his honor while he was still alive.

22nd.

1500   Pedro Alvarez Cabral discovered Brazil.

1870   Nikolai Lenin was born.

1881   Alexander Kerensky was born. (See September 15th and November 7th entries.)

1889   Homesteaders swarmed into the Oklahoma Territory.

1904   J. Robert Oppenheimer was born. (See July 16th entry.)

1954   The Army-McCarthy hearings were televised. (See February 21st entry.).

History—like politics—makes strange bedfellows. Today, for example, marks the birth of two post-Czarist Russian leaders. Born in 1881, Alexander Kerensky led the revolution that displaced Czar Nicholas II in 1917, and established a moderate democratic government. Born in 1870, Bolshevik leader Vladimir Ilyitch Ulyanov—better known as Nikolai Lenin—returned from exile to overthrow Kerensky and his moderates, establishing a socialist regime. Kerensky himself was exiled by Lenin.

Land ownership seemed to be a hot topic on this day in history. In 1500, explorer Pedro Alvarez Cabral discovered the territory of Brazil and claimed this vast area of South America for Portugal—a nation who was not about to lose its claim to the New World to either Spain or England. In 1889, the great Oklahoma Land Rush took place. Homesteaders and carpetbaggers gathered at the border days earlier, and at the sounding of a gun on this day, the assembled crowd of covered wagons, horses, carts, carriages, and shoe leather swarmed into the Oklahoma Territory staking—and sometimes jumping—claims to the free land. Next to gold, land has impassioned people to risk everything more than any other commodity. As populations grow and land gets scarcer, this passion will surely grow. Or, as Mark Twain commented, "I've heard they don't make any more of it and therefore the price is going up."

On J. Robert Oppenheimer's birthday, it is wise for all of us to remember that all great discoveries have the potential for both good or evil. It was on this day in 1904, that a peaceful, soft-spoken man was born in New York City. This son of a successful textile merchant excelled in physics, chemistry, and Oriental philosophy at Harvard University. He became fascinated with atomic structure while studying at Cambridge University's Cavendish Laboratory. Robert J. Oppenheimer worked on the first atomic power experiments and later became director of the Los Alamos Laboratory in New Mexico. On July 16, 1945, this theoretical physicist introduced the world to an awesome power that had the potential of serving humankind for both good and evil. On that day, Almogordo, New Mexico, became the site of the world's first nuclear explosion.

23rd.

The feast day of St. George.

1564 William Shakespeare was born. (See March 11th entry.)

1616 William Shakespeare died. (See above.)

1635 A boundary dispute between Maryland and Virginia erupted into a naval skirmish off the coast of Virginia.

1988 A federal ban on smoking during domestic airline flights of two hours or less went into effect.

1995 The US observed a national day of mourning for the victims of the Oklahoma City blast. (See April 19th entry.)

This is the feast day of St. George, the patron saint of England. George was not British; and there is no indication that he ever crossed the English Channel. According to accounts, he was born in the Near East and died in Palestine around the fourth century. Hundreds of years later, he turned up as a saint whose name was invoked in England before the Norman conquest. The stories about his slaying of a dragon emerged centuries after that.

If there is one name that symbolizes the written word and the glow of theater lights, it is William Shakespeare. He was probably born on this date in 1564, and very definitely died on this same date in 1616. Every now and then, life itself lives up to Shakespeare's dramatic and historical sensibilities. Certainly, our own lives remind us that "all the world's a stage." Look around you. There are still Hamlets, King Lears, Julius Caesars, and even Macbeths serving as heads of state. There are contemporary comedies of errors and a great deal of much ado about nothing. Shakespeare's writings survive because they are excellent training grounds for the realities of life today.

Could you imagine reading in the paper tomorrow morning that a war was brewing between Vermont and New Hampshire, or that Nevada was amassing troops on the Utah border? And yet, on this day in 1635, a border dispute between Virginia and Maryland erupted into a naval skirmish off the coast of Virginia.

Since the Civil War there have been no great battles fought on North American soil. Even terrorism was regarded as something we had to beware of while travelling overseas. The bombing of New York's World Trade Center in 1993, brought home the fact that foreign radicals could bring their cowardly brand of destruction across our borders. But until the 1995 bombing of the Alfred P. Murrah Federal Building in Oklahoma City, no one believed that an American could be capable of such an horrific and senseless act.

24th.

1704 First regularly issued American newspaper started publication.

1800 The U.S. Library of Congress was established.

1833 The soda fountain was patented.

1898 Spain declared war on the U.S. (See April 25th entry.)

1962 MIT executed the first satellite relay of a TV signal.

1970 China launched its first satellite.

What American institution born on this day is black and white and read all over? In 1704, the first regularly issued American newspaper, the *Boston News Letter*, started publication.

Jacob Ebert and George Dulty are not exactly household names. But on this very day, in 1833, they received the first patent for the soda fountain. Ours is a soda fountain society. We've made major advances in the bottling and canning of soft drinks. And new flavors continue to hit the market each year. Did you ever stop to think that the soda is one of the ways America has colonized the world? Soda fountain psychology has shaped our social life—it's the "pause that refreshes," the elixir of youthful masses.

The U.S. Library of Congress was established on this day, in 1800, with $5,000 in donated funds and Thomas Jefferson's entire book collection. Today, this vast depository of American literature, letters, sound recordings and photographs stands as a monument to our intellectual heritage.

The world got a little bit smaller on this day in 1962. Scientists at the Massachusetts Institute of Technology successfully transmitted the first satellite relay of a television signal sent from Camp Parks, California, to Westford, Massachusetts. This momentous achievement made it possible for the entire world to sit back and watch a live event as it happened in one small corner. Knowledge and information should never be limited to a select portion of a given population. And satellite technology obviously isn't, because in 1970, the People's Republic of China launched their first satellite.

25th.

1864 Guglielmo Marconi was born. (See March 27th entry.)

1898 The U.S. formally declared war on Spain. (See April 24th entry.)

1918 Ella Fitzgerald was born.

1945 U.S. and U.S.S.R. troops met in friendship.

1945 The United Nations Conference opened. (See January 1st, January 9th, and October 24th entries.)

Turn on the radio and spin down the dial. Station after station broadcasts all kinds of music, news, chat, advertising, interviews, and other information to the world. One man would be particularly pleased if he were alive to see, or rather hear, this endless variety of stations, not to mention emergency broadcast services and two-way radio communications. Today is Guglielmo Marconi's birthday. Born in 1864 in Bologna, Italy, Marconi was the father of the wireless radio which revolutionized worldwide communications. But this day marks a number of other communications high-water marks as well. In 1945, as the Second World War was drawing toward a close in Europe, American and Soviet soldiers met at the Elbe River, and a group of international dignitaries met in San Francisco at the opening of the United Nations Conference. At that magic moment, the east and west joined forces on two separate fronts, despite the language barrier. In 1918, a female diplomat who never worried about speaking any particular language was born. Jazz legend Ella Fitzgerald communicated to international audiences through her singing, bringing diverse peoples together in a common love of jazz.

26th.

Confederate Memorial Day in the southern United States.

1780   John James Audubon was born.

1986   The world's worst nuclear disaster occurred in Chernobyl, U.S.S.R.

1992   Worshippers celebrated Russian Orthodox Easter for the first time in seventy-four years in Moscow, Russia.

1995   The U.S. observed a minute of silence. (See April 19th entry.)

Confederate Memorial Day, is still observed in the southern states. It honors those who sacrificed their lives in hopes of changing the future for their successors. A region's grief is somehow part of a familial heritage; a nation's grief is of almost epic proportions. It's been said that silence speaks louder than words. On this day in 1995, a nation screamed out its anguish over the loss of innocents and innocence with a national minute of silence to honor the victims of the Oklahoma City bombing.

John James Audubon was in love with America's birds. Born on this day in 1785, he drew and wrote about the uniqueness of North American wildlife with a master's touch. But some generations later, the society that bore his name—the Audubon Society—was regarded as a membership of oddballs. Bird watchers at that time had no place in a world that revered only artificial or contrived beauty. Luckily, society at large has come to share Audubon's view of natural beauty.

There are times when the unthinkable does occur. On this day in 1992, worshippers celebrated Russian Orthodox Easter for the first time in seventy-four years in Moscow, Russia. Religious rites of any kind had been banned by the Communist Party since the establishment of the Soviet Socialist Republic in 1918. It was considered to be an impossible turn of events for many years and by many generations. On this same day in 1986, the world's worst nuclear disaster occurred in the Soviet city of Chernobyl. A reactor meltdown in a nuclear based power plant exposed hundreds of thousands of civilians to dangerous levels of radioactive material which spread throughout most of Europe in the months that followed, carried by the wind and rain. No one could even measure the true extent of the damage until a few years later.

27th.

1791 Samuel F.P. Morse was born. (See February 21st and May 24th entries.)

1822 Ulysses S. Grant was born.

1937 The U.S. Social Security System made its first benefit payments.

This is an historic anniversary for the United States. But in 1937, few Americans realized how momentous it was going to turn out to be. On this day, the first insurance payments were made to retired and unemployed individuals under the Social Security Act of 1935. It is difficult to contemplate what would have happened in the ensuing generations if there had been no pension system. Regardless of its problems and defects, it was the first time the United States had committed itself to do something for citizens in need other than provide outright charity for those unable to work.

Today is the birthday of a man who changed his name and went on to fame. Hiram Ulysses Grant was born in 1822. And when this Ohio native entered West Point, he mistakenly enrolled as Ulysses S. Grant. He kept that name for the rest of his life. Grant commanded the Union army during the Civil War and became a U.S. President in 1868. To put it kindly, history records his presidency as undistinguished. Afterwards, in private life, he was bilked in an investment scam and spent the rest of his private life writing his memoirs. Royalties from his writings at least paid off his debts and provided for his family. Grant was an honest man who reinforced the latent American belief that great generals don't necessarily make good Presidents. It was sixty-six years before another professional soldier, Dwight D. Eisenhower, lived in the White House.

28th.

1758 James Monroe was born. (See December 2nd entry.)

1789 A mutiny took place on the *H.M.S. Bounty*. (See September 9th entry.)

1817 Rush-Bagot Agreement was written. (See April 16th entry.)

1993 The first "Take Our Daughters to Work Day" took place.

Most everybody knows the story of the mutiny on the *H.M.S. Bounty*. Fewer people realize that it was a true story, not a Hollywood fictionalization. It was on this day, in 1789, that Fletcher Christian led an uprising of the *H.M.S. Bounty*'s crew against its captain—William Bligh. After the facts became legendary and the best-selling book was transferred to the motion-picture screen, Captain Bligh's name became synonymous with an imprudent adherence to rules and regulations. Bligh and eighteen crew members survived being set adrift on the open sea by Christian and his mutineers. But Breadfruit Bligh, as he was later called, never learned an all-important lesson: that executives should have some level of compassion for employees' needs. Placed in a managerial role two more times, Bligh encountered mutinies at each of his posts.

A unique twist on an old tradition was established in Manhattan on this day in 1993. The first "Take Our Daughters to Work Day" was celebrated in offices, stores, factories, and everywhere else mothers work. The New York-based Ms. Foundation established the day to boost the self-esteem of the nation's young women and to open a world of opportunities to them.

29th.

1863 William Randolph Hearst was born. (See February 15th entry.)

1894 Coxey's Army marched on Washington D.C.

1901 Emperor Hirohito was born. (See November 10th entry.)

1913 The zipper was patented.

1931 President Herbert Hoover received the King of Siam.

If you think times have changed, are you aware of the story of Coxey's army? In 1894, on this day, an Ohioan named Jacob S. Coxey led a group of about four hundred unemployed men on a march to Washington, D.C. Coxey was arrested for trespassing at the Capitol Building, and his army subsequently dispersed. Coxey's Army became a symbol for raggedy groups and parades that marched on behalf of lost causes. But what Coxey really wanted was to have the government finance a public-works program. He thought this could be done simply by printing five hundred million dollars in new money.

On this date in 1863, William Randolph Hearst was born in San Francisco. Some historians believe Hearst helped to start the Spanish-American War. Hearst's newspaper, the *New York Journal*, kept calling for a confrontation until it was officially declared. The war was a success for the United States and for Hearst. But in later years, the Hearst newspaper chain shrank, and the lands that had won their liberty from Spanish rule did not prove to be islands of political serenity and happiness. The war for circulation in New York between Hearst and Joseph Pulitzer produced a whole era of sensationalist journalism. It was sardonic that the press had a field day in the 1970s when Hearst's granddaughter, Patty, was kidnapped. Sensationalism in the reporting of the news has not changed much since Hearst's heyday.

Today was the beginning of Japan's Showa—or bright peace—dynasty. In 1901, Emperor Hirohito was born at Tokyo's Aoyama Palace. He was the twenty-fourth direct descendant of Jimmu, Japan's first emperor. But Hirohito distinguished himself as Japan's first modern emperor. He broke the age-old precedent of Imperial silence in 1945, when he broadcast Japan's acceptance of the Potsdam Declaration on the radio. He broke a 1,500-year tradition in 1959, by allowing his son, Crown Prince Akhito, to marry a commoner. During the 1970s, he became history's first reigning Japanese monarch to tour both Europe and the United States.

It was an historic day at the White House, in 1931, when President Herbert Hoover welcomed the King of Siam. It was the first time an absolute monarch traveled to the United States and entered the doors of the White House.

Gideon Sundback of Hoboken, New Jersey, received a patent on this day in 1913. This simple event gives all of us some reason for concern on occasion because Mr. Sundback had invented a separable fastener. The zipper made getting dressed and undressed a lot easier than meddling with buttons.

30th.

1789   George Washington was inaugurated as President of the United States. (See January 20th and March 4th entries.)

1798   The U.S. Department of the Navy was established. (See March 27th entry.)

1803   The United States doubled in size through the Louisiana Purchase. (See April 22nd and December 30th entries.)

1889   The first George Washington Bridge opened, linking New York City and the state of New Jersey. (See October 24th entry.)

Today is a memorable American anniversary. It was on this date, in 1789, that George Washington was sworn in as President of the United States on the balcony of Federal Hall in New York City. The first inaugural speech in America was uttered at that ceremony. Although many more followed, Washington's words are worth hearing once again: "The foundation of our national policy will be laid in the pure and immutable principles of private morality."

On this day in 1889, the centennial of George Washington's inauguration, the ribbon was cut to open the George Washington Bridge in New York City. At the time, it connected the community of Washington Heights, New York, with the farmland and forests of Fort Lee, New Jersey, as well as all points west. But it only stood for forty-two years before it was replaced with the far larger bridge that spans the Hudson River today.

Historically, this is a great day for organizing and acquiring. It was on this date, in 1789, that the United States Department of the Navy was established by an act of Congress; since that time it's grown to become the strongest, most powerful navy in the world. The Louisiana Purchase took place on this day in 1803, when the United States purchased enough land from the French to double the size of the fledgling country for a price of $15 million. Needless to say, it's worth a bit more than that now. Also on this day in 1900, the U.S. annexed Hawaii, gaining some of the most beautiful islands in the world.

May

The month of May derives its name from Maia, the goddess of spring and fertility. But in the United States, May has been designated as Older Americans Month, honoring the nation's senior citizens, the fastest growing segment of our population. May is also Mental Health Month. The human mind is an intricate, organic computer. Each of us is the sole owner and operator of a semi-intuitive, parallel processor of cognitive data.

1st.

1707 May Day observed throughout the world under a variety of names.

1707 Great Britain was formed.

1786 Mozart's *The Marriage of Figaro* premiered.

1884 Construction of the first skyscraper began.

1931 The Empire State Building was dedicated.

May Day has traditionally been a day of celebration. In Europe, it was celebrated by peasants with garland festivals and dances around May poles. In former Soviet Russia, the May Day Parade in Moscow's Red Square was a show of military and political might. In the United States, it is sometimes observed as Loyalty Day; but our principal observance is called Law Day, which is dedicated to respect for the law and its enforcers.

Today is an anniversary of great unions. In 1786, Mozart's *The Marriage of Figaro* premiered in Vienna, Austria. But a much more historic—yet harmonious—union took place in 1707. England and Scotland formed the nation of Great Britain on this date, and although it was not always a marriage made in heaven, the association did make Britain truly great.

Touching the sky doesn't always mean your feet have to leave the ground, as today's anniversaries will attest. In 1884, construction of the first skyscraper—the Home Insurance Building—began at the corner of LaSalle and Adams Streets in Chicago, Illinois. The first building to be called a skyscraper was only ten stories tall. But on this same date in 1931, the Empire State Building was dedicated in New York City. Taller skyscrapers have been built since those days; and even taller structures have already been conceived. But they couldn't have happened without these first groundbreaking buildings to pave the way.

2nd.

1945 The German city of Berlin surrendered to the Russian Army.

1952 The first jet airplane passenger service was launched.

1991 Pope John Paul II recognized the success of capitalism. (See January 5th, January 25th, May 4th, August 18th, November 27th, and December 2nd entries.)

On this day in 1945, the German city of Berlin surrendered to Russian Allied forces during the Second World War. It is important to remember this high-water mark in history. Russia—which had been invaded and occupied in two World Wars—became a conquering nation when it entered Germany's capital. The Russian forces went on to conquer the Japanese troops in Manchuria soon after.

Sometimes it is hard to imagine how one single action can inspire the world to follow suit. However, commercial jet airline passenger service marks such an anniversary today. In 1952, the first passenger flight took off from London, England, and landed in Johannesburg, South Africa. Little did anyone on that flight know, at the time, that jet-setting would become a way of life in less than a decade.

In his ninth encyclical, Pope John Paul II recognized the success of capitalism. But he also denounced the economic system for sometimes achieving results at the expense of the poor and of morality on this day 1991.

3rd.

1469 Niccolo Machiavelli was born.

1765 The first U.S. medical school was founded.

1898 Golda Meir was born. (See March 17th entry.)

1907 United States Chief Justice Evans Hughes said: "The Constitution is what the judges say it is."

1933 Nellie Taylor was sworn in as the first female director of the U.S. Mint.

1979 Margaret Thatcher became England's first female Prime Minister.

Today is the anniversary of a breakthrough in American medicine. The first U.S. medical school to offer a full-fledged diploma program opened on this day in 1765, at what is now called the University of Pennsylvania.

On Niccolo Machiavelli's birthday, it is worth noting that his recipe for dictatorial rulership remains as valid today as when he wrote it. Born in Florence, Italy, in 1469, Machiavelli wrote that morality had to yield to political power. To him, the reality of politics was that anything goes; a philosophy which he documented in his masterwork, *The Prince*.

Laws are fine, and the U.S. Constitution is one of the finest. But it was one of our great jurists—Chief Justice Charles Evans Hughes—who said on this day in 1907, that "the Constitution is what the judges say it is." Justice, in the end, depends not simply on the law but on the way people construe the law.

Today is a triple-header landmark in women's history. It's Golda Meir's birthday. Born in Kiev, Ukraine in 1898, Meir grew to become an ardent Zionist. She eventually emigrated to the Land of Milk and Honey—Israel—and became its first female prime minister. In 1979, Margaret Thatcher became England's first female prime minister. She had already set a new precedent by becoming the Conservative Party's first female leader, but Thatcher broke all the rules of tradition by being elected to the nation's highest political position. And the international political arena was not the only gentlemen's club rousted on this day. In 1933, many people believed women couldn't handle money. That is, until Nellie Taylor was sworn in as the first female director of the U.S. Mint.

4th.

1493 Pope Alexander VI divided the New World. (See June 7th entry.)

1836 The Ancient Order of Hibernians was founded.

1927 The Academy of Motion Picture Arts and Sciences was founded. (See May 16th entry.)

1932 Al Capone entered a federal penitentiary.

1970 Four students were killed at Kent State University.

On this day in 1836, one of America's many minorities founded a fraternal brotherhood in New York City called the Ancient Order of Hibernians. If they were founding it today, they might have simply called it the Ancient Order of the Irish. To escape religious and political oppression and a devastating famine, the Irish emigrated to America during the nineteenth century. They fought racial prejudice once they landed in Boston and New York. Eventually, the Irish not only won respect and tolerance; they rolled up their sleeves and helped to build their new country. Immigrants from other lands soon followed in their footsteps. Thank goodness, there is no longer a sign in any American workplace saying: "No Irish need apply."

Violence is unfortunately part of American life. On this day in 1970, four students were killed by National Guardsmen on the campus of Kent State University in Ohio. Student unrest, over America's involvement in the Vietnam War and the national draft policy, had erupted. Student takeovers of campus buildings, demonstrations, and manifestos were all too common, as was the violence on both sides of the protests. The incident at Kent State brought the nation up short. Years later, there was another confrontation on the site of the incident. The demonstrators sought to prevent the construction of a building on a site they felt should be preserved as a memorial.

Al Capone was the king of organized crime in Chicago during the 1920s; there seemed to be no way to bring him to justice during that heated decade. But there was. On this day in 1932, Al Capone entered the federal penitentiary at Atlanta, Georgia. He had not been convicted for any of his principal and obvious crimes: He went to jail for income tax evasion.

5th.

1818   Karl Marx was born.

1891   New York's Carnegie Hall held its opening concert. (See December 15th entry.)

1920   Nicola Sacco and Bartolomeo Vanzetti were arrested. (See July 14th entry.)

1935   John Scopes, a biology teacher, was arrested. (See March 13th entry.)

1945   Denmark was liberated from Nazi occupation. (Liberation Day in Denmark)

In 1977, the Governor of Massachusetts held a public ceremony to admit that the prosecution of the cobbler Nicola Sacco and the fish peddler Bartolomeo Vanzetti had been improperly conducted. The event occurred fifty years too late. The Italian immigrants, Sacco and Vanzetti, were arrested on this date in 1920, for manslaughter committed during a payroll robbery. It was felt by many at the time, and by more subsequently, that they had been tried, convicted, and executed by a hostile court and jury in an unfair trial because they were anarchists. The Sacco-Vanzetti case was a widely known cause celebre in American judicial history.

Today is Liberation Day in Denmark, which commemorates the end of the Nazi German occupation of that country in 1945. It also recalls the Danes' behavior under that occupation. When the Nazis took over, they wanted to force Danish Jews to wear yellow Stars of David and be subjected to the same indignities suffered by victims in other Nazi-occupied lands. The Danes refused to comply. Ultimately citizens succeeded in smuggling every Danish Jew out of the country to the neutral nation of Sweden at the risk of their own lives.

Today is Karl Marx's birthday. Born in Treves, Prussia in 1818, Marx became the de facto patron saint of the proletariat. Like many of the other "isms" that emerged during the nineteenth century, Marxism subscribed to Darwin's theory of survival of the fittest. In Marx's case, he believed the working classes, not the social elite and royalty, were most fit to rule.

6th.

1840   First postage stamps were issued.

1856   Sigmund Freud was born.

1895   Rudolph Valentino was born. (See August 23rd entry.)

1954   Roger Bannister broke the four-minute barrier for the mile run.

Today is the postage stamp's birthday. In 1840, the British postal service issued the "black penny" stamp. It was the first stamp of its kind. Since then, postage stamps have become big business both as a means of mailing letters and as valuable collectibles.

Humanity seems to be constantly setting and resetting goals for itself. For generations, runners aimed for the four-minute mile, which it seemed would never be conquered. Then, on this date in 1954, an Oxford University medical student named Roger Bannister ran the mile in 3 minutes, 59.4 seconds.

Sigmund Freud was born on this day in 1856, in Freiberg, Moravia. Few men have explored new frontiers like Freud's pioneering encounters with the subconscious and developing the field of psychology. He was obsessed and extreme in his views. But without his unyielding efforts, others might not have been impelled to follow his example.

7th.

1833   Johannes Brahms was born.

1840   Peter Ilyitch Tchaikovsky was born.

1915   The *Lusitania* was sunk by a German submarine.

1945   Nazi forces surrendered to General Eisenhower.

The British ocean liner *Lusitania* was not the first civilian ship sunk by German submarines during the First World War. But it was the first major passenger ship attacked in that war. When it was torpedoed in the Atlantic Ocean on this date in 1915, it played a major role in turning American sympathies toward the Allies and away from Germany. On this anniversary, remember it for a remark made by the American theatrical producer Charles Frohman, who was aboard the *Lusitania*. He allegedly said, as he was going to his Maker, "Why fear death? It is the most beautiful adventure in life."

In 1945, the surrender of the Nazi forces to General Dwight D. Eisenhower's army took place on this day in Reims, France. However, the cease-fire and proclamation of VE Day—Victory in Europe Day—didn't take effect until the next day.

Today is the birthday of two of the world's greatest romantic composers. In 1833, Johannes Brahms was born in Hamburg, Germany. And in 1840, Peter Illyitch Tchaikovsky was born in Votkinsk, Russia.

8th.

1828   Jean Henri Dunant was born. (World Red Cross Day)

1884   Harry S Truman was born.

1945   Victory in Europe was declared during the Second World War. (VE Day) (See May 7th entry.)

1973   American Indian Movement militants surrendered to government officials at Wounded Knee, South Dakota. (See February 27th and December 29th entries.)

Today is World Red Cross Day which is observed on this service organization founder's birthday. Jean Henri Dunant was born in 1828 in Geneva, Switzerland. His merciful efforts toward helping those in distress throughout the world earned him the position of co-winner of the first Nobel Peace Prize.

For President Harry Truman, his sixty-first birthday in 1945 was an unforgettable one. He had only been President of the United States for thirty-eight days, and on this birthday, the war in Europe ended. For Truman—who was born in Lamar, Missouri, in 1884—it was quite a day. People have disagreed about his role in world history, although he generally receives quite high marks. There is no disagreement, however, about the fact that Truman was the author and the exemplar of the most terse description ever given of the U.S. Presidency. Truman said: "The buck stops here."

9th.

1800   John Brown was born. (See October 16th entry.)

1914   Mother's Day was proclaimed.

1923   A law limiting liquor prescriptions was struck down.

1926   Lt. Commander Richard E. Byrd flew near the North Pole. (See May 12th and April 6th entries.)

1944   First eye bank opened.

1961   Newton N. Minow referred to the quality of television programming as a "vast wasteland."

Seventeen years after Robert Peary and Matthew Henson reached the top of the world, two men attempted to fly over the same point. Today marks the anniversary of this event. In 1926, Lt. Commander Richard E. Byrd and Floyd Bennett flew near the North Pole in a Fokker monoplane. They reached 87.75 degrees north before they turned back. The press and public heralded them as heroes. But there were those who doubted they had achieved their goal. They had not dropped the American flag from the plane as they had promised. Three days later, Roald Amundsen, the famous South Pole explorer, flew over the ninety-degree mark in a dirigible. But his achievement went relatively unnoticed. Many times, history discovers the truth after the fact. This was the case seventy years later, when Byrd's diary revealed that he might not have made it after all.

A new kind of bank opened on this day in 1944. It was the eye bank at New York Hospital: a source for healthy organs that could be transplanted in patients with impaired vision.

Right and wrong are relative terms. If they are hard to define at times, it is even harder when the goal is worthy but the methods are extreme. That was certainly true in the case of John Brown, who was born on this date in 1800 in Torrington, Connecticut. Brown fought against slavery. He felt so strongly about it that he killed for his convictions. He created a new land known as "bloody Kansas," and he met his Waterloo at Harper's Ferry, where a U.S. military unit captured him. The unit's commander was Robert E. Lee, who went on to command the Confederate Army while the Union Army sang "John Brown's body lies amoldering in the grave but his soul goes marching on."

On this day in 1961, Newton N. Minow, who was chairman of the Federal Communications Commission, referred to the quality of television programming as a "vast wasteland" during a speech. That vast wasteland has since become a powerful source for up-to-the-minute news and commentary as well as entertainment medium.

Isn't it refreshing to know that among the many holidays we celebrate in this nation which commemorate great deeds—Columbus Day, Memorial Day, Veterans Day, and President's Day—there is a special day set aside for some of the great deeds that could only be accomplished by the women of our nation—Mother's Day. On this day in 1914, President Woodrow Wilson proclaimed the designation of a national Mother's Day.

When a bad law is repealed there are bound to be cheers. On this day in 1923, Judge John C. Knox struck down a law that prevented doctors from prescribing more than one pint of liquor for each patient every ten days. Those cheers were no doubt accompanied by the sounds of glasses clinking together. A *New York Times* article at the time pointed out that there was "no reason why a physician, in the legitimate exercise of his discretion should not hold a man needed a highball or a glass of wine or beer as a stimulant after a hard day's manual work or nervous strain."

10th.

1869   First transcontinental railroad link completed.

1899   Fred Astaire was born.

1933   Nazis burned books.

1940   Winston Churchill became Prime Minister of Great Britain.

1994   Nelson Mandela was sworn in as South Africa's first native-African president. (See July 18th entry.)

The railroad sparked the nation's industrial development back in the 1800s. If covered wagons helped open the West, the railroad rolled out the welcome mat and made it mature. There were big doings at Promontory, Utah, on this date in 1869. Representatives of the Union Pacific Railroad drove a golden spike into the ground, completing the first full transcontinental railroad connection.

Printed books and oral storytelling traditions store ideas that later generations can discover. On this date in 1933, a group of fanatics thought they could change that. The German Nazis burned all the books of which they disapproved—20,000 copies. It was the book burners' golden hour. And of course, it didn't work. The Nazis were ultimately ground into the dust. The messages of those books were remembered.

Do the times make the men or the men make the times? The man who took office as Great Britain's Prime Minister, on this date in 1940, is a case in point. He had been a successful author and lecturer, but more of a gadfly than a politician. Winston Churchill was sixty-six years old when he was offered his nation's highest office.

Fred Austerlitz was born on this day in 1899 in Omaha, Nebraska. Years of dance lessons paid off when he and his sister Adele changed their last name to Astaire and took their act on the road. They quickly rose to stardom, playing the vaudeville circuit and eventually landing lead roles on Broadway during the 1920s. Adele got married in 1932, and Fred went out to Hollywood where he immortalized his seamless dance style on celluloid with style and grace.

An historic turning point occurred on this day in 1994. Since its early settlement by the Boers and the British in the 1800s, South Africa had maintained its rule of apartheid-segregation and discrimination between races. Native Africans were considered third-class citizens as were East Indians, who had emigrated to South Africa in the late 19th century. Bitter clashes, demonstrations, and political arrests were part of daily life. One political prisoner, Nelson Mandela, had spent years in a South African jail for opposing apartheid. He was eventually released in the 1980s as that nation began to lift its bans because of international political pressure. On this particular day, the former political prisoner Nelson Mandela was sworn in as South Africa's first Native-African president.

11th.

1854 Ottmar Mergenthaler was born.

1888 Irving Berlin was born.

1910 Glacier National Park was established.

Every time we sing "God Bless America" or hum our dreams for a "White Christmas" we pay tribute to Irving Berlin's genius. "God Bless America" was written by a man who was born in Temum, Russia, in 1888, and raised in New York's Lower East Side tenements. Berlin's songs also express America's hopes, aspirations, and attitudes from "Oh, How I Hate to Get Up in the Morning" to "You're Not Sick, You're Just in Love."

In the late 1800s, this country had an absolute explosion of print. Newspapers flourished; the book business boomed. All this was largely due to Ottmar Mergenthaler, who was born on this date in 1854, in Hachtel Germany. Mergenthaler emigrated to the United States when he was eighteen years old. As a young man, he invented a machine that mechanically set printing type. It was called the Linotype. In one fell swoop, Merganthaler's machine changed printing from a slow, hands-on trade into a mass-production enterprise. The Linotype increased daily newspaper circulation and made books more affordable.

The million-acre Glacier National Park is a monument to North America's natural beauty: a cherished heirloom we can all appreciate. On this day in 1910, this spectacular parcel of American wilderness was designated as a national park. Nestled on the northern border of Montana, it's land where active glaciers continue to shape the craggy mountains, lush alpine meadows, crystal-blue lakes and green valleys.

12th.

1926 Roald Amundsen reached the North Pole in a dirigible. (See May 9th entry.)

1949 Soviet land blockade of West Berlin ended.

1978 The Commerce Department announced that hurricanes would no longer be named exclusively after women.

1980 The first nonstop crossing of North America in a hot air balloon was made. (See June 5th and November 21st entries.)

1985 Amy Eilberg became the first female rabbi in the Conservative Jewish movement. (See February 11th and March 12th entries.)

Today is the anniversary of a significant western victory. In 1949, after eleven long months, Soviet troops stopped their blockade of all land routes to West Berlin, Germany. It did not occur as a result of any sudden upsurge of conscience, but simply because the Western powers had rendered the blockade useless by operating the world's greatest relief operation: the Berlin Airlift.

We use the term Florence Nightingale as a synonym for a kind, ministering angel. The real Florence Nightingale was born on this date in 1820 in Florence, Italy. She was an indomitable British lady who transformed nursing into a noble profession; contributed greatly to the organizational structure of the modern hospital; and changed the general concept of medical care.

Today is a dual anniversary for equality that should remind all of us that there are two sides to every endeavor—even the women's movement. On the serious side, this the day in 1985 that Amy Eilberg became the first female rabbi ordained into the Conservative

Jewish movement. It was a victory that had taken women's rights advocates decades to achieve. However, on a lighter note, advocates of gender equality also won a more dubious victory at the U.S. Commerce Department on this day in 1978, when the department announced that hurricanes would no longer be named exclusively after women. It's doubtful, however that it will ever change poets' and songwriters' personification of storms. After all, "they call the wind Harold" just doesn't have the same ring to it.

13th.

1607   Jamestown, Virginia, was founded.

1842   Sir Arthur Seymour Sullivan was born. (See November 18th entry.)

1940   Winston Churchill rallied England to battle.

1992   The crew of the shuttle *Endeavor* walk in space to rescue a damaged satellite.

This is the anniversary of the first permanent English settlement in continental America. In 1607, Virginia's Jamestown colony was established on this date. We have a tendency to concentrate on New England's Pilgrim colony, but Virginia was settled first. Pocahontas and Captain John Smith were an item way before Priscilla Mullen met John Alden and Miles Standish. As a matter of fact, history records that the Pilgrims themselves were planning to settle in Virginia when they boarded the *Mayflower*. It's a good thing they didn't, It might have taken longer to establish the thirteen colonies if everyone had settled in one place.

Patriotism and dedication were the key concepts Great Britain's Prime Minister Winston Churchill used to rally Parliament and the nation to war. Speaking to the House of Commons on this day in 1940, Churchill said: "I have nothing to offer but blood, toil, tears and sweat."

In 1992, astronauts Pierre Thout, Tom Akers, and Richard Hieb made history on this day when they grabbed a wayward four-ton satellite. The space shuttle *Endeavor* was launched to repair a damaged satellite which the three man had walk in space to retrieve. It was a first for a space shuttle crew. But that wasn't all. They then had to wrestle the satellite into the space shuttle itself for repairs using only their gloved hands. That mission also was the site of another historic event. Astronaut Kathy Thornton became the first mother to walk in space.

14th.

1804 The Lewis and Clark expedition began.

1942 Women's Auxiliary Army Corps (WAACs) was founded.

1944 George Lucas was born.

1946 Robert Jarvik was born.

1952 David Byrne was born.

1973 *Skylab One*, America's first manned space station was launched. (See July 11th entry.)

In 1942, on this date, the Women's Auxiliary Army Corps was established as a U.S. Army unit. The WAACs were enlisted into non-combat units during the Second World War. In later years, women were recognized as regulars rather than auxiliaries, and their military career opportunities broadened considerably.

The Lewis and Clark expedition left St. Louis, Missouri, to explore the western frontier on this date in 1804. After mapping much of what was to become the great American west, Meriweather Lewis and William Clark returned to St. Louis in September, 1806. Commissioned by President Thomas Jefferson, Lewis and Clark were the pioneers of American government-financed exploration.

It's been said again and again that great minds think alike. Three people born on this day are perfect examples to the contrary. George Lucas, born in 1944, created the *Star Wars* film series. Robert Jarvik, born in 1946, created the first working artificial heart. And David Byrne, born in 1952, pioneered punk music with his band Talking Heads before pursuing a highly-successful solo career. Each found success by pursuing his personal dream. Perhaps the saying should be: Great minds think what they like.

15th.

Peace Officers' Memorial Day.

1918 First experimental airmail route in the U.S. was started.

1924 The U.S. Congress instituted immigration quotas. (See May 19th entry.)

1930   United Airlines began employing stewardesses.

1940   Nylon stockings went on sale.

Keeping the peace is a high-risk occupation. And peace officers deserve the public's cooperation. Today is Peace Officers' Memorial Day which commemorates the men and women who devote their lives to keeping the peace.

On this day, in 1940, the age of synthetics really began when nylon stockings first went on sale. Since then we have had dacron, rayon, polyester, kevlar, polar fleece, and a great number of new household words added to our shopping lists.

The loftiest ideas can succeed if they fulfill a public demand. Today marks the anniversary of some airworthy examples. In 1918, the first experimental U.S. airmail service began carrying mail to and from New York, Philadelphia, and Washington, D.C. The new system was an overnight success as more and more executives demanded to have their letters and packages airmailed for fast delivery. However, the best example of an overnight success story occurred on this day in 1930. That's when United Airlines' stewardesses began serving passengers on the company's San Francisco, California, to Cheyenne, Wyoming, flights.

16th

1801   William H. Seward was born in Florida, New York. (See March 30th entry.)

1868   The impeachment of President Andrew Johnson failed.

1929   First Oscars were presented at the Academy Awards. (See May 4th entry.)

1966   The Cultural Revolution began.

1975   Junko Tabei became the first woman to reach the summit of Mount Everest. (See May 29th entry.)

Today marks an anniversary that was chronicled in President John F. Kennedy's book, *Profiles in Courage*. In 1868, President Andrew Johnson faced impeachment proceedings as a result of a dispute with the U.S. Congress over withdrawals that the president made from the Bank of the United States. Senator Edmund G. Ross of Kansas—a man who opposed much of Johnson's political thinking—stood up and voted according to his conscience. His was the deciding vote that saved the president. It meant the end of Senator Ross's political career, and he knew it. But he did what he felt was right.

Today is Oscar's birthday. Oscar, as if you didn't know, is the award presented by the Academy of Motion Picture Arts and Sciences. In 1929, five Oscars made their debut at a Hollywood dinner. And Oscar has been imitated everywhere ever since. There's hardly an art form or an industry that does not have its own equivalent of the Oscar: the Emmy, the Grammy, the Tony, the Desi, and the Coty, to name just a few. Oscar had a good idea. Recognition by one's colleagues is sometimes the sweetest recognition of all.

On this day in 1975, Mount Everest was conquered. It had been climbed before. But on this day, Mount Everest was conquered by a woman. An experienced Japanese mountaineer, Junko Tabei, took to the Himalayan slopes and climbed the world's tallest mountain, reaching its summit.

A dark decade began on this day in 1966, when the Communist Party's Politburo approved an edict authored by Chairman Mao Zhedong. It started The Great Proletarian Cultural Revolution. Schools were closed and the Red Guard—an elite troop of young, zealous students—was formed to attack traditional values and so-called bourgeois thinking. According to Mao, the people had to learn to live by a pure interpretation of Chairman Mao's original manifesto. Intellectuals, military leaders, business people, and politicians were dragged out into the streets, forced to wear dunce caps, and were publicly criticized by Red Guardsmen. An entire nation was tortured and terrorized into submission by this young army. At the end of its ten-year purge, tens of thousands had been killed and millions of people's lives were ruined. An entire generation of children grew up without a proper education.

17th.

1749 Edward Jenner was born.

1792 New York Stock Exchange was founded.

1845 The rubber band was patented. (See March 30th entry.)

1954 Racial segregation in public schools was declared unconstitutional.

1987 The U.S. Navy frigate *Stark* was struck by missiles.

Today is the New York Stock Exchange's birthday. Since it opened in 1792, the Exchange has sometimes been castigated as the speculators' playground; a stock manipulators' oasis. It's had its share of intrigues and conspiracies, but its birthday is a good time to be reminded that the concept of public stock ownership has given millions of small shareholders a chance to own a "piece of the action."

On this date in 1954, in a unanimous decision written by Chief Justice Earl Warren, the U.S. Supreme Court swept away America's ancient heritage of racial segregation and declared that "separate educational facilities are inherently unequal." It was the dawning of racial equality in American education.

This is Edward Jenner's birthday. Born on this date in 1749 in Berkeley, England, Doctor Jenner developed a new medical concept called a vaccination. Thanks to his discovery, smallpox ceased to be a worldwide plague, and numerous diseases have been prevented or mitigated by immunization processes based on Dr. Jenner's concept.

Thirty-seven American sailors were killed in 1987 when an Iraqi warplane attacked the U.S. Navy frigate *Stark* without warning in the Persian Gulf. It struck the vessel with two guided missiles. Iraqi President Saddam Hussein issued an official apology. Then Iraq and the United States characterized the attack as a mistake. But three years later, the U.S. was at war with Iraq, defending Kuwait from invasion.

18th.

1804   Napoleon became Emperor of France.

1910   Haley's comet was seen from the earth.

1933   The Tennessee Valley Authority (TVA) was authorized.

1980   Mount St. Helens erupted.

Napoleon Bonaparte was a Corsican soldier enlisted in the French army who became the First French Republican general after the French Revolution. But that was not enough for this ambitious young man. On this date in 1804, Napoleon became the Emperor of France. Under his reign, France attempted to conquer Europe and the world—an occupational disease that affects many self-made monarchs and dictators.

The Tennessee Valley Authority was authorized on this date in 1933. It was established to develop the hydroelectric and water resources of the Tennessee River, including the power dam at Muscle Shoals, Alabama; and to assist in the economic and social development of the entire valley. Despite bitter opposition from both public and private interest groups, it can be conservatively said that the TVA changed the face of the South.

Nature certainly made its presence known on this day in history. This is the anniversary of a visit from Haley's Comet. In 1910, the enormous comet was seen from the earth as it moved across the sun. It was a brilliant spectacle few people who witnessed it would ever forget. But the fearsome power of nature has also been evident on this date. In 1980, Mount St. Helens erupted in Washington state. It was the mountain's largest eruption in 123 years. People were evacuated from their homes for hundreds of miles around as volcanic ash rained down upon them. Unfortunately, sixty people died during the spectacular event.

19th.

1536   Anne Boleyn was beheaded.

1602   Martha's Vineyard was first sighted by Captain Bartholomew Gosnold.

1832   The first Democratic National Convention was held. (See August 28th entry.)

1846   The first steamship arrived in Hawaii. (See May 22nd entry.)

1848   The first department store opened. (See April 13th entry.)

1881   The American Red Cross founded by Clara Barton. (See May 8th and May 21st entries.)

1884   The Ringling Brothers Circus first performed. (See June 3rd entry.)

1898   Postcards were first authorized by the U.S. Post Office. (See April 16th, May 6th, and July 7th entries.)

1900   The Simplon Tunnel opened as the world's longest railroad tunnel.

1914   Greyhound Bus Company was founded.

1916   Britain first applied "summer time" (Daylight Savings Time).

1921   Immigration quotas were established. (See May 15th entry.)

1935 T.E. Lawrence (Lawrence of Arabia) died in England from injuries sustained in a motorcycle crash. (See July 6th and August 15th entries.)

1992 Vice President Dan Quayle pronounced a "poverty of values" in America's inner cities.

1994 The FDA approved of the first genetically-engineered tomato. (See April 12th and June 16th entries.)

1995 NASA's administrator unveiled plans to slash thousands of aerospace jobs and to overhaul the entire agency.

1996 A large asteroid approached within 281,000 miles of the earth.

2161 Eight out of nine planets in the solar system will align on the same side of the sun; a pattern known as syzygy.

Over the course of history, many people have lost their heads. And on this day, a queen lost hers. In 1536, Henry VIII of England's second wife and mother of Elizabeth I— Anne Boleyn—was beheaded in the Tower of London.

On this date in 1921, the U.S. Congress decided to limit America's "open door" policy somewhat, by establishing immigration quotas. To this day, immigration continues, though thankfully some of the ethnic discriminations built into the intial quota system were eventually eradicated after the Second World War.

Many of us have been accused of being penny-wise and pound foolish. And today's anniversaries provide us with some lofty food for thought. On this day in 1995, NASA's administrator unveiled plans to slash thousands of aerospace jobs and to overhaul the entire agency as part of a federal cost-cutting plan. After all, paying people to look up at the stars seemed like a good place to slash a budget. However, on this same day in 1996, a group of extremely surprised NASA astronomers observed an astronomical near hit. A large asteroid approached earth within 281,000 miles—a distance just greater than the moon. It startled not only the astronomers who discovered it, but the budget-cutters who had said it was useless to pay people to look up at the stars. We have to look ahead and plan ahead for the unknown despite present trends. We can only hope NASA's people are better prepared on this same day in the year 2161. That's when eight out of nine planets in the solar system will align on the same side of the sun in a rare formation known as syzygy.

Historically speaking, this is a great day for travel. In 1602, Captain Bartholomew Gosnold first sighted the island of Martha's Vineyard off Cape Cod. In 1900, the twelve-mile-long Simplon Tunnel opened as the world's longest railroad tunnel, linking Switzerland to Italy through the Alps. In 1914, the Greyhound Bus Company was founded. And to give us an extra hour of daylight during the summer, England introduced Daylight Savings Time (originally called "summer time") on this day in 1916.

This was the day, in 1992, that Vice President Dan Quayle denounced what he called the "poverty of values" in America's inner cities during a speech in San Francisco. At that same event, he also criticized the television show *Murphy Brown* for having its title character bear a child out of wedlock.

20th.

1775 Mecklenburg County, North Carolina, declared its independence from British rule. (Mecklenburg Independence Day)

1830 The first railroad timetable was published.

1927 Charles Lindbergh began his solo transatlantic flight.

1932 Amelia Earhart took off on her first solo flight.

1941 First airborne invasion took place.

Today is Mecklenburg Independence Day. In 1775, Charlotte, North Carolina—located in Mecklenburg County—was the site of a convention which adopted a declaration of independence from British rule. The participants sent words to that effect to the North Carolina delegation at the Continental Congress meeting in Philadelphia, Pennsylvania.

On this day in 1927, the young American aviator Charles A. Lindbergh took off from Roosevelt Field, New York, and headed toward Paris, France. It seemed like an incredible risk. Hour after hour, the world held its breath and waited for news of the *Spirit of St. Louis*. Lindbergh—later nicknamed the Lone Eagle—was supposed to land at Le Bourget at 7: 30 PM the following evening. He didn't. But news came that he had been seen flying over Ireland, and then over England. He finally landed shortly after 10 PM. What happened thereafter is a story for another day.

It is a sardonic twist of fate that, on the anniversary of Charles A. Lindbergh's first transatlantic flight, a less heroic aviation first was also achieved. In 1941, Nazi

Germany captured the island of Crete in history's first totally airborne invasion. The whole face of warfare changed; and so did its financial costs. The menace of a surprise attack became infinitely greater.

This is the anniversary of the day man—and woman—conquered the skies above. In 1927, American aviator Charles A. Lindbergh took off from Roosevelt Field, New York, bound for Paris, France. And in 1932, American aviatrix Amelia Earhart took off from Newfoundland, heading for Ireland.

Before this day was marked with memorable events in aviation history like Charles Lindbergh and Amelia Earhart's first solo transatlantic flights, another event changed the way we thought of land-based travel. In 1830, the first railroad timetable was published in a Baltimore, Maryland, newspaper. The arrival and departure times of the nation's first railroad train—the Baltimore & Ohio—were of critical importance to passengers and cargo shippers wishing to take advantage of this new, luxurious means of rapid locomotion.

21st.

1881 American National Red Cross founded.

1918 The House of Representatives passed the Nineteenth Amendment to the U.S. Constitution. (See February 27th, August 26th, and December 10th entries.)

1927 Charles Lindbergh landed in Paris, France. (See May 20th entry.)

1955 The first transcontinental round-trip solo flight was completed. (See January 25th, July 22nd, and December 17th entries.)

Today is the American National Red Cross' birthday. In 1881, Clara Barton founded the organization in Washington, D.C.: a North American counterpart to the famed organization established in Switzerland by Jean Henri Dunant.

22nd.

1813   Richard Wagner was born.

1819   The American steamboat *Savannah* made the first transatlantic crossing. (National Maritime Day)

1859   Sir Arthur Conan Doyle was born. (See January 6th entry.)

1947   The Truman Doctrine went into effect.

On this day in 1819, the American-built steamboat *Savannah* was launched from Savannah Harbor, beginning its journey across the Atlantic. This anniversary is commemorated every year as National Maritime Day.

Today marks the anniversary of the Truman Doctrine's enactment. Outlined by President Harry Truman in 1947, the Truman Doctrine was intended to limit and contain Soviet expansion by providing U.S. aid for countries threatened by Communist takeover. The passage of this legislation approved an initial appropriation of $400 million in financial aid to Greece and Turkey.

German composer Richard Wagner was born on this day in 1813. Inspired by ancient Teutonic legends of gods, heroes, and heroines, Wagner was truly a pop star of his time. His music was raucous, loud, and not nearly as refined as his predecessors. His new sound earned him little respect from more established composers such as his father-in-law Franz Liszt who thought little of his radical son-in-law's work.

23rd.

1734   Friedrich Anton Mesmer was born.

1785   Benjamin Franklin created his own pair of bifocals.

1922   The play *Abie's Irish Rose* opened on Broadway in New York City.

1934   Nylon was first produced by Dr. Wallace H. Carothers, a research chemist at Du Pont laboratories. (See May 15th entry.)

Benjamin Franklin was a man of many talents, including invention. And today is the anniversary of his most famous creation. In 1785, he described his design in a letter written to his daughter. It was a very simple idea. Franklin needed two pairs of spectacles: one pair for reading, one pair for seeing at a distance. He got tired of switching from one pair to another, so he constructed a pair of spectacles that had both types of lenses in each frame: the upper portion worked for seeing at a distance and the lower portion worked for reading. Thus, bifocals were born.

Not too many people have ever heard of the play, *Abie's Irish Rose*. The title pretty much tells you the plot. It is particularly relevant today because this is the anniversary of its premiere. In 1922, the critics gave it a rather unfriendly reception. As a result, it only ran for 2,327 performances and became one of the longest running plays in theatrical history.

It's possible that people were hypnotized before 1734, but you can be sure they were never mesmerized. It was on this day that Friedrich Anton Mesmer, the father of modern hypnosis, was born. His namesake process has since become an apt adjective to describe anything that holds our attention.

24th.

1819   Queen Victoria of England was born. (Celebrated on the Monday closest to the date as Victoria Day) (See January 2nd, January 22nd, February 10th, and June 20th entries.)

1844   Samuel F.B. Morse sent first telegraph message. (See February 21st and April 27th entries.)

1883   The Brooklyn Bridge opened.

"What hath God wrought!" Samuel F.B. Morse, an artist born in Charlestown, Massachusetts, sent those words in the first message telegraphed from Washington, D.C. to Baltimore, Maryland, on this date in 1844. The fifty-three-year-old Morse was being devout and modest. The telegraph was what Morse himself had wrought along with an international language that could be communicated across it: the language of dots and dashes known as Morse Code.

This is the Brooklyn Bridge's birthday. In 1883, the Brooklyn Bridge which links the borough of Brooklyn to the borough of Manhattan was opened. It also paved the way to a glorious opportunity for generations of con men thereafter. Nobody will ever know how many times the Brooklyn Bridge has been sold to a gullible visitor.

Victoria Regina was born on this day. In 1819, Great Britain's monarch and India's empress, Queen Victoria, was born in Kensington, England. Few monarchs have reigned as long or have been as revered as Victoria. Few people have left their imprint on an entire era. Her popularity was based on what she stood for: integrity, responsibility, and duty.

25th.

735 AD St. Bede died.

1787 First session of the Constitutional Convention convened.

1803 Ralph Waldo Emerson was born.

Today is the anniversary of the U.S. Constitutional Convention's first session. In 1787, the representatives that gathered in Philadelphia eventually adopted a final draft of the nation's Constitution. But this was not supposed to be the convention's first session. It had been scheduled to convene on May 14th. But only the representatives of Virginia and Pennsylvania were there on time. A quorum didn't convene until this day.

This is American poet and essayist Ralph Waldo Emerson's birthday. He was born in Boston, Massachusetts, in 1803. It was Emerson, who said: "Nothing great was ever achieved without enthusiasm." That's not to say that we should all launch ourselves headlong into whatever we do. Emerson also said, "He has not learned the first lesson of life who does not every day surmount a fear."

The final act of a great man is often more memorable than any other deed executed during his life. On this day in 735 AD, the Anglo-Saxon scholar Bede awoke in his monk's cell at the Jarrow monastery. He was ready to dictate the last chapter of his latest translation: the Gospel according to St. John. "Take up your pen and ink and write quickly," he told his scribe. Upon completion of his translation, Bede knelt down to pray and died.

26th.

1886 Asa Yoelson was born.

1954 The Egyptian Pharaoh Cheops' funeral ship was found.

1979 Israel formally returned El Arish to Egypt. (See May 27th entry.)

The Pharaoh Cheops ordered the construction of Egypt's Great Pyramids thousands of years ago. When he died, he was buried in a funeral ship built for his other-world journey. Though it remained motionless for thousands of years, on this date, in 1954, Cheops' funeral ship reached another world. It was uncovered near the Pyramid of Giza.

When Asa Yoelson was born on this day in Srednike, Russia, in 1886, his parents had no idea they would emigrate to the United States. But they soon did. They never could have dreamt that their son would become a jazz singer—they hoped he would become a cantor at the local synagogue. But Asa Yoelson changed his name to Al Jolson. He sang his way up from Rialto vaudeville theaters to Ziegfeld's Follies and finally to the motion picture screen. Jolson was the first singer to be heard on film. Thousands of other highly talented performers have followed since then. And it would be nice to think that his famous line still rings truc: "You ain't heard nothin' yet, folks."

Actions speak much louder than words, as an event that happened on this day clearly proves. In 1979, Israel formally returned El Arish to Egypt under the terms of a peace pact. The capital of the Sinai peninsula had been occupied by Israeli forces for over a decade. This deed showed both Egypt and the world that Israel meant to keep its promise to instigate a peaceful coexistence between the two nations. The next day, the border between Israel and Egypt was opened.

27th.

1647 Achsah Young was hanged as a witch in Massachusetts.

1818 Amelia Bloomer was born.

1819 Julia Ward Howe was born.

1894   Dashiell Hammett was born. (See June 20th entry.)

1923   Henry Kissinger was born.

1979   Egyptian President Anwar Sadat and Israeli Prime Minister Menachem Begin announced the opening of the border between Egypt and Israel. (See May 26th entry.)

Achsah Young is not a particularly famous figure. She was the first person inscribed in the annals of colonial America for being executed as a witch. It happened in Windsor, Connecticut, on this date in 1647. Some people dispute this fact. Margaret Jones—who was executed in 1648—is given the dubious honor by a few historians.

Amelia Bloomer is primarily remembered in history for an old-fashioned article of feminine apparel. In 1818, Amelia Jenks was born on this date in Hiram, New York. She grew up, married, and became Mrs. Bloomer. She was an outspoken suffragist who felt that feminine apparel was a handicap and who took to wearing trousers and bloomers. She was ridiculed for her stance on women's rights, but it didn't stop her from fighting. Today is also Julia Ward Howe's birthday. Born in New York City in 1819, Ms. Howe was not only a suffragist; she fought for the abolition of slavery and wrote the lyrics to the "Battle Hymn of the Republic."

Art often mirrors real life. This statement was never truer than in the case of author and screenplay writer Dashiell Hammett. Born on this day in 1894, Hammett was the originator of the hard-boiled school of fictional detective writing. He had a lot of experience from which to draw his characters. Before he enlisted into the army during the First World War, Hammett had spent eight years working as a Pinkerton detective. While receiving treatment for tuberculosis—which he contracted during the war— Hammett started writing short stories and novellas. In 1930, his novel about a detective named Sam Spade was published. *The Maltese Falcon* won Hammett critical acclaim. Two years later, the first of the Thin Man novels hit the bestseller lists. The hard-edged Nick Charles and his gutsy society wife Nora were America's favorite sleuthing couple. And it's often been said that Nora's character was based on Hammett's real-life love, playwright Lillian Hellman.

This is Henry Kissinger's birthday. In 1923, Kissinger was born in Furth, Germany. If history had taken a different turn, this masterful diplomat would have stayed in Germany; and later on, history would—no doubt—have taken a very different turn. But the fact is he and his family emigrated to the United States. Kissinger grew up to become one of history's most celebrated diplomats. He made history when he was appointed Secretary of State. He was the first Jewish-American to hold the position; and he was the first Secretary of State to speak with a German accent. Kissinger also made history by breaking away from precedents; by being aware that public opinion was a powerful force; and by working about three times harder than most people.

28th.

1892 The Sierra Club was organized by John Muir in San Francisco. (See April 21st entry.)

1908 Ian Fleming was born.

1923 The U.S. Attorney General determined that it was legal for women to wear trousers where and when they please. (See May 27th entry.)

1928 The Dodge Brothers, Inc., and the Chrysler Corporation merged. (See January 14th entry.)

1929 The first all-color talking picture *On With The Show* was exhibited. (See August 8th and October 6th entries.)

1934 The Dionne quintuplets were born.

1940 The Dunkirk evacuation began.

1953 *Melody*, the first animated, three-dimensional cartoon in Technicolor, premiered. (See September 19th entry.)

1961 Amnesty International was founded.

1987 A West German pilot landed a private plane in Moscow's Red Square.

Most of us are born alone, so to speak; some of us are born twins; fewer of us are born triplets. On this day in 1934, Mrs. Oliva Dionne gave birth to quintuplets. The Dionne Quints were a wonder of the modern world. Their family doctor became a world celebrity. Nobody would have dreamed that, thanks to new fertility drugs, multiple births would become more common in later years. A natural miracle in one generation sometimes becomes a commonplace scientific procedure in the next.

In a period of about a week in 1940, more than 300,000 Allied Forces were evacuated from the French shores near Dunkirk, a bitter defeat by the Nazis on the European continent during the Second World War. Ships, fishing boats, sailing craft of every shape and size crossed the English Channel to rescue the stranded troops in one of the world's largest volunteer missions. The Dunkirk evacuation did more than bring the fighting men out of what seemed a final, inescapable trap. It also gave new heart to the British people who gave their time and effort toward the cause.

A nineteen-year-old West German pilot, Mathias Rust, stunned the world when he landed a private plane in Moscow's Red Square after evading Soviet air defenses. He went undetected because he flew across the Russian countryside at low altitude. Why did he do it? Why do teenagers do anything? To him it was an adventure, nothing more. However, for several Soviet military officials who could not explain how a foreign aircraft could cross so much protected airspace it was the end of their careers.

Mathias Rust couldn't have picked a more appropriate day to land his plane in Red Square. This is Ian Fleming's birthday. A former British intelligence agent, Fleming kept audiences shaken, not stirred for decades with his James Bond adventure stories. But unlike 007, Rust wasn't there to rescue anyone or blow anything up, his intentions were as peaceful as those of an organization born on this day—Amnesty International—which has been fighting against human rights abuses worldwide since 1961.

29th.

1736   Patrick Henry was born.

1903   Bob Hope was born.

1917   John F. Kennedy was born. (See November 22nd entry.)

1953   Edmund Hillary and Tensing Norkay scaled Mount Everest. (See May 16th entry.)

Today marks a high point in history. On this day in 1953, Sir Edmund Hillary and Tensing Norkay climbed higher than any human beings had ever been before. They became the first men to scale the world's tallest peak high in the Himalayas—Mount

Everest. As climbs go, Everest is far from the most technically challenging. Yet few climbers who have made the ascent would deny that for other reasons it is the world's most difficult. The air is far too thin to support human life for any length of time, and the weather is unpredictable and unforgiving. So why do so many adventurers follow in Sir Edmund's footsteps? Perhaps it's for the same reason he gave in an interview: "Because it is there."

Today was the birthday of both Patrick Henry and John F. Kennedy, two eloquent American speakers. It's also the birthday of another great spokesman, Bob Hope. Even though he was born in England, Hope embraced and embodied the American spirit as much as native sons Henry and Kennedy. And he took that spirit on the road to American radio and television audiences as well as American military bases around the world.

30th.

Memorial Day (celebrated on the last Monday of the month).

1431 Joan of Arc burned at the stake. (See January 6th entry.)

1901 The Hall of Fame was dedicated in Bronx, New York.

1934 Alexei Arkhipovich Leonov was born. (See March 18th entry.)

Today used to be Memorial Day when it was defined by a date. Memorial Day is now celebrated on the last Monday in May. That gives us a three-day weekend, which may or may not add to our commemoration of the men and women of the armed forces who died in service to our country. But it does add somewhat to the pleasure of the moment, and marks our nation's unofficial transition from spring to summer.

This is the Hall of Fame's anniversary. It is some measure of fame itself that most people now are likely to ask which hall of fame—baseball's, football's, rock 'n' roll's or what? The sad fact is that the Hall of Fame that was dedicated in the Bronx on this day in 1901, is less famous than some of its namesakes.

31st.

1043 Lady Godiva rode naked through the market square in Coventry, England.

1790 The U.S. copyright law was enacted. (See April 10th entry.)

1868 The nation's first Memorial Day parade took place in Ironton, Ohio. (See May 30th entry.)

1884 Dr. John Harvey Kellogg applied for a patent for flaked cereal.

1930 Clint Eastwood was born.

1954 President Dwight D. Eisenhower spoke about revolutionaries and rebels.

1962 Adolf Eichmann was executed.

This is the anniversary of Adolf Eichmann's execution by the State of Israel. Eichmann was hunted down as a mass murderer of Jews during the Second World War. His hanging wrote a new chapter in international law and terrified other fugitive Nazis who were hiding in various places around the world.

It was on this date in 1954 that Dwight D. Eisenhower made a speech at Columbia University's bicentennial. The President of the United States and the former President of Columbia University said: "Here in America, we are descended in blood and in spirit from revolutionists and rebels—men and women who dared to dissent from accepted doctrine. As their heirs, we may never confuse honest dissent with disloyal subversion."

Today is Clint Eastwood's birthday. Some of you may know him as the former mayor of Carmel, California. Others may remember his dark, silent role as the Man with No Name in 1960s Italian westerns such as *A Fistful of Dollars* and *The Good, the Bad, and the Ugly*. But most probably think of his hard-boiled portrayal of the grizzled San Francisco police detective Harry Callahan in *Magnum Force*. We love our screen heroes, even with the rough edges of human character Eastwood is so famous for bringing to the screen. With each new premiere theatergoers seem to enter with Callahan's classic attitude, "Go ahead, make my day."

History's most sensational events have a habit of becoming—or at least giving birth to—legends and folklore. Today's anniversary is no exception. In 1043, a short horseback ride earned Lady Godiva immortality. She and her husband Leofric founded a monastery in Coventry, England. When her husband began to demand excessive taxes from the residents of the village that grew around the monastery, she protested. He agreed to lower the villagers' taxes on one condition: She would have to ride through the Coventry market square naked. She did.

It's a big day for flakes. It was on this day in 1884, that Dr. John Harvey Kellogg applied for a patent for his flaked corn cereal. The manufacturing process was discovered by accident. He and his brother William were trying to find a way to make corn more digestible for the patients at their sanitarium in Battle Creek, Michigan. They were both called away from their work for a few hours, and their corn gruel became dried flakes. Thus, by glorious accident, breakfast was born.

June

April showers may bring May flowers, but June heralds the end of the school year and the beginning of summer vacation. This is the time when the majority of Americans take to the roads and the skies to see the country, visit relatives, and bask in the sunshine. This particular month is also traditionally the Marriage Month. More brides step up to the altar in June than in any other month in the year. For young and old summer holds wonderful carefree moments that could be summed up in a line from an old Jimmy Buffett song, "life is just a tire swing."

1st.

1801   Brigham Young was born.

1813   Captain James Lawrence said: "Don't give up the ship."

1926   Norma Jean Baker was born.

1933   J.P. Morgan was photographed with a midget on his lap.

1980   Cable News Network made its debut.

Of all the watchwords chronicled in American history, none has been quoted more than the immortal words: "Don't give up the ship." According to reports the *U.S.S. Chesapeake*'s Captain James Lawrence uttered them as he lay dying aboard his ship on this day in 1813. Some record the statement as the *U.S.S. Franklin*'s Captain James Mugford's dying words in 1776. Generally, Captain Lawrence is regarded as the revered author of this ringing cry that became the U.S. Navy's motto. The fact is that Lawrence's vessel was not only defeated by the British ship *H.M.S. Shannon* but was also boarded and captured. Despite the Captain's fighting words, we did give up the ship.

Public attention is easily diverted. On great example occurred during a U.S. Senate hearing held on this date in 1933. One of the world's greatest financiers—J. Pierpont Morgan, Jr.—was waiting to be questioned about the current economic state. It was the Depression, after all. A circus press agent suddenly placed a female midget on Morgan's lap and took a photograph. You won't find much in the history books about that Senate hearing, but you'll find Morgan and the woman in one history book after another.

Today is Brigham Young's birthday. He was born on this day in 1801 in the green hills of Whittingham, Vermont. Young not only believed in miracles, he led one: the epochal Mormon trek across the wild continent to Utah's Great Salt Lake. High in the Rocky Mountains, Young and his followers founded Salt Lake City. Young was both a religious leader and a doer. He had twenty-seven wives and was survived by forty-seven children. While he lived, polygamy was still an accepted Mormon practice, although it was outlawed in the rest of the nation.

The icon of 1950s American femininity was born on this day. In 1926, Norma Jean Baker was born in Los Angeles, California. She always wanted to be an actress, and when she grew up she dyed her hair blond and changed her name to Marilyn Monroe. People noticed Marilyn. She had all the charm, innocence, and sex appeal that was necessary to be the ideal all-American bombshell. She rose from a cameo role in a Marx brothers film to stardom in less than five years. She was *Playboy Magazine's* first cover girl. When she married the all-American male, baseball player Joe DiMaggio, her fans loved her even more.

Back in 1980, people didn't think there were many frontiers left to explore. But they changed their minds when Cable News Network made its debut on this day. CNN was the world's first all-news cable television station. Within a decade, the network surpassed television giants like ABC, NBC, and CBS at getting the news first; they also set a precedent by delivering news and commentary twenty-four hours a day. CNN brought the realities of the Persian Gulf War into the world's living rooms. It continues to be on the scene throughout the nation and the world.

2nd.

1740 Marquis de Sade was born.

1896 Great Britain granted Guglielmo Marconi the first wireless radio patent. (See March 27th and April 25th entries.)

1924 The U.S. Congress granted Native Americans citizenship.

1953 Queen Elizabeth II was crowned at Westminster Abbey. (See April 21st entry.)

Today is the Marquis de Sade's birthday. Cynicism is not required to observe that de Sade was born before his time. It's difficult to say whether this French nobleman, born in 1740, would have been a contemporary cult leader, a porno film producer, an adult magazine publisher, or a romance novelist. Maybe he would have done all of the above. In real life, he spent his last decade in a lunatic asylum.

Today marks the anniversary of the second Elizabethan age. In 1953, Great Britain's Queen Elizabeth II was crowned at Westminster Abbey. Surrounded by heads of state, princes and dukes, lords and ladies, Elizabeth's coronation followed a tradition that dates back to the Middle Ages. But Elizabeth II also broke new ground: She allowed the ceremony to be televised. Tens of thousands of her loyal subjects became the first British commoners to attend a royal coronation.

An unusual footnote was written into the annals of American history on this day. The aboriginal peoples of North America had inhabited the continent from coast to coast for thousands of years. But in 1924, the U.S. Congress granted Native Americans their right to national citizenship for the first time. Treaties had been made since the establishment of the Jamestown and Plymouth colonies—and many of them were broken at one time or another with little regard for the original tenants of the land. This was the first step toward recognition.

3rd.

1621 The Dutch West India Company received a charter for Nieue Amsterdam.

1808 Jefferson Davis was born. (See February 18th entry.)

1835 P.T. Barnum's circus made its first tour of the United States.

1906 Josephine Baker was born.

1916 The National Defense Act was authorized.

1937 Edward, Duke of Windsor, married Wallis Warfield Simpson. (See June 19th and June 23th entries.)

This is the anniversary of the National Defense Act. It was neither the first, the last, the biggest, nor the smallest defense legislation in our history. But in 1916, this act established the Reserve Officers Training Corps. The ROTC has certainly had its ups and downs, but through it all there has been one concept worth commending today: the idea of a civilian-officer. It meant that the armed forces could benefit from having officers who were not strictly military academy officers.

When Great Britain's King Edward VIII dramatically abdicated in 1936 to marry the woman he loved, the world gasped and sighed. He chose to live as a commoner rather than to rule England without her. On this day, in 1937, that historic love story reached its moment of romantic glory in Mons, France. Edward, Duke of Windsor, married Mrs. Wallis Warfield Simpson, an American divorcee. They did indeed live happily ever after until his death in 1972.

Jefferson Davis was the President of the Confederate States of America, and today is his birthday. Born in Christian County, Kentucky, in 1808, Davis was a West Pointer and a brilliant military leader in the Mexican War. He was a Mississippi state senator and later became the U.S. Secretary of War. Then he returned to the Senate. He was not considered an extremist even when he reluctantly followed his state out of the Union. After Robert E. Lee's surrender, he tried to continue the war long enough to negotiate more favorable terms, but he was captured in May, 1865. Held prisoner in Virginia, he was shackled until public outcry ended that barbarism. He was indicted for treason in 1866, released on bail in 1867, and never brought to trial. Until he died in 1889, the U.S. continued to revoke his citizenship.

Today marks the anniversary of the greatest show on earth. In 1835, P.T. Barnum's circus made its first tour of the United States. Barnum had made his name by presenting the most unique individuals and deeds at his Manhattan museums. After two infernos leveled those structures, he set his sights on the big top. The circus he created was as much a childhood heirloom as soda fountains and five-and-dime stores for decades. Life under the big top continues to fascinate both young and old audiences alike in such sophisticated metropolises as New York, Paris, Moscow, and London, as much as it does in smaller towns around the world.

When the Dutch West India Company received a charter to establish a New World settlement called Nieue Amsterdam in 1621, neither the government nor the trading company had any idea what would develop from this simple act. On this day, New York City was born. The Dutch West India Company's settlement quickly outgrew its original boundaries at the southern tip of Manhattan island which had been purchased from the natives for $24 worth of trinkets. Soon it stretched across five boroughs.

A talented actress, comedienne, singer, and dancer who could laugh at herself was born on this day in 1906. Josephine Baker's long legs, lanky figure, and funny faces didn't hold much promise in American eyes. It didn't stop her from pursuing her dreams. She landed a job as the dresser for blues singer Bessie Smith and toured Harlem's thriving 1920s nightclub scene even though she saw more face powder than footlights. One day, she was offered a job as a dancer in a jazz revue that was bound for Paris. Naturally, she took the job. Baker quickly became the toast of Paris' Follies Bergere. Audiences loved the uninhibited way she sang and gyrated, revealing herself as an accomplished dancer and a natural comic. During the 1940s and 1950s, French film-going audiences flocked to see her. Josephine Baker never became the toast of America, but France proclaimed her their national treasure.

4th.

Old Maids' Day. (See February 28th entry.)

1738   King George III of England was born.

1896   Henry Ford tested his horseless "quadricycle" carriage through Detroit's pre-dawn streets. (See January 14th, July 30th, and October 1st entries.)

Today used to be celebrated as Old Maids' Day, which was originated in 1946. It doesn't get much attention anymore. This is not a manifestation of a mere alteration in vocabulary to satisfy feminists. It is simply that singleness is no longer regarded as a debility.

Great Britain's King George III was born in London on this date in 1738. It is somewhat due to his stubbornness and ill-temper that the American colonies first rebelled and then declared their independence.

5th.

1723   Adam Smith was born.

1783   Joseph and Jacques Montgolfier demonstrated their hot-air balloon. (See November 21st entry.)

1884   William Tecumseh Sherman refused the presidential nomination.

1915   Women's suffrage was introduced in Denmark.

1947   The Marshall Plan was proposed. (See April 3rd entry.)

1967   The Six-Day War began.

1975   The Suez Canal was reopened.

Historian Thomas Carlyle called economics the dismal science. If it is a science at all, we can thank, among others, Adam Smith, who was born on this day in 1723, in Kirkcaldy, Scotland. Smith was not the first political economist, but he put the subject all together, in 1776, in his book which was entitled, *Inquiry into the Nature of the Causes of the Wealth of Nations*. We have had a number of economic debates since then. Economics has become not so much the dismal science as the disputatious one.

The great Civil War general, William Tecumseh Sherman, was asked to run as a presidential candidate. But on this date in 1884, he sent a clear, profound message which went something like this: "If nominated, I will not accept; if elected, I will not serve." Only a few potential candidates made similar declarations in the century that followed.

It is an ironic twist of fate that the Six-Day War's anniversary also marks the day the Suez Canal was reopened. In 1967, the Six-Day War began between Israel and its neighboring Arab nations. After the six days were over, the ideological and political battles didn't end. That took years to amiably negotiate. In 1975, The Suez Canal reopened for the first time since the Six-Day War. International shipping lanes between the Mediterranean and the Indian Ocean were once again operational.

6th.

1765   Nathan Hale was born.

1911   Professor Hiram Bingham set sail in search of the last Incan city. (See July 24th entry.)

1944   The Allied forces landed on the beaches of Normandy. (D-Day)

1968   Senator Robert F. Kennedy was assassinated.

1984   The Indian army attacked Sikh extremists at the Golden Temple of Amristar. (See January 19th and November 19th entries.)

If it had not been planned and carried out, the world would be a very different and very unpleasant place. D-Day ensured the western hemisphere's freedom and today is its anniversary. D-Day marked the landing of the Allied Forces on the beaches of Normandy in 1944.

In war, millions have been killed; millions of bullets have found their mark. Yet, the bullet which found its mark on this day in 1968, shocked the world. New York Senator Robert F. Kennedy died in Los Angeles, California, from bullet wounds. Robert Kennedy's assassination was the overture to America's long, hot summer of civil discontent.

It's Nathan Hale's birthday. Born on this date in 1775 in Coventry, Connecticut, Hale was executed as a spy when he was twenty-one years old. According to legend, as he stood on the gallows, he said: "I regret that I have but one life to lose for my country."

7th.

Freedom of the Press Day.

1494 Spain and Portugal signed the Treaty of Tordesillas, agreeing to divide the new World between them. (See May 4th entry.)

1841 Henry D. Thoreau wrote: "Man stands to revere, he kneels to pray."

Freedom of the press—whether as a special day or as an institution—has not often been observed throughout the Americas. Nevertheless, today is Freedom of the Press Day which was originated by the Inter-American Press Association.

Prayer is a noble institution, but we must not confuse reverence and prayer. Reverence is a sign of respect; prayer is a plea for divine intervention. On this day in 1841, the author Henry D. Thoreau noted that: "Man stands to revere, he kneels to pray."

When Spain and Portugal signed the Treaty of Tordesillas, agreeing to divide the New World between them on this day in 1494, it never occurred to them that eventually, the settlers and residents of the New World would have their own opinions of who should govern them. But no one at the time could have possibly imagined populations growing to the size they are today, much as we can hardly imagine a planet with double the current number of people.

8th.

1869 Frank Lloyd Wright was born.

1869 The suction vacuum cleaner was patented.

1959 The U.S. Postal service delivered the mail by missile.

1964 Former President Dwight D. Eisenhower addressed the National Governors Conference.

1965 U.S. forces were authorized to go into combat in South Vietnam.

On this date, in 1965, President Lyndon B. Johnson authorized U.S. forces to go into combat against the Vietcong in South Vietnam. It was neither the first nor the last step in our escalated role in that conflict. And Johnson was neither the first nor the last President to deal with it.

Not many architects achieve Frank Lloyd Wright's fame. Born in Richland Center, Wisconsin, on this day in 1869, Wright's most famous works include Tokyo's Imperial Hotel, Manhattan's Guggenheim Museum, and striking homes like Falling Water, the Robie House, and his own Talliesin. He pioneered the concept of synthesizing a structure to its surroundings, camping on the land, and becoming acquainted with it before designing the building. For him, architecture was a design for living.

Repressive laws are all too often prompted by the excesses of individuals and the failure of others to stand together. On this day, in 1964, former President Dwight D. Eisenhower delivered an address to the National Governors Conference, calling for better self-government. In his speech, he said: "Our best protection against bigger government in Washington is better government in the states."

The United States Postal Service has been dedicated to finding faster more efficient means of moving our mail since it was established in the 1700s. It successfully experimented with a number of new modes of transportation while the public was still trying to figure out how they worked. Trains, trucks, and planes were all employed by the pioneering postal service almost as quickly as they were invented. But on this day in 1959, this efficient government department tried delivering letters by what appeared to be the fastest means ever—by missile. Officials gathered in Mayport, Florida, to view the momentous occasion. The *U.S.S. Barbero* naval submarine launched a guided missile containing 3,000 letters from its post at the Naval Auxiliary Air Station. It promptly dove straight to the bottom of the sea.

To say that on this day, in 1869, one new invention truly sucked is not a disparaging statement. Soon this sucky implement—the bane of dust bunnies—found its way into virtually every house making life a little less gritty for all of us. This invention was and is the suction vacuum cleaner, which was patented by Ives McGaffey of Chicago.

9th.

1791 John Howard Payne was born.

1892 Cole Porter was born.

1935 The Jonkers Diamond was sent by transatlantic mail.

This is the day when, in 1935, the fabulous, 700-plus-carat Jonkers Diamond was safely transported across the Atlantic. It was mailed from England to the United States for thirty-five cents postage.

This is John Howard Payne's birthday. He was born on this date in 1791 in New York City. Payne was the author of dozens of plays and an actor of some repute, but most people only remember his one claim to fame. Payne wrote the song "Home Sweet Home."

Cole Porter was born on this date in 1893 in Peru, Indiana. His Broadway hits were innumerable: his lyrics were sophisticated; his music was catchy and clever. Merely reciting the titles of some of his songs provides an upbeat rhythm of its own: "Anything Goes," "Just One of Those Things," "Don't Fence Me In," "Wake Up and Dream," and "You're the Top."

10th.

1922 Judy Garland was born.

1940 Italy attacked France.

1942 Lidice, Czechoslovakia was wiped out.

1946 Mussolini was overthrown, and Italy became a republic.

Today marks the anniversary of both a low and high point in Italian history. In 1940, Italy joined forces with Nazi Germany in attacking France. Under Mussolini's dictatorship, Italy's action was described by President Franklin D. Roosevelt as, ". . . the hand that held the dagger has stuck it into the back of its neighbor." But in 1946, the same country overthrew its dictator, and formally became a republic.

Do you recognize the name Lidice? Do you have to stop and think about it? Don't be disturbed if that is the case, because Lidice is not a happy memory. On this day, in 1942, after Gestapo leader Reinhard Heydrich was killed, Nazi forces wiped out the entire town of Lidice, Czechoslovakia. Even in the midst of the Second World War, this was a shocking event.

Loved by one and all for her singing and acting, Frances Ethel Gumm was born on this date in 1922. Perhaps you know her by another name. This young girl from Grand Rapids, Minnesota, changed her name to Judy Garland and became a star before she even entered high school.

11th.

1910 Jacques Cousteau was born.

1937 Stalin's great Soviet "purge" ended.

1950 Ben Hogan made his comeback on the professional golf circuit.

This was the day, in 1937, when Josef Stalin's great Soviet "purge" reached its climax. After a secret military trial, Marshal Tukhachevski and seven other high-ranking officers were convicted of conspiring with the Germans and sentenced to death. They were shot the next day. Earlier in the year, thirteen civilian leaders who had fallen out of favor with Soviet Premier Stalin, had been convicted and executed. With this execution, Stalin managed to terrorize and suppress all opposition to his call for pure socialism. He also branded any concept that was not his own as anti-socialist, Leninist, Trotskyite, or simply traitorous. What makes this case even more interesting is that Stalin signed a non-aggression treaty with Germany two years later. The U.S.S.R. remained conveniently neutral until it became more convenient to side with the Allies.

Every act of athletic heroism is memorable. That is particularly true when an athlete makes a comeback. Today is the anniversary of such an event. In 1950, professional golfer Ben Hogan thrilled the nation when he won the U.S. Open Golf Championship. Hogan had been a champion long before then. But more than a year earlier, he had been seriously injured in a car accident. It appeared he would never play again. But Hogan was determined. He worked. He struggled. He exercised. He kept trying. And he won.

We often think of pioneering explorers as individuals who discover uncharted lands, scale the highest peaks, or reach for the stars. But today is the birthday of an explorer who discovered uncharted lands and solved many mysteries under the sea. French naval officer and undersea explorer Jacques Cousteau was born on this day in 1911. Besides crossing deep into this mysterious frontier, Cousteau also developed a process for using television cameras underwater and invented the aqualung diving apparatus.

12th.

1776   The Virginia Convention adopted a Declaration of Rights.

1939   The Baseball Hall of Fame opened.

1943   The Alcan Highway was opened to traffic. (See November 20th entry.)

1979   Bryan Allen flew the first man-powered aircraft.

1991   The Chicago Bulls won their first NBA title. (See June 19th and June 20th entries.)

Today's anniversary has been largely overlooked. It's a shame, because it was really a red-letter day in American history. It was on this date, in 1776, that the Virginia Declaration of Rights—largely written by George Mason—was adopted by the Virginia Convention while the Continental Congress met in Philadelphia. Perhaps if you read a few passages you will see why this precursor to the Declaration of Independence so important. Article One: "That all men are by nature equally free and independent and have certain inherent rights . . . the enjoyment of life and liberty . . . and pursuing and obtaining happiness." Article Two: "That all power is . . . derived from the people." The Virginia Declaration of Rights made some other points as well, like insistence on freedom of the press and freedom of worship. All in all, this remarkable document's influence is obvious.

Today is the day when the Baseball Hall of Fame opened in 1939 in Cooperstown, New York. Just like the Hall of Fame in the Bronx, the Rock 'n' Roll Hall of Fame in Cleveland, and many others, this monument to baseball is an example of America's desire to recognize and honor accomplishment by both individuals and groups.

The Alaska Highway had taken years to complete, linking our northernmost state to points south. It was officially opened in the dead of winter on November 20th, 1942. However, on this day in 1943, the Alaska Highway had its first traffic, winding its way through the northern wilderness between Dawson Creek, British Columbia, in Canada, and Fairbanks, Alaska. The road was bumpy and potholed in places from the climatic extremes that part of the world experiences annually; and it wasn't completely paved until 1994, but the highway we now call the Alcan has become a legend. And the 25,000 cars, jeeps, vans, RVs, and trucks that brave the trip each summer attest to our growing love of wilderness adventure.

In 1979, on this very same day, an adventurer named Bryan Allen flew the first viable man-powered aircraft across the English Channel. The twenty-six-year-old cyclist braved the piercing winds and cold in the *Gossamer Albatross* to prove that gas engines weren't a necessity to air travel.

13th.

323 BC Alexander the Great died.

1898 The Yukon Territory entered into the confederation of Canada. (See July 1st entry.)

1944 Missiles were first used in warfare. (See March 16th entry.)

1966 The U.S. Supreme Court issued the Miranda decision.

1967 First African-American Supreme Court Justice was nominated.

1979 President Jimmy Carter proposed a superfund to clean up hazardous waste.

This is the day when Alexander the Great was proven right for saying he had no more worlds to conquer. He had felt that he had done it all, overtaking Persia and portions of India as well as establishing settlements along the way. However, while he was in Babylon, plotting his next conquest, he fell ill after a banquet and—on this day in 323 BC—died of a fever.

The anniversary of a landmark nomination is always a cause for celebration. In 1967, Thurgood Marshall was nominated to the U.S. Supreme Court by President Lyndon B. Johnson. It was a long time in coming, but it came. Marshall became the Supreme Court's first African-American justice, and went on to a truly distinguished career.

This is the anniversary of a landmark decision that ensured the rights of those suspected of committing a crime. In 1966, the U.S. Supreme Court handed down the Miranda decision which states: If you are arrested for a crime, you have the right to remain silent and not make any statement at all; any statement you make may and probably will be used against you in a court of law; you have the right to have a lawyer present to advise you either prior to any questioning or during any questioning; if you are unable to hire a lawyer, you have the right to have a lawyer appointed to counsel with you prior to or during any questioning; and you have the right to terminate the interview at any time.

Our nation's natural resources are fragile and finite, and in the course of our industrial progress, suffered greatly from mismanagement and misuse. On this day in 1979, President Jimmy Carter joined the ranks of conservation-minded Executives in Chief like Theodore Roosevelt, Franklin D. Roosevelt, and Richard M. Nixon when he proposed a superfund to clean up hazardous waste. He also set aside vast tracts of land as wilderness areas to be preserved for future generations.

14th.

Flag Day.

1775　The U.S. Army was founded.

1811　Harriet Beecher Stowe was born.

1946　Donald Trump was born.

1953　President Dwight D. Eisenhower spoke at Dartmouth College.

1982　Argentine forces surrendered the Falkland Islands. (See April 13th entry.)

Today is Flag Day. It's the anniversary of the day we adopted the Stars and Stripes as our national banner. Since 1777, the Stars and Stripes have waved over the land of the free and the home of the brave.

Today is Harriet Beecher Stowe's birthday. In 1811, Harriet Beecher Stowe was born in Litchfield, Connecticut. As an adult, she wrote a book whose alternate title was, *Life Among the Lowly.* You never heard of it? Yes you have. The full title was, *Uncle Tom's Cabin or, Life Among the Lowly.* Her story first appeared in book form in 1852. It whipped up abolitionist sentiments in the North long before the Civil War. And its influence lasted long after that war. Today, when we call someone a Simon Legree, we are recalling one of Stowe's characters; and if Uncle Tom does not mean today what it did to Mrs. Stowe, it is still drawn from her book.

There are those among us who have a fear of books. That thought was on President Dwight D. Eisenhower's mind on this day in 1953 when he addressed an audience at Dartmouth College. "Don't join the book burners," he warned. "Don't think you are going to conceal faults by concealing evidence that they ever existed."

Since it's Donald Trump's birthday, reflect on a few words from this Manhattan real estate developer who was born in 1946. Trump once said "if you're going to be thinking anyway, you might as well think big."

This is the birthday of the U.S. Army. It was founded on this day in 1775, when the Continental Congress in Philadelphia authorized the recruitment of ten companies of riflemen to serve for one year. There is an old Army adage: If it moves salute it, if it doesn't move, paint it.

15th.

The feast day of St. Vitus.

The second installment of the U.S. estimated tax is due.

1215 King John I of England signed the Magna Carta.

1381 British peasant revolted against the poll tax.

1648 Margaret Jones became the first person executed in Massachusetts for witchcraft. (See May 27th entry.)

1752 Benjamin Franklin proved that lightning contained electricity.

1844   Vulcanized rubber was patented. (See December 29th entry.)

1860   The first settlers arrived in Idaho.

1884   Harry Langdon was born.

1907   The Second International Peace Conference opened.

1909   The cork-centered baseball was patented.

1911   Pioneer Day was declared a state holiday in Idaho.

1913   New Yorker Carrie Chapman-Catt opened the first Women's Suffrage Congress.

1925   A New York City ordinance requiring cab drivers to wear white collars on the job went into effect.

1932   Mario Cuomo was born.

1951   Jim Belushi was born.

Today is the feast day of St. Vitus. In Germany, it is said that if you dance before a statue of St. Vitus on his day, you'll be assured a year's good health. This patron saint of comedians, dancers, and Sicilians is invoked against epilepsy, lightning, snakebite, attacks by wild animals, and oversleeping. Certainly people who were born today like silent-screen comedian Harry Langdon, former New York Governor Mario Cuomo, and comedic actor Jim Belushi have been blessed by St. Vitus. And Ben Franklin definitely picked the right day to prove that lightning contained electricity. At least he became enlightened instead of lighted by his discovery.

This is a good day to go fly a kite. It was on this day, in 1752, that Benjamin Franklin flew a kite with a key tied to its string and proved that lightning contained electricity. Franklin's accomplishment is about as much fun as the cork-centered baseball that was patented on this very day in 1909. Despite the fact that these two discoveries share an anniversary over a hundred years passed before the next logical step—the night game—took place.

We all have something in common with King John of England, on this, the anniversary of the day he begrudgingly signed the Magna Carta in 1215. The last article of the document read: "that the men in our kingdom shall have and hold all the aforesaid liberties, rights, and concessions well and peacefully." In essence, King John lost some of his power without recourse when he signed the Magna Carta. This is also the day when you write a check for the second U.S. estimated income tax installment.

If you think that writing a check for the second U.S. estimated income tax installment—which is due today—is cause for revolt, perhaps another event that occurred on this day might give you cause for thought. In 1381, a bloody peasant revolt ended in London. For three days, peasants descended upon the city of London to protest the poll tax. King Richard II had imposed a one-shilling levy on every person over fourteen years of age. It was the third tax leveled on the common people in four years. It took no account for each individual's means or circumstances. So the overtaxed public went on a rampage. The rioting ended when the king himself rode into the angry crowd, revoked the tax, and promised to abolish serfdom.

It's a groundbreaking day for pioneers. The citizens of Idaho call today Pioneer Day. In 1860 the first pioneering settlers arrived in the territory that soon became the state of Idaho. Other pioneering efforts have also happened on this day. In 1907, pioneers in world politics convened at the Second International Peace Conference in The Hague, Netherlands. And six years later, the women's rights pioneer Carrie Chapman-Catt opened the first Women's Suffrage Congress in Budapest, Hungary.

16th.

1329   The Black Prince—Edward, Prince of Wales—was born.

1838   John Quincy Adams began a three-week speech.

1858   Abraham Lincoln warned of a house divided.

1902   *The Wizard of Oz* premiered.

1980   The U.S. Supreme Court ruled that scientists who developed new life forms in laboratories could patent their creations. (See April 12th entry.)

History records that on this very day in 1838, former U.S. President John Quincy Adams—then serving in the House of Representatives—rose and began a speech opposing the Texas annexation. The history books tell us that his speech lasted three weeks.

On this date in 1858, the Republican Party assembled in Springfield, Illinois. It had just nominated Abraham Lincoln as a candidate for the U.S. Senate. He lost that particular election, but his words on that day still echo through the corridors of time. Lincoln said to his audience: " 'A house divided against itself cannot stand.' I believe this government cannot endure permanently half slave and half free."

Theatergoers set their sights somewhere over the rainbow on this day in 1902. That's when *The Wizard of Oz* had its stage premiere.

Today is the Black Prince's birthday. In 1329, Edward, Prince of Wales, was born. He gained his dark nickname partially because of the color of his armor. But Edward also earned his dubious title for his ruthless brutality toward his enemies and his relentless cruelty on the battlefield. Even on his deathbed, Edward refused to forgive his enemies.

17th.

1775 The Battle of Bunker Hill occurred. (Bunker Hill Day)

1816 Billy Barker was born. (See August 21st entry.)

1947 First round-the-world airline service commenced.

1954 Army-McCarthy televised hearings ended. (See February 21st and April 22nd entries.)

1972 A break-in at the Democratic National Headquarters in the Watergate complex was discovered. (See January 4th and February 7th entries.)

This is the anniversary of the day when an American commander said, "Don't fire 'til you see the whites of their eyes." It was said in 1775, at the Battle of Bunker Hill in Boston, Massachusetts. The troops held their fire until the British troops were nearly upon them. But this was no demonstration of chivalry or courage. Guns at that time were so inaccurate that firing any sooner would have been a waste of ammunition.

Today is the anniversary of the first round-the-world passenger airline flight. A Pan-American Airline plane took off from New York's LaGuardia Field. It didn't take eighty days to fly around the world, but it did take a lot longer than the same trip takes today by jet.

18th.

1798 Robert Goodloe Harper gave his "millions for defense" toast.

1815 The Battle of Waterloo took place. (See February 26th entry.)

1873 Suffragist Susan B. Anthony was fined $100 for attempting to vote in the 1872 U.S. Presidential Election. (See February 15th entry.)

1928 Amelia Earhart became the first woman to fly across the Atlantic Ocean. (See January 11th and May 20th entries.)

1977 The U.S. space shuttle *Enterprise* carried a crew aloft for the first time. (See January 24th and April 6th entries.)

1983 Sally K. Ride became America's first woman in space as she and four other astronauts blasted off aboard the U.S. space shuttle *Challenger*. (See April 19th, June 24th, and August 30th entries.)

What would happen today if someone toasted a guest of honor in the way Robert Goodloe Harper did at a dinner held for diplomat John Marshall who had just completed a mission to France. On this date, in 1798, Harper declared: "Millions for defense, but not a cent for tribute." Of course, the figure would be revised to billions if it were quoted today.

19th.

1885 The Statue of Liberty arrived in the United States.

1896 Bessie Wallis Warfield was born. (See June 3rd and June 23rd entries.)

1903 Lou Gehrig was born.

1917 The royal British family adopted the name Windsor.

1934 Federal Communications Commission was created.

1984 Michael Jordan was signed to the Chicago Bulls. (See June 12th and June 20th entries.)

There are few symbols more closely related to the spirit of America than the Statue of Liberty. Today is the day when "Lady Liberty" arrived. In 1885, she landed at Bedloe's Island in New York Harbor. This noble symbol was a gift from France. She was created in Paris by Frederic Bartholdi around a metal skeleton designed by Alexandre Eiffel. She was transported by ship in parts; and reassembled on the spot where she still proudly stands.

Back in 1934, on this date, Congress created the Federal Communications Commission. Its job is to regulate interstate and international communications by radio, telephone, telegraph, and cable. And its influence now expands to television, fiber optics, remote networks, modems, cellular and satellite phones.

Two events that were part of major news headlines in the 1930s began on this day. In 1917, Great Britain's royal family adopted the name Windsor to replace Saxe-Coburg-Gotha. When Queen Victoria married Prince Albert, the nation's union with a royal house of Germany was sealed. But during the First World War, political and public sentiments changed; so King George V made that unprecedented name change to disassociate the royal family from its German origins. All succeeding monarchs from that day forward have had the last name of Windsor. George's successor, King Edward also made news when he abdicated his title, became the Duke of Windsor, and married a woman who was born on this day in 1896. Bessie Wallis Warfield became the famous divorcée Mrs. Wallis Simpson, and as you probably know she eventually bore the title Duchess of Windsor.

When Michael Jordan was signed to the lowly Chicago Bulls basketball club on this date in 1984, the team's general manager was quoted as saying, "Jordan isn't going to turn this franchise around." But the University of North Carolina at Chapel Hill varsity player, Olympic gold medalist, and the NBA's number one draft pick, took the team from last place to win three consecutive championships between 1990 and 1992, and more after that.

A great American who became the inspiration for millions was born on this day in 1903. Baseball player Lou Gehrig joined professional sports and quickly rose to fame. Nicknamed the "Pride of the Yankees," Gehrig played with another all-time hero, Babe Ruth, but before he could beat the Babe's career high, he was stricken with the debilitating nervous disorder ALS and retired from the game.

20th.

1756	Over one hundred British prisoners suffocated at the Black Hole of Calcutta.
1782	The Great Seal of the United States was adopted by Congress.
1837	Victoria became Queen of England. (See January 2nd, January 22nd, February 10th, and May 24th entries.)
1893	Lizzie Borden was acquitted of murder.
1993	The Chicago Bulls became the first team to win three successive NBA championships in twenty-seven years. (See June 12th and June 19th entries.)
1907	Lillian Hellman was born. (See May 27th entry.)

It would be wonderful if some events never happened. But we cannot change history, only keep it as reminder so that we might never let it repeat itself. Today is the anniversary of an incident known as the Black Hole of Calcutta. One hundred forty-six British soldiers were placed in a tiny dungeon that was so crowded only twenty-three survived the fateful night in 1756. The governor of Bengal, Narwab Suraj ad Dawlah, had ordered his army to overtake the East India Company's garrison in Calcutta to protest Great Britain's expansion into India.

The Great Seal of the United States was adopted on this very day by the U.S. Congress back in 1782. That was before we even had a constitution! The nation's symbol featured an eagle holding an olive branch, and the legend, "E Pluribus Unum," which, in Latin, means "one from many."

Every generation has its crime of the century. Today we have the anniversary of a not-guilty verdict handed down for such a crime. This verdict did not, however, put an end to the strangely persistent legend. In 1893, Lizzie Borden was acquitted in New Bedford, Massachusetts, of the murders of her father and her stepmother. You may not know that she was acquitted. You are more likely to know the children's rhyme which goes: "Lizzie Borden took an ax. / Gave her mother forty whacks. / When she saw what she had done. / She gave her father forty-one."

On this day in 1905, a champion of human rights was born in New Orleans. Playwright Lillian Hellman became a well-known playwright and screenwriter penning stories that blatantly attacked injustice, exploitation, and selfishness in human nature. *The Children's Hour*, *Little Foxes*, and *Watch on the Rhine* exposed the effect a malicious child, a manipulating family, and an irresponsible, carefree generation had on individual lives and on their surroundings.

21st.

The summer solstice takes place. (See December 22nd entry.)

1834 The reaping machine was patented.

1948 The long-playing record was demonstrated.

Although the summer solstice isn't always precisely punctual, today is often the first day of the summer season. When "summer is icumen in," as the Scottish poet Robert Burns put it, our major purpose in life is, or should be, to keep cool.

Today is a record anniversary. In 1948, the long-playing record was demonstrated by CBS Laboratories' Dr. Peter Goldmark. The LP—with its high-fidelity recording and its extended playing time—ushered in the advent of new medium for recording sounds and launched a forty-year tidal wave of gold and platinum records. The LP— and its smaller cousin the 45—have since been replaced by cassette tapes and compact discs, though there are still purists who swear that nothing sounds better than a carefully dusted vinyl platter.

As the old saying goes: "Ye shall reap what ye shall sow." And today's anniversary reaped a good profit for inventor Cyrus McCormick. In 1834, McCormick received a patent for his reaping machine. The bountiful harvest it provided ushered in a new age of agriculture.

22nd.

1611 Henry Hudson was set adrift. (See August 3rd and September 3rd entry.)

1921 Joseph Papp was born.

1937   Joe Louis became world heavyweight boxing champion.

1938   Joe Louis defended his title as world heavyweight boxing champion and won.

1964   Three civil rights workers were slain in Mississippi.

1970   The voting age was lowered to eighteen by law.

1985   President Ronald Reagan honored the remains of four Marines.

There is a story about an old vaudevillian whose act was falling flat—so flat that he was yanked off the stage and a local youngster was brought in as an emergency fill-in. The youngster was a smash hit and the next day the local critic wrote that the old vaudevillian's act "had died that others might live." We are inclined to take some martyrs' deaths that lightly—but not others. In one of history's more somber notes, on this date in 1964, three civil-rights workers disappeared in Mississippi. Comedian and activist Dick Gregory convinced publisher Hugh Hefner to post a $25,000 reward and eventually their murderers were found. The bodies were discovered two weeks later.

One reason not all people are alike is that we come from different generations. In 1970, on this day, President Richard M. Nixon lowered the voting age from twenty-one to eighteen years old. There were those who saw disaster ahead. After the Twenty-sixth Amendment ratified the law on June 30, 1971, young adults could vote not only in national elections, but state and local elections as well.

If it's worth doing well, it's worth doing twice, and today's anniversary will prove this point. Joe Louis became world heavyweight boxing champion on this day in both 1937 and 1938. He won the title when he knocked out James Braddock in Chicago. The next year, he knocked out German contender Max Schmeling in New York City.

On this day in 1611, Henry Hudson, his son, and six other crew members were set adrift by mutineers in what is now called Hudson's Bay. The explorer had been commissioned by the Russian Muscovy Company and the Dutch East India Company to find the fabled Northwest Passage to Asia. He had discovered the island of Manhattan and the Hudson River. But drifting aimlessly during a long, harsh winter on this huge inland sea—which eventually bore his name—tempers flared among the crew of his ship, *Discovery*. A mutiny resulted. Hudson and his crew were never found. The mutineers sailed back to England, but the ringleaders did not return. They were killed in a battle with Inuit tribesmen.

On this day in 1985, President Ronald Reagan received the coffins of four Marines killed in an attack on a San Salvador café. At the ceremony, the president solemnly vowed that the slayers of these brave man would "not evade justice on earth any more than they can escape the judgment of God."

When Joseph Papp was born on this day in 1921, most Americans still thought of Shakespeare's plays as generally unentertaining, long-haired, intellectual stuff. But when Papp opened New York's Public Theater and produced the acclaimed summertime Shakespeare in the Park series, a lot of Average Joe's changed their minds. Papp's productions brought Shakespeare and other playwrights' works to modern audiences in much the same way Shakespeare himself presented his plays at the Globe Theater. The sets weren't elaborate; the actors were talented but relatively unknown; the tickets didn't cost a fortune; the shows were highly entertaining on many intellectual and non-intellectual levels. As a result, American theater gained a whole new audience.

23rd.

963 AD   Luxembourg became a principality.

1868   The capital letter typewriter was patented.

1894   Edward VIII, Duke of Windsor, was born. (See June 3rd, June 19th, and December 10th entries.)

1912   Alan M. Turing was born.

1931   Aviators Wiley Post and Harold Catty took off from New York for a flight around the world. (See July 22nd entry.)

1938   U.S. Congress created the Civil Aeronautics Authority.

1961   The International Treaty of Scientific Cooperation and Peaceful Use of Antarctica was signed.

Won't you wish a happy birthday to the principality of Luxembourg which was founded on this date in 963 AD? The birthday has to be happy because Luxembourg has survived occupations and invasions by more powerful neighbors—and every other country is more powerful than Luxembourg except in its ability to survive. Good countries, like other good things, sometimes come in small packages.

Today we commemorate a chilly subject—Antarctica. On this date in 1961, an international treaty for scientific cooperation and the peaceful use of the Antarctic continent

Joan of Arc was born January 6, 1412. She was burned at
the stake on May 30, 1431.

Sir Francis Drake and the British fleet
routed the Spanish Armada July 29, 1588.

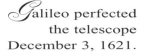

Galileo perfected
the telescope
December 3, 1621.

Marie Antoinette was born November 2, 1755.

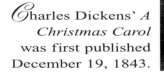olfgang Amadeus Mozart was born January 27, 1756.

*C*harles Dickens' *A Christmas Carol* was first published December 19, 1843.

The first transcontinental railroad link was completed May 10, 1869.

𝒢eneral George Armstrong Custer made his last stand against Sioux warriors led by Chief Sitting Bull at Little Big Horn, Montana June 25, 1876.

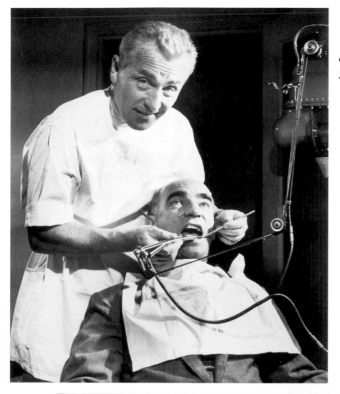

The electric dentist drill was patented January 26, 1875.

The first gas pump was delivered to a gasoline dealer September 5, 1885. Henry Ford introduced the Model T October 1, 1908.

$\mathcal{S}$ir Charlie Chaplin was born April 16, 1889.

ℬabe Ruth was born
February 6, 1895.

𝒯he editorial entitled "Yes,
Virginia, there is a Santa Claus"
was published September 21, 1897.

$\mathscr{W}$ilbur and Orville Wright made their first airplane flight December 17, 1903.

The Nineteenth Amendment to the U.S. Constitution was ratified giving women the right to vote August 26, 1920.

Hirohito became Emporer of Japan November 10, 1926

Amelia Earhart became the first woman to fly across the Atlantic Ocean June 18, 1928 and the first woman to fly solo across the Pacific January 11-12, 1935. She and her navigator Fred Noonan disappeared over the Pacific Ocean July 2, 1937.

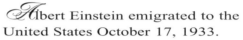Albert Einstein emigrated to the United States October 17, 1933.

Joe Louis became world heavyweight boxing champion June 22, 1937 and successfully defended his title exactly one year later June 22, 1938.

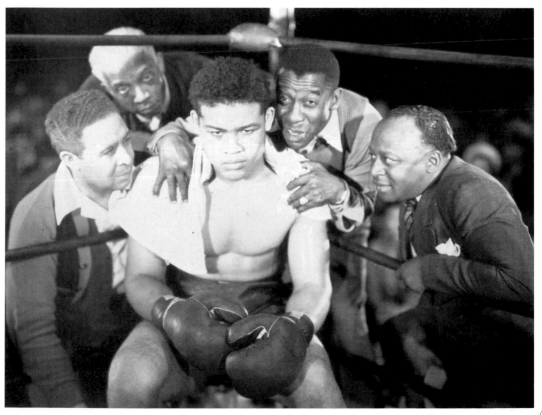

American sailors celebrate VJ day at Pearl Habor, Hawaii. Although their formal surrender would not come for a few weeks, the Japanese forces stopped fighting on August 14, 1945.

Dr. Jonas Salk announced a polio vaccine March 26, 1953.

Astronaut John Glenn orbited the earth
February 20, 1962.

*T*he Reverend Dr. Martin Luther King, Jr. was born January 15, 1929. He delivered his eloquent "I have a dream" speech to civil rights marchers in Washington, D.C. on August 28, 1963.

*P*resident Richard Nixon announced his resignation August 8, 1974.

was signed. It will be a cold day when that treaty ends. Meanwhile, we can benefit from knowing that none of the treaty nations are planning a mass migration of their populous there in the near future.

History records that on this date, in 1868, Christopher Sholes, a Wisconsin journalist and state senator, received a patent for a contraption called a "Type-Writer." This particular typewriter printed only capital letters—it didn't have a shift key. But it sparked an evolution in business equipment that has led to pocket-sized computers with complete though minute keyboards, and enough memory to store all kinds of information—despite the fact that many of them also type in capital letters only.

A lot of controversy has arisen over Edward VIII, Duke of Windsor, in the past few years. Was the son of Great Britain's King George V really a German spy? Born on this day in 1894, it was a well-known fact that before Edward took the throne he wanted to sign a friendship agreement with the German government. The royal house of Windsor did have German connections which his father officially declared as severed during the First World War. Did Parliament really allow him to abdicate his title and marry a commoner just to get rid of him? The mystery has not yet been solved, though new evidence is still being uncovered.

During the 1930s, America took to the skies. On this day in 1931, aviators Wiley Post and Harold Catty took off from New York City for their epic flight around the world. And seven years later to the day, the U.S. Congress created the Civil Aeronautics Authority to regulate air traffic. The skies had become crowded with airmail routes, passenger flights, and barnstorming stunt pilots in the thirty years following the Wright Brothers' first flight at Kitty Hawk, North Carolina. Now known as the Federal Aviation Administration, this arm of government continues to monitor the thousands of aircraft that fly in America's crowded airspace.

No one had ever heard of digital computers when British mathematician Alan Mathison Turing was born in 1912. Artificial intelligence was just a wild-eyed fantasy in a few obscure science tests. While studying for his masters degree at Cambridge University's King's College, Turing took long walks through the river-side meadows down to the village of Grantchester. On one of his afternoon strolls, he conceived of a universal computing machine; and in 1937, he published his theory entitled "On Computable Numbers." After the Second World War, Turing headed a project to create the ACE—Automatic Computing Engine. Three years later, he directed the construction of the Manchester Automatic Digital Machine. And in 1950, Turing predicted that computers would eventually think like humans. Sadly, he never lived to see his prophecy come to the fruition it has reached.

24th.

1497 John Cabot sighted land between Halifax and southern Labrador.

1763 Empress Josephine of France was born. (See March 9th entry.)

1947 Flying saucers were reported near Mount Rainier, Washington.

1948 The Berlin Blockade began. (See May 12th entry.)

1983 Sally Ride became America's first female astronaut to return to earth. (See April 19th entry.)

Today is an historic anniversary. In 1947, flying saucers were sighted over Mount Rainier, Washington. Kenneth Arnold of Boise, Idaho swore that he saw "shining saucer-like objects . . . Not just one, but nine." That was it. In later years, the reports were considerably more detailed, up to and including accounts of alien abductions, descriptions of "gray men" and so forth. There is little evidence that these people were deliberately trying to con the public, but the government explained the sightings as marsh gas mirages, weather balloons, or atmospheric phenomena. People didn't seem terribly anxious to believe those explanations either.

The space shuttle *Challenger* safely landed on this day in 1983, at Edward's Air Force Base. This may not seem that newsworthy until you consider that one of the crew members was Sally Ride, our first female astronaut to travel into space.

Five years after Christopher Columbus reached the New World, exploring the islands in the Caribbean, and returned to Spain to report his discoveries, a courageous British navigator sighted the coastline between Halifax, Newfoundland, and southern Labrador. On this day in 1497, John Cabot made the first recorded discovery of the North American mainland. History tells us that the Vikings had landed on this continent five centuries earlier, but they left no written record of their epic journey. John Cabot did.

25th.

1876 General George Armstrong Custer made his last stand. (See December 5th entry.)

1903 George Orwell was born.

1950 The Korean War began.

Today is the anniversary of one of the U.S. military's darker days. This is the day in which Custer went to his last stand. In 1876, General George Armstrong Custer and his entire command of over two hundred men were wiped out by the Sioux nation at Little Big Horn, Montana. Only one horse—who was named Comanche—survived.

Some anniversaries leave stern memories. Long after Custer's Last Stand took place in 1876, another questionable military event occurred. In 1950, North Korea invaded South Korea, sparking the Korean War. Countless casualties and a relatively unaltered border resulted. And the battle continues across opposite sides of international conference tables—featuring streams of speeches from both sides.

George Orwell, who was born on this day in 1903, kept his feet planted firmly on the ground as he wove prophetic visions of civilization's future right here on earth. His prophecies concerning life in the year 1984 were not far from wrong; and his commentary on civilization's degeneration in his novel, *Animal Farm*, provide the theme for today. The animals in his story fought for and won their freedom from a tyrannical farmer, establishing an egalitarian government based on equal rights and the democratic process. The lust for power overtook some of the pigs, and slowly the social scales shifted from absolute equality to a privileged class structure where some animals became more equal than others.

26th.

1819   Abner Doubleday was born

1866   George Edward Carnavon was born. (See November 4th and February 16th entries.)

1945   The United Nations Charter was signed in San Francisco, California. (See January 1st, January 9th, April 25th, and October 24th entries.)

1948   The Berlin airlift began. (See May 12th entry.)

Today is Abner Doubleday's birthday. Born in 1819, in Ballston Spa, New York, Doubleday invented America's national pasttime: baseball.

27th.

1844   Mormon leaders Joseph and Hyrum Smith were murdered by a mob in Carthage, Illinois. (See April 6th entry.)

1880   Helen Keller was born.

1936   President Franklin D. Roosevelt delivered his "rendezvous with destiny" speech.

1969   Patrons at Manhattan's Stonewall Inn clashed with police during a raid.

We generally think of courage in terms of combat—either on the battlefield or on the playing fields. Today we should be thinking of a far greater kind of courage. Today is Helen Keller's birthday. Born in 1880, in Tuscumbia, Alabama, Helen Keller was diagnosed blind, deaf, and mute. In her time, many physically challenged people were placed in lunatic asylums. But thanks to inventor Alexander Graham Bell—whose wife was hearing-impaired—and her visually-impaired teacher Anne Sullivan, Keller learned to speak. She learned to read lips by touching the lips and throat of the individual speaking. She learned to read Braille. She became a professional writer and crusaded for better treatment of visually- and hearing-impaired individuals.

When President Franklin D. Roosevelt was renominated on this day, in 1936, he sounded a rallying call for his time. "This generation," Roosevelt proclaimed, "has a rendezvous with destiny."

Today marks some somber footnotes in the history of America's fight for freedom. In 1844, Mormon leaders Joseph and Hyrum Smith were murdered by a mob in Carthage, Illinois. The First Church of Latter Day Saints had been exiled from New York State and a number of other places before attempting to settle in the Midwestern town. But local people were enraged by the idea of having these so-called heretics who practiced polygamy in their Christian town. The Mormons were run out on a rail once again. In 1969, patrons of Manhattan's Stonewall Inn clashed with police during a raid. Homosexuality was treated as a crime in New York City and the incident at this bar became the focal point of gay rights' advocates for years to come.

28th.

1491 Henry VIII of England was born.

1902 Richard Rodgers was born. (See July 12th entry.)

1914 Gavrilo Princip assassinated Austria's Archduke Francis Ferdinand.

1919 The Treaty of Versailles was signed. (See March 19th entry.)

1976 Terrorists hijacked a passenger jet to Entebbe, Uganda. (See July 4th entry.)

Today is Richard Rodgers' birthday. Born in New York City in 1902, he started out writing songs for amateur boys' club shows. His music quickly matured to familiar, yet haunting, melodies that made him a giant in the theatrical world. The music "Slaughter on Tenth Avenue" and "My Funny Valentine" soon gave way to the scores for groundbreaking musicals like *Oklahoma*, *South Pacific*, *The King and I*, and *Flower Drum Song* which were written with lyricist Oscar Hammerstein III.

How many of us know the name of Gavrilo Princip. It is one of history's quirks that some of the people who kindled epic flames are so little recognized. Gavrilo Princip was a Serbian revolutionary who fought for his nation's freedom from Austro-Hungarian rule. We should remember his name because today is the anniversary of an incident that triggered the First World War. On this day, in 1914, Princip assassinated Austro-Hungary's heir apparent Archduke Francis Ferdinand and his wife Sofia in Sarajevo, Bosnia-Herzegovina.

The fact that the anniversaries of both the beginning and end of the First World War occur on the same day is poetic. In 1919, most of the nations involved in that great war signed the Treaty of Versailles and agreed to organize an international League of Nations, except one—the United States.

On this date in 1976, terrorist hijackers seized an Air France plane and flew it to Entebbe, Uganda. They held the passengers—mostly Israelis—as hostages. The world was aghast. A week later, a daring Israeli raid freed the hostages and quashed the terrorists' plans.

The Lord, it's said, works in strange and wondrous ways. An event in 1491 was perhaps more of the former and less of the latter. The founder of the Church of England was born on this day. Great Britain's King Henry VIII was born in Greenwich, England. Henry VIII had more wives than most monarchs; was a glutton for good food; reputedly wrote songs like "Greensleeves;" and generally did more of everything than most people—including fighting with the Catholic Church.

29th.

1566 The Stationers Company was granted a monopoly.

1577 Peter Paul Rubens was born.

1767 Britain passed the Townshend Revenue Act.

1900 Antoine de Saint-Exupéry was born.

1928 Al Smith was nominated as a presidential candidate.

1946 British authorities arrested more than 2,700 Zionists. (See August 31st and September 29th entries.)

1967 Israel united east and west Jerusalem.

1995 The space shuttle *Atlantis* linked up with the *Mir* space station.

A monopoly was created on this day in 1566. Great Britain's Queen Mary had granted the Stationers Company guild the power to be the nation's sole booksellers eight years earlier. But on this date they gained a total monopoly on the business of publishing. The guild consisted of printers, booksellers, and publishers nicknamed for the stalls or stations they set up to sell their wares. Their monopoly meant that every book title had to be registered in the company's roster in advance. "Illegal" books were confiscated and burned. No guild member was allowed to publish the same book as another member. Healthy competition wasn't even considered. No edition could exceed 1,250 copies. Best-sellers had to be reset and reprinted so printers would have steady work. Book prices soared in the absence of competition. Soon no one could afford to buy their products.

Peter Paul Rubens was born on this date in 1577, in Westphalia to a Flemish family. Unlike many starving artists of his time, Rubens did very well indeed—not merely in the mastery of his art but also in the size of his purse. If you visit Rubens' house in

Antwerp, you will see quite an establishment. It is fair to say that, even though so many people have delighted in his work, in a material sense he got a lot more out of it.

We are generally familiar with the reasons for the Boston Tea Party in 1773. This so-called party protested the import tax levied by Britain on its colonies. But few remember that the whole thing really began on this date. In 1767, King George III gave his approval to the Townshend Acts which had been proposed by Chancellor of the Exchequer Charles Townshend. The acts taxed imports of glass, paper, lead, paints and tea to the colonies. The tea tax was retained long after the colonists boycotted and successfully repealed the other levies. Slowly but surely the resentment against "taxation without representation" laid the groundwork for the American Revolution.

It was considered almost revolutionary that John F. Kennedy, a Catholic, was elected President. But before that day, another Catholic candidate had won a major party Presidential nomination and today is the anniversary of that event. In 1924, Alfred E. Smith was denied the Democratic nomination because he was a Catholic. In 1928, he was not rejected. Another bastion of religious discrimination in America was breached.

An adventurer with a romantic soul was born on this day. In 1900, Antoine de Saint-Exupéry was born in Lyon, France. His escapades as a test pilot, military reconnaissance pilot, and aviator were enough to fill a hundred adventure novels; and he penned quite a few of them himself. Saint-Exupéry wrote popular books like *Night Flight*; *Wind, Sand, and Storm*; and *Flight to Arras*, when he wasn't involved in real-life adventures. But his most famous work was a children's fable entitled *The Little Prince*. The moral of this classic story holds a fundamental secret to happiness: The best things in life are the simplest ones.

The first joint American-Russian space mission had taken place during a thaw in the Cold War, in 1975. The ice finally melted away twenty years later. And on this day in 1995, the U.S. space shuttle *Atlantis* linked up with Russia's *Mir* space station in outer space. It was the first of seven scheduled missions to prepare both nations for a joint pioneering effort—the construction of an international space station. Its purpose sounds like something from the pages of a science fiction novel: the station will serve as a scientific laboratory and launching platform for a planned expedition to Mars.

Many Arab nations resented Great Britain's involvement in the Holy Land following the First World War. But as the Second World War came to an end, troubles in British-held Palestine escalated. Tens of thousands of displaced European Jews moved to overtake the Holy Land in the name of Zionism—a radical religious and political movement that had originated in eastern Europe. Terrorism erupted in Jerusalem, and on this day in 1946, British authorities arrested more than 2,700 Zionists in the hope that it might end the plague of bombings and sniper attacks. It didn't. Two years later, Great Britain was forced to leave Palestine, and Israel was born. Jerusalem was split in half so that Islamic holy places would not fall under Zionist jurisdiction. On this same day in 1967, Israel ignored international protests and united the city. The incident ignited a full-scale war. Neither side was willing to compromise their religious beliefs for the sake of political peace.

30th.

1572   Great Britain's Poor law was passed.

1870   Ada Kepley became the first female law school graduate.

1906   The Meat Inspection Act became law.

1906   The Pure Food and Drug Act became law.

1936   *Gone with the Wind* was published.

1971   The Twenty-sixth Amendment to the U.S. Constitution was enacted. (See June 22nd entry.)

Welfare reform has been instituted in many different ways throughout history. On this day in 1572, Great Britain's Queen Elizabeth I instituted that nation's first Poor Law. This system gave statutory assistance to the poor who were unemployed or vagrant. Church parishes were responsible for distributing this government-funded aid. Those applicants who were willing and able to work were given tools and placed in paying jobs. Those who couldn't work—such as the elderly or infirm—were cared for in their own homes. Able-bodied individuals who were work-shy were publicly punished as vagrants.

The world's most popular Civil War novel was written generations after the actual incident. Margaret Mitchell's epic *Gone with the Wind* was first published on this date in 1936. The novel was an all-time best seller and the film adaptation was a box office sensation more than once.

This nation prides itself on providing its people with foods and medicines which are safe to consume. And today marks the anniversary of the reason why. In 1906, the U.S. Congress established both the Meat Inspection Act and the Pure Food and Drug Act. Scientists and doctors had discovered that poorly-prepared or mishandled ingredients, foods, and medications had killed many Americans. Not all producers were following sterile or standardized methods of processing, packaging, or storing these vital commodities. By enacting strict guidelines and regular inspections, the government ensured the public's safety. Thanks to these measures, botulism and other preventable illnesses were nearly eradicated; the physically deforming effects of drugs like Thalidomide were discovered; and the public was educated on how to properly cook and handle raw meats and poultry.

One talent many American women have is the ability to outthink and outtalk any American man. And on this day in 1870, Ada Kepley became one of the first American women to take professional advantage of that talent. She was the nation's first female law school graduate.

July

While most of us think of July as the middle of vacation season—a time for back-yard cookouts and napping under a shaded tree in a hammock—the world seems to revolve around the word freedom. The list of nations that gained their freedom during this particular month attests to this seasonal trend. From Canada and the United States to Peru and other points south, the July watchwords were independence and freedom. The echoes of "*liberté, egalité, fraternité*" chimed through France, Belgium, and the north African coastal nation of Algeria. During the month of July in 321 AD, freedom from work was proclaimed by the Roman emperor Constantine. Now that's something for which we can all hum the V for victory theme as Winston Churchill did in 1941. But some of you surely agree with Horace Greeley who said in July: "Go west, young man! Go west!" The freedom of the wide open spaces are near and dear to all of us.

1st.

Freedom Day.

Canada Day.

1847 The U.S. Post Office issued the first adhesive-backed stamps. (See Septmber 22 and November 1st entries.)

1863 The Battle of Gettysburg began.

1867 The provinces of Nova Scotia, New Brunswick, Quebec, and Ontario officially became the Dominion of Canada.

1873 The province of Prince Edward Island joined into the confederation of Canada.

1898 Theodore Roosevelt and the Rough Riders charged San Juan Hill. (See October 27 entry.)

1963 The U.S. Post Office inaugurated the postal zip-code system.

1966 Medicare went into effect.

Today is Freedom Day. Many nations—including our own—gained their freedom during this particular month of the year. Canada became a self-governing British dominion on this day in 1867. France had its first revolution on July 14. Nations such as Algeria, Argentina, Colombia, Belgium, Peru, Liberia and Venezuela also gained self-government and freedom during this month.

Today marks the anniversary of the Battle of Gettysburg, a three-day-long confrontation that took place in 1863. President Abraham Lincoln said we must remember this battle so that from its honored dead "we take increased devotion to that cause for which they gave the last full measure of devotion." In the largest sense, their cause was to fight for what Lincoln described as a "government of the people, by the people, for the people [that] shall not perish from the earth."

The concept of providing health care for senior U.S. citizens became a reality on this date. In 1966, Medicare became part of the services offered to American citizens. In the intervening years Medicare has been accused of making a few people rich; it has also been credited with helping more people to live healthier and longer lives.

Today is Canada Day: a day to commemorate this northern nation's freedom from British rule. In 1867, the provinces of Nova Scotia, New Brunswick, Quebec, and Ontario became a confederation under an Act of Parliament known as the British North America Act. Canada's representatives sat down at the bargaining table and negotiated a peaceful step-by-step settlement which guaranteed them self-government. Neighboring territories like Prince Edward Island soon joined them. As a dominion, Canada still owed its allegiance to the British crown and to Parliament, eventually receiving total independence in 1982. But unlike its southern neighbor—the United States—Canada did not bear arms to gain its freedom.

Today is the ideal day to salute the U.S. Post Office, who issued the first adhesive-backed stamps on this day 1847, and kept us from searching for a pot of glue while mailing out our bill payments. On this same day in 1963, the Postal Service made it easier for our creditors to get our checks when it inaugurated the postal zip-code system. The reason for mentioning these particular events is simple. When are we going to end this reign of revolving credit; and stop echoing Theodore Roosevelt's immortal cry heard this day in 1898 when he and the Rough Riders took Cuba's San Juan Hill— "Charge!"

2nd.

1566 French astrologer, physician, and visionary Nostradamus died. (See December 14th entry.)

1776 The Continental Congress declared American independence.

1777 Vermont became the first American colony to abolish slavery. (See January 1st and March 6th entries.)

1937 Amelia Earhart and navigator Fred Noonan disappeared over the Pacific Ocean. (See January 11th, May 20th, and June 18th entries.)

1947 A UFO crashed near Roswell, New Mexico. (See June 24th, October 26th, and December 17th entries.)

1950 The motion picture *Plan 9 From Outer Space*, premiered.

1964 President Lyndon B. Johnson signed the Civil Rights Act into law.

1982 Larry Walters rose 16,000 feet into the air. (See November 21st entry.)

Some of you are undoubtedly getting ready to celebrate Independence Day in two more days. However, today is the real anniversary of our independence. On this day in 1776, the Continental Congress declared that the colonies "are, and of right ought to be free and independent States." Congressional member John Adams wrote to his wife that, quote: "The Second of July, 1776, will be the most memorable epoch in the history of America. I am apt to believe that it will be celebrated by succeeding generations as the great anniversary festival...It ought to be so solemnized with pomp and parade, with shows, games and sports, guns, bells, bonfires and illuminations, from one end of this continent to the other, from this time forward, forevermore." And of course we have done just that, but not on July 2. After passing this resolution, the assembly decided to adopt a full declaration on July Fourth.

A century after the Battle of Gettysburg—and almost to the day—a law was enacted that ensured equal freedoms for all Americans. On this date in 1964, President Lyndon B. Johnson signed the Civil Rights Act. It was not the end of the fight for equal rights that had pitted neighbor against neighbor, brother against brother during the Civil War. But the Civil Rights Act did win the battle for government recognition that there had been a denial of full citizenship for certain segments of our population.

Sometimes its hard to believe what you see. Take for example three events that occurred on this day. In 1947, an object crashed near Roswell, New Mexico. Eyewitness accounts gave rise to the speculation that the UFO was an alien-manned spacecraft. But despite numerous civilian reports, the U.S. Air Force announced that the unknown object was a weather balloon. And in 1982, Larry Walters rose 16,000 feet into the air, using a lawn chair and forty-two helium weather balloons. He was arrested by authorities for violating Los Angeles air space after a United Airlines pilot radioed to the airport that he had just passed a man in a lawn chair with a gun while landing his passenger jetliner. Some of the facts are pretty unbelievable, but with any luck they will make more sense than Ed Wood's sci-fi vampire film, *Plan 9 from Outer Space*, which premiered on this day in 1950.

3rd.

321 AD   Sunday was designated as a day of rest.

1775   George Washington took command of the Continental Army. (See February 22nd and December 4th entries.)

1878   George M. Cohan was born.

On this date in 1775, a forty-three-year-old Virginia country gentleman and soldier named George Washington assumed command of the Continental Army at Cambridge, Massachusetts. He did not make a particularly spectacular start, but ultimately, Washington turned out to be a pretty good man for the job.

George M. Cohan was one of America's top song-and-dance men. This unashamed and effervescent flag waver wrote "You're a Grand Old Flag" and "I'm a Yankee Doodle Dandy." Now today happens to be George M. Cohan's birthday. Born in Providence, Rhode Island, in 1878, Cohan's father decided to designate his son's birthdate as the Fourth of July. So George M. became in his own words "a real live nephew of my Uncle Sam, born on the Fourth of July."

We should all take a rest and reflect today on an important event that took place centuries ago on this very day. In 321 AD, the Roman Emperor Constantine proclaimed *dies solis*—or Sunday—as a day of rest and religious observance so his Christian soldiers could attend services and his pagan troops could offer prayers to their gods. It is an ancient tradition that one hopes will never change.

4th.

Independence Day in the United States.

1807 Giuseppe Garibaldi was born.

1826 Stephen Foster was born. (See January 13th entry.)

1826 Three U.S. Presidents died (1826 and 1831) and one President was born (1872).

1845 Henry D. Thoreau went to live near Walden Pond. (See July 12th entry.)

1862 Lewis Carroll first told Alice Liddell the story of Alice in Wonderland. (See January 27th entry.)

1976 Israeli commandos raided Entebbe airport in Uganda and rescued 103 hostages on a hijacked airliner. (See June 28th entry.)

Independence Day is a celebration: a day to enjoy the unalienable right to the pursuit of happiness. Back in 1776, the men who signed the Declaration of Independence on this date said, and meant it literally, that "we mutually pledge to each other our lives, our fortunes, and our sacred honor."

Is history a matter of chance or is there some great director guiding its course? When we consider this day, we find some interesting facts. Two of the men who signed the Declaration of Independence died years later on exactly the same day in 1826. President Thomas Jefferson and President John Adams—whose lives were so closely intertwined in both destiny and friendship—died fifty years to the day after they signed the Declaration of Independence. And five years later, President James Monroe—author of the Monroe Doctrine—passed away in 1831. But in 1872, future President Calvin Coolidge was born in Plymouth, Vermont.

The father of Italian independence and unity was born on this date. In 1807, Giuseppe Garibaldi was born in Nice, France. He tried, in vain, to incorporate his birthplace into Italy rather than France. But even for Garibaldi the Fourth of July commemorated another event. When his fortunes were at a low ebb and his patriotic efforts got him into trouble, Garibaldi found refuge in America.

The story of Alice's adventures underground was first told on this date. In 1862, Lewis Carroll and an Oxford University schoolmate, Robinson Duckworth, took Lorina, Alice, and Edith Liddell on a boating trip to the town of Godstaw. Carroll entertained the group by relating his story while they lunched on the riverbank. In the six months that followed, Carroll wrote down his tales; and—at Alice's request—entitled his work *Alice's Adventures Underground*.

5th.

1810 P.T. Barnum was born.

1811 Venezuela gained its independence.

1865 William Booth founded the Salvation Army in London.

Today is Phineas T. Barnum's birthday. Born in 1810 in Bethel, Connecticut, Barnum is still regarded as America's greatest showman. He very adroitly followed his own maxim: "There's a sucker born every minute." But despite this flippancy, Barnum greatly contributed to America's vitality, excitement, education, and even its sophistication. He created a circus that became known as "the greatest show on earth"; he brought soprano Jenny Lind to America; and he tried to palm off Jumbo the African elephant as the world's last surviving mastodon. He brought his customers flocking. But when he wanted to get rid of them, he pointed them to a door marked "Egress." Only after they had gone through it did they realize that egress meant exit. Barnum didn't take life seriously, and as a result, he succeeded in persuading others to enjoy it a little more.

On this day in 1811, Venezuela became the first South American nation to declare its independence from Spanish rule. Native son Simon Bolivar led the fight for his country's freedom, and the virus of freedom spread to the rest of the continent.

We are gathered here today on the anniversary of a meeting that changed the lives of many good Christian men and women. In 1865, a Methodist minister named William Booth held the first meeting of the Christian Revival Association in London's East End. His mission was to establish "stations" where the poor and homeless could be fed and housed. This somewhat militarist movement—of one fervent evangelist—is better known as the Salvation Army. And that's the name Booth chose for his troops in 1878. Throughout eighty nations, Booth's soldiers still volunteer their services and sign the Articles of War against degradation, depravity, and despondency.

6th.

1747   John Paul Jones was born.

1885   Louis Pasteur successfully used his anti-rabies vaccine. (See December 27th entry.)

1917   T.E. Lawrence and a small group of Arab revolutionaries captured the Turkish garrison at Aqaba. (See August 15th entry.)

1933   The first all-star baseball game was played.

If the average American were asked to name our greatest naval heroes, John Paul Jones would be high on the list. John Paul was not named Jones. In 1747, he was born simply as John Paul, in Kirkcudbrightshire, Scotland. As commander of his own British ship he had been charged with flogging a seaman to death and murdering a mutineer. With the law hot on his tail, he fled to Virginia; and changed his last name to Jones. During the American Revolution, he took a commission in the infant American Navy. He became the only American to bring the Revolution to England, raiding towns and harbors along the coast. The high point of his career was the epic battle between his ship,

Bonhomme Richard, and the British warship *Serapis*. In the heat of this confrontation, Jones allegedly declared: "I have not yet begun to fight!" When the Revolution was over, Jones became a forgotten man. After the war comes diplomacy—which was not one of Jones' virtues. So he lived out his life in Paris, waiting for another American commission. He died in 1792 at the age of forty-five. His new commission arrived one month after his funeral. In 1905, his remains were discovered and brought to the final honor of a resting place at the U.S. Naval Academy at Annapolis. That is the not always heroic saga of John Paul Jones.

Americans pride themselves on being team players. Baseball, basketball, football, and hockey are all team sports. Therefore, when the first major league baseball all-star game was played on this day at Chicago's Wrigley Field, it was regarded as a sort of circus attraction. The concept of all-star games bloomed after this event took place in 1933.

Mind can win over matter despite the odds. An event that occurred in 1917 illustrates this point. Turkey was allied with Germany, fighting against the British during the First World War. At the same time, Saudi Arabia and Palestine were fighting for their freedom from Turkish rule. Both British troops and Arab rebels needed supplies, but no one could pass the watchful eye of the two huge long-range guns that monitored the route. The heavily armed garrison at Aqaba overlooked the shipping channel from Cairo to Palestine. With a relative handful of Arab horsemen, a British officer named T.E. Lawrence captured the garrison on this date. Better known as Lawrence of Arabia, it was he who deduced that the Turkish army never anticipated a desert attack. So he took advantage of the garrison's unarmed side.

7th.

1535 Sir Thomas More was executed.

1846 Commodore John D. Sloat proclaimed California for U.S.

1839 John D. Rockefeller was born.

1908 Nelson A. Rockefeller was born.

Everybody has his or her own personal definition of utopia. The original concept of a utopia—that is to say, the word "utopia" itself—was created by Thomas More. For most of his life, it seemed that More had not only coined the word but found his own ideal world. More's novel, *Utopia*, centered around a mythical island named—you guessed it—Utopia. His mythical paradise was a metaphor for England. Utopia was filled with creature comforts but lacked individual freedom. The book was received as a satire on government and humanity, not as an idealistic vision at all. Real life seemed a lot kinder to More. He was knighted. He became King Henry VIII's favorite; the royal chancellor's favorite; and the people's favorite. But his troubles began and ended when Henry VIII named himself the supreme head of the Church of England. More felt the king could not rule both church and state. On this day in 1535, More was beheaded.

On this day in 1846, U.S. Naval Commodore John D. Sloat landed at Monterey and claimed California for the United States. The Mexican War was on, and there was a good bit of fighting before the annexation took hold. But when gold was discovered at Sutter's Mill less than two years later, California was an American territory and the boom began.

Both John D. Rockefeller, Sr. and his grandson and Nelson A. Rockefeller were born on this day. The founder of the Standard Oil Company, John D. Rockefeller was born in 1839. As a young man, this ambitious entrepreneur switched from dealing grains, meats and commodities to selling a new product—crude oil. His business rapidly grew as the machine age became more dependent on fossil fuel, and eventually it became the first great U.S. business trust. It wasn't long before that monopoly came under fire with the passing of the Sherman Anti-Trust Act in 1890. But around that same time, Rockefeller turned his remarkable drive toward more charitable causes including the establishment of the University of Chicago and the Rockefeller Foundation. By contrast, his grandson—Nelson Rockefeller—rose to greatness in the political arena. As director of a Standard Oil affiliate in Venezuela, Nelson became fluent in Spanish. That asset landed him an appointment at the State Department during the Second World War. From there, he became leader of the Republican Party's moderate wing; New York's governor for four terms; a presidential candidate; and U.S. Vice President under Gerald Ford. Like his father and grandfather, Nelson was also a patron of education and the arts, founding New York's Museum of Primitive Art and serving as a trustee for the Museum of Modern Art.

8th.

1776 The Declaration of Independence was first read to the public.

1835 The Liberty Bell cracked.

1885 *The Wall Street Journal* was first published.

1896 William Jennings Bryan gave his "cross of gold" speech.

On this day in 1835, the Liberty Bell cracked while it chimed in honor of Chief Justice John Marshall who had recently died. This day is now observed as Liberty Bell Day. The Liberty Bell stands silent in Philadelphia. It rings only in our memories and our hearts.

We sometimes forget how different our times are from those in the past. Today brings a reminder. In 1776, the Declaration of Independence was signed, but it took four more days before it was publicly read. Today marks the anniversary of that first public reading in Philadelphia. The next day it was read aloud to General George Washington's troops in New York. It took two days to prepare copies for shipment to all the colonies. It took another month until all the copies were signed.

Today marks the anniversary of a speech made at the 1896 Democratic National Convention. At this assembly, Nebraska delegate William Jennings Bryan said: "You shall not press down upon the brow of labor this crown of thorns; you shall not crucify mankind upon a cross of gold." His oratory electrified the convention. A few days later, this thirty-six-year-old Demosthenes was nominated as the Democratic presidential candidate.

Today, in 1885, was the day that the first *Wall Street Journal* was published. Even the daily that generations of financial wizards have relied upon to forecast the future couldn't have predicted the state of the world today. But as it has already established an Internet edition, it is once again showing us the direction the world is heading.

9th.

1776   The Declaration of Independence was read to George Washington's troops in New York. (See July 8th entry.)

1819   Elias Howe was born.

1850   Millard Fillmore became President of the United States. (See March 31st entry.)

1991   The International Olympic Committee readmitted South Africa. (See February 2nd and May 10th entries.)

Today is Elias Howe's birthday. Just in case that makes you feel like asking "how now," let me tell you about Mr. Howe. You may not recognize his name. He was the man who invented the sewing machine. Born on this day in 1819 in Spencer, Massachusetts, Howe wasn't a comedian, but he has certainly kept us in stitches.

Some U.S. Presidents have been more famous than others. One past President is so little remembered that a presumably tongue-in-cheek society was organized to remind the nation that he ever existed. Millard Fillmore acceded to office when President Zachary Taylor died on this day in 1850. Millard Fillmore decided that the Union must be preserved, so he supported the Fugitive Slave Act just to keep the nation together. After that, his own party refused to renominate him. In 1852, he sent Commodore Matthew C. Perry to Japan in order to negotiate a trade agreement. In 1856, he tried to get back into the White House as the Know-Nothing party's candidate. He lost that election and went back home to Buffalo, New York.

10th.

1509 John Calvin was born.

1947 Arlo Guthrie was born. (See July 14th entry.)

1991 Boris N. Yeltsin took the oath of office as the first elected president of the Russian Republic. (See January 14th entry.)

1991 President George Bush lifted economic sanctions against South Africa. (See February 2nd and May 10th entries.)

On this day in 1509, an influential religious leader was born in Noyon, France. John Calvin's religious ideals, which became known as Calvinism, influenced the development of Puritanism, the Protestant work ethic, and the concept of congregationalism—with a small "c." John Calvin believed in austerity, and America's founding fathers lived according to that Puritan ideal.

Today is Arlo Guthrie's birthday. Born on this day in 1947, Arlo took after his father Woody and became a performer and songwriter. To commemorate the event, we should start the day off by quoting one of his most popular songs. "Good morning, America. How are ya'?"

Modern democracy is perhaps our most valuable export. Though berating our system, complaining about taxes, and mistrusting politicians has been a national pastime since our nation's birth; the truth is that over the past centuries it's proven itself to be the best system of government in the world. It was on this day, in fact, that Boris Yeltsin took the oath of office as the first popularly-elected president of the Russian Republic.

The carrot or the stick. Reward or punishment. Will a person change their behavior faster if you reward them for each step or punish them for not moving quickly enough. On the issue of equality, we changed our national stance toward South Africa on this date, in 1991, when President George Bush lifted U.S. economic sanctions against that nation, citing a "profound transformation."

11th.

1274 Robert the Bruce was born.

1767 John Quincy Adams was born.

1804 Alexander Hamilton challenged Aaron Burr to a duel. (See January 11th entry.)

1896 Sir Wilfrid Laurier became the first French Canadian Prime Minister of Canada and opened up the Canadian Prairies to immigration.

1899 E.B. White was born.

1979 The *Skylab* space station fell to earth.

The Adams family has played a remarkable role in American history; and John Quincy Adams was one of its prime protagonists. John Quincy Adams—whose birthday is today—was not your usual U.S. President. Born in 1767, in Braintree, Massachusetts, Adams was the only President who was the son of another President. After he left the White House, he served in the House of Representatives until his death.

As you may or may not recall, Scotland's king—Robert the Bruce—was about to give up the fight for independence from British rule when he saw a spider spinning its web. At first, the spider failed. But it continued to spin and spin and spin until it finally finished its web. Robert realized that if a little spider could prevail, then he could do the same. He continued to fight and ultimately won. That's the story of Robert the Bruce, who was born on this day in 1274, in Turnberry, Scotland.

When journalist and author E.B. White was born on this day in 1899, the world was entering a drastic transitional phase that challenged every fiber of what society felt was right or wrong. Adventure, war, and automation rapidly became part of White's world. After the

First World War, he went to Alaska as a reporter for *The Seattle Times*, and while still in his twenties, he became a writer for *The New Yorker* and *Harper's* magazines. Famous for his indignant commentaries, this naturalist who preferred Thoreau's view of life and the environment reveled in scrutinizing a peculiar species called modern human. White deplored mechanization, automation, and modernization, voicing a weariness that many people at the time experienced. As one of his characters once commented: "No wonder I'm sitting here in this dreary joint at the end of this woebegone afternoon, lying about my bizarre thoughts to a doctor who looks, come to think of it, rather tired."

Picture wagon trains streaming across endless prairies past seas of plains buffalo; sodbusters literally raising houses from the soil; and filling fertile land with waving grain. America? Yes, but this happened in Canada as well. Today is the day, in 1896, that Sir Wilfrid Laurier became the first French Canadian Prime Minister of Canada. During his term in office the Canadian Prairies were opened up to immigration. To quote Horace Greeley, *"Va, l'ouest jeune homme, va, l'ouest!"* Settlers arrived from Scotland, the Ukraine, France, and Great Britain, braving the bitter-cold winters and torrid tundra summers of the Canadian wilderness in the hope of establishing a new life.

Chicken Little was right. It was on this day, in 1979, that the abandoned *Skylab* space station burned up in the atmosphere and showered debris over the Indian Ocean and Australia. Sometimes it pays to keep your eye to the sky rather than down on the ground below your feet when looking for signs of trouble.

12th.

102 BC   Julius Caesar was born. (See March 15th entry.)

1817   Henry D. Thoreau was born. (See July 4th entry.)

1862   U.S. Congressional Medal of Honor was established.

1895   Oscar Hammerstein was born. (See June 28th entry.)

On this date in 1862, the Congressional Medal of Honor was authorized. It still remains America's highest recognition of valor in the cause of freedom.

Julius Caesar built the Roman empire. Born on this day in 102 BC, Caesar was the first monarch of this vast ancient empire. But in the end, he fell prey to the same lust for power that had led him to the top. He died at the hands of assassins—one of whom was his closest friend.

Henry David Thoreau was an escapist. The philosopher from Concord, Massachusetts, was born on this date in 1817. Thoreau did not want to be governed; and he did not want to be part of government. Thoreau wanted to live a natural existence without human intervention. In 1845, he chose the Fourth of July as the day when he moved into a rustic hut on Walden Pond. His deed reaped some of America's most influential literature.

13th.

1787   The Northwest Ordinance was enacted by Congress.

1865   Horace Greeley wrote: "Go west young man, go west . . . ."

1977   The second New York blackout paralyzed the city. (See November 9th entry.)

In 1787, the United States was still an infant nation governed by a loose code known as the Articles of Confederation. But on this date a law was enacted that became the basis of our geographical and national growth—the Northwest Ordinance. The law outlined how the territory north of the Ohio River should be governed; and how those lands would evolve into states. It established territorial self-government as a step toward statehood. And it required all U.S. territories to grant their citizens the right to freedom of worship, trial by jury, and opportunities to receive public education.

It is sometimes both comforting and shocking to recall what some wise men have said in the past. On this day, in 1865, Horace Greeley delivered a few comments you might be interested in hearing. He wrote in *The New York Tribune* that "Washington is not a place to live in. The rents are high, the food is bad, the dust is disgusting and the morals are deplorable. Go West, young man, go West, and grow up with the country."

14th.

1789   French Revolutionaries stormed the Bastille. (Bastille Day)

1912   Woody Guthrie was born. (See July 10th entry.)

1913   Gerald R. Ford was born.

1921 Nicola Sacco and Bartolomeo Vanzetti were convicted of manslaughter. (See May 5th entry.)

Today is Bastille Day which commemorates the storming of the Bastille prison in Paris during the French Revolution. In 1789, this incident was seen as a great victory for the rights of the common man. But it also marked the beginning of the infamous Reign of Terror.

Sometimes, a person's place in history is secured by accident—not only by design. Today is Gerald R. Ford's birthday. He became President of the United States during a time of crisis precipitated by an absolutely unprecedented series of events. But his demeanor in office helped to ensure further peaceful chapters. Born on this day in 1913 in Omaha, Nebraska, Gerald Ford was not elected President; he wasn't even elected Vice President. He was the Republican minority leader in the House of Representatives when Vice President Spiro Agnew pleaded no contest to charges of falsifying tax returns, was fined, and resigned his office. Two days later, on December 6, 1973, President Richard M. Nixon nominated Ford to succeed Agnew, and Ford took the office. Less than a year later, Nixon himself resigned because of the Watergate impeachment hearings and Ford acceded to the presidency. It was quite a shock for the nation—and for Gerald Ford as well. But he put the country back on an even keel.

Woody Guthrie was a staunch advocate of the common man, composing songs about the hardships and achievements of both farmers and factory workers during the Great Depression. This traveling American minstrel—who was born on this day in 1912— also wrote some inspiring lyrics about the grandeur of this great nation: "This land is your land / This land is my land / From California / To the New York Island / From the redwood forest / To the Gulf Stream waters / This land was made for you and me."

15th.

The feast of St. Swithin's.

1606 Rembrandt Harmens van Rijn was born.

1870 The provinces of Manitoba and the Northwest Territories entered into the confederation of Canada. (See July 1st entry.)

Today is St. Swithin's Day. Legend has it that if it rains today it will continue to rain for forty days. If, on the other hand, it remains fair today, it won't rain for forty days. No rain for forty days in England is a veritable impossibility. And for St. Swithin—who was the Bishop of Winchester, England—the idea of no rain for forty days was obviously the expectation of a miracle.

Rembrandt Harmens van Rijn was born in Leyden, Holland, on this date in 1606. He came from a well-to-do family, and in his time he was a highly-acclaimed painter. But he outlived his time. He went bankrupt. He kept on painting, producing some of his greatest work. But the public had passed him by. When he died, his greatness seemed to be behind him. Of course it didn't work out that way at all. In the intervening centuries, his greatness grew and flourished.

16th.

1921   The Chicago Black Sox Trial began.

1945   The first atom bomb test took place in New Mexico. (See April 22nd entry.)

1969   The *Apollo 11* space mission was launched. (See July 20th entry.)

1973   The Nixon tapings were revealed. (See January 4th entry.)

Two scientific miracles that changed the world occurred on this day. They both were prompted by war, but eventually were used in the name of peace. The first atom bomb was tested at Los Alamos, New Mexico, on this date in 1945. Less than a month later, this device proved to be man's deadliest weapon. And as one of its inventors—Richard Oppenheimer—later mused upon his discovery: "I have become death, killer of millions." We now harness this power to energize the world. Also on this date, in 1969, Neil Armstrong, Edwin Aldrin, Jr. and Michael Collins, blasted off from Cape Kennedy, Florida in the *Apollo 11* space capsule. Their destination was the moon. The rockets used to bomb Europe in the Second World War were transformed into the engines that help us reach for the stars.

It was on this day in 1973, that the existence of tape-recorded versions of President Nixon's White House conversations were disclosed, revealing vital information about the Watergate break-in and cover-up. Nixon's refusal to surrender those tapes led to his resignation a year later.

It's an appropriate day to wear black socks. On this day in 1921, the Chicago Black Sox Trial began. Eight White Sox baseball players were accused of throwing the 1919 World Series. It was considered a dark day for baseball.

17th.

1938   Douglas Corrigan flew in the wrong direction.

1955   Arco, Idaho, became the first city to have atomic-powered electrical service. (See July 16th entry.)

1955   Disneyland opened in Anaheim, California.

1975   The *Soyuz 19* linked with *Apollo 18* in space. (See March 18th entry.)

It's Disneyland's birthday. The world-famous amusement park which was developed by animator Walt Disney opened in Anaheim, California, on this date in 1955.

Douglas Corrigan was just another American airplane pilot until he took off from New York on this day in 1938. He was supposed to fly to California, but the next day he landed in Dublin, Ireland, instead. From that point, Douglas Corrigan was nicknamed "Wrong Way" Corrigan. The world strongly suspected that "Wrong Way" Corrigan knew where he was going all along even though he swore he didn't.

On this day in history, progress took a peaceful turn exactly ten years and one day after we feared the worst. In 1955, the world witnessed the establishment of the first atomic-powered electrical service in Arco: a small town located near Atomic City in eastern Idaho.

There was a thaw in the Cold War in 1975. On this day, the Soviet *Soyuz 19* space craft linked with the U.S. *Apollo 18* space craft. The first cosmonaut to walk in space, Alexei Leonov, and his crew member Valery Kubasov not only met astronauts Thomas P. Stafford, Donald K. Slayton, and Vance D. Brand, they worked together over the next forty-four hours to conduct scientific and technical experiments that were of mutual benefit.

18th.

64 *AD*   Rome burned and Nero fiddled. (See December 15th entry.)

1918   Nelson Mandela was born. (See May 10th entry.)

1921   John Glenn was born. (See February 20th entry.)

1940   President Franklin D. Roosevelt was nominated for a third term.

There were two times in American history when we came closer to having a king than most of us suspect. The first time was when some people proposed George Washington should be crowned the king of the United States. Washington himself disapproved. The second time occurred on this day in 1940, when President Franklin Delano Roosevelt decided to defy the old two-term tradition and accepted the nomination for a third term of office. Roosevelt was re-elected, and was later elected to a fourth term. Soon after his death, an amendment to the U.S. Constitution limited the Presidential incumbency to two elected terms. There is, of course, a provision for a little elasticity when a President dies in office. Generally, the Vice President is entitled to two elected terms in addition to his period of accession. But the installation of a permanently indispensable man or woman as Chief Executive is specifically unconstitutional.

We are all familiar with the story of Nero's fiddling while Rome burned, and today marks that anniversary. It started on this day in 64 AD, and when it was over, there were those who blamed the fire on Nero himself. But the emperor picked a likely group of scapegoats—the Christians. It was the perfect excuse for persecuting them.

19th.

1813   The Sisters of Charity was founded. (See August 28th entry.)

1848   The first women's rights convention convened.

1860   Lizzie Borden was born. (See June 20th entry.)

1941   V for victory theme was introduced by Winston Churchill.

One of history's longest battles has been the fight for women's rights. Today marks a milestone in that struggle. On this day in 1848, the first women's rights convention was held in Seneca Falls, New York. At this assembly, Elizabeth Cady Stanton declared that "man cannot fulfill his destiny alone" and Amelia Bloomer wore her signature garments.

Except for national anthems, we do not normally associate a specific musical piece with a specific state of mind. But about this day in 1941, Great Britain's Prime Minister Winston Churchill conceived the idea of using a musical Morse code theme to symbolize the letter V for victory. It was recognizable on the air and yet somewhat undetectable because it was a familiar succession of musical notes. It was, in fact, the first four notes of the theme of Beethoven's *Fifth Symphony*. Ever since, that theme has meant V for victory. During the Second World War, it signified hope to thousands of Europeans listening to their radios in Nazi-occupied nations.

20th.

1871 The province of British Columbia entered into the confederation of Canada. (See July 1st entry.)

1919 Sir Edmund Hillary was born. (See May 29th entry.)

1969 Neil Armstrong walked on the moon. (See July 16th entry.)

On this day in 1969, a human being first set foot on the moon and walked on its surface. That "one small step for man, one giant leap for mankind" was taken by *Apollo 11* astronaut Neil Armstrong. A few moments later, his teammate Edwin "Buzz" Aldrin, Jr., took that same giant step.

21st.

1816 Paul Reuter was born.

1861 The Confederate Army won the Battle of Bull Run near Manassas, Virginia.

1899 Ernest Hemingway was born.

1911   Marshall McLuhan was born.

1921   The first time a battleship was ever sunk by an airplane.

1930   U.S. Veterans Administration was established.

We are so accustomed to air-powered warfare that it is sometimes surprising to recall that an aviator had to sink a battleship during peacetime to get America's military leaders to pay attention. On this very day in 1921, aviation pioneer General Billy Mitchell flew off with a payload of makeshift aerial bombs and sank the former German battleship *Ostfriesland* off Hampton Roads, Virginia. That momentous display of air power didn't fully persuade his superiors. Consequently, when the Second World War broke out, there weren't enough aircraft carriers to maneuver what had become regarded as the greatest weapons of that war—fighter planes.

Author and adventurer Ernest Hemingway was born on this day in 1899, in Oak Park, Illinois. He lived in the disillusioned post-First World War era of the 1920s and 1930s, capturing those few precious moments in time and recording them for posterity. He became an anachronism thereafter. *A Farewell to Arms* and *For Whom the Bell Tolls* assured his place in literary history, but it was *The Old Man and the Sea*, the story of an elderly Cuban fisherman's struggle to catch a giant fish, that earned him a Pulitzer and then a Nobel Prize. Hemingway's life was as dramatic as the fiction he wrote. The illusion and disillusionment; the heroism and the frailty; the emotions he experienced and described seem as real and relevant today.

If you were asked what group has grown the most in our times, you probably would say it was the elderly. And maybe that's right. But suppose you were asked what single group that encompasses both young and old has grown? The answer would be veterans. On this date in 1930, the Veterans Administration was established to preside over the rights and welfare of our millions of First World War veterans. That was before the Second World War; before the Korean War; before the Vietnam War; before the Persian Gulf War. If the veterans were a large group in the 1930s, think about their numbers today. They may not be enrolled in the American Legion or the VFW as they were in the past, but they are still a sizable constituency indeed.

The Confederate Army won the Battle of Bull Run on this day in 1861. The bloody confrontation that occurred near Manassas, Virginia, spurred a flood of news reports that elicited a number of publicized comments. The world's richest man—Andrew Carnegie—uttered one of them. He was reported as saying: "War should become as obsolete as cannibalism."

As writer Marshall McLuhan—who was born on this day in 1911—once said: "The medium is the message." Certainly Paul Reuter, founder of Reuters News Service, agreed. Born on this same day in 1816, it was Reuter who realized that news should be delivered in a timely fashion. He tried everything, including homing pigeons to move late-breaking news items across Europe for publication in the growing number of newspapers.

22nd.

1587 Settlers arrived on Roanoke Island, Virginia. (See August 18th entry.)

1620 The Pilgrims set out from Holland destined for the New World. (See November 19th and November 21st entries.)

1793 Sir Alexander Mackenzie arrived at Canada's Pacific coast.

1890 Rose Fitzgerald Kennedy was born.

1933 Wiley Post completed the first around the world airplane flight in seven days, eighteen hours, and forty-five minutes. (See June 23rd entry.)

1934 John Dillinger was killed in Chicago, Illinois, 1934.

In 1620, the exiled British Pilgrims started out from Holland for the New World on this day aboard the ship *Speedwell*. They landed at Plymouth, England, where they transferred to the *Mayflower*. The rest is history. One wonders what would have happened if they had followed their original plan and landed in Virginia. They never would have sighted Cape Cod and Plymouth Rock nor established the first British settlement on the northeast American coast. Interestingly, on this same day, in 1587, another group of British settlers landed on Roanoke Island, off Virginia. They expected to be welcomed by a group that preceded them. But there was no one left. And when a third group arrived some years later, the second company had also disappeared. The story of Roanoke's Lost Colony is still a mystery to this day. There is no mystery about the Plymouth Pilgrims except for what might have happened if they had sailed to Virginia.

Today marks the anniversary of John Dillinger's death. In 1934, Public enemy number one was shot down by FBI agents as he left Chicago's Biograph movie theater. That event captured the public's imagination. The media's enthusiasm for the criminal "hall of fame" fanned the flames of sensationalism, making heroes out of villains. Public enemy number one had to work harder to maintain his dubious position.

A great American matriarch—Rose Fitzgerald Kennedy—was born on this day in 1890, in Boston, Massachusetts. Rose Fitzgerald Kennedy saw her son John rise to the Presidency and be assassinated. She lost another son, Robert, who was on the road to Presidential nomination when he was assassinated. She lost a son and daughter earlier, before these two tragedies. But through it all she carried on, providing inspiration and encouragement.

An epic journey ended on this day in 1793, when Sir Alexander Mackenzie stood for the first time on the Canadian Pacific coast. He had walked across the entire breadth of the uncharted North American continent, exploring the natural wonders of Quebec's rolling hills, Ontario's lakes and rivers, Manitoba and Saskatchewan's lush prairies, Alberta's majestic mountains, and British Columbia's ancient coastal rain forests. As he stood along the shore of the mighty Pacific Ocean, he realized his journey had come to a successful end.

23rd.

1886   Steve Brodie jumped off the Brooklyn Bridge and survived.

1904   The ice cream cone was invented.

1996   The U.S. Womens Olympic gymnastics team earned their first gold medal.

On this day, in 1886, saloon keeper Steve Brodie jumped off the Brooklyn Bridge and lived to tell the tale. The fact that there is and was a Brooklyn Bridge; and a Steve Brodie who lived to tell the tale are all established facts. The only uncertainty is whether he ever jumped off the Brooklyn Bridge as he claimed. True or not, Brodie contributed an American colloquialism. A "brodie" is a blunder. To "make a Brodie" is to make a mistake. These contributions to our popular language may not have been what Brodie had in mind when he was fished out of the water below the bridge and claimed to have survived a jump. It just goes to show that history can be made by taking a dive or claiming to have done so.

The ice cream cone is said to have been invented on this day in 1904, in St. Louis, Missouri. When you stop and think what the ice cream cone has done for the dairy business and retail trade, not to mention the dispositions of human beings, you've got to regard today's birthday as a blessed event that most assuredly deserves a place in history. Let's face it. It's very nice to have something around that is made to take a licking.

The 1996 Summer Olympics in Atlanta, Georgia, was where Kerri Strug made a final vault despite torn ligaments in her left ankle as the U.S. women gymnasts clinched their first-ever Olympic team gold medal. Few people may remember her heroic effort, but history will always remember that event as the first time the U.S. Womens Olympic gymnastics team earned a gold medal. We look at our medalists, our sports heros, our record holders as being super-human. But they aren't. On the other hand, their effort is, their commitment, their determination, and their ability to see through the pain and stay focussed on their goals are monumental. No one would have criticized Kerri Strug for quitting. She was injured and in pain. However, no one would have awarded her a medal either. She earned it by giving her best when she was given the opportunity to do so.

24th.

1783 Simon Bolivar was born.

1847 Brigham Young and the first Mormons arrived at Salt Lake, Utah. (Utah Pioneer Day) (See January 6th and June 1st entries.)

1911 Machu Picchu was discovered. (See June 6th entry.)

1929 Kellogg-Briand Treaty declared in effect (See January 15th entry.)

Simon Bolivar has been called the George Washington of South America. The nations of Venezuela, Colombia, Ecuador, Panama, Peru and Bolivia officially named him "Libertador"—The Liberator—and Bolivia was named after him. Simon Bolivar, who was born on this date in 1783, in Caracas, Venezuela, led a continent to independence.

Sometimes when you search hard for something; you don't always know you've reached your goal when you're there. That was the case when Hiram Bingham climbed to a Peruvian mountain top with a native guide and walked through a mysterious city in the clouds. On this day in 1911, Bingham discovered one of the last Incan cities—Machu Picchu. The young Yale history professor had been searching for this mythical place ever since he read about it in the accounts of the Spanish explorers who had failed to uncover its whereabouts. But Bingham didn't know he had succeeded in his quest as he surveyed the vine-covered stone walls and buildings. It wasn't until he had searched a few other places and returned to New York that he realized his search was over. The next year, Bingham returned to the city in the clouds and documented his findings for the National Geographic Society.

25th.

National Farm Safety Week.

1952 Puerto Rico became a self-governing commonwealth of the United States. (Commonwealth Day in Puerto Rico)

1978 Louise Brown was born.

1984 Soviet cosmonaut Svetlana Savitskaya became the first woman to walk in space.

This is the beginning of National Farm Safety Week. We think back so fondly to the bucolic, rustic charms of the country farm that we forget the risks. Farming is a physically and financially risky business. Even when farming ran on horse-and-donkey power, it was physically taxing and dangerous. Urban dwellers believe that cities are dangerous. But cities have no monopoly on risk. Perhaps it would be helpful to remember, at least during National Farm Safety Week, that where the grass is greener it is also apt to be slipperier as well.

On this day in 1952, the Commonwealth of Puerto Rico became a self-governing territory of the United States. The designation was just short of statehood status. At the time, this change was expected to solve the island's status problem. But we learned soon enough that the hope was premature. Commonwealth Day certainly deserves to be considered a noble attempt and a good start.

The world was awestruck when Louise Brown was born in England on this day. In 1978, Louise Brown became the world's first known test-tube baby. After a number of disappointing attempts, Louise's parents chose to try this new and radical form of conception. The experiment was an overwhelming success.

There are few things in this world that only men can do; and walking in space is not one of them. On this day in 1984, Soviet cosmonaut Svetlana Savitskaya became the first woman to walk in space.

26th.

1856 George Bernard Shaw was born.

1875 Carl Jung was born.

1908 The Federal Bureau of Investigation was established.

1947 U.S. Department of Defense was established.

1953 Fidel Castro led a futile attack and was captured in Cuba.

Today is the FBI's birthday. Established by Attorney General Charles J. Bonaparte on this date in 1908, the Federal Bureau of Investigation assumed an important role in modernizing the science and methods of crime prevention, crime detection, and law enforcement. And on a similar note, the job of national defense was also condensed on this day. In 1947, the U.S. Department of Defense was established under the Armed Forces Unification Act. It signaled the recognition that there had to be one combined overall military command.

Fidel Castro has ruled Cuba for so long that today's anniversary seems like an echo from another planet. On this day, in 1953, the young revolutionary led a futile attack on a Cuban Army barracks at Santiago. He was captured and sent to prison. But this adventure gave his movement its name—the July 26th movement. And the next time he struck he succeeded.

Thanks to a man who was born on this day in Kesswil, Switzerland, the world realized that the human mind was influenced by far more than potty training and unrealized childhood fantasies. In 1875, the founder of analytic psychology, Carl Jung came into this world. His theories delved deeper into the human psyche than Freud's psychoanalytic methods. He proposed the concepts of extroverted and introverted individual personalities. He believed that man's institutions such as religion, literature, and oral tradition were provocative manifestations of a collective consciousness that was stimulated by social interaction. Jung helped us to realize that for every individual's action there is a potential for a similar, synchronous action taking place somewhere else in the world.

When George Bernard Shaw was twenty years old, he decided to become a writer, and moved from his birthplace—Dublin, Ireland—to the great city of London, England, where his mother and sister already lived. Born on this day in 1856, Shaw did not have a promising start to his chosen career. In fact, he failed so miserably as a novelist he was starving and penniless. But just as he was ready to quit, he was offered a job writing book reviews for the *Pall Mall Gazette*. Then he got offers to write art criticism for *The World* and theater reviews for *The Saturday Review*. Twenty years after he had made his fateful decision to become a writer, his first play—*Arms and the Man*—premiered on the London stage. Shaw was an overnight success. During the next twenty years he created a body of memorable plays including *Major Barbara* and *Pygmalion* which was eventually remade into the musical *My Fair Lady*.

27th.

1866 The Atlantic telegraph cable between England and the U.S. was completed.

1909 Orville Wright tested the U.S. Army's first airplane for one hour, twelve minutes. (See August 19th and December 17th entries.)

1940 *Billboard* magazine began publishing bestseller charts.

1940 Bugs Bunny made his debut. (See September 19th entry.)

1953 The Korean War armistice was signed in Panmunjom, Korea.

1995 The Korean War Veterans Memorial was dedicated.

The Atlantic telegraph cable between England and the United States was completed on this date in 1866. From that day forward, news crossed the ocean instantly. And that, in turn, speeded up the tempo of world events to a relatively rapid pace.

On this day in 1953, an armistice agreement was signed at Panmunjom, on the border between North and South Korea. After more than two years of seemingly endless negotiations, this agreement allegedly ended the Korean War. This still chilly and tenuous truce reminds us that a tense peace has only one positive facet—it is better than a hot war.

Top 10. Top 40. Top 100. There are so many bestseller lists and pop charts these days. It's hard to imagine the concept has only been around since this day in 1940, when *Billboard* magazine first published its list of bestselling albums and singles.

"Only those are fit to live," said General Douglas MacArthur, "who are not afraid to die." In Washington, on this day in 1995, President Clinton and South Korean President Kim Young-sam jointly dedicated the Korean War Veterans Memorial to a very select group of Americans who, by General MacArthur's definition, were truly fit to live.

28th.

1868 The Fourteenth Amendment was ratified.

1914 The First World War began when Austria-Hungary declared war on Serbia. (See June 28th entry.)

1945 A U.S. Bomber crashed into Empire State Building.

1958 Terry Fox was born.

Today marks the anniversary of the Fourteenth Amendment to the U.S. Constitution. This is the amendment that guarantees due process of law to all citizens. Announced on this date in 1868, the Fourteenth Amendment was enacted after the Civil War to extend the federal guarantee of due process to govern state as well as federal matters. It was an extension of Constitutional supremacy; and a forerunner of the further protection of civil rights. It took another century to move from this amendment to the civil rights legislation of the 1960s, but it was an historic step.

On this day in 1945, the Second World War was coming toward its end. But at home, a U.S. bomber crashed into the Empire State Building in New York City. The building stood firm. The bomber was destroyed. It was Saturday, so only thirteen people were killed on the ground. Designers had been improving airplanes and skyscrapers for years, but nobody ever imagined that one would crash into the other.

Terry Fox was born on this date in 1958. The story of this remarkable Canadian's life was all too short, but his courage serves as eternal inspiration for us all. When Terry was nineteen years old, he started a marathon run at the "Mile 0" marker of the Trans-Canada Highway in Victoria, British Columbia. His goal was to run the full length of the highway to Prince Edward Island on the east coast to raise the nation's and the world's awareness of cancer. This would have been a monumental task for any runner.

But Terry Fox wasn't just another marathon runner. Fox himself had fallen to the disease; and the disease eventually cut short his heroic Run Against Cancer and his life. His run was cut short in Thunder Bay, Ontario, when the cancer spread to his lungs.

29th.

1588 Sir Francis Drake and the British fleet routed the Spanish Armada.

1883 Benito Mussolini was born.

1905 Dag Hammarskjöld was born. (See April 7th entry.)

1957 President Dwight D. Eisenhower signed the National Aeronautics and Space act, creating NASA.

Although the story of David and Goliath encourages us to believe that a little guy can sometimes be more than a match for a big one, we don't usually apply that rule to military encounters. But every time a military machine gains too much confidence, it is a good idea to think of the Spanish Armada which was reputedly the mightiest war machine ever assembled. It turned out to be somewhat less than that. On this day in 1588, thanks to the indomitable spirit of Sir Francis Drake, the British fleet under his command, and inclement weather, the Spanish Armada was totally routed and Great Britain was saved.

This is Benito Mussolini's birthday. Born in 1883, this father of modern fascism and a classic demagogue, was the son of a blacksmith. Before he rose to power as dictator of Italy, he had been an editor of the socialist paper *Avanti*; and he founded the facist publication *Popolo d'Italia* after serving in the First World War. By 1922, his blackshirted army—a band of political thugs—marched on Rome and declared Mussolini as government head: a position he held until he was captured and executed in 1945.

One of the world's most influential peacemakers was born on this day in Jonkoping. The second Secretary-General of the United Nations, Dag Hammarskjöld was born, in 1883, to Sweden's Prime Minister Hjalmin Hammarskjöld. While on a peace mission to meet President Moisi Tshombe of Katanga in the African Congo in 1961, Dag Hammarskjöld died in a plane crash. But before his fateful death, he had presided over numerous international conflicts that were on the brink of igniting new world wars. The Suez Canal controversy; the Belgian Congo's fight for independence; the border crisis between Lebanon and Jordan; and the continuing conflicts between the Arab nations and the newly formed state of Israel all came within the diplomatic jurisdiction of this protagonist of international peace. His efforts won him a posthumously awarded Nobel Peace Prize and the respect of the entire world. Too often we honor our military leaders rather than our peacemakers.

A remarkable step upward was made on this day in 1957. President Dwight D. Eisenhower signed the National Aeronautics and Space Act which created the NASA program, beginning the race to be the first nation to put a man into space and to send a spacecraft capable of landing on the moon's surface.

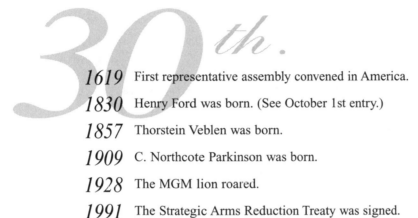

1619 First representative assembly convened in America.

1830 Henry Ford was born. (See October 1st entry.)

1857 Thorstein Veblen was born.

1909 C. Northcote Parkinson was born.

1928 The MGM lion roared.

1991 The Strategic Arms Reduction Treaty was signed.

Today is the anniversary of the first legislative assembly held in America. The representatives met at Jamestown, Virginia, on this day, in 1619. It was a brief meeting, which in itself makes this legislative session even more unique.

On this day in 1863, Henry Ford was born near the town of Dearborn, Michigan. The man who did more than any other person to mass produce and popularize the automobile in America was famous for saying that you could have your car in any color you wanted—as long as it was black. Ford turned out millions of black Model Ts between 1908 and 1927. A lesser-known fact is that Henry Ford also had a passion for soybeans. Certain that it was versatile enough to feed the world and all its appetites, Ford once served a sixteen-course banquet of dishes made with soybeans, and he always kept a few pitchers of soy milk on hand. When Ford found a good thing, he held on to it.

In honor of a man who was born in Wisconsin in 1857, it is time say a few words about Thorstein Veblen. He was a scholar who, in 1899, gave us the "theory of the leisure class." Veblen's theory was simply that he was against consumerism. As he remarked, "Conspicuous consumption of valuable goods is a means of reputability to the gentleman of leisure."

Where would the world be if C. Northcote Parkinson had not discovered "Parkinson's Law?" Born on this day in 1909 in Durham, England, Parkinson brought us up short in the 1950s with his basic law of human behavior which states that "work expands so as to fill the time available for its completion."

The MGM lion roared for the first time on this day in 1928. The famous film production company—MGM—had added sound to its roster of special effects. So as a way of launching the world's first "talkie" they let their lion introduce the feature attraction. The company continues to announce its motion picture films and television programs in this same manner today.

The Cold War melted down on this day in 1991, when the Strategic Arms Reduction Treaty was signed by U.S. President George Bush and Soviet Premier Mikhail Gorbachev. The nuclear arms race didn't just come to a halt. Both nations agreed to disarm and disband projects like Star Wars, Minutemen missiles, and other doomsday mechanisms.

31st.

1777 The Marquis de Lafayette was made a major-general in the American Continental Army.

1912 U.S. government prohibited movies and photos of prize fights in an effort to reduce portrayals of violence in the media.

1921 Whitney M. Young, Jr. was born.

1922 Eighteen-year-old Ralph Samuelson rode the world's first water skis.

1971 The *Apollo 15* astronauts drove a car on the moon.

1981 Arnette Hubbard became president of the National Bar Association.

Today marks the anniversary of history's strangest automobile ride. In 1971, *Apollo 15* astronauts David R. Scott and James B. Irwin began three days of exploration on the moon's surface driving a specially designed electric car. Millions of earthlings watched the trip on television via satellite transmission.

Whitney M. Young, Jr. was born on this date in 1921, in Lincoln Ridge, Kentucky. This outstanding African-American leader is remembered for many events in his life, but his remarks in a 1970 speech which he made in New York City, serve as inspiration for my theme today. "We may have come over in different ships," said he, "but we're all in the same boat now."

Can you trust a teenager to be responsible? It was on this day in 1922 that eighteen-year-old Ralph Samuelson showed pioneering efforts when he successfully tested the first waterskis. But on this same day in 1777, another teenager proved himself even more capable. The Marquis de Lafayette, a nineteen-year-old French nobleman, became a major-general in the American Continental Army, and proved himself worthy of his post.

Public outcry against violence in the media is not nearly as new as you might think. In fact, on this day in 1912 the United States government banned movies and photos of prize fights in an effort to reduce portrayals of violence.

"Change," said John F. Kennedy, "is the law of life." A great change in the life of law took place on this day in 1981, when Arnette Hubbard became the first female president of the National Bar Association.

August

In some parts of this country, the days of August have a special name: the dog days of summer. Not meant to demean the canine species, this designation is an apt description of the doggedly hot temperatures most regions encounter during this sweltering month. And summer heat does seem to raise people's tempers. It's not uncommon to hear people barking about the heat and the humidity, nipping at comments as if they're meant to be insults. But on the brighter side, the dog days of summer also symbolize the laid back attitude we should all aspire to achieve when the temperatures rise.

1st.

1291   The Republic of Switzerland was founded. (Swiss Independence Day)

1625   The British Parliament moved to Oxford.

1770   William Clark was born. (See May 14th entry.)

1790   First U.S. Census was taken.

1819   Herman Melville was born. (See November 18th entry.)

Today is Swiss Independence Day. There isn't anything novel about the concept of Swiss independence, but rather, because the reverse is true. This anniversary marks the founding of the Republic of Switzerland in 1291. That, in turn, makes this country the oldest such government still in existence.

Mark Twain said there are three kinds of lies—lies, damned lies, and statistics. The first U.S. census was taken on this day in 1790. The government was curious to find out how many people lived in the entire country. It was discovered that there were four million Americans or about 15 percent of today's population count.

The British Parliament made an unprecedented move on this day in 1625. The members of this august governing body had been convening in London for hundreds of years. But on this day, they assembled sixty miles north in the university city of Oxford. It wasn't a wartime security measure per se, but it was meant as a preventive action mounted against a lethal invasion. The black plague had been raging through London, killing thousands of people per week. Parliament moved in an attempt to save itself from decimation.

American author Herman Melville was born on this day in 1819, in Caroll County, Maryland. He didn't create volumes of monumental work during his lifetime, but he did write a voluminous piece of literature entitled *Moby Dick*. The tale of Captain Ahab and the great white whale epitomized man's unending battle with his own unnatural nature.

William Clark was born on this day in 1770. He was appointed by President Thomas Jefferson to join Meriweather Lewis on an expedition to explore the recently acquired Louisiana Territory. Lewis and Clark's observations of this vast northwestern wilderness—its indigenous people, wildlife, and terrain—are well known. In return for his services, President Jefferson made Clark a brigadier general of the Louisiana Territory militia and awarded him a vast section of the new land. He also made Clark the territory's superintendent of Indian Affairs. Throughout the remainder of his career, Clark regularly appealed to the federal government for the just and humane treatment of Native Americans.

2nd.

1873   Andrew Hallidie operated his first cable car in San Francisco. (See February 23rd entry.)

1909   The U.S. War Department purchased its first airplane.

1922   Alexander Graham Bell died. (See January 25th, March 3rd, and March 7th entries.)

1939   Albert Einstein wrote a letter to President Franklin D. Roosevelt. (See March 14th entry.)

1964   Gulf of Tonkin incident took place. (See August 7th entry.)

The future of the world sometimes changes without our even realizing it. That may well have happened on this day back in 1909, when the U.S. War Department bought the first airplane from Wilbur and Orville Wright.

On this day in 1964, the North Vietnamese attacked a U.S. destroyer within the international waters of the Gulf of Tonkin. That's the way we were told it happened thereafter by President Lyndon B. Johnson and his aides. As a result, the U.S. Congress adopted the Gulf of Tonkin Resolution a few days later, which gave the President broad powers to use the armed forces without a declaration of war.

When the telephone's inventor, Alexander Graham Bell, died on this day in 1922, he did not receive a twenty-one-gun salute nor a final trumpet call. But the United States phone system did shut down for two whole minutes. It might be the only time in history that telephones throughout this nation went silent in unison for more than two whole seconds.

3rd.

1460 James II of Scotland was killed.

1492 Christopher Columbus sailed from Spain. (See October 12th entry.)

1610 Henry Hudson entered the inland sea that was later named Hudson's Bay. (See June 22nd entry.)

1948 Whittaker Chambers accused Alger Hiss. (See January 21st entry.)

On this day, in the year 1492, Christopher Columbus set out from the port of Palos, Spain, to look for a sea route across the Atlantic to India. What a glorious failure he had! And how many other discoveries—like that of the New World—were made by people who were really looking for something else. Coincidentally, Henry Hudson entered Hudson's Bay on this same day in 1610. Hudson and the crew of the *Discovery* were searching for the Northwest Passage from the Atlantic to the Pacific.

On the anniversary of King James II of Scotland's death, we should pay due respect to the solemnity of the moment. In 1460, James II and his army were laying siege to the English garrison at Roxburgh Castle. The twenty-nine-year-old monarch's wife sent word that she was coming for a visit. Elated at his wife's arrival, he ordered his artillery men to prepare a special salute. As Queen Mary made her way to the encampment, the cannon salute began. But unfortunately, James was standing in front of one of his own cannons and was killed instantly.

4th.

1735 John Peter Zenger was acquitted.

1790 The Revenue Marine Service was founded. (Coast Guard Day)

1914 England declared war on Germany; and the United States declared its neutrality.

One of the great pleasures of American life is our right to criticize our government and its leaders. That right really began on this day, in 1735, when Governor William Crosby of New York acquitted John Peter Zenger—a printer and publisher of the *New York Weekly Journal*—of libel charges. Zenger's defense was that the statements he had printed in his newspaper about New York's royal governor were true. His acquittal was regarded as an evolutionary landmark in America's freedom of expression.

Today is Coast Guard Day which celebrates the founding, in 1790, of the Revenue Marine Service. We now know this branch of the Department of Transportation as the U.S. Coast Guard. It isn't in the news very often. The Coast Guard just doesn't have time, considering the length of the coastlines it patrols and the number of incidents it investigates on a daily basis.

After Austro-Hungary declared war on Serbia, Germany declared war on Russia and on France and then invaded Belgium. The First World War had begun. When England declared war on Germany on this day in 1914—because of its commitment to its allies and because of Germany's invasion of Belgium—the German Chancellor made a classic, self-righteous statement about its British cousin. German Chancellor Theobald von Bethmann-Hollweg said, ". . . just for a scrap of paper, Great Britain is going to make war on a kindred nation. . . ." In one respect, he was not far from wrong. King Edward of England had close German relatives. But England's loyalty to its neighbors ran deeper. And definitely deeper than that of the United States who declared neutrality.

5th.

1864 Admiral David Farragut damned the torpedoes.

1884 Cornerstone of Statue of Liberty laid. (See June 19th entry.)

1924 The comic strip *Little Orphan Annie* first appeared. (See October 7th entry.)

1957 *American Bandstand* was first televised.

Most of our battle cries are either appeals to our memory or blunt questions—like "Remember the Alamo!" or "Do you want to live forever?" However, one battle cry that was first uttered on this day seems to summarize a pretty general American attitude. It was said by Admiral David Glasgow Farragut at the Battle of Mobile Bay during the Civil War in 1864. What he said was: "Damn the torpedoes, full speed ahead!"

It is often said that art reflects the times in which it was created and today's anniversaries are sparkling examples of this statement. In 1924, the comic strip *Little Orphan Annie* first appeared in daily newspapers. The optimistic little girl—with her dog Sandy—never let tragedy get the best of her. She uplifted readers who found themselves sunk in the depths of despair during the Great Depression era that soon followed. Also on this date, in 1957, *American Bandstand* premiered on the relatively new medium of television. Its host, Dick Clark, introduced generations of young audiences to a new musical form called rock 'n' roll. Every week, the hottest bands played the latest tunes while a live audience danced the newest steps. The program quickly galvanized a generation who felt increasingly detached from the rest of society.

6th.

1497   John Cabot returned from the New World.

1809   Alfred Lord Tennyson was born.

1881   Sir Alexander Fleming was born.

1926   Warner Bros. Studios premiered the first talking pictures.

1927   Andy Warhol was born.

1945   The crew of the *Enola Gay* dropped the first atomic bomb on Hiroshima, Japan.

Today was a very big day in 1926. The world discovered that the movies could talk. The Warner Brothers motion-picture company premiered two short films in New York City. Called Vitaphone films, the shorts contained live sound: actors could finally be heard as well as seen. All of a sudden, silent-screen actors had to worry about their voices—not just their looks—and they had to memorize their lines.

Today marks the anniversary of the Hiroshima bombing. When the atom bomb was dropped by the crew of the *Enola Gay* on this Japanese city in 1945, it was more than the shattering premiere of a brand new weapon. The world did not stand still thereafter. In Hiroshima, we learned the real effects of atomic power on something we had not tested at Los Alamos, New Mexico—real people. We learned the horrifying effects of radiation not just days but years later. We learned that man had no control over the terrible might of the microscopic atom.

You may recognize the name of Sir Alexander Fleming—not because he happened to have been born on this day in 1881, in Lochfield, Scotland—but because he grew up to discover a lifesaver. Fleming isolated the antibiotic known as penicillin.

"Men may come and men may go, But I go on forever." Do not be alarmed. It is a quotation from Alfred Lord Tennyson. Great Britain's poet laureate was born on this day in 1809 in Somersby, England. And it is Tennyson who also reminded us of a virtue we should always aspire to develop. He wrote: "My strength is as the strength of ten, because my heart is pure."

On this day, in 1497, the Genovese navigator John Cabot returned from his voyage aboard the *Matthew*. Licensed by Great Britain's Henry VII, Cabot had sailed to the New World and claimed Nova Scotia in the name of his mentor as he planted the Tudor flag on its shores. The entire voyage cost the king £10, plus an annuity of £20 to Cabot.

Andy Warhol was born on this day in 1927. At one point this pop art master and experimental filmmaker declared that, in the future, everyone will have at least fifteen minutes of fame. And in many ways his prediction has come true. The Internet, the WorldWide Web, chat rooms, and other advances have made everyone into a potential media star.

7th.

1794 The Whiskey Rebellion took place.

1882 The feud between the Hatfields of West Virginia and McCoys of Kentucky erupted.

1942 Battle of Guadalcanal took place.

1964 The Gulf of Tonkin Resolution was passed. (See August 2nd entry.)

Today was the day, in 1794, when President George Washington issued a proclamation telling a group of Western Pennsylvanian farmers to go peacefully back to their homes and to stop their Whiskey Rebellion. Washington's words were not enough. He had to issue a second proclamation a month and a half later and sent troops to persuade the rebels. It is worth noting that, even though the fight over excise taxes imposed on whiskey-making was quelled that time, the Internal Revenue Service is still engaged in games of wits with some rural whiskey makers in this country.

When the U.S. Marines landed at Guadalcanal on this day in 1942, it was more than merely the start of a bitter battle between U.S. and Japanese forces. It was the turning point in the Pacific theater confrontation during the Second World War. It was the first time the United States had taken the offensive.

It all started in 1878, when Randolph McCoy accused Floyd Hatfield of stealing a hog. But when Ellison Hatfield was fatally stabbed by three McCoys on this day during the 1882 election, animosity turned into a desire for revenge. During the next eight years, the fiery feud between the Hatfields and the McCoys raged across state borders. Their legend even had its Romeo and Juliet—Rosanna McCoy and John Hatfield.

8th.

1940 Battle of Britain began.

1950 President Harry S Truman denounced repression of freedom.

1974 President Nixon announced his resignation. (See July 16th entry.)

The theater of war used to play out its acts to a select audience. War was conducted on a battlefield by fighting men, while the civilians waited for the results. That changed in modern times. And on this day in 1940, a major random attack began which was later called the Battle of Britain or "The Blitz." The German air force waged a sustained series of daytime air attacks against both British home territory and the Royal Air Force. Their targets were not strictly limited to airfields or army bases. They rained bombs on British cities as well. The Blitz eventually ended because the British people responded with a new burst of determination. It was their spirit that ultimately defeated the purpose of the attacks.

Government is a double-edged sword. Devised to protect its people, it can also stifle the rights of individuals in the desire to work for the common good. President Harry S Truman warned us of these consequences on this date in 1950, when he said: "Once a government is committed to silencing the voice of opposition, it has only one way to go, and that is down the path of increasingly repressive measures, until it becomes a source of terror to all its citizens and creates a country where everyone lives in fear."

9th.

1790 The *Columbia* arrived in Boston Harbor.

1930 Betty Boop made her debut. (See July 27th and September 19th entries.)

1936 Jesse Owens became the first Olympian to win four medals. (See September 12th entry.)

1945 The U.S. Air Force dropped the second atomic bomb over Nagasaki, Japan. (See August 6th entry.)

1974 Gerald R. Ford succeeded Richard M. Nixon as U.S. President. (See July 14th entry.)

1988 New York's daily lottery number was 888.

Sometimes we are told that an individual cannot fight city hall. Today we should remember just how much one person can affect the world. When Adolf Hitler hosted the 1936 Summer Olympics in Berlin, he wanted to prove that Aryan superiority was not limited to intellect. It included athletic prowess. In front of thousands of spectators and the world media, African-American runner Jesse Owens became the first person to win four Olympic medals. He stood on the winner's platform as living proof that individual achievement can outweigh perceived group strength and transcends racial, political, and economic barriers.

There are times when taking a gamble on the improbable pays. The day after the eighth day of August—which is the eighth month—in the year 1988, New York's daily lottery number was 888. For the people who bet on the improbable, it was a winning combination. For those who didn't, it meant missing out on the chance of a lifetime.

The American flag officially became a flag seen 'round the world on this day in 1790. The sailing ship *Columbia* returned to Boston Harbor after a three-year circumnavigation, becoming the first ship to carry the American flag around the world.

Only three days after the first atomic bomb was dropped on Hiroshima, the U.S. Air Force once again flew high above Japan and released a second bomb. This time the target was the industrial city of Nagasaki, and the death toll was estimated at 74,000 people. As tragic as this loss of civilian life was, it is also credited with bringing an end to the Second World War. Had the war continued for another year, the death toll would have likely been many times higher. There are few evils greater than war. But the Nagasaki bombing also marks a positive note in history. Despite nuclear proliferation, it marks the last time any nation used such a device of mass destruction in combat.

10th.

1833   The city of Chicago was incorporated as a village.

1846   The Smithsonian Institution was established.

1946   President Bill Clinton was born.

When Chicago was incorporated as a village on this day in 1833, nobody could have foreseen that it would become a major American industrial hub; that it would burn to the ground and rise again as a metropolis; that it would be the capital of crime during the Prohibition; and it would be watched by the whole world when it hosted the 1968 Democratic convention. It is a city that is known for its colorful local politics; and known for the themes it has inspired in American literature. All great cities have grown from humble beginnings and—despite their problems—have invigorated not only their residents, but the world.

The Smithsonian Institution was approved by an Act of Congress on this day in 1846. Its establishment was the dying request of James Smithson of London, England, who had bequeathed its initial funding. Since then, various units of the Smithsonian have been endowed by other private philanthropists—the Freer Gallery, the Mellon and Kress Collections, the Hirshhorn and many, many others. Public and private funds have built this jewel in the crown of American museums. Private initiative started it. Public enthusiasm followed.

William Jefferson Clinton was born on this day in 1946. Legend has it that Bill Clinton's uncle brought him into town once when Bill was still an infant, leaned his nephew up in a cardboard crib on the general store counter; and said to the people around him: "Take a good look at that boy, 'cause some day he's gonna be governor of Arkansas." Well, some day came, and Bill was governor. But he didn't stop there. He went on to become President of the United States.

11th.

1909 The S-O-S distress signal was first used by an American ship—the Arapahoe—off Cape Hatteras, North Carolina. (See November 22nd entry.)

1921 Alex Haley was born.

1934 The first federal prisoners arrived at Alcatraz Island. (See October 12th entry.)

1954 Vietnam was partitioned.

1965 Riots broke out in the Watts district of Los Angeles, California.

King Solomon was asked to judge between two women each claiming to be the mother of a certain baby. Solomon suggested that the solution was to cut the baby in half and divide the remains between the two parties. One woman said, "No, let her have the child." Solomon knew that she was the real mother. She cared enough to give of herself to save her child. Partitions of wealth or of land can be like this tale of King Solomon. Those who agree to divide may not do so to be reasonable. On this day, in 1954, the French withdrew from what was French Indochina. Under the terms of a Geneva agreement, the territory was divided into two separate nations. The people of the two Vietnams voiced their opinions soon after. Many of them left Communist North Vietnam to take refuge in South Vietnam. All too soon, there was war. And when it ended, the North ruled all of Vietnam.

On this day in 1965, six days of rioting began in the Watts district of Los Angeles, California. It came as a surprise to most of the country that the idyllic dream factory—the land of the lotus eaters—had the same social problems as less-glamorous cities. It also shocked residents of the city itself.

After we learn about the birds and the bees the question: "Where did I come from?" takes on a new meaning. One man's search for answers to this question inspired the rest of the nation to do the same. Alex Haley, who was born on this day in 1921, penned his journey through the successive generations back to his roots in a tribe in Africa. When he published his discoveries as a novel, *Roots* not only became an instant bestseller, it became the first made-for-television miniseries.

12th.

1862   Julius Rosenwald was born.

1881   Cecil B. DeMille was born.

1948   Mrs. Kasenkina jumped from a window to escape deportation.

1961   The Berlin wall was built. (See November 20th entry.)

Dictatorships are sometimes like long-winded speakers. They prefer a captive audience. On this day, in 1961, Communist East Germany literally created a captive audience. Overnight, the Communist government put up a wall sealing off East Berlin from West Berlin. The purpose was obviously to keep East Germans from leaving. But some brave people leapt to their freedom over the heavily fortified barricade. Like the Walls of Jericho, in 1989, the Berlin Wall came tumbling down. The city once again became whole, and its people were free to choose where they lived.

The struggle for personal freedom has many times meant jumping over walls to escape oppression. Not all attempts were successful. Mrs. Olga Kasenkina had been sent to America to teach Soviet diplomats' children in New York City. Then she was ordered to return home. As she was being deported on this day in 1948, she broke away from consulate officials and leapt through a window at the Soviet embassy. Rather than spending her life in Stalinist Russia, she chose freedom at all costs. This happened long before a rash of defectors became an international embarrassment for Soviet Russia and other socialist nations.

Julius Rosenwald was born on this day in 1862, in Springfield, Illinois. His name may not mean much to you, but his mail-order business helped build a growing nation. Rosenwald's Sears, Roebuck, and Company brought the luxuries of civilization to remote settlements when America's west was young. He amassed a fortune as he built his company into a huge retail institution. With his goals achieved, Rosenwald started sharing his success with the nation. He became a great philanthropist in his later years.

Cecil B. DeMille was born on this day in 1881, in Ashfield, Massachusetts. Real life has always been hard put to equal the sheer spectacle of a DeMille production such as the *Ben Hur* or *The Ten Commandments*. Maybe life would be a lot more interesting if it could be staged by a Cecil B. DeMille, but who has that kind of budget?

13th.

1818   Lucy Stone was born.

1899   Alfred Hitchcock was born.

1969   The 3,000-mile welcome for *Apollo 11* astronauts.

Whoever said that you can't be in two places at once must have felt foolish on this day in 1969. Three *Apollo 11* astronauts—Neil Armstrong, Edwin Aldrin and Michael Collins—flew to New York, Chicago, and Los Angeles on the same day to attend civic receptions in their honor. One thing Michael Collins said during the course of that day deserves to be said again now. He said: "We share with you the hope that we citizens of earth who can solve the problems of leaving the earth can also solve the problems of staying on it."

Alfred Hitchcock was born on this date in 1899, in London, England. This master of the thriller once remarked: "In the entire history of sadism, the television commercial is the only instance where man has invented a torture and then provided the victims with an escape. What is interesting is that so few people avail themselves of the opportunity."

When Lucy Stone married Mr. Henry Blackwell she became known as Mrs. Lucy Stone. Born on this day, in 1818, in West Brookfield, Massachusetts, this women's suffrage movement leader was particularly interested in enabling women to keep their maiden names. It was a long hard fight. And when she died in 1893, the battle still had not been won. Little did anyone know that nearly a century later, professional women everywhere would follow Mrs. Stone's example.

14th.

1900   The Boxer Rebellion ended.

1935   The Social Security Law was established. (See April 27th entry.)

1941   The Atlantic Charter was signed by England and the United States.

1945   VJ Day.

When the leaders of two great nations meet at sea and issue a statement of principle, it has to have a certain element of drama. The situation was very dramatic when on this date in 1941, President Franklin D. Roosevelt and Prime Minister Winston Churchill issued the Atlantic Charter simultaneously in Washington D.C. and London. They had held a three-day conference aboard the British fighting ship *H.M.S. Prince of Wales* and the U.S. cruiser *Augusta* to discuss their potential post-war goals: no more territorial aggrandizement; respecting the wishes of territorial inhabitants as to territorial changes; recognizing the people's right to decide on their own form of government; easing restrictions on international trade and insuring equal access to raw materials; cooperating to provide better economic security for people all over the world; freedom from want and fear; freedom of the seas; and the ultimate establishment of a permanent structure of peace. Fifteen nations—including Soviet Russia—endorsed the Atlantic Charter in less than two months. And the effects of that agreement can still be found throughout the world today.

Today marks a critical a landmark in Second World War history. In 1945, this was VJ Day. Japanese forces formally surrendered on September 2nd aboard the U.S. battleship *Missouri*, but this was the day the Japanese stopped fighting.

The Boxers were put down on this day in 1900. After a fifty-six-day siege of European and American families living in Beijing and other parts of China, the Boxers ended their bloody rampage when 10,000 British, American, French, and German forces marched into the capital city to rescue the stranded diplomats, missionaries, businessmen, men, women, and children. The Boxers were members of a patriotic martial arts society that strongly protested the western influences that had swiftly spread throughout the nation in less than fifty years. More than 1,500 Europeans had been killed before the rebellion ended. But the event was only the beginning of the rapid demise of the western occupation of Asia.

15th.

1057 Macbeth died.

1769 Napoleon Bonaparte was born.

1865 Sir Joseph Lister discovered the antiseptic process. (See April 5th entry.)

1888 T.E. Lawrence was born. (See July 6th entry.)

1914 The Panama Canal was opened.

When the Panama Canal opened on this date in 1914, it was considered one of the wonders of the modern world. Countless laborers had suffered in the dense Central American jungles, battling heat, humidity, snakes, and malaria to build it. A half century later, people realized that the canal wasn't wide enough for modern freighters and cruise ships to pass through. Forgetting the political wrangling and maneuvering that centered around the canal, it became a monument to the rapidity of change.

Today is Napoleon Bonaparte's birthday. Born in 1769 in Ajaccio, Corsica, Napoleon was a small man who cast a gigantic shadow over most of Europe, Egypt, and part of Mexico. A lot of people have imagined themselves to be Napoleon and succeeded only in meeting their Waterloo.

A notable anniversary that inspired a tragic play marks this date. In 1057, Macbeth of Moray was mortally wounded by Malcolm near Aberdeen, Scotland. Macbeth had placed his claim on the Scottish throne because he was married to King Kenneth III's granddaughter. In 1047, he had killed his only rival, Duncan, in battle and grabbed the throne. As the saying goes, violence begets violence. Macbeth's death did not end the fight for the Scottish crown. It continued for generations.

On this day, in 1888, an enigma was born. Thomas Edward Lawrence came from a middle-class Edwardian background and showed great promise as an archaeologist when he studied at Oxford University. He had fallen in love with the desert after bicycling from England to Palestine, and his passion grew as he joined an excavation team in Saudi Arabia at the beginning of the First World War. Lawrence joined the British army as a cartographer and expert in Arab culture when the war reached the desert. A spark of inspiration spurred him on to lead a handful of Arab rebels and overtake a Turkish garrison at Aqaba; and from that day forward, he was known as Lawrence of Arabia. His fame grew as news of his exploits reached Europe and America. But instead of reaping glory's benefits, he hid in the shadows. He changed his name and joined the R.A.F., working on motorcycle and hydrofoil designs; and writing his epic chronicle, *Seven Pillars of Wisdom*. He found peace in obscurity until he died in 1935, when he was laid to rest in Britain's highest place of honor—Westminster Abbey. An average person would have reveled in fame, but Lawrence was no ordinary man. His accomplishments transformed the Near and Middle East's future, but he never perceived his deeds as historical turning points. He had not chased his destiny, it found him.

16th.

1894   George Meany was born.

1996   A gorilla saved a young child.

George Meany was born on this day in 1894. He grew to become the American Federation of Labor's vigorous and vital leader: a post he held well into his eighties.

Many people are convinced that wild, untamed animals are a danger to humans. That's why zoos build deep moats or put up shatter-proof glass around their exhibits to protect visitors from harm. But one does begin wonder about this attitude when we recall an incident that happened on this day in 1996. A three-year-old boy accidentally fell fifteen feet into the gorilla pen at the Brookfield Zoo near Chicago, Illinois. As he lay unconscious, a rare female western lowland gorilla named Binti-Jua picked up the child, cradled him in her arms, carried his unconscious body to the cage door, and protected him until his rescuers arrived. A similar incident took place at the Great Britain's Jersey Zoo a few years earlier. A dominant male silverback gorilla gently patted and then stood guard over a young boy who had fallen into that exhibit.

17th.

1786   Davy Crockett was born. (See February 23rd entry on the Alamo.)

1892   Mae West was born.

1896   Gold was discovered in Klondike territory.

Not too many women have given their name to a distinctive garment. In the case of bloomers, they were named after the first person who wore them. In the case of the Mae West, the device named after the shape of the woman it resembles. The Mae West was an inflatable life preserver that was widely used during the Second World War. For reasons we needn't go into the soldiers and seamen who wore them nicknamed them for the raunchy blonde bombshell who had graced the silver screen since the 1930s. For Mae West, it was a lovely salute. Born on this day in 1892—or thereabouts—in Brooklyn, New York, Mae West put more innuendo into a few words than anyone after her. "Come up and see me some time" always seemed steamier when delivered with West's classic style.

There is a four-letter word that has inspired more hope in mankind and opened more new lands than any other. The word is gold. The search for gold started the settlement of California in 1849; of British Columbia in 1856; and of Alaska and the Yukon territories on this day in 1896. This was the day that George Carmack, Skookum Jim, and Tagish Charlie discovered gold on Bonanza Creek in the Canadian Klondike. Officials were barring fortune-hunters from crossing the border into Canada unless they had enough funds and provisions to stake themselves for a full year in the wilderness. But that didn't stop the 100,000 adventurers who sought their fortunes during the next two years. Thanks to the Klondike gold rush, Alaska became an American territory. Some brave-hearted people still search for the pot of gold at the end of the Arctic rainbow. But the key word always has been that four-letter one—gold.

18th.

1587   Virginia Dare was born. (See July 22nd entry.)

1853   The milk condensation process was patented.

1883   Pope Leo XIII declared his law of history.

On this day, in 1853, Gail Borden received a patent for an improved method of condensing milk. His invention ultimately led to the foundation of the Borden Company.

When Pope Leo XIII opened the Vatican Archives on this date in 1883, his remarks condensed a great deal of morality into a very small package. He said, "The first law of history is not to dare to utter falsehood; the second is not to fear to speak the truth."

Today is Virginia Dare's birthday. The first child born to English parents in the New World was born on Roanoke Island in Virginia on this day in 1587. Virginia, her parents, and the whole Roanoke settlement, disappeared shortly after that off the face of the earth.

On This Day in History

19th.

1851 Captain Gennadi Nevelskoy raised the Russian flag on Sakhalin Island.

1870 Bernard M. Baruch was born.

1871 Orville Wright was born (celebrated as National Aviation Day).

1919 Malcolm Forbes was born.

Today is National Aviation Day which commemorates the birth of Orville Wright. Born in 1871, in Dayton, Ohio, Orville and his brother Wilbur invented the airplane. When they set out to make a heavier-than-air propeller-driven machine fly off the ground, they looked for a place with a big wind. Once they found it at Kitty Hawk, North Carolina.

Bernard M. Baruch was probably America's most notable elder statesman. Born on this day in 1870, in Camden, South Carolina, Baruch advised every President from Woodrow Wilson to John F. Kennedy. He would sit on a park bench and hold impromptu press conferences as easily as he moved within the inner circles of power. In his last years, he was hard of hearing and wore a hearing aid. There was always a suspicion that one of his assets in delicate conversations was that he could decide what he wanted to hear.

Sakhalin Island, just north of Japan, has been the scene of a number of international incidents. But on this day, in 1851, one event not only led to a naval captain's demotion, it spurred a tidal wave of Russian expansion. Czarist Russian military and political leaders believed that the Amur River in Siberia emptied into the Sea of Okhotsk. Naval Captain Gennadi Nevelskoy had been sent to explore the region for future settlement. But he discovered that his superiors were wrong; this mighty river actually ended at the Pacific Ocean. In his excitement, Nevelskoy raised the Russian flag on the eastern shore of Sakhalin Island directly across from the river's mouth. On his return, he was demoted to the post of sailor because he had acted without orders from his superiors. They did, however, take advantage of this revelation. Nearly a decade later, Manchurian China ceded that portion of the Amur River region; and the Russian city of Vladivostok was established at the river's mouth. Japan eventually ceded Nevelskoy's island to the Czar as well.

Since it's Malcolm Forbes' birthday, we should reflect on a few words this eloquent publisher, who was born in 1919, once said. "I don't waste too much time philosophizing about wealth," Forbes commented, "I just recommend it to everyone."

20th.

1741   Alaska was discovered.

1833   Benjamin Harrison was born.

1940   British Prime Minister Winston Churchill paid tribute to the Royal Air Force, stating, "Never in the field of human conflict was so much owed by so many to so few." (See November 30th entry.)

1977   NASA launched the *Voyager Two* space probe.

About this time of the year, in 1741, the Danish explorer Vitus Bering discovered Alaska while heading a Russian expedition through the Arctic. Little did Bering realize that a century later his discovery would become known as Seward's Folly; and would be the site of a third rush for gold. Bering couldn't have foreseen that two centuries later this peninsula would still be one of the last relatively uninhabited wildernesses left on earth—a place where nature stills reigns supreme.

Most American Presidents have some particular claim to fame, and Benjamin Harrison has a unique right to that honor. Born on this day in 1833, in North Bend, Ohio, Harrison was the grandson of the President William Henry Harrison, who served the shortest term in history. But that was not Benjamin's particular claim to Presidential distinction. It was simply that Benjamin Harrison—who succeeded Grover Cleveland as President—also preceded Grover Cleveland as President. He beat Cleveland in one election, then lost to him the next time around. This would have been inspirational if you happened to be Grover Cleveland; and rather irritating if you were Benjamin Harrison.

Mankind set out toward deep space on this day in 1977. *Voyager Two*—a small space probe—became our first tenuous venture into the vast unknown. But it had a second purpose beyond retrieving information. Carrying a twelve-inch copper phonograph record containing greetings in dozens of languages, samples of music and sounds of nature, and abstract images of a man and a woman, it was our first calling card to life in distant galaxies. However, if intelligent life out there ever comes across it, they will probably play that record between episodes of *I Love Lucy* or *Gilligan's Island* as television and radio signals have been departing the earth for parts unknown since the dawn of broadcasting, like a view through the curtains straight into our living rooms.

21st.

1862 Billy Barker struck gold in western Canada. (See June 17th entry.)

1939 German-Russian non-aggression treaty was announced.

1951 Construction of the first nuclear submarine was ordered.

1959 The Hawaiian Islands achieved American statehood.

Aloha! Today is the anniversary of Hawaii's admission as the fiftieth state—and the first state outside the North American mainland. Even though Captain James Cook named the island group the Sandwich Islands after his mentor the Earl of Sandwich, it was the Americans who overtook the Hawaiian Islands, replacing the royal family with a territorial government. It took almost a century before the islands achieved statehood and the right to an electoral vote in Federal elections.

On this date in 1939, the Soviet Union (which had been claiming to be the only true opponent of Nazism) and Nazi Germany (which had set itself up as the prime enemy of Communism) announced that they had agreed to a ten-year non-aggression treaty. It was signed formally three days later. The so-called non-aggression treaty proved to be the fuse that ignited the Second World War. In no time, the Nazis and the Communists greedily divided Poland between them. Not too long afterward, they fought each other.

Back on this day in 1951, the U.S. ordered the construction of the first nuclear-powered submarine. The same power used in the atomic bombs during the Second World War was ordered to be harnessed as an alternative energy source.

A British canal man and sailor named Billy Barker struck gold in western Canada on this day in 1862. When Barker arrived in British Columbia's northern Cariboo mountains, a few thousand other adventurers had already staked their claims in the 1856 gold rush. He couldn't find a plot anywhere near the big veins that were already discovered, so he decided to try his hand below the canyon on Williams Creek. Other prospectors gathered to laugh at Billy's folly, as he dug deeper and deeper. Fifty-two feet later, he struck one of the area's richest finds. It was worth $600,000 when gold was worth only $20 an ounce. Billy went through his fortune fairly quickly. So he dug up another strike equally as rich a few miles south. But his beautiful second wife frittered that fortune away. In the end, Billy Barker died penniless.

22nd.

1741 George Friedrich Handel started writing *The Messiah*. (See September 14th entry.)

1851 The America's Cup was first won. (See September 18th entry.)

1902 Theodore Roosevelt became the first U.S. President to drive an automobile. (See October 27th entry.)

1903 Baseball's World Series was first suggested.

1920 Ray Bradbury was born.

Yacht racing is not your average spectator sport, but a particular yacht race has captured the public's fancy for more than a century—the America's Cup. On this day in 1851, the U.S. schooner *America* won the race against the British schooner *Aurora* to win a silver cup trophy in British waters and international honors. From that day forward the race has been known as the America's Cup. It was defended by American sailors and yachts for well over a century thereafter and remained in U.S. possession until recently. Great Britain's Sir Thomas Lipton tried many times; he lost the races but his great sportsmanship won American hearts.

Barney Dreyfuss used to own the Pittsburgh Pirates baseball team. This may not give him a resounding claim to fame. But we are told that Dreyfuss wrote a letter on this day, in 1903, that entitles him to a place in history. Writing to an American League club owner, this National Leaguer said, "The time has come for the National and American Leagues to organize a World Series." And later that year the first World Series was held. Now, of course, we have world series in one sport after another. And if you look at them, you'll find that most of them are misnamed since they are actually restricted to one country. We sometimes mistake our world for the entire world.

Author Ray Bradbury was born on this date in 1920, and grew up in Waukegan, Illinois and Los Angeles, California. While he was in high school, he launched his own magazine—*Futuria Fantasia*. Within a few years, he was selling his stories to pulp magazines; and later, to major publications like *The New Yorker* and *The Saturday Evening Post*. Bradbury's fantasy and science fiction narrate the interrelationship of technology, society, and the individual in terrifyingly precise detail. But one story—which was first featured in *Playboy Magazine* because other publishers were scared to print it—told of a world where firemen burned books because the government decided their contents made a television-addicted, pill-popping society unequal and unhappy. One of *Fahrenheit 451*'s characters—an old English professor—describes books in a particularly profound way: "This book has pores. It has features. This book can go under a microscope. You'd find life under the glass, streaming past in infinite profusion . . . They show the pores in the face of life." We cannot deny the power of well-written ideas; nor the empowerment great books inspire in a receptive audience.

23*rd*.

1838 The first American women's college held its first graduation.

1926 Rudolf Valentino died. (See May 6th entry.)

1927 Nicola Sacco and Bartolomeo Vanzetti were executed. (See May 5th entry.)

On this day in 1926, the great romantic film idol Rudolph Valentino died in New York City. His passing—at the age of thirty-one—plunged countless females of all ages into an orgy of public grief across the country.

The sad case of a misconducted trial and appeal ended on this day in 1927. Two Italian immigrants—Nicola Sacco and Bartolomeo Vanzetti—were executed for the alleged murder of a guard during a payroll robbery. During the long period before they met their end, Vanzetti wrote to Judge Thayer: "Never in our full life could we hope to do such work for tolerance, for justice, for man's understanding of man as now we do by accident."

When the first American women's college, Mount Holyoke Female Seminary, opened in South Hadley, Massachusetts, the public generally felt women needed refinement, not higher education. On this day in 1838, the college graduated its first students. This may not have had a profound effect on the male population in their day, but to twist a famous line that was written nearly a century later: For today's women, men bend on their knees to women with degrees.

24th.

79 AD The city of Pompeii was destroyed.

1562 Great Britain reminted its coins.

1814 British forces burned Washington, D.C.

1949 The North Atlantic Treaty went into effect. (See March 18th entry.)

1959 Daniel K. Inouye of Hawaii was sworn in as the first Japanese-American in the House of Representatives.

1959 Hiram L. Fong of Hawaii was sworn in as the first Chinese-American in the U.S. Senate.

Back in the year 79 AD, on this day, Mount Vesuvius erupted. Before it was finished, two Roman cities—Herculaneum and Pompeii—were wiped out. The ruins of Pompeii remind us how suddenly and how thoroughly a living city can cease to exist.

On this day in 1814, Washington, D.C. was burned to the ground by the British. It happened during the War of 1812. And unlike Mount Vesuvius' destruction of Pompeii, or General Sherman's razing of Atlanta, the British Army was infinitely more selective. They didn't burn the whole city; they concentrated on the White House and other government buildings. Then they marched north to Baltimore, where they were repulsed at the Battle of Fort McHenry. The nation's capitol was rebuilt, and after a suitable lapse of time, Great Britain and America became the best of friends who are separated only by their mutual illusion that they speak the same language.

Saving a penny here and a nickel there makes good sense in most cases, but in 1562, it was a source of embarrassment to the British government. In an attempt to economize on the cost of minting money, King Henry VIII had coins made from metals like iron and lead that were worth less than the face value they represented. The public felt its money wasn't worth the metal it was minted on and refused to accept it. So on this day, the government finished reminting all of the nation's coins worth their face value in solid silver.

Americans are descended from many different groups that immigrated in hopes of attaining a better life. On this day in 1959, two native sons of immigrant parents achieved some pretty high goals. Daniel K. Inouye of Hawaii was sworn in as the first Japanese-American congressman to the U.S. House of Representatives; Hiram L. Fong of Hawaii was sworn in as the first Chinese-American U.S. senator.

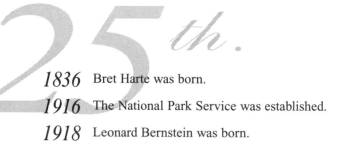

1836   Bret Harte was born.

1916   The National Park Service was established.

1918   Leonard Bernstein was born.

Today is the National Park Service's birthday. In 1916, this department was established to protect tracts of our nation's wilderness from development. The first National Park Service director was paid $4,500 a year. That says a lot about inflation. It also says a lot about the increased popularity of our national parks. These protected areas get more crowded each year, and the job of maintaining and protecting them gets more and more difficult. The wide open spaces just aren't as wide or as open as they used to be. But we can all breath a little freer because of the job well done by this worthwhile governmental department.

One of America's most famous composers and conductors was born in Lawrence, Massachusetts, on this day in 1918. At the age of twenty-five, Leonard Bernstein was already known as the famous symphony conductor who brought the New York Philharmonic to new glory. He was also an accomplished composer. His *Jeremiah* symphony brought him public acclaim. And, in his spare time, he wrote the scores for popular musicals like *West Side Story* and *Candide*. Bernstein moved with ease between these two facets of the music world, proving that the classicism spans all forms of music from symphonies to songs if placed in talented hands.

Some talented people rise and shine brighter as the years go by, while others rise like meteors and fall the same way. One of writing's meteors was Bret Harte, who was born on this day in 1836, in Albany, New York. Harte wrote exciting and grubbily humorous accounts of Western life like "The Luck of Roaring Camp" and "The Outcasts of Poker Flat." Within a decade, he burned himself out as an author, while friends and colleagues like Mark Twain kept shining, burning brighter with each new work. Bret Harte, however, described how his audience eventually felt when his star began to dim on the literary horizon when he wrote: ". . . he smiled a kind of sickly smile, and curled up on the floor, / And the subsequent proceedings interested him no more."

26th.

55 BC Roman forces under Julius Caesar invaded Britain.

1873 Lee DeForest was born.

1883 The volcano Krakatoa erupted with increasingly large explosions killing 36,000 people.

1920 The Nineteenth Amendment to the U.S. Constitution was ratified.

Today marks a milestone in the fight for women's rights. On this day in 1920, the Nineteenth Amendment to the U.S. Constitution was ratified, giving women the right to vote. It did not end discrimination against American women, but it armed them with a new secret weapon: the vote.

American inventor Lee DeForest was one of a relatively small group of brilliant men who took Marconi's radio and developed it into the device that transmits sight and sound signals into your home—the television. He was also a pioneer in the development of talking pictures. Today is Lee DeForest's birthday. He was born in Council Bluffs, Iowa, in 1873.

This is the anniversary of the original British Invasion. Long before the Beatles and the Rolling Stones arrived on American shores, the Romans invaded the British Isles. When Julius Caesar became the ruler of Britain in 55 BC, his engineers shaped the landscape. Amazingly, much of the Romans' work still remains to this day. The Roman roads, canals, and aqueducts that crisscross the country, connect cities like London, Bath, and Cambridge—which were all founded by the Romans.

When the tiny island of Krakatau—located in Indonesia between Java and Sumatra—became the site of a volcanic eruption on this day in 1883, it was an environmental disaster of global proportions. The eruption, the island's collapse, and the subsequent tsunami took an estimated 36,000 lives. But the airborne smoke and ash quickly circled the globe, blocking out the sun and causing Dickensean weather conditions for a few years. In fact, it was those dreary, dark, bitter cold winters and wet, chilly, and all too brief summers that set the scenes in Dickens' works.

27th.

1783 The first hydrogen balloon was tested.

1859 Colonel Edwin L. Drake dug the first oil well.

1882 Sam Goldwyn was born.

1908 Lyndon Baynes Johnson was born.

1927 Bill Brock flew the *Pride of Detroit* over London.

1938 George Eyston set an automobile land-speed record.

1939 Captain Erich Warshitz flew the first jet plane.

1954 The first white men crossed the Northwest passage from the Atlantic to the Pacific.

1979 The Soviet spacecraft *Soyuz 15* went into orbit and met with a Soviet space station.

When Colonel Edwin L. Drake struck oil in Pennsylvania on this day in 1859, the world had its first oil well. The world got the better end of the deal. Colonel Drake was broke within fifteen years. He kept producing oil, and waiting, but it just wasn't a precious commodity in those days. His story is quite different from the one about the two desert prospectors who struck it rich. They were looking for gold and found water. You see— as Thomas Edison put it—everything comes to him who hustles while he waits.

President Lyndon Baynes Johnson, who was born on this day in 1908, came to office when John F. Kennedy was assassinated. This first Texan president ushered us into the space race, signed the Civil Rights Act, and declared a war on poverty during his terms in office. He once said: "Presidents learn—perhaps sooner than others—that our destiny is fashioned by what all of us do—by the deeds and desires of each citizen—as one tiny drop of water after another ultimately makes a big river."

Today is Sam Goldfish's birthday. You all know who he is. As a young man, Sam moved to America from Poland and got into the glove business. He did pretty well, but then he discovered the movies. He and his new partners hired Cecil B. DeMille, a young untried director. Their gamble was a hit. Then Sam Goldfish joined Edgar Selwyn and started Goldwyn Studios. The name stuck. He became Sam Goldwyn, one of Hollywood's greatest producers. Opinionated and honest, he coined comments like: "A verbal contract isn't worth the paper it's written on." When asked once for his opinion of a film script, he replied: "I read part of it all the way through."

Historically, this has been a good day for reaching new frontiers. It all started in 1783, when J.A.C. Charles tested the first hydrogen balloon. His experiment paved the way for modern aviation. In 1927, Bill Brock flew over London in the *Pride of Detroit* on his way to completing the first flight around the world. Back on land, race car driver George Eyston set a 345-miles-per-hour land-speed record in 1938. The next year, German pilot Erich Warshitz flew the first jet plane through the skies. During the summer of 1954, the Arctic Circle's Northwest Passage was finally conquered in a pair of icebreakers. And in 1979, *Soyuz 15*, a manned Soviet spacecraft, went into orbit and rendezvoused with a space station. Whether by air or land or sea, this day has favored those who "boldly go where no man has gone before."

28th.

1774 Mother Elizabeth Seton was born. (See July 19th entry.)

1922 The first radio commercial was aired.

1958 *The New York Times* broke the TV quiz-show scandal story.

1963 A civil rights march took place in Washington, D.C.

1968 Antiwar demonstrators harassed the Democratic convention in Chicago, Illinois.

Today marks the anniversary of two demonstrations that altered the course of American history. In 1963, an inspiring civil rights march was held in Washington, D.C., led by the Reverend Dr. Martin Luther King, Jr. This demonstration is well-remembered because of his eloquent "I have a dream" speech. The Civil Rights Act was passed less than a year after this peaceful event. In 1968, an antiwar demonstration held in Chicago during the Democratic National Convention ended in a violent confrontation between protesters and police. After a shocking mediafest which was fueled by dramatics—like alleged Chicago Seven conspirator Bobby Seal being bound and gagged at his own trial—two generations of Americans learned an eye-opening lesson about the communications gap that had grown between them. Taking a lesson from these two events, it is a good time to remember the words of President Lyndon Johnson who once said, "Let us reason together."

It is recorded in some history books that on this day in 1922, the commercial message was born. It aired on WEAF—a New York radio station—and the world hasn't been the same since. In fact, on this same day, the television industry marks a black-letter day in its history. The producers of the popular quiz show *21* had routinely given contestants the answers to questions in advance. The show was so convincingly rigged that participants like college professor Charles Van Doren were transformed into national heroes overnight. In 1958, *The New York Times* broke the scandal wide open with a front-page story. The news injured the viewing public's faith in heroes, the advertisers' confidence in the medium credibility, and changed broadcasters' minds about what should be televised.

America's first Roman Catholic saint was born on this day in 1774. Mother Elizabeth Seton was a native New Yorker. After she had married and started a family, her husband passed away from a chronic illness in 1803. Seton converted to Roman Catholicism a few years later; and opened an elementary school in Baltimore, Maryland, where several young women were entrusted to her care. From that beginning, America's first religious society, the Sisters of Charity was formed in 1813, with Sister Seton as its first mother superior. Saint Elizabeth Seton didn't start America's first Catholic elementary school, but she is considered the founder of the American parochial school system.

29th.

1896 Chop suey was invented in New York City.

1901 Carry Nation tried to visit John L. Sullivan. (See November 25th entry.)

1922 W.A. Dwiggins defined advertising.

We like to think that the United States is a pacesetter among the world's nations, but until recently we rarely considered American cuisine as one of our high points. But on this date in 1896, a truly American dish was invented—chop suey. It's true. According to the record books, chop suey was first concocted in New York City by visiting Chinese ambassador Li Huang-Chang's chef while he was staying at the Waldorf-Astoria Hotel.

It's been a long time since anybody went around the country smashing saloons with a hatchet, crusading against the evils of alcohol. Have you ever heard of Carry Nation who left Kansas at the turn of the century to put everyone on the wagon? On this day, in 1901, Ms. Nation was in New York City, and she was on the war path. We are told that she paid a well-publicized visit to a saloon run by John L. Sullivan, the former heavyweight boxing champion. But John L. was nowhere in sight. He sent her a message that he was sick in bed.

It was on this day in 1922, that illustrator and designer W.A. Dwiggins was quoted in the *Boston Transcript* as defining advertising design as "the only form of graphic design that gets home to everybody." The power of advertising is even more obvious today since it's carried in not only newspapers, magazines, radio, and billboards. Since Dwiggins time, advertising has embraced television, motion pictures, the Internet, and the WorldWide Web. Today, the average American is exposed to nearly 1,500 pieces of advertising daily, proving that this form of graphic design is the only one that will find you at home, at work, and at play.

30th.

1963 The hotline between the U.S. and Moscow was established.

1967 Thurgood Marshall took his seat on the U.S. Supreme Court. (See June 13th entry.)

1983 Guion Bluford Jr. became the first African-American astronaut in space when he blasted off aboard the space shuttle *Challenger*. (See April 19th entry.)

In 1963, a favorite prop for screenwriters of the time came into existence: the hotline between the White House in Washington, D.C. and the Kremlin in Moscow was placed into operation. No one knows if the two telephones depicted in the motions pictures *Dr. Stranglove* and *Fail Safe* were really tinted fire-engine red. But then, again, the motion pictures themselves were filmed in black-and-white.

Two men took gigantic steps in their given professions on this day in history. In 1967, Thurgood Marshall took his seat on the U.S. Supreme Court. Appointed by President Lyndon Baynes Johnson, Marshall was the first African-American justice to step up to the nation's highest court bench. In 1983, astronaut Guion Bluford, Jr., took off as a member of the space shuttle *Challenger*'s crew. Bluford was the first African-American astronaut to take a giant leap into space.

1887 Thomas Edison patented the kinetoscope.

1903 A Packard automobile completed the first transcontinental car trip.

1947 The U.S. Investigating Committee recommended that Great Britain give up control of Palestine. (See June 29th and September 29th entries.)

In 1887, Thomas Edison invented something called the kinetoscope—or at least he had it patented. This was the day the patent was granted for his device which allowed an individual to peer through a peephole to watch images that appeared to move. Edison's invention opened up a whole new world of entertainment and information delivery that is still enjoyed around the world.

A monumental feat was accomplished on this day when, in 1903, a Packard automobile reached New York City from San Francisco, California. It was the first time anyone had ever attempted to drive across the country without a horse. The trip took fifty-two days—not the four or five days it now takes. Then again, the Packard averaged about ten to twenty miles per hour.

September

Now is the time when we traditionally conclude the rites of summer with the long Labor Day weekend. Intended to be a salute to working people, Labor Day has become a celebration of the end of the vacation season, signaling that it's time to go back to work. But it's also a warning to children that it's time to hit the books and go back to school. The month of September does remind us that even though hard work may be difficult to digest at times, we all savor the fruits of our labors.

1st.

1866   James J. Corbett was born.

1875   Edgar Rice Burroughs was born.

1905   The provinces of Saskatchewan and Alberta entered into the confederation of Canada. (See July 1st entry.)

1939   The Second World War began.

1972   Bobby Fisher won the international chess championship against Boris Spassky in Reykjavik, Iceland. (See March 9th entry.)

Despite the world's general hope that the First World War was the war to end all wars, the Second World War began twenty years later, on this very day in 1939. It was ignited when Germany invaded Poland and was not extinguished until two atomic bombs were dropped upon Germany's ally, Japan.

Gentleman Jim Corbett was well-dressed, eloquent, and moved gracefully in polite society. He was the man who beat the legendary John L. Sullivan for the world heavyweight boxing title. He was a superb boxer—not a slugger or brawler. This native San Franciscan was also a new kind of professional fighter who played by the Marquess of Queensberry rules. Born on this day in 1866, James J. Corbett became a successful lecturer and actor after his pugilistic career ended. We've had a succession of accomplished, articulate fighters since Corbett's day, but it was Gentleman Jim who broke the old thick-headed mold. He demonstrated that technique and style could be more than a match for brute force.

Edgar Rice Burroughs was born in Chicago on this day in 1875. He had served in the U.S. cavalry, fighting against the Apache Indians out west until he was discharged: it was discovered that he was under age. After pursuing one or two colorful occupations, Burroughs decided to focus his attention on improving the quality of the dime novel. And in 1914, his first novel, *Tarzan of the Apes*, was published. The success of this and the subsequent novels made Burroughs a millionaire, especially when they were eventually translated into radio broadcasts and feature films.

2nd.

1789 U.S. Treasury Department was established.

1901 U.S. Vice President Theodore Roosevelt gave his "speak softly and carry a big stick" speech. (See October 27th entry.)

1945 Japanese forces formally surrendered to the Allies. (See August 14th entry.)

The U.S. Treasury Department was established on this day in 1789. The Constitutional government had been operating for five months or so before the Treasury Department came into existence, which shows that our priorities have certainly changed since that day. Apparently, when this nation started, we were less convinced that money talks. In the beginning, of course, government was not big business; the income tax was more than a century away. People could, and many did, live off the land. The services provided by the government were minimal. But times have changed. The U.S. Treasury Department today, thanks to the Internal Revenue Service, has fingers in a lot of pies.

"Speak softly and carry a big stick." Vice President Theodore Roosevelt made that famous statement about his foreign relations policy on this day, in 1901, at a Minnesota state fair. His words must have carried some weight with the voters. Certainly when he became President the next year, he wasn't the last person in that office to softly warn an aggressor nation, and then send in the marines whether it was on the shores of North Africa or the South China Seas.

3rd.

1609 Henry Hudson discovered the island of Manhattan. (See June 22nd and August 3rd entries.)

1783 Treaty of Paris ended the American Revolutionary War.

1856 Louis Henry Sullivan was born.

1882   The first municipal electric power station was built by Thomas Edison. (See September 30th entry.)

1888   George Eastman patented his roll film camera and registered his Kodak name.

1939   Britain and France entered the Second World War.

According to history, sometime around this date in 1609, explorer Henry Hudson discovered Manhattan Island. One reason there is some uncertainty about the date is that when he first saw Manhattan, he really wasn't sure that it was an island. In that respect, Hudson was no different from many recent visitors. The only way to figure out how Manhattan works is to be there for awhile.

Today commemorates a sort of microcosm of extremes—an anniversary of one war's end and the start of another. On this day, in 1783, the American Revolution formally ended when Great Britain and the U.S. signed the Treaty of Paris. But in 1939, this was the day that Great Britain and France declared the war against Germany.

In the past century or so, we have renovated the earth, the shape of the cities, and the whole concept of architecture. The man who influenced this facelift in the twentieth century was the architect Louis Henry Sullivan, who was born on this day in 1856 in Boston, Massachusetts. Sullivan built the prototype of the modern skyscraper back in 1890, in St. Louis, Missouri. He trained future modern designers like Frank Lloyd Wright; and pioneered the concept that a structure's form is dependent upon its function.

Electrical lighting was on everyone's wish list after its inventor, Thomas Edison, introduced it to the world. To meet the demand in New York City, Edison built and put into operation the first municipal power station—the Pearl Street Station. It happened on this day in 1882. Hundreds of thousands of power stations have been built since then. Some run on conventional turbine engines, while others use water or nuclear energy to supply electricity.

On this day in 1888, George Eastman patented his roll film camera and registered his Kodak name. In light of this picturesque historic moment, we can thank Mr. Eastman for allowing those of us with less than photogenic memories to remember pleasant moments and historic occasions in a flash or at least with the turn of a photo album page.

4th.

1781   The village of Los Angeles was founded.

1909   Eleven thousand Boy Scouts held their first parade.

1951   The first transcontinental live television broadcast was aired.

Let's all wish El Pueblo de Nuestra Senora de la Reina de los Angeles de Porcincula a happy birthday because it was founded on this day in 1781. And we should also thank whoever was responsible for shortening its name to Los Angeles. Because of its spectacular growth in the twentieth century, we like to think of Los Angeles as a totally modern phenomenon born of the movie business—a lotus land described as "seventeen suburbs in search of a city" and "an asylum that's run by the inmates." But the fact is that for most Americans, Los Angeles—rightly or wrongly—symbolizes the good life. Los Angelenos have to work for a living just like the rest of us; and they worry about water and smog just like the rest of us. Nevertheless, we seem to need a symbol of the good life and we have one situated on our southwestern shores.

On this day in 1951, Americans on both coasts were able watch the same live television picture at the same time. The first nationwide broadcast featured President Harry S Truman's speech at the Japanese Peace Treaty Conference in San Francisco, California.

Scouting proudly salutes an important anniversary today. In 1909, the Boy Scouts held their first national parade at London's Crystal Palace. Less than two years after its conception, Great Britain's Boy Scouts Organization was eleven thousand members strong. Lord Robert Baden-Powell's Scouts participated in wholesome activities like water safety, camping, hiking, and wood crafting. According to its founder, scouting built strong bodies, keen minds, and sound character. In 1907, Baden-Powell had taken twenty boys from various backgrounds on a camping trip to Brownsea Island. That autumn, the first troops were formed. You can't keep a good idea down, especially when it incorporates ideals and values that both young and old can appreciate.

5th.

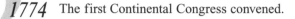

1774   The first Continental Congress convened.

1836   Sam Houston was elected president of the Republic of Texas. (See April 21st entry.)

1882   The nation's first Labor Day parade was held in New York City.

1885   The first gas pump was delivered to a gasoline dealer. (See January 7th entry.)

1939   The United States proclaimed its neutrality in the Second World War. (See December 8th entry.)

A cynic once remarked that when nobody talks it's a crisis and when everybody talks it's a Congress. Today marks the anniversary of a lot of serious talks—the start of the First Continental Congress. Most Americans know that the Second Continental Congress adopted the Declaration of Independence. But the First Continental Congress flowered on this day in 1774, and fathered the historic gathering that met the following year.

Today is the perfect time to salute the working men and women of America. It was, after all, on this day in 1882 that thousands of workers took to the streets of New York to participate in the nation's first Labor Day parade. You may wonder exactly who is a laborer? The people who built our cities, one brick at a time are laborers. They paved our streets, and keep them paved. They stitched the clothes on our backs, after they harvested the cotton, and have woven the cloth. Laborers from across the nation put the food on our tables. As each of us participates in our daily lives, we are the present generation of America's labor force: receiving a great country from our predecessors and passing a better one to those who will follow us.

6th.

1620   Pilgrims set sail from Plymouth, England. (See July 22nd entry.)

1837   The first coeducational college opened in Oberlin, Ohio.

1860   Jane Addams was born.

1966 The television program *Star Trek* premiered.

1989 Ben Johnson's victories were stricken from the record books.

The first full admission of women to an American college filled with men happened on this day. In 1837, Oberlin Collegiate Institute—now called Oberlin College—which is located in Oberlin, Ohio, became America's first coeducational institution of higher learning. Four women and thirty men began their studies together.

There used to be a saying that women's work was never done. Fortunately, a good deal of progress has been made by women who went beyond the limits of what used to be regarded as women's work. One pioneer was Jane Addams, who was born on this day in 1860 in Cedarville, Illinois. Addams devoted her life to making life better for others. She founded Chicago's Hull House; she was a women's rights leader; and she fought for world peace. In 1931, she and Columbia University's President, Nicholas Murray Butler, were jointly awarded the Nobel Peace Prize. Addams was the first American woman to receive that honor.

Captain's log, stardate 1966. These are the voyages of the Starship Enterprise, its five year mission is to go where no man has gone before. Well, the voyage has lasted far longer than Captain Kirk's original estimate, but there's no denying that *Star Trek* went where no television series had ever gone before. It was radical for its day because it portrayed men and women, minorities and non-minorities, working together as equals. It portrayed the universality of values, ethics, and diplomacy. Each episode was an intentional morality play, showing right winning over wrong in every instance. And yet somehow it still managed to keep generations of Trekkies entertained.

"Winning isn't everything," said Vince Lombardi, "It's the *only* thing." In the field of competitive sports that may be true. Setting and breaking records is any atheleto's ultimate dream. But if attaining that dream means cheating, there can be no winning, as there is no longer a fair competition. It was in this spirit that the Amateur Atheletic Federation stripped Ben Johnson of his track records on this day in 1989, after tests showed that he had used performance enhancing drugs.

7th.

1533 Great Britain's Queen Elizabeth I born. (See November 17th entry.)

1892 James J. Corbett beat John L. Sullivan. (See September 1st entry.)

1936 The Boulder Dam (Hoover Dam) went into operation.

You may not know it, but England's Queen Elizabeth I was born on this day in 1533. During her reign William Shakespeare and others made the English language positively sing. Apparently this lyrical language was not lost on her. When Sir Walter Raleigh wrote to her, "Fain would I climb, yet fear I to fall." Elizabeth replied, "If thy heart fails thee, climb not at all."

Electrical power is a prime necessity in this nation. It was the same back in 1930. Growing cities and settlements in the west needed electricity as much as their eastern counterparts. So to meet their demand, the government spent six years harnessing the power of the Colorado River as it rushed through the Black Canyon at the Arizona-Nevada border. In 1936, Boulder Dam—which was later renamed Hoover Dam—was completed and went into operation on this very day. Besides supplying the west with much-needed energy, the project that President Herbert Hoover had authorized created a new body of water. Lake Mead has been a cool, relaxing oasis for vacationers ever since.

8th.

1157 King Richard the Lion-Hearted was born. (See April 17th entry.)

1565 The first permanent European settlement in North America was established.

1921 Margaret Gorman was crowned Miss America. (See September 17 entry.)

1990 The Ellis Island National Historical Site opened.

This is King Richard the Lion-Hearted's birthday. Born in Oxford, England in 1157, Richard spent most of his life outside of his kingdom, and didn't quite have a glittering historical record to match his reputation. Maybe some of his fame rested on his fondness for troubadours and his own talent for writing lyrics. Maybe the troubadours that spread his legend considered him to be one of their own. Possibly the moral of this story is that if you write your own legend maybe history will be good to you.

Pulling up roots and laying new foundations in strange territory takes a lot of courage. Fear of the unknown stops a lot of us from taking steps that could change our lives for the better. It was on this day that the first permanent European settlement in North America was established at St. Augustine, Florida in 1565. Spanish explorers had been landing in the New World for over five decades before this momentous event. But this day marked the first time settlers came to build homes in this unknown land.

After decades of renovation and refurbishment, Ellis Island reopened its ornate doors as a historical site on this day in 1990. For millions of European immigrants, Ellis Island had been their gateway to America. But on this particular day, the E-shaped island which had been built primarily on landfill in New York Harbor suddenly became the prize in a political tug-of-war between New York and New Jersey. Each state claimed it and the accompanying tourism revenues. In 1998, the courts finally sided with New Jersey.

9th.

1754 William Bligh was born. (See April 28th entry.)

1776 The United Colonies became the United States.

1850 California became a state.

This is California's birthday. Or more exactly, this is the anniversary of California's admission to the United States as the thirty-first state. Gold had been discovered the year before California became a state, in 1850, and the rush continues today. The richest state in the world's richest nation inspires many Americans and immigrants to seek to fulfill the American dreams of fame, glory, wealth, and the good life along California's sunny coast.

We generally observe the United States' birthday on the Fourth of July. But if you want to be technical, we didn't become the United States until this day. In 1776, the Continental Congress decided to change the name of the rebellious United Colonies to the United States. So today is indeed the United States' birthday—at least in name.

10th.

1297   The Scottish defeated the British at the Battle of Sterling.

1813   U.S. Naval Commodore Oliver Perry defeated the British.

1913   The first coast-to-coast paved road in the U.S. opened.

1929   Arnold Palmer was born.

The Battle of Sterling took place on this day. In 1297, Scottish rebel forces, led by William Wallace and Andrew Murray, ambushed the Earl of Surrey's army on the bridge at Forth near Sterling. The Earl's three hundred cavalrymen and ten thousand foot soldiers were quickly defeated by a handful of highlanders.

This may be hard to believe, but today, back in 1913, the first coast-to-coast paved U.S. road was unveiled. Up to that time, portions of our transcontinental highway were just dirt roads. This smooth throughway was named the Lincoln Highway. You might know it as Interstate 80 which flows through the Great Plains and past the Great Salt Lake on its way to San Francisco's Golden Gate. The people who created the Lincoln Highway had the foresight to realize that cars and trucks—not horses and trains—would become a major source of transportation for freedom-loving Americans. And over the years, this and many other interstate highways have come to symbolize American pride in freedom of movement.

Not all great naval battles took place on the open seas. In fact, a critical U.S. naval battle occurred on a lake—the Battle of Lake Erie. On this day in 1813, Commodore Oliver Hazard Perry described his defeat of the British fleet in a succinct message that has been a model for clarity and brevity ever since. "We have met the enemy," Perry said, "and they are ours."

Today is Arnold Palmer's birthday. Born in 1929, this great golfer who hails from Youngstown, Pennsylvania, is known for his playing efficiency, style, and personality. Those talents won him a regiment of admirers—Arnie's Army. The same skills also earned him millions of dollars in prize money and endorsements. Talent can only take a person so far. It takes good interpersonal skills to make any star shine in the public eye.

11th.

1783 Benjamin Franklin wrote about the Treaty of Paris.

1862 O. Henry was born.

1885 D.H. Lawrence was born.

William Sydney Porter was born on this day in 1862, in Greensboro, North Carolina. Under his pen name—O. Henry—this American writer narrated unforgettable stories and was a master manipulator of trick endings and surprising twists. He wrote equally unforgettable short stories about cowboys and about Latin America. But his most famous setting was the city that he called "Baghdad on the subway"—New York City.

Benjamin Franklin was seventy-seven years old when—with John Adams and John Jay—he negotiated a peace settlement with Great Britain in Paris, France. On this date in 1783, shortly after the Treaty of Paris was signed, Franklin wrote to a friend that, "There never was a good war or a bad peace." He didn't waste words. After all, as Franklin observed, time is money.

Lady Chatterley's Lover—for those of you who might be unfamiliar with the title—is a classic romantic tale that was banned for decades due to its graphic content. Today is its author's birthday. D.H. Lawrence, who also wrote *Women in Love*, was born on this day in 1885. Concentrating his energies on the conflicts between male and female perceptions of love and sex, Lawrence went against the grain of social acceptability. Yet a century after his birth, his work is considered to be classic, not pornographic.

12th.

1866 *The Black Crook* premiered in New York City.

1880 H.L. Mencken was born. (See December 28th entry.)

1913 Jesse Owens was born. (See August 9th entry.)

1953 Nikita Khrushchev became Soviet Russia's Premier. (See April 17th and October 30th entries.)

This was the day, in 1866, when a new form of American entertainment premiered in New York City. The show was entitled *The Black Crook*. It was the first American presentation to feature beautiful showgirls. The idea spread like wildfire after that.

Back in 1953, this was the day when Nikita Khrushchev became the First Secretary of the U.S.S.R.'s Communist Party, a position which automatically brought him front and center. Khrushchev loved to talk, and in one of his famous public appearances, he brought a new technique to the public forum. He pounded his shoe on the table to add emphasis to a point in the course of a United Nations discussion.

On December 28, 1917, the long-defunct *New York Evening Mail* ran an article purporting to give the history of the bathtub. It was an obvious spoof. It discussed the invention of the bathtub at length, alleging that the tub was invented in Cincinnati in the 1840s, that Millard Fillmore had been the first U.S. President to take a bath in the White House, and an entire litany of other absurdities. The trouble was, the article's author, H.L. Mencken, had written the article so convincingly that even after he printed an explanation of the hoax, his article continued to be quoted by medical men, professional journals and societies as a factual study on the advancement of personal hygiene. Today is the anniversary of his birth which occurred in 1880. Bits and pieces of the myth he created still exist as fact and custom. The pen can be mightier than the sword, especially since its message can have a long-lasting effect whether it depicts the truth or simply a hoax.

13th.

1759 The Battle of Quebec took place.

1788 First U.S. national election was authorized.

1993 Yitzhak Rabin of Israel and Yasser Arafat, PLO chairman, signed the Middle East peace accord.

The Battle of Quebec marks the day when the army led by General Wolfe defeated the forces led by General Montcalm. On this day in 1759, this battle between British and French troops became a turning point in Canadian history. This battle was not of tremendous historical importance, but its story has a moral to tell. In the end, both leaders were killed. And although one side defeated the other in battle, neither leader survived to celebrate victory or to suffer failure. That is not the normal course of events for a military encounter. We have always had some leaders who lead the way.

When the U.S. Congress, on this day in 1788, decided that the first national election would take place on the first Wednesday in January, 1789, they were mindful that many people would want to make speeches. So they gave each candidate plenty of time.

Today marks the anniversary of an historic meeting between Israeli Prime Minister Yitzak Rabin and PLO chairman Yasser Arafat. In 1993, these two leaders, whose peoples had been at war for nearly half a century, met in Washington, D.C., signed a peace accord, and shook hands. It took a remarkable diplomatic effort on both sides, as well as the United States, to bring the two together. Since that time there has still been terrorist violence between the two countries; Yitzak Rabin was killed by one of his own people who disagreed with the peace effort; and things haven't changed that much. But no effort toward peace—which generally implies a cessation of the killing of soldiers and other innocents—is unimportant.

14th.

1741 George Friedrich Handel completed *The Messiah*. (See August 22nd entry.)

1814 Francis Scott Key wrote "The Star Spangled Banner."

1849 Ivan Pavlov was born.

1883 Margaret Sanger was born

Very early in the morning on this day in 1814 at Baltimore Harbor, Francis Scott Key wrote the words to a song as he watched and waited to see whether the American flag was still flying. It was a signal that the United States had turned away the British invaders in the War of 1812. "Oh say can you see, by the dawn's early light," Francis Scott Key wrote, asking whether the flag was still there. When those lines were written, the British had burned government buildings and the White House in our nation's capital. Francis Scott Key wrote of the rockets' red glare and bombs bursting in air. If the British had succeeded in taking Baltimore, it would have been the end. Luckily, they didn't.

The German composer George Friedrich Handel had held his "farewell concert" in the spring of 1741. But somehow, toward the end of summer he was inspired to write another work. Many consider it to be his greatest achievement. He started writing on August 22nd, and finished on this day. Handel's *Messiah* wasn't given its first performance until the next spring, but this was the day that Handel himself sang a Hallelujah chorus.

Many reactions are the result of what we call conditioned reflexes. Some people's hearts beat faster when the flag goes marching by. Some people get hungry when they hear the dinner bell ring. Some products have a particular odor deliberately applied to trigger a craving or an appreciation. The scientist who pioneered the study of conditioned reflexes was Ivan Pavlov, born on this day in 1849 in Ryazan, Russia. Pavlov showed the world how a dog could be trained to react one way or another to two distinctly different stimuli.

Margaret Higgins Sanger, who was born on this day in 1883, was trained as a nurse. But she devoted her life to birth control, until her death in 1966. When Sanger began championing her cause, birth control was a dirty word. Contraceptive information was classified as obscene and censored by the post office. She was arrested on obscenity charges—although the case never went to trial. The dispute continued even after her death, but at least the issue was discussed with a freedom that had been previously denied. Thanks to Sanger's single-minded efforts, people can speak more freely today about birth control.

15th.

1867   William Howard Taft was born.

1890   Agatha Christie was born. (See November 25th entry.)

1917   Russia was proclaimed a republic by Alexander Kerensky. (See April 22nd and November 7th entries.)

Not too many people in U.S. history have been chosen to serve as President and as Chief Justice. William Howard Taft—who was born on this day in 1857, in Cincinnati—was President for four years and Chief Justice of the United States for nine years. He also headed a distinguished Ohio political family. Unlike many United States presidents, William Howard Taft has one unusual distinction. His words are rarely ever quotes. In fact, most of his printed quotes were judicial decisions.

One of the world's greatest mystery writers was born on this day in 1890. Agatha Christie was educated at home by her mother and spent her childhood growing up in the

Derbyshire countryside. She began writing detective stories while working as a nurse during the First World War. She continued honing her craft after the war as her first— and short-lived—marriage disintegrated. In 1920, she introduced the world to the Belgian detective Hercule Poirot in *The Mysterious Affair at Styles*. Later, her loyal fans were treated to the exploits of Miss Marple. It's certainly no mystery why her books sold over a hundred million copies in numerous languages. Yet in real life, the mystery of her short disappearance after the break up of her first marriage has never been solved.

Alexander Kerensky was an idealistic attorney in Czarist Russia who frequently defended revolutionary intellectuals accused of political offenses. He entered politics and championed concepts like freedom of speech, freedom of the press, the right of assembly, freedom to worship, universal suffrage, and equal rights for women. But unlike some of his clients and political peers, Kerensky supported Russian involvement in the First World War. In 1917, Kerensky urged the dissolution of the monarchy during the February Revolution. And on this day in that same year, Russia was proclaimed a republic by Alexander Kerensky after Czar Nicholas II abdicated his throne. Kerensky's dream came true. But it was short-lived. He was ousted during the October Revolution and Vladimir Lenin took his place as the voice of the people.

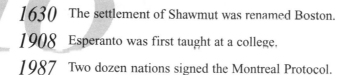

1630 The settlement of Shawmut was renamed Boston.

1908 Esperanto was first taught at a college.

1987 Two dozen nations signed the Montreal Protocol.

Many immigrants to the United States have chosen new names. On this day in 1630, a community of new arrivals did just that. The Massachusetts settlement of Shawmut changed its name to Boston, in honor of a town located in Devonshire, England. One wonders whether the language or the history of America would have been the same if Boston had remained Shawmut. Names—like other words—create mental images and impressions. Would we be remembering the Shawmut Massacre or the Shawmut Tea Party? Would Shawmut baked beans taste as sweet?

Many years ago, a language called Esperanto was devised to enable people around the world to speak to each other. On this day in 1908, Clark University—located in

Worcester, Massachusetts—initiated a course in the universal language of Esperanto. Who knows how long the course remained in the Clark curriculum? But Esperanto—though still alive—was not as widely accepted as its sponsors had hoped. English and French became common diplomatic languages in the decades that followed.

On this day in 1987, two dozen nations signed the Montreal Protocol. This agreement which was designed to save the earth's ozone layer by urging nations to curb harmful emissions.

17th.

1787   The U.S. Constitution was completed and signed. (See March 4th entry.)

1796   George Washington gave his farewell speech.

1920   The American Professional Football Association—a precursor of the NFL—was formed in Canton, Ohio. (See February 2nd entry.)

1939   Supreme Court Justice David H. Souter was born. (See October 2nd entry.)

1967   The television program *Mission Impossible* premiered.

1994   Heather Whitestone of Alabama became the first deaf woman to be crowned Miss America. (See September 8th entry)

Having lived through a number of presidential farewell addresses, it's difficult to understand one thing about George Washington's parting speech. The content is no problem. The puzzle is that he dated it September 17th, but never delivered it. Instead he published it on September 19th, 1796. So maybe today is its anniversary—and maybe not. We can assume it was on this day that he said, "Citizens by birth or choice of a common country, that country has a right to concentrate your affections." He also asked Americans to "Observe good faith and justice toward all nations. Cultivate peace and harmony with all."

It seems awfully appropriate that on this day in 1967, the program *Mission Impossible* premiered on television, Although no one has any intention of self-destructing in five seconds, many of us have had the opportunity to say: "This is your mission if you choose to accept it."

Today is Heather Whitestone's birthday. The name doesn't ring a bell? It was also on this day, in 1994, that Heather became the first deaf Miss America in the pageant's seventy-five-year history when she was crowned at age twenty-one, in Atlantic City. As a child, it took Heather six years just to learn how to pronounce her last name. How did she get so far in life? As she said in a finalist interview to pageant host Regis Philbin, "My good attitude helped me get through hard times and believe in myself."

18th.

1709   Samuel Johnson was born.

1793   George Washington laid the Capitol Building's cornerstone.

1851   *The New York Times* published its first issue.

1905   Greta Garbo was born.

1947   The Air Force was established as a separate branch of the military.

1977   Ted Turner won the America's Cup in his yacht *Courageous*. (See August 22nd entry.)

1983   George Meegan finished a six-year-long walk.

This is the anniversary of a very solemn and important event in our nation's history. In 1793, President George Washington placed the cornerstone on the Capitol Building in Washington, D.C. Unfortunately, the history books do not document what the President said on that momentous occasion. Yet, little needs to be said about the enormity of the event. It wasn't soon after that cornerstone was laid that the foundations of government were established on that same spot.

British author Samuel Johnson was born on this day in 1709. Doctor Johnson once criticized the poet Dryden by saying: "He delighted to tread upon the brink of meaning." One only wishes to be on the cutting edge of thought without teetering on the cliff of miscomprehension.

Greta Garbo was born on this date in 1905, in Stockholm, Sweden. Apart from her impressive screen performances, she was also famous for her constant search for solitude. "I want to be let alone," were supposedly Garbo's watchwords. But most of us are more curious and more social than the elusive Miss Garbo. In fact, most of us want to know everything that's going on around us. In the words of the motto of *The New York Times*, which published its first issue on this day in 1851, we want to know "all the news that's fit to print."

As a popular song commented, walk a mile in my shoes. But on this day in 1983, a British adventurer named George Meegan finished a 19,021-mile walk from the southernmost tip of South America to Prudhoe Bay, Alaska. It took him six years to reach his goal.

The Air Force joined the ranks of the Armed Forces on this day in 1947. Previously a division of the Army, air combat had played such a major role in the Second World War, it was decided that the time had come to recognize the importance of our defense strength in the skies above.

19th.

1777   The U.S. won the first Battle of Saratoga.

1796   George Washington published his farewell address. (See September 17th entry.)

1881   President James A. Garfield was assassinated.

1928   Adam West was born.

1934   Bruno Hauptmann was arrested.

1959   Nikita Khrushchev visited Los Angeles.

1983   St. Kitts and Nevis declared independence from England.

1984   Great Britain and China announced their agreement to transfer Hong Kong in 1997 to Chinese rule. (See December 19th entry.)

The man who masqueraded as television's mild mannered millionaire Bruce Wayne—and as Batman—was born in Walla Walla, Washington, on this day in 1928. Adam West was a star among an endless stream of famous co-stars and celebrities making cameo appearances. Burgess Meredith, Eartha Kitt, Sammy Davis, Jr., Cesar Romero, Frank Gorshen, and many other actors made appearances on this show which defined the term "camp" for most Americans.

This was a day of upsets and endings. On the same day that George Washington published his farewell address, the U.S. had won the first Battle of Saratoga, in 1777, which came as a great surprise to the better equipped British troops. President James A. Garfield was felled by an assassins bullet in 1881. Bruno Hauptman, a German carpenter, was arrested for the abduction and murder of Charles Lindbergh's baby, in one of the most highly-publicized kidnapping cases in the twentieth century. On a more pleasant note, the Caribbean island's of St. Kitts and Nevis bid England a fond farewell as they peacefully gained their independence on this day in 1983.

On this day in 1959, United States relations with the Soviet Union felt a slight strain. Soviet leader Nikita Khrushchev reportedly became furious during a visit to Los Angeles when he was informed that, for security reasons, he wouldn't be allowed to visit Disneyland.

20th.

1519 Portugese navigator Ferdinand Magellan set out from Spain to find a western passage to Indonesia's Spice Islands. (See November 28th entry.)

1884 The Equal Rights Party was formed.

1946 President Harry S Truman asked Secretary of Commerce Henry A. Wallace to resign.

1973 Billie Jean King beat Bobby Riggs.

Back in 1973, this was expected to be a very exciting day. Veteran tennis star Bobby Riggs was scheduled to play the outstanding woman player, Billie Jean King. It was touted as the battle of the sexes. Naturally, what the match proved was that a great young female champion could beat a once-great, over-the-hill male champion. Gender has little to do with ability, although nothing can eliminate the ravages of time.

In 1946, Secretary of Commerce Henry A. Wallace delivered an address on September 12th in which he strongly criticized America's policy toward Russia. Eight days later, on this date, President Harry S Truman reacted. He asked Wallace to resign.

There is nothing we can do, it's often been said, that has not been done before. There has been some conjecture recently that before long there might be a woman running for president. But it won't be a first. On this day in 1884 the Equal Rights Party was formed, and nominated Belva Ann Bennett Lockwood for president. Needless to say, she didn't win. But it was the first step.

21st.

The autumnal equinox generally occurs.

1866 H.G. Wells was born.

1897 The editorial entitled "Yes, Virginia, there is a Santa Claus," was published.

Although the autumnal equinox sometimes plays games with the calendar and autumn sneaks in a day late or a day early, this is the usual day for welcoming the new season. Besides signaling the advent of cool temperatures and blustering winds, autumn sports a brilliant palette of oranges, reds, and browns born from summer's pastel shades. And the autumn harvests remind us that it's time to stock up and prepare for the long winter that lay just ahead.

In 1897, an editorial was published in *The New York Sun* newspaper that has remained a Christmas tradition. On this day, an article entitled, "Yes, Virginia, there is a Santa Claus" first appeared.

One man is largely responsible for a Martian invasion, invisibility, and time travel. Science fiction writer H.G. Wells was born on this day in 1866, in Bromley, England. His works have thrilled generations of readers. Perhaps little that took place in *The War of the Worlds*, *The Invisible Man*, or *The Time Machine* will ever occur in real life, but his writings did contain elements of the Internet and other predictions which have subsequently come true. To quote Wells' time traveler, "You must follow me carefully. I shall have to controvert one or two ideas that are almost universally accepted."

22nd.

1776 Nathan Hale was hung. (See June 6th entry.)

1789 The U.S. Post Office was established. (See July 1st and November 1st entries.)

1981 The world's fastest train took its inaugural run.

The U.S. Post Office was established on this day in 1789. Delivering the mail in those years was an arduous and uncertain task. And things haven't gotten any easier today. In fact, as we computerize communications, we seem to have just as much trouble getting messages across on the Internet as our forefathers did with horse-driven technology.

The world's fastest train took its inaugural run from Paris to Lyons, France at 156 mph for three hundred miles on this day in 1981. Although that is far faster than passenger rail services in most parts of the world, it was soon antiquated by even speedier trains running the same routes. In 1990, France's TGV trains attained speeds of up to 186 mph, with estimates of up to 217 mph by the year 2000.

23rd.

1518 The Royal College of Physicians was established.

1642 Harvard University held its first commencement.

1779 John Paul Jones uttered his famous battle cry. (See July 6th entry.)

1846 Neptune was discovered by German astronomer Johann Gottfried Galle.

During the reign of Great Britain's King Henry VIII, the craft guilds were in flower. Each profession had its own local union, where apprentices learned their craft, journeymen refined their technique, and master craftsmen handed down their skills. From bootmakers to printers, every craft was protected by a chartered guild. In 1518, Henry VIII granted Thomas Linacre a guild charter to establish a guild of craftsman trained in the diagnosis and treatment of disease. The Royal College of Physicians was established to protect citizens from medical charlatans and quacks who often applied cures that were more fatal than the illness being treated. Barbers and surgeons soon followed, creating their own guild. But that's another story.

To commence something is to set forth or set out to do something in the world. And although a commencement ceremony celebrates the end of years of study and preparation, it also ushers in the beginning of a new life. The first American college commencement took place on this day in 1642. It wasn't the same kind of convocation ceremony that we are partial to these days. But for the new graduates of Harvard College, it was a great event.

It's amazing what you can do when you set your sights on the stars. On this day in 1846, German astronomer Johann Gottfried Galle discovered the planet Neptune. It wasn't the last celestial body to be observed, but Galle's discovery was momentous none the less. At the time, no one believed there were any planets after Uranus which had been discovered in 1781.

24th.

1755 John Marshall was born.

1896 F. Scott Fitzgerald was born.

1954 *The Tonight Show* premiered on television. (See October 23rd entry.)

1969 The Chicago Seven trial began. (See August 28th entry.)

1988 The first female Episcopal assistant bishop was ordained. (See February 11th and March 12th entries.)

1996 A treaty to end all testing and development of nuclear weapons was signed.

This is Chief Justice John Marshall's birthday. He was born in Midland, Virginia, on this day in 1755. "The people made the Constitution," Justice Marshall said in an 1821 decision, "and the people can unmake it. It is the creature of their own will, and lives only by their will."

It was more than a year after antiwar demonstrations erupted into a riot during the 1968 Democratic National Convention, that the demonstration leaders—the Chicago Seven—went on trial. On this day in 1969, defense attorney William Kunstler began his opening remarks.

One of the most essential pieces of advice ever given to any aspiring author is to write what you know: to choose subjects and characters from your own life and draw richness and depth from them. This is the birthday of F. Scott Fitzgerald. He was one author who became famous by following that wisdom. His novel, *The Great Gatsby*, was about a consummate 1920s playboy and about the reckless abandon of the Prohibition party scene. But the tale could have been a page out of F. Scott and Zelda Fitzgerald's social diary.

"I don't know what weapons will be used to fight the next world war," Albert Einstein is credited with saying, "but the one after that will be fought with sticks and stones." The world's major nuclear powers took a small step away from that possibility when they signed a treaty to end all testing and development of nuclear weapons on this day in 1996. This is an advance that Einstein—one of the creators of the atomic bomb—would have truly appreciated. He was an outspoken opponent of nuclear weapons from the start: "The discovery of nuclear chain reactions need not bring about the destruction of mankind any more than did the discovery of matches. We only must do everything in our power to safeguard against its abuse. Only a supranational organization, equipped with a sufficiently strong executive power, can protect us."

25th.

1513 Vasco Nuñez de Balboa discovered the Pacific Ocean.

1690 First American newspaper was published.

1789 Bill of Rights was submitted to the states.

1890 The U.S. Congress established Yosemite National Park. (See April 21st entry.)

1912 The Ford Motor Company instituted an 8-hour, 5-day work week.

1981 Sandra Day O'Connor became the first female Supreme Court Justice.

The Bill of Rights, which guarantees so many of our basic freedoms wasn't in the Constitution when the first Congress met, so the Congress did something about it. On this day in 1789, Congress sent each state twelve proposed Amendments to the Constitution. Ten of those amendments—known as the Bill of Rights—were ratified. From that moment on, Americans were assured freedoms not available in other lands by a government that pledged to defend their rights to that freedom.

The first American newspaper was a rather modest three-page publication entitled *Publick Occurrences, Both Foreign and Domestic*, which was published on this day in 1690 in Boston. It was never published again, because the Massachusetts Governor didn't like it. In those days what the Governor didn't like was neither published nor speechified.

Back in 1513, Spanish explorer Vasco Nuñez de Balboa and his crew were tracking through the thick hot jungle environment of the Isthmus of Panama. Like his predecessors, Balboa was searching for a passage to Asia and the riches of the New World. However, on this particular day, Balboa discovered a seemingly placid body of water. He stood in the shallows on the beach and, on behalf of the king, claimed the Pacific— meaning calm and quiet—Ocean for Spain.

Besides being a transportation pioneer, Henry Ford proved to be an innovator in business management as well. He adapted some of Eli Whitney's production concepts, like the assembly line and interchangeable parts. But on this day in 1912, Ford's motor company instituted something we can all appreciate—an eight-hour, five-day work week.

As far as what is worn under the robes, justice can be blind. But society, like the wheels of justice, grinds exceedingly slow. But the wheels do grind. A long-standing injustice came to an end on this date in 1981. Sandra Day O'Connor became the first female U.S. Supreme Court justice.

26th.

1774   Johnny Appleseed was born.

1815   The Act of the Holy Alliance was signed.

1898   George Gershwin was born. (See September 30th entry.)

1919   President Woodrow Wilson collapsed. (See December 28th entry.)

1960   The first Nixon-Kennedy debate was televised.

This was a very big day for the spoken word, back in 1960. The first televised Presidential debates were aired nationwide. Candidates John F. Kennedy and Richard M. Nixon started a trend in national election campaigns with their televised, face-to-face confrontation. The power of words and their delivery—not to mention a close shave—were never more dramatically illustrated. It became a common forum for presidential campaigns in the future, offering both voters a chance to contrast and compare the opinions of the candidates without media bias.

In 1919, on this day, President Woodrow Wilson collapsed. He had been on the road conducting a forty-date speaking tour. His mission was to garner the nation's support for the Treaty of Versailles. Unfortunately, he did not rally the people to accept the far-reaching, global nature of the treaty which would have involved the United States in the international political arena for the first time. It would take another world war and three more decades before Americans were convinced that they were not an isolated entity, but rather one of world's major hubs.

In the name of Christianity, many politically-directed activities have taken shape. The Crusades, the Spanish conquest of the Americas, and the European Inquisitions are just a few of those deeds. On this day in 1815, the Act of the Holy Alliance was signed by the Czar of Russia, the Emperor of Austro-Hungary, and the King of Prussia. The agreement stated that: "They will consider themselves as members of one and the same Christian nation." Gradually other Christian monarchs throughout Europe signed the act with the exception of two key figures: Great Britain's king and the pope himself.

When Jacob Gershowitz's parents bought a piano for his brother Ira, they quickly discovered that Jacob had a remarkable talent: he could listen to a song, then sit down in front of the keys and tentatively play it. Encouraged by his parents, Jacob took lessons. Born on this day in 1898, Jacob Gershowitz found a career in music under the name George Gershwin, and went on to write such masterpieces as *Rhapsody in Blue*, *An American in Paris*, and *Porgy and Bess*—an opera which was highly controversial when it opened, as it dealt with the issue of black poverty in the South. Though he passed away in 1937, his music continues to live.

Today marks the birth, in 1774, of a simple American icon. According to popular legend, John Chapman—better known as Johnny Appleseed—slung a sack of apple seeds over his shoulder and set out from his home in New York State. He headed for the frontier, planting trees which would not bear fruit for his consumption, but for anyone who might happen upon them in the future. Chapman gave saplings to the natives and new settlers. In addition to the apple trees and a coterie of medicinal herbs, he planted seeds of a different sort. He would sit under the shade of one of his trees, and invite passers by to join him while he read passages from the Bible and other books.

27th.

1722 Samuel Adams was born.

1825 The first locomotive to haul a passenger train was operated by George Stephenson in England.

1840 Thomas Nast was born. (See November 7th entry.)

It's Samuel Adams' birthday. He was a firebrand in his time: the leader of the Stamp Act resistance and a prime instigator of the Boston Tea Party. John Adams' second cousin from Boston was born in 1722. And one thing is certain. When Sam Adams spoke, things happened. Everyone should definitely bear in mind Sam Adams' injunction: "Let us contemplate our forefathers, and posterity, and resolve to maintain the rights bequeathed to us from the former, for the sake of the latter."

Every time you see the Democratic donkey or the Republican elephant, you are viewing the inspiration of the great political cartoonist, Thomas Nast, who flourished at the turn of the century. This was the day Thomas Nast was born, in 1840, in Germany. His family emigrated to America when he was six years old. Nast's creations—like The Tammany Tiger and Boss Tweed cartoons—did a great deal to harden public opinion against the corrupt Tammany Ring that controlled New York City politics during the late nineteenth century. Nast knew the power of images and used that power to tell stories that needed to be told to those who didn't necessarily understand the same language.

When, on this day in 1825, the first locomotive to haul a passenger train was operated by George Stephenson in England, there was more than passengers and cargo on board. The industrial future was there—perched atop the billowing stack—never once looking back at the agrarian past which was quickly enveloped by the thick coal smoke.

28th.

1066   William the Conqueror invaded England and claimed the English throne. (See October 14th entry.)

1820   Friedrich Engels was born.

1920   A grand jury indicted eight members of the Chicago White Sox. (See July 16th entry.)

1996   The U.S. House of Representatives passed legislation to reduce the number of illegal immigrants.

The reason why Karl Marx's name is known everywhere is largely because of a man who is relatively unknown. Friedrich Engels co-authored the Communist Manifesto along with Marx, and edited a considerable portion of Marx's writings. This German author was born on this day back in 1820.

What price could you place on your honor and reputation? It was on this day in 1920 that eight members of the Chicago White Sox were indicted in the infamous Black Sox scandal: charged with throwing the 1919 World Series in exchange for bribes. They received the money, but it cost them their right to play ball ever again. It cost them the victory they would surely have earned had they played the way they had all season. And worst of all, it stripped their fans of the heroes they'd idolized.

America may be the land of opportunity. But it seems that along with seizing an opportunity comes the desire to prevent any more newcomers from joining the competition. With few exceptions, we are a land of immigrants. Yet throughout our country's history, there has been discrimination against new arrivals by their predecessors. People emigrating from third-world countries are more likely to need public assistance, and it's been that way from the start. Thanksgiving itself is a symbol of gratitude to the Native Americans who supplied the first Pilgrims with food to survive their first winter. But with burgeoning welfare roles, overcrowded public schools, and expenses landing on the shoulders of taxpayers it's understandable that on this day in 1996, landmark legislation to reduce the number of illegal immigrants was passed in the U.S. House of Representatives as part of a federal-spending bill.

29th.

1899 U.S. Navy Admiral George Dewey received a hero's welcome in New York.

1923 Great Britain began ruling Palestine under a League of Nations mandate. (See June 29th and August 31st entries.)

1938 The Munich Agreement was signed.

This was a very festive day in 1899. New York City gave a hero's welcome to Admiral George Dewey on his return from the Spanish-American War. Dewey became famous for his historic naval victory at Manila Bay. He also became famous for saying to his flagship's captain, "You may fire when you are ready, Gridley." Nothing Dewey said later ever dimmed the flame of that one short sentence.

Four men met in Munich, Germany, on this day in 1938: British Prime Minister Neville Chamberlain, French Premier Edouard Daladier, Italian Premier Benito Mussolini and German Reichfuehrer Adolf Hitler. They negotiated and agreed to the partitioning of Czechoslovakia. Neville Chamberlain announced it was the beginning of "peace in our time." That peace—and Chamberlain's job—lasted less than a year.

30th.

1846   Ether was first used as an anesthetic. (See December 11th entry.)

1882   The first American hydroelectric plant opened in Appleton, Wisconsin. (See September 3rd entry.)

1935   *Porgy and Bess* premiered in Boston. (See September 26th entry.)

Ether was introduced as an anesthetic on this day in 1846 by dentist William Morton. It had a profound affect on those who encountered it. No one could stay awake to register a negative criticism. Yet many people appreciated it's ability to dull any negative reaction to an operative procedure.

One of the big hits in George Gershwin's musical *Porgy and Bess*—which premiered in Boston on this day in 1935—was a song entitled "It Ain't Necessarily So." A lot of things we assume fall in that category. They "ain't necessarily so." One thing is for sure, however. Gershwin's musical challenged the public's acceptance of segregation and poverty for African-Americans living in the southern states. And it opened the stage to a new theme for its musical productions—real life.

October

Right between the lazy days of summer and the chilly days of autumn, there's a time when the days are sunny and warm, but the nights are crisp and cool. It's called Indian Summer. The green leaves of summer begin to change their hue to yellow, orange, and burnt red; pumpkins and maize ripen in the fields. The name also serves to remind us of the days when Native Americans harvested nature's bountiful array of nuts, fruits, and vegetables; fished its clear running rivers for salmon and trout; hunted the herds of wild buffalo; and stalked the mountains for bear, moose, and deer. Nature had blessed these people with everything they needed just before the winter snows began to fall in Indian Summer. And the people respected and nurtured nature's gifts throughout the year in return.

1st.

1908 Henry Ford introduced the Model T. (See July 30th entry.)

1918 The Lost Battalion was trapped in the Argonne Forest.

1939 Winston Churchill made a mysterious forecast.

There was a famous American First World War fighting unit known as the Lost Battalion. It earned its name when trapped in the Argonne Forest of France—surrounded by the Germans—on this day in 1918. The unit members held out against unbelievable odds until they were rescued on October 8th.

On this day in 1908, Henry Ford introduced the Model T automobile, known affectionately as the Tin Lizzie. Model T manufacture employed assembly lines, interchangeable parts, and mass production—unlike its custom-built European counterparts such as the Mercedes and the Bugatti. Even though Ford borrowed some of his production methods from Eli Whitney and other inventors, he was the first to apply it to such a complex piece of machinery that appealed to so many people.

History records that on this date in 1939, Winston Churchill said, "I cannot forecast to you the action of Russia. It is a riddle wrapped in a mystery inside an enigma." Churchill was wise to admit that no crystal ball or logical progression could predict the future actions of something and someone over whom he exerted no control.

2nd.

1835 The first battle of the Texas Revolution took place as American settlers defeated a Mexican cavalry. (See March 2nd entry.)

1836 Charles Darwin returned to England. (See February 12th entry.)

1869 The Mahatma Mohandas K. Gandhi was born.

1890 Groucho Marx was born.

1990 The Senate confirmed the Supreme Court nomination of Justice David H. Souter. (See September 17th entry.)

Mohandas K. Gandhi was the great modern apostle of nonviolent civil disobedience. The Mahatma used those tactics to gain respect for East Indians living in South Africa. He used the same strategy to lead his native India to independence from British rule. Gandhi was born on this day in 1869. In a strange twist of fate, he himself met a violent death, in New Delhi, in 1948. But Mahatma Gandhi taught the world that if you speak peacefully and make sense, people will listen and will act on what you say.

Groucho Marx was legendary for his wit. Like other famous actors, Groucho listed different years for his birth at different times in his life. We are certain that he was born in Manhattan on this day, but we're not to sure if it was in 1890, 1891, 1889, never mind. It was Groucho who said once that he would never join any club that would accept him as a member. And as a matter of fact, he remained in a league all of his own.

3rd.

1789 Thanksgiving Day proclamations were made, 1789 and 1863.

1876 Johns Hopkins University opened.

1925 Gore Vidal was born.

It's a little early for Thanksgiving, but this day has a very clear connection with that occasion. In 1789, President George Washington proclaimed the first national Thanksgiving Day. It was to be observed on November 26th in honor of the adoption of the U.S. Constitution. On the same day in 1863, President Abraham Lincoln designated the last Thursday in November as Thanksgiving Day. It's because of the proclamations made by Washington and Lincoln that we have come to cherish a great American tradition by gathering with friends and family to partake of a feast.

There isn't a university in this country whose name is misstated more often than Johns Hopkins. This institute of higher learning opened in Baltimore on this day in 1876. There's a story about a distinguished Johns Hopkins University president who was asked to speak in Pittsburgh. He was introduced most generously and graciously as the President of John Hopkins University. That's the usual error—no "s" in the first word, which is Johns, not John. So he thanked the gentleman who had introduced him. As he started his speech he commented how happy he was to be in "Pittburgh."

Author Gore Vidal was born on this day in 1925. He commented once in an interview that "Literature takes a skill beyond just listening. You have to be able to take a line of prose . . . and become as one with the other end of that prose. A great writer can do that for you, and a great reader can do that for any writer."

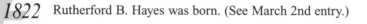

1822   Rutherford B. Hayes was born. (See March 2nd entry.)

1853   Turkey declared war on Russia. (See October 25th entry.)

1957   The *Sputnik* satellite orbited the earth.

1958   Transatlantic jet plane service began.

On this date in 1957, the Russians launched the first *Sputnik* satellite into orbit around the earth. It was a startling scientific achievement. The event jolted the United States into an all-out effort to expand its limited space technology.

A British airline company put the first transatlantic passenger jet service into operation on this day in 1958. It's interesting that it took longer to launch that service than to put a satellite into orbit. It's similar to the answer Walter Pitkin—the author of *Life Begins at 40*—gave when asked about the difference between a two-hundred-word article and a fifteen-hundred-word article on the same subject. He simply replied, "the fifteen-hundred-word article you can have tomorrow; the two-hundred-word one will take a week." An article's length is not necessarily a measure of its difficulty. The merits of brevity far outdo the vice of empty glibness.

Most wars end with a settlement of the conflicts that ignited them. Today marks the start of a war which ended in a stalemate. On this day in 1853, Turkey declared war on Russia. The discord had erupted over who had ultimate control of the Near East— particularly the Crimean Peninsula. Russia, an orthodox Christian empire, demanded its right to protect Christian subjects living in the Islamic Ottoman-Turkish empire. The declaration soon exploded into an international free-for-all. Russia had been arguing with France over the control of certain holy places in Palestine. So, France sided with Turkey. Great Britain was determined to gain control of the Suez Canal which was also in the Ottoman Empire. It sided with Turkey. Russia's long-time ally, Austro-Hungary, just wanted to be on the winning side. It sided with Turkey. In the end, thousands of lives were lost and no one won the Crimean War. One nation, however, lost more than soldiers' lives. Austro-Hungary lost Russia's much-needed military and financial support when the war ended.

5th.

1830 President Chester Alan Arthur was born.

1944 President Franklin Delano Roosevelt spoke about world peace.

1947 The first presidential television broadcast was made from the White House.

1981 Raoul Wallenberg was granted honorary U.S. citizenship.

Back on this day, in 1947, Harry S Truman became the first U.S. President to televise a speech from the White House. There weren't too many television sets yet, and the President's speech was not the hit of the week. He was asking the nation to observe meatless Tuesdays, eggless-and-chickenless Thursdays, and to eat one less slice of bread daily for the sake of providing food for postwar Europe. But the public responded favorably. It would be nice to believe it was because President Franklin D. Roosevelt had made a speech on this same day, in 1944, in which he said: "We owe it to our posterity, we owe it to our heritage of freedom, we owe it to our god, to devote the rest of our lives and all our capabilities to the building of a solid, durable structure of world peace."

In 1880, Chester Alan Arthur was placed on the Republican presidential ticket with James A. Garfield as a sop to the old-line spoils-minded party wing. When President Garfield was assassinated, everyone thought a crass political phase was automatically going to follow. But President Arthur turned out to be something else again. He prosecuted dishonest officials; secured the passage of the Civil Service Act; and did what historians generally regard as a good job. Chester Alan Arthur was born on this day, in 1830, in Fairfield, Vermont. His story reminds us that you can't simply apply past performance as a basis for future deeds.

The United States has rarely granted individuals honorary citizenship. And on this day in 1981, the nation awarded this rare honor for the second time in its history to former Swedish diplomat Raoul Wallenberg. During the Second World War, Wallenberg was credited with saving thousands of Hungarian-Jewish lives by issuing them Swedish identification papers in Nazi-occupied Hungary. The award was posthumously given to this courageous war-hero who disappeared in 1945. Because he was living in Hungary when Soviet troops overtook Nazi forces, he was arrested by Stalinist officials and vanished into the Soviet prison system.

6th.

1889 Thomas Edison showed his first motion pictures.

1927 Al Jolson spoke in *The Jazz Singer*.

1994 Michael Jordan announced his retirement from professional basketball to play professional baseball. (See February 17th entry.)

Today is a double-feature anniversary. In 1889, inventor Thomas Edison showed his first motion pictures in West Orange, New Jersey. And thirty-eight years later, in 1927, singer/actor Al Jolson spoke in the first "talkie"—*The Jazz Singer* which premiered in New York City. We learned to see—via the camera and film—before we learned to speak on celluloid.

7th.

1826 The first gravity-powered railroad went into operation.

1849 James Whitcomb Riley was born. (See August 5th entry.)

1881 Great Britain's Prime Minister William Gladstone commented on civilization's resources.

1954 Marian Anderson became the first African-American opera singer to join New York's Metropolitan opera.

Today is the birthday of the first American railroad. In 1826, the Granite Railway—powered by a horse and the force of gravity—began operation. It ran from Quincy to Milton, Massachusetts, carrying granite rock down to the waterfront.

The Hoosier poet James Whitcomb Riley was born on this day in 1849, in Greenfield, Indiana. He was *Little Orphan Annie*'s creator and warned that the goblins'll get you if you don't watch out. It is a nice suspense-filled touch to put the blame on unidentified goblins; but remember that Pogo's creator Walt Kelly pointed the finger a lot closer to home. "We have met the enemy," Pogo said, "and he is us."

Back on this date in 1881, British politician William E. Gladstone made a sweeping statement. He stood up in Parliament and said, "The resources of civilization are not yet exhausted." This was obviously not a prophecy.

You may not be familiar with Marion Anderson, but she opened a stage door on this day in 1954, and changed the face of opera, much to the delight of opera fans around the world. As the first African-American to join New York's Metropolitan Opera, Anderson must have had plenty of butterflies in her stomach when she made her debut. But her phenomenal vocal ability quickly won audiences.

8th.

1838   John Hay was born.

1871   The Great Chicago Fire started. (Celebrated as the start of Fire Prevention Week)

1941   The Reverend Jesse Jackson was born.

Let us pause for a moment to remember Mrs. O'Leary's cow. That bovine supposedly kicked over a lantern in the O'Leary barn on this day in 1871, and started the Great Chicago Fire. In sixteen hours, 3.5 squares miles of that growing city was razed to the ground.

John Hay combined a distinguished diplomatic career with an equally distinguished career as a poet and author. Since he was born on this day in 1838, We are reminded of some of his more famous maxims. For example, he once wrote: "Who would succeed in the world should be wise in the use of his pronouns. Utter the you twenty times where you once utter the I." He wrote something else which is very good advice for anyone tempted to stay too long at the fair. "True luck," he said, "consists not in holding the best of the cards at the table; luckiest is he who knows just when to rise and go home."

America's first African-American presidential candidate was born in Greenville, South Carolina on this day in 1941. During the 1960s civil-rights movement, Jesse Jackson was asked by the Reverend Dr. Martin Luther King, Jr. to head the Chicago branch of the Southern Christian Leadership Council's economic arm—Operation Breadbasket. Jackson quickly became the project's national director. He had convinced African-American businesses to supply employment for young people and to feature African-American products in key neighborhoods. In 1968, Jackson was ordained as a Baptist minister at the Chicago Theological Seminary. And three years later, Jackson headed Operation PUSH which was dedicated to combating racism, and promoting scholarship and hard work among youth. In 1983, he became the nation's first African-American Presidential candidate; and although he didn't win the election, Jackson made his point to the entire world.

9th.

1000 AD Leif Erikson landed in North America.

1701 Yale University was chartered.

1940 John Lennon was born.

Today is Leif Erikson Day. This anniversay commemorates the supposed landing of the Viking explorer on the North American mainland near Newfoundland in 1000 AD. Erikson and his party didn't stay for long, instead they set sail for the more hospitable climbs of the Greenland coast.

This is the day when, in 1701, the Collegiate School of Connecticut was chartered. This institution of higher learning was later named Yale University. This institution has turned out some of America's greatest leaders—and turned down some of America's great leaders as well. That's the hazard of any selection system. Yale's motto speaks of "light and truth." Yet, each of us sees the truth in our own light.

Today is John Lennon's birthday. The boy who grew up to become a member of the rock band, the Beatles, was born in Liverpool in 1940. In honor of his all-too-short life, we should take a moment to imagine; to imagine where his life would have taken him were he alive today. Before he died, he had been devoting more and more time and energy to a number of worthy causes, using the fame and influence he'd accumulated in music toward a hope of world peace. You might say he was a dreamer, but he wasn't the only one.

10th.

1813 Giuseppe Verdi was born.

1865 John Hyatts patented the billiard ball.

1886 The tuxedo was born.

1955 David Lee Roth was born.

Some of you may not know that the original tuxedo jacket was midnight blue—not jet black. And you probably don't know that this formal attire was named after an actual place. Back in 1886, on this date, an autumn ball was held at a very elite retreat known as Tuxedo Park, New York. Some of the male guests wore a new type of dinner jacket. Unlike some garments that have been named after their first wearer, the garment eventually took its nickname from this elegant setting.

Today is Giuseppe Verdi's birthday. In 1813, this operatic composer was born in Le Roncole, Italy. Even if you are unfamiliar with the opera *Aida*, you have to be impressed by this composer's lyrical name alone. But would you be equally amused by his name's English translation? Somehow, a Joseph Green opera doesn't sound quite the same.

Today is the day inventor John Hyatts patented the billiard ball in 1865. A few of us have felt we've been standing behind one of Mr. Hyatts' inventions for sometime now. But incidentally, today is also singer David Lee Roth's birthday. And honor of that event we should follow the lyrics of one of his hits and "go ahead and jump."

11th.

1521 Great Britain's King Henry VIII denounced Martin Luther's teachings.

1779 Brigadier General Casimir Pulaski died. (General Pulaski Memorial Day)

1884 Eleanor Roosevelt was born.

1932 The Democratic National Committee sponsored a television program.

1962 Pope John XXIII's Ecumenical Council convened. (See January 25th entry.)

Casimir Pulaski was a hero in the fight for Polish independence before he came to the United States in 1777. Two years later, Pulaski led a charge against British forces in Savannah, Georgia. He was mortally wounded and died two days later. Today is General Pulaski Memorial Day which commemorates the passing of Brigadier General Casimir Pulaski.

Eleanor Roosevelt elevated the role of First Lady to a stature on par with that of the Commander in Chief. And she became the only First Lady to be honored with her own statue at a presidential memorial. Anna Eleanor Roosevelt was born on this day in 1884 in New York City. She was President Theodore Roosevelt's niece, and had married her cousin, Franklin Delano Roosevelt. Throughout her life, she was an awkward public speaker. But the courage of her convictions and her undeniable determination to succeed won public attention for both civil and human rights at home and abroad even when she was eventually appointed as an ambassador to the Untied Nations.

Christianity's defenders often made strange bedfellows in history's final analysis. Great Britain's King Henry VIII publicly denounced the teachings of Martin Luther in a book entitled, *Assertion of the Sacraments*. On this day in 1521, King Henry presented a published copy to Pope Leo X. But the king's printed reprisal of Martin Luther's teachings didn't stop Cambridge University scholars and British printing presses from spreading the Protestant founder's word. The moral of this story comes from an old adage: People who live in glass houses shouldn't throw stones.

The first political telecast took place on this exact day in 1923. Sponsored by the Democratic National Committee, it was broadcast from New York. Few people were able to receive or view that program, but it was the beginning of a relationship that proliferates today. Paid announcements and programs are as much a part of political campaigns as the whistle-stop tours of long ago. As every politician knows, you have to be seen by the people to be elected by the people.

12th.

1492   Christopher Columbus discovered the New World.

1917   Lions International was founded.

1933   Alcatraz became a federal prison. (See August 11th entry.)

1960   Soviet Premier Nikita Khrushchev disrupted a United Nations General Assembly session. (See April 17th entry.)

Christopher Columbus arrived in the Bahamas on this day in 1492, so you might logically suppose that this would be Columbus Day. It used to be that simple, but it isn't anymore. Columbus Day is now observed on the second Monday of October. It is customary, on Columbus Day, to salute Columbus' Italian heritage; to spare a fond memory for Queen Isabella of Spain who financed his exploration for a new route to India; and perhaps to sympathize with the Native Americans who were perfectly happy until Columbus landed.

For some reason, our fraternal organizations seem to adopt animal names like the Moose, Golden Eagles, and Elks. In fact, on this very day in 1917, the Lions International was founded in Dallas, Texas.

13th.

1775 The U.S. Naval Fleet was authorized.

1792 President George Washington laid the cornerstone of the Executive Mansion.

1860 The first aerial photograph was taken.

1925 Lady Margaret Thatcher was born. (See February 11th entry.)

Some people lay down cornerstones for others to build upon. On this day in 1792, President George Washington laid the cornerstone of the Executive Mansion in Washington, D.C. He started the project, but he wasn't around to see it completed. He died in 1799. John Adams became the mansion's first resident in 1800.

The United States Navy was officially authorized on this day in 1775. The first fleet consisted of a handful of sailing ships as our sole sea-going line of defense. In the centuries that have followed, we have expanded our naval might to include aircraft carriers, nuclear-powered submarines, and any number of transport freighters. All great nations have been measured by the size of their naval fleet from Great Britain and Spain in the past to our own U.S. Navy.

You might say that the concept of looking at the big picture began on this day. In 1860, the first aerial photo was taken in the United States from a hot air balloon floating over Boston, Massachusetts.

14th.

1066 The Battle of Hastings took place.

1644 William Penn was born.

1890 President Dwight D. Eisenhower was born.

1947 U.S. Air Force Captain Chuck Yeager became the first person to fly faster than the speed of sound as he tested a rocket-powered research plane.

1964 The Reverend Dr. Martin Luther King, Jr. won the Nobel Peace Prize for his work in promoting human rights.

1986 Elie Wiesel won the Nobel Peace Prize for his work in promoting human rights.

In 1890, Dwight D. Eisenhower—military leader and the thirty-fourth U.S. President—was born on this day. Ike was not regarded as an outstanding public speaker, but he spoke in eloquent terms at Columbia University's Bicentennial Celebration in 1964. He referred to "the revolutionary doctrine of the divine rights of the common man." That statement cannot be improved upon as the idyllic definition of modern American life.

Today is William Penn's birthday. Pennsylvania's founder was born in London, England, in 1644. When he arrived in the colonies, Penn made peace with the Native Americans; established a tradition of brotherhood and decency; and built Philadelphia—The City of Brotherly Love. Ironically, after he returned to England, the people who supervised his colony didn't do a very good job. As a matter of fact, Penn went to debtor's prison for a while. History tells us that he was about to sell Pennsylvania when he suffered a stroke.

One of history's turning points occurred on this day. It was the start of the Norman Conquest of the British Isles. In 1066, William the Conqueror defeated the Anglo-Saxons at the Battle of Hastings. The conquest was aided by conflicts among the Anglo-Saxons themselves, but this confrontation sealed their fate. The Normans' true conquest of Britain took many more years as words and traditions blended together, ultimately creating a rich heritage.

Two noble heroes in the fight for human and civil rights were honored on this day when they received the Nobel Peace Prize. In 1964, The Reverend Dr. Martin Luther King,

Jr., received this coveted award for his work in championing African-American civil rights. And in 1986, Romanian-American activist Elie Wiesel won the award for internationally promoting human rights.

Today is the anniversary of a landmark in aviation history. In 1947, test pilot Chuck Yeager flew an X-1 rocket plane into the history books as the first man to break the sound barrier. Yeager didn't stop there, he kept seeking higher heights and loftier barriers for many more years. But on this day, Yeager reached the edge of the unlimited frontier open up above him and he got a glimpse of heaven.

15th.

1881 P.G. Wodehouse was born.

1928 The *Graf Zeppelin* made the first commercial transatlantic flight.

1965 First draft card was burned.

Author P.G. Wodehouse was a nonagenarian when he died in the 1970s. He was born on this day in 1881, in an England that passed away when he was still young. Scatterbrained Lords like Bertie and impeccable butlers like Jeeves disappeared from Wodehouse's world during the Second World War. Yet the innocent, civilized universe he created continues to entertain millions of readers.

You may not know it, but today is the anniversary of the day in 1928 when the *Graf Zeppelin*, a predecessor of the infamous *Hindenburg*, made the first commercial transatlantic air flight. For passenger travel, the airships were a luxurious marvel. But for transoceanic communications, it meant that documents could cross the ocean in three days, instead of the seven or eight it took by ship. It may not seem very fast by our modern standards, but the *Graf Zeppelin* set a record in its day.

It was on this very day, in 1965, that the first draft card was burned in protest of the United States' escalating military involvement in Vietnam. And on this same day in 1969, those flames of protest swept across the nation in the form of demonstrations and a candlelight vigil outside the White House. Freedom of speech and the freedom to assemble are both guaranteed by our own Constitution. So even though many Americans did not agree with the government's foreign and military policies, they continued to exercise their rights to publicly express their opinions.

16th.

1758   Noah Webster was born.

1854   Oscar Wilde was born. (See January 3rd entry.)

1859   Abolitionist John Brown staged a raid on the U.S. arsenal at Harper's Ferry, Virginia. (See May 9th entry.)

Today is a good time to think about the meanings of the words we write and speak because it's Noah Webster's birthday. Noah—the unabridged—Webster of dictionary fame was born in 1758 in West Hartford, Connecticut. Thanks to him, not one of us is ever at a complete loss for words or a definition.

Oscar Fingall O'Flahertie Wilde may have been the most adept wordsmith of the English language. Born on this day in 1854, Wilde was not only a great playwright; he also authored a few notable epigrams and pithy sayings. If he had been born in 1954, he would have been publicly honored and lionized in the publishing world. But Oscar Wilde was born out of his time. In his novel *The Picture of Dorian Gray*, Wilde wrote that "the only way to get rid of a temptation is to yield to it." His refusal to abide by society's sexual standards brought him vilification, persecution, and eventual infamy.

17th.

1933   Albert Einstein emigrated to the U.S. (See March 14th entry.)

1973   A group of Arab nations started an oil boycott. (See March 13 entry.)

1979   Mother Teresa was awarded the Nobel Peace Prize for her work with the destitute of Calcutta over three decades.

On this date in 1973, the western hemisphere woke up to a critical energy shortage when the oil-producing Arab states imposed a boycott. We've been looking for ways to conserve our own oil resources and find new energy alternatives ever since.

It has been said that there is no greater charity than to give selflessly to those who have no means to repay. Compassion and charity are particularly appropriate topics for today, as this is the anniversary of the day, in 1979, when Mother Theresa received the Nobel Peace Prize in recognition of her three decades of work with Calcutta's most destitute citizens.

18th.

1648 First American labor organization was founded.

1767 The Mason-Dixon Line was established.

1867 The U.S. officially took ownership of the Alaska territory. (See March 30th entry.)

The Mason-Dixon Line was officially adopted on this day. In 1767, the border between Maryland and Pennsylvania became the border between the northern states and the southern states and it's been that way ever since.

Both trade associations and labor unions have their roots in the medieval guilds. On this day, in 1648, Boston's shoemakers, barrelmakers, and tubmakers were given official permission to set up their own guild. They eventually went their separate ways when they no longer shared a common cause. We tend to forget what all crafts-people have in common, emphasizing only their differences. Newscaster Eric Sevareid sometimes used to stress the common interest. He pointed out that when two people are sitting in a boat, it doesn't make much sense for one of them to point an accusing finger at the other and say, "Your end of the boat is sinking."

19th.

1605 Sir Thomas Browne was born.

1781 Lord Cornwallis surrendered at Yorktown, Virginia.

1936 Journalist H.R. Ekins completed an around the world flight in 18.5 days.

Today marks the anniversary of Lord Cornwallis' surrender at Yorktown, Virginia. This event, in 1781, actually ended the American Revolutionary War.

When H.R. Ekins—a reporter for *The New York World Telegram*—completed an around-the-world airline trip in 18.5 days on this day in 1936, his story made headlines all over the world. It was especially newsworthy because he beat two other competing journalists to both the finish line and the scoop.

This is the birthday of the seventeenth-century physician and writer, Sir Thomas Browne, who was born in London in 1605. His name is not very well known today, but some of his thoughts and phrases are immortal. It was Thomas Browne who wrote, "There is no road or ready way to virtue," and "Charity begins at home." Another of Sir Thomas Browne's observations was that "The whole world was made for man."

20th.

1792   George Washington wrote about religious differences.

1867   Benjamin Disraeli wrote about change.

1944   General Douglas MacArthur stepped ashore at Leyte, in the Philippines. (See January 9th entry.)

1973   The "Saturday night massacre" occurred in Washington, D.C.

While writing a letter about this time of year in 1792, President George Washington made some observations about the causes of the world's troubles, and came to a decisive conclusion. "Of all the animosities which have existed among mankind," he wrote, "those which are caused by a difference of sentiments in religion appear to be the most inveterate and distressing, and ought to be deprecated."

British Prime Minister Benjamin Disraeli lived in a time of whirlwind changes. And a lot of people were afraid of them. Back in 1867, as the late October landscape showed its seasonal alterations, Disraeli commented that "Change is inevitable in a progressive country. Change is constant." That is the eternal contradiction: Change is constant.

In 1973, the "Saturday night massacre" took place at the White House. This may seem a rather lurid description, but it's not far from wrong. On that Saturday night, President

Richard Nixon fired the special Watergate prosecutor Archibald Cox, Attorney General Elliot Richardson, and Deputy Attorney General William D. Ruckelshaus. To many people it signaled the beginning of President Nixon's end. Everything went downhill from then until he resigned.

21st.

Whale Watching Week.

1833 Alfred Nobel was born. (See December 10th entry.)

1879 Thomas A. Edison demonstrated the incandescent electric lamp.

1920 Timothy Leary was born.

A number of years ago, the Honolulu-based First Society of Whale Watchers ordained this day as the start of International Whale Watching Week. We have learned much about whales since that first week. The fact that whales migrate in herds and communicate with each other through a language of echoing sounds. We have discovered numerous types of whales from Wright whales and gray whales to the mysterious, single-horned Narwhals and pale-gray Beluga whales. Yet we have still to understand how we can live in harmony with these huge, but gentle giants of the sea.

Alfred Nobel was born on this day in 1833, in Stockholm, Sweden. He made his fortune as an inventor and manufacturer of high explosives and detonators. When he died, he left his fortune for the establishment of the Nobel Prizes for the advancement of the peaceful arts and sciences, including the fine art of peace itself.

Today is Edison Lamp Day, the day that Thomas A. Edison demonstrated the incandescent electric lamp in 1879. And less than a half century later on this day, a controversial figure who also believed in turning things on was born. It's also Timothy Leary's birthday. The psychologist who coined the beat generation mantra, "Tune in, turn on, and drop out," was born in 1920.

22*nd.*

1746   Princeton University was chartered. (See February 13th, October 3rd, and October 9th entries.)

1797   André Garnerin demonstrated the parachute.

1918   The Great Influenza Epidemic began.

André J. Garnerin is not one of those names that rings bells. Not even his French countrymen and women have him enshrined in their hearts. But on this day, in 1797, André Garnerin gave the first public demonstration of his invention: the parachute. He jumped from a balloon to show how his creation worked. And luckily, it did work. The parachute was originally designed to enable people to escape from the early balloons during an emergency, and to land safely. But since that day, it's saved the lives of pilots manning single-engine, double-engine, jet-propelled, and turbine-propelled aircraft. It's inspired extreme sports enthusiasts to risk their lives by jumping off high mountain cliffs with nothing more than a parachute. And it's provided skysurfers with the ideal means to keep them and their surfboards afloat in the clouds.

At this time, in 1918, a worldwide influenza epidemic went on a rampage. During the First World War, over eighteen million people died from the flu virus—not from guns or grenades. For years afterward, we patted ourselves on the back. We thought that medical science had found a way to diffuse microscopic bombs like influenza. Then, as you may recall, in the 1970s, the U.S. government instituted a nationwide swine flu vaccination program. It reduced fatalities, but there was some question about the vaccine's harmful effects. And in the early 1990s, another influenza epidemic swept through the U.S. so severely that it reduced our national average life expectancy by a few points.

23*rd.*

The swallows leave San Juan Capistrano. (See March 19th entry.)

1925   Johnny Carson was born.

Although Nebraska claims him as a native son—and he has returned that compliment—the fact is Johnny Carson was born in Corning, Iowa, on this day in 1925. He grew up in Nebraska and aged gracefully in the nation's bedrooms as the host of television's *Tonight Show.*

24th.

National Popcorn Week. (See February 22nd entry.)

1931 The George Washington Bridge opened.

1945 The United Nations' charter was adopted. (celebrated as United Nations Day) (See January 1st, January 9th, April 25th, and June 26th entries.)

For reasons best known to popcorn manufacturers, the last week of October was designated as National Popcorn Week. Popcorn is an American legacy and National Popcorn Week is literally an event you can take with a few grains of salt. But today is also United Nations Day, which marks the U.N. Charter's adoption in 1945. Adlai Stevenson remarked on United Nations Day in 1963, that "The journey of a thousand leagues, we say, begins with a single step. So we must never neglect any work of peace that is within our reach, however small." Stevenson then added that "Our efforts will be erratic, and the world will remain a dangerous place to live." And the world's activities continue to pop right before our very eyes.

A wonderful event took place on this day in 1931. An event that alleviated the traffic crush on rush-hour traffic crossing the Hudson River to Manhattan. The George Washington Bridge opened, with four lanes going each way on two levels. That was an enormous amount of space. Of course, it didn't take long for commuters to fill those lanes.

25th.

St. Crispin's Day.

1854 The charge of the Light Brigade took place. (See October 4th entry.)

Today is the feast day of St. Crispin, the patron saint of shoemakers. Since more of us are working out daily in running shoes and crosstrainers; rediscovering nature in our hiking boots; and scaling walls and cliffs in climbing shoes, there ought to be a major resurgence of festivities honoring this guardian of the footwear manufacturers who protect our feet from bruises, bunions, and blisters.

In 1854 on this day, the doomed British Light Brigade charged into the valley of death. It's a lot easier to quote Tennyson's poem than to remember the details of the Crimean War's Battle of Balaklava. We remember lines like "Theirs not to make reply, / Theirs not to reason why, / Theirs but to do and die."

26th.

1785   The first jackasses arrived in America.

1881   A shoot-out took place at the O.K. Corral.

1947   Hillary Rodham Clinton was born.

1955   The U.S. Air Force officially reported that there were no such things as flying saucers.

Every now and then, history turns up an anniversary that has not had its proper due. Today is such a day. In 1785, we are told, two jackasses arrived in Boston Harbor from Spain. These were not ordinary jackasses. They were a gift from the King of Spain to President George Washington. They were sent to the fledgling nation so they could be mated with mares to produce America's first native mules.

On this day, in 1955, the U.S. Air Force officially proclaimed that flying saucers were nothing more than delusions and myths. But the public went right on seeing flying saucers and describing visits with mysterious space creatures. It takes more than an official denial to defeat the power of folklore. From the days of dragons to flying saucers, history has shown us that people believe what they want to believe. And no amount of official documentation will ever make them see anything different.

Today is First Lady Hillary Rodham Clinton's birthday. It might come as a surprise that in most other nations—including our northern neighbor, Canada—the spotlight doesn't fall on elected officials' spouses. Polls which include questions about leaders' wives are as American as the phenomenon of First Ladies publicly influencing government policy. This is hardly new. George Washington, John Adams, James Madison, and Franklin D. Roosevelt—to name just a few—all had strong partners working with them in the White House. Eleanor Roosevelt even became a United Nations ambassador after she left office. Born on this day, in 1947, Hillary Rodham Clinton has joined a long and distinguished list of truly American heroines.

The infamous shoot-out at the O.K. Corral took place on this day in 1881. It's a rather romantic notion: a high-noon shoot-out between Sheriff Wyatt Earp—accompanied by his two brothers, and Doc Holliday—and members of the Ike Clanton gang. But in reality, this bloody incident in Tombstone, Arizona, left three men dead and two more ravaged by gunshot wounds. If that incident were replayed today, law enforcement officials might have captured the Clanton gang without firing a shot. And they'd all be serving sentences for weapons possession, conspiring to commit manslaughter, as well as their previous felonies.

27th.

1858 President Theodore Roosevelt was born. (See August 22nd entry.)

1914 Dylan Thomas was born.

1938 DuPont announced the invention of nylon.

1939 John Cleese was born.

1975 Menachim Begin and Anwar al-Sadat won the Nobel Peace Prize. (See November 11th entry.)

Theodore Roosevelt—who was born in New York City on this day in 1858—exemplified his own policy. He spoke softly and carried a big stick. As Governor of New York, he was a trust-busting, anti-corruption crusader. He was so hated by political bosses, they persuaded him to run for the vice-presidency just to get rid of him. President McKinley was assassinated six months after the 1900 election and Roosevelt found himself in the White House. As U.S. President, big business found him to be a tough opponent and nature conservationists discovered that he was their strongest advocate. Good people can't be kept down and good causes can't be swept under the rug. And as Teddy himself might have said "Bully for the honest man."

Dylan Thomas is best remembered for the lines, "Do not go gentle into that good night, / Old age should burn and rave at close of day; / Rage, rage against the dying of the light." Born on this day in 1914, in Carmarthenshire, Wales, Dylan Thomas' words inspire us to ask why so many people are willing to "go gentle into that good night" of old age without lifting a finger to improve their quality of life.

Today is British comedian John Cleese's birthday. So let's talk a bit about his strife. No, wife. No, life. He was born on this day in 1939. In England, of course, you silly people. Pay attention. He wrote and performed with Monty Python's Flying Circus. So to celebrate this gentleman's terrific talent, we should now go on to something completely different.

You could say the fabric of life changed on this day in 1938. Dupont Chemical Company research teams based in New York and London and led by Dr. Wallace Carothers, introduced a new fiber. Named for the two international cities that cooperated in bringing this synthetic into existence, nylon—which stands for New York and London—was born. Stretching far beyond hosiery and leisure suits, nylon and its successors have found their way into our daily lives in a myriad of ways.

28th.

The feast day of St. Jude.

1813 Thomas Jefferson wrote about natural aristocracy.

1886 Statue of Liberty was dedicated. (See June 19th entry.)

1919 The U.S. Congress overrode President Wilson's veto and enacted the Volstead Prohibition Act.

Today is the feast day of St. Jude, the patron saint of the impossible. You've seen those classified ads thanking this saint for helping them through trying times. In the Bible, Matthew (13:55) describes Saint Jude as the "brethren" of Jesus. In the Hebrew language, the word "brethren" indicates a near relationship. During his lifetime he traveled throughout Mesopotamia preaching and converting the willing to Christianity. He died a martyr's death, and his body now rests in the Vatican.

Writing to his friend and colleague John Adams on this date in 1813, Thomas Jefferson had a few kind words to say about the aristocracy. "I agree with you," he wrote, "that there is a natural aristocracy among men. The grounds of this are virtue and talents." More important than what he said, is what he did not say. Jefferson did not associate aristocracy with lineage, birthright, and wealth. He did not attribute it to certain groups, but to all men with virtue and talents.

Today marks the anniversary of a day when the U.S. Congress put politics ahead of government. On this day in 1919, Congress overrode President Wilson's veto and enacted the Volstead Prohibition Act. The law lasted eight years. What it proved was not only that an unpopular law would be rebelled against, but that it was simple to make criminals out of a large segment of the population. Luckily, more level heads prevailed in 1927.

29th.

1618   Sir Walter Raleigh was executed.

1896   Robert G. Ingersoll commented on property ownership.

1929   The Wall Street stock market crashed.

History remembers Sir Walter Raleigh as a great courtier—the man who spread his coat over the mud to protect a noble lady's shoes. But Raleigh was a far more adventurous man than that. This pioneering explorer of the New World got into serious trouble with the Crown. When he was executed on this day in 1618, he became increasingly popular in memory. That, of course, was small comfort to the late Sir Walter Raleigh.

On October 29, 1929—as the show business paper *Variety* so tersely noted—Wall Street laid an egg. Stock market prices collapsed, and the twentieth century's worst economic depression rose from its ashes. Many people believe that the Great Depression ended because the Second World War began. Everybody who lived through that depression tells their descendants that no matter how bad things are they were worse then.

A former Illinois Attorney General and eloquent orator Robert G. Ingersoll made an unique observation. On this day in 1896, he said: "Few rich men own their property, the property owns them."

30th.

1938 Orson Welles and the Mercury Theater broadcast *The War of the Worlds*.

1961 Nikita Khrushchev ordered the de-Stalinization of the U.S.S.R. (See April 17th and September 12th entries.)

It started out as a radio dramatization by a young actor-director named Orson Welles, who had adapted a version of H.G. Wells' novel, *The War of the Worlds*. It aired on this evening, in 1938, over a coast-to-coast network. *The War of the Worlds* was so realistic that part of the nation actually believed Martians had invaded New Jersey. Telephone lines were jammed; people contemplated suicide; and some took ill with anxiety. It took days to persuade the public that it had only been a radio show.

When Soviet Premier Nikita Khrushchev chose to emphasize his regime's break with Josef Stalin's previous dictatorship, he chose a very simple strategy. He ordered Stalin's name edited out of books and magazines. On this day in 1961, he also ordered that Josef Stalin's remains were to be moved from his mausoleum in Red Square.

31st.

Halloween.

National UNICEF Day.

1517 Martin Luther posted his ninety-five Theses. (See January 3rd and November 10th entries.)

1956 U.S. Navy Rear Admiral G.J. Duefek became the first person to land an airplane at the South Pole.

There are a lot of Halloween superstitions and traditions that have survived, even though witches floating around on their brooms probably need an air-traffic controller today.

So, with all due deference to the occasion, we should all try to keep in good spirits while the goblins and ghouls roam outside.

When Martin Luther posted his ninety-five Theses on the church door in Wittenberg, Germany, on this day in 1517, he started a revolution: a Protestant Revolution. History does not provide for retakes. We will never know whether a little less intransigence might have prevented or delayed for centuries the schism between Catholicism and Protestantism. What we do know is that those who are unwilling to accept the status quo often change it more than they intended.

This is National UNICEF Day which is observed on behalf of the United Nations Children's Fund. Children speak a direct, uninhibited, single-minded language of their own. We should be mindful that this can be a virtue even in adulthood.

It was no trick, on this day in the spring of 1956—yes, October 31, 1956—that U.S. Navy Rear Admiral G.J. Duefek entered the aviation record books. He became the first person to land an airplane at the South Pole. It may have been a chilly treat for the man whose wish came true at the center of the Antarctic. But it took skill not tricks to get him there.

November

November is when the north winds begin to blow and herald the coming of winter. This month is also a time of migration: gray whales swim south to the warm waters of Mexico; ducks, geese, cranes, and even monarch butterflies fly south to escape the ice and snow; and many people now fly south to Florida and Arizona to warm their weary bones.

1st.

1788 The U.S. Continental Congress closed.

1864 The U.S. Post Office introduced the money order. (See July 1st and September 22nd entries.)

1870 The U.S. Weather Bureau made its first observations.

1913 Notre Dame beat Army 35 to 13 at West Point; popularized the forward pass; and brought team captain Knute Rockne to fame. (See March 4th entry.)

1918 The Hapsburg monarchy came to an end.

1950 Charles Cooper of the Boston Celtics became the NBA's first African-American player.

1952 The U.S. tested its first H-bomb.

This is the day when, in 1870, the United States Weather Bureau made its first observations. It wasn't called the weather bureau back then because it was part of the U.S. Army Signal Corps. On this particular day reports were telegraphed from twenty-four places around the U.S. and the first national weather report was born.

In 1952, the United States conducted a test explosion of a hydrogen bomb at Eniwetok Island in the Pacific. It was such an awesome test that it probably strengthened the resolve of sensible people everywhere never to employ such a weapon. Later developments and events proved that anyone could make one anywhere.

Two governments went out of business on this day in history. In 1788, the U.S. Continental Congress closed after conducting business for fourteen years. It was later replaced by the House of Representatives and the U.S. Senate. In 1918, the Hapsburg monarchy which had ruled the Austro-Hungarian empire for centuries also came to an end. Two separate republics were proclaimed to replace the old system. The Hungarian Republic was proclaimed in Budapest; and the Austrian Republic was proclaimed in Vienna.

It got a whole lot safer to send money through the mail on this day in 1864. The U.S. Post Office introduced the money order.

A professional basketball milestone took place on this day, which opened the doors for a number of its greatest heroes. In 1950, Charles Cooper of the Boston Celtics became the NBA's first African-American player. Since that day, many great players—inspirational heroes to basketball fans and aspiring players—have stepped on and off the professional basketball court. Wilt Chamberlain, Julius Irving, Magic Johnson, Michael Jordan, Isaiah Thomas, and Kareem Abdul-Jabar are just a few of the men who were given the opportunity to play the game thanks to Charles Cooper.

2nd.

1755   Marie Antoinette was born.

1865   Warren G. Harding was born.

1920   Warren G. Harding was elected U.S. President.

1920   The Harding-Cox election results were reported on the radio.

Marie Antoinette was an Austrian princess who married France's crown prince in 1770. Naturally, she became queen when he succeeded to the throne in 1774; and she was guillotined during the French Revolution in 1793. Marie Antoinette was born in Vienna on this day in 1755, and is remembered not for any of the events noted, but for a line she allegedly said when told that the people had no bread. "Let them eat cake," Marie Antoinette replied. The fact is that long before Marie Antoinette was born, "Let them eat bread" was a wisecrack similar to "Tell them to go into the garden and eat worms." Her remark was also attributed to a French queen of a previous century.

Very few American homes had radios on this day in 1920. But the ones who did were able to follow the Presidential election results from the comfort of their own homes. It was the first radio news broadcast of an election, and the start of general public interest in national affairs.

The 1920 presidential election had one rather unusual aspect. Born in 1865, in Corsica, Ohio, Republican candidate Warren G. Harding was celebrating his birthday. On his fifty-fifth birthday, he was elected President of the United States. History will record that as a far-better birthday present for Warren G. Harding than for the American people. During his term, the Teapot Dome scandal broke. Harding was the candidate who was allegedly nominated in "a smoke-filled room" by a group of political bosses. When he died—and was succeeded by Vice President Calvin Coolidge—few people felt the nation was the loser.

3rd.

1801 Karl Baedeker was born.

1900 The first automobile show opened. (See November 5th entry.)

1964 President Lyndon Baynes Johnson won by a landslide.

1992 Bill Clinton was elected president of the United States. (See August 10th entry.)

On this day in 1964, Lyndon B. Johnson—who had succeeded President Kennedy after his assassination—won the Presidential election over Senator Barry Goldwater by the largest popular-vote plurality in the nation's history. Four years later, LBJ faced up to the facts and announced he would not run for re-election. If he had run, he might easily have been defeated because of the events in Vietnam during his term. From the most popular President ever to one whose chances of re-election were dubious was quite a change. It doesn't make public opinion seem particularly stable. And it reminds us that opinions are triggered by events that ebb and flow with time.

Karl Baedeker made a career of selling his opinions. Born on this day in 1801, in Essen, Germany, Baedeker was the pioneer writer and publisher of a popular international travel guide series. Indeed, his name became synonymous with the word guidebook.

4th.

1825 The first vessel to traverse the Erie Canal arrived in New York.

1879 Will Rogers was born.

1879 The cash register was patented.

1916   Walter Cronkite was born.

1922   The entrance to King Tutankhamen's tomb was discovered. (See February 16th and June 26th entries.)

Today is Will Rogers birthday. Born in Oolagah, Oklahoma, in 1879, Rogers began his career as a vaudeville trick-rope artist, but he soon discovered that audiences liked to hear him talk. Government and politics were his targets. He went on to a brilliant career as a monologist, lecturer, newspaper columnist, and movie actor. When the U.S. Congress makes a joke, he once said, it's a law, and when they make a law it's a joke. He also said, "I do not belong to any organized party. I am a Democrat." At first, when he said these sorts of things on network radio in the 1930s, people were shocked. But his good-humored and brilliant delivery made the needling of sacred institutions a popular mass entertainment.

Walter Cronkite was by no means the first television news broadcaster; he was, however, the first to become a national institution. When Cronkite concluded his report by saying that's the way things were, we believed him. During his vintage years, television became the prime news medium for millions of Americans. Broadcast news was still a dream when Walter Cronkite was born on this day in 1916, in St. Joseph, Missouri.

The cash register was granted a patent on this day in 1879. A lot of time slipped by between the cash register's invention and the emergence of the computer. But the machine became the answer to business people's prayers on this day in 1879. We started punching keys instead of handwriting receipts.

An historic event revealed the secrets of one man's past on this day. In 1922, archaeologist Howard Carter and his patron George Edward Carnavon did not heed the curse of the pharoah inscribed on the tomb entrance which said: "Any man who enters this tomb I will pounce upon like a cobra." The next year, they didn't heed the words engraved on the burial chamber: "May he inside remain uninjured, the son of Ra." The discovery of King Tutankhamen's tomb in Egypt's Valley of the Kings was an immediate media sensation. The world contracted mummy fever. Even though a cobra did not pounce on the archaeologists, the Egyptian government did. Officials accused the team of grave robbing, and eventually forced Carter to donate his finds to the Cairo Museum. A mosquito bit Carnavon while he was visiting the tomb. He died from infections and complications less than two months after the burial chamber's seals were broken.

Is anyone here familiar with Clinton's Ditch? No, it isn't a Presidential bailout. In 1825, the Erie Canal—nicknamed for its creator, General Clinton—provided a vital connection from the Hudson River all the way across New York State to Lake Erie. At first, most people thought the idea was absurd and potentially disastrous. But on this day, the first vessel to traverse the Erie Canal arrived in New York City. The trip from Buffalo took nine days, which may seem long in these times, but it was a vast improvement over the weeks of grueling overland travel it took before Clinton's Ditch was built.

5th.

Guy Fawkes Day.

1855 Eugene V. Debs was born.

1895 The first American automobile patent was granted.

Guy Fawkes Day is the basis for lighthearted celebration throughout Great Britain, even though it commemorates a very serious event. The leader of the Gunpowder Plot, Guy Fawkes, was captured by authorities on this day in 1605 as he was about to blow up the House of Lords. He and a number of coconspirators were tried and executed. Over the centuries, the serious nature of Guy Fawkes' arrest has faded into childhood whimsy.

The first U.S. patent for an automobile was issued on this date, in 1895, to George B. Selden who had actually invented this creation much earlier than his rival, Henry Ford. He held off filing his patent while he tried to find backers. He still hadn't gotten either the money or the patent when other people started building automobiles. His patent did garner funding from a few manufacturers. But Henry Ford refused to pay him. He claimed his Model T wasn't based on Selden's design. In the end, Ford made more money.

The name of Eugene V. Debs is not well known today. In the early 1900s, his name was both honored and reviled. Born on this day in 1855 in Terre Haute, Indiana, Debs was a labor leader, a socialist, and a Socialist Party presidential candidate. In his time, socialism was not only regarded as an extreme left-wing movement, it was absolute treason in America. What made matters worse was that Debs was an American working man—not a foreign intellectual. He contradicted popular belief. He later became a venerated figure among liberals and even non-socialists; some of his ideals were eventually incorporated into modern American political platforms.

6th.

1854   John Philip Sousa was born.

1860   Abraham Lincoln was elected U.S. President.

1869   The first intercollegiate football game took place.

As we consider our present political assets, we may not see another Lincoln on the horizon. But even if we don't, we see a nation less divided, stronger, and a great deal larger than it was in Lincoln's time. Did you know that two days after the election, Lincoln wrote to Vice President Hannibal Hamlin, suggesting that it might be a good idea if they met? They had been elected on this date in 1860, without ever meeting each other.

On this day in 1869, Rutgers University and Princeton University played the first intercollegiate football game, in New Brunswick, New Jersey. Football, like basketball, has been the great "democratizer" of American college education. It has financed the expansion of student bodies and facilities; given college educations to those who might not have otherwise afforded them; and inspired a great deal of alumni loyalty.

American marching bands and march music owe a great deal to John Philip Sousa, who was born in Washington, D.C., on this day in 1854. Nicknamed the "March King," Sousa wrote a number of high-energy, emotion-filled themes like "The Stars and Stripes Forever," and led some of the greatest marching bands of his time.

7th.

1837   Abolitionist Elijah P. Lovejoy was murdered by a mob. (See November 9th entry.)

1867   Madame Marie Curie was born. (See December 21st entry.)

1874   *Harper's Weekly* featured a Republican elephant. (See September 27th entry.)

1917   The Bolshevik Revolution began. (See April 22nd and September 15th entries.)

1918   Billy Graham was born.

1972   President Richard M. Nixon was re-elected. (See January 9th entry.)

1989   L. Douglas Wilder of Virginia became the first elected African-American governor. (See January 11th entry.)

On this day in 1917, Vladimir Lenin and his Bolshevik followers started a revolution against Alexander Kerensky's provisional democratic government. The Russian Revolution did not begin as a Communist movement; the Czar was overthrown and replaced by a democratic coalition. But that government seemed to be content to make only a small portion of the reforms the people demanded. They had tasted power. Czar Nicholas II had not swayed to public demand; neither had Alexander Kerensky. On this day in 1917, the Bolsheviks opted for armed force as the people's weapon of change.

Billy Graham came a long way in the world from Charlotte, North Carolina, where he was born on this day in 1918. As the greatest evangelist of his time, Graham became the friend of presidents and a missionary to the world.

The world of science is oftentimes thought to be a man's domain. But Madame Marie Curie—who was born on this day in 1867—was a definitive exception to that myth. This dedicated Polish-born French physicist won two Nobel Prizes. In 1903, she shared this most-coveted award in physics with Henri Becquerel and her husband Pierre Curie for their research and discovery of radioactive elements and properties. And in 1911, Madame Curie was the sole honoree in the field of chemistry for her successful isolation of pure radium.

8th.

1923   The Nazi beer hall putsch took place.

1932   Franklin D. Roosevelt was first elected President. (See January 30th entry.)

1942   U.S. and British forces invaded Nazi-occupied North Africa.

On November 8, 1923, Adolf Hitler and his followers broke into a Münich beer hall and proclaimed a new German government. They had a few thousand adherents, but they

NOVEMBER

had miscalculated both the government's and the public's attitude. Not only did the announcement fail to garner applause, Hitler was arrested a few days later and sent to prison.

In 1942, U.S. and British forces invaded Nazi-held North Africa. This day was a major turning point in the outcome of the Second World War. The Allied forces switched roles from a defensive to an offensive posture.

9th.

1802 Elijah P. Lovejoy was born. (See November 7th entry.)

1934 Carl Sagan was born.

1938 Krystalnacht took place.

1965 New York City encountered its first blackout. (See July 13th entry.)

1976 The U.N. General Assembly approved ten resolutions condemning South African apartheid.

1989 The Berlin Wall crumbled. (See August 12th entry.)

Back in 1965, on this day—or, more exactly, this night—most of the northeastern United States, and New York City in particular, experienced a massive power failure. It was a black night in the city, but it proved to be peaceful and cooperative. In fact, nine months later, there was a baby boom on the eastern seaboard. Twelve years later, during the long, hot summer of 1977, New York City had another blackout; but that time looters had a field day.

Elijah P. Lovejoy was a newspaper editor. He was also a fiery abolitionist. Born on this day in 1802, in Albion, Maine, Lovejoy established a newspaper in Alton, Illinois. His coverage of the abolitionist movement irritated some of the people in the town, and his presses were destroyed many times. On November 7, 1837, he was murdered by a mob while trying to defend his newspaper.

Apartheid has had many faces in our long history. And it played a major role on this day for the worse and the better. In 1938, Nazi rabble-rousers roamed the streets of German cities looting and destroying Jewish-owned buildings. Shattering glass rang throughout the night and littered the paths of horrified passersby the following morning.

Krystalnacht was the overture to a reign of terror that accelerated from apartheid to genocide. The solemn memory of Krystalnacht still echoed in 1976, when the U.N. General Assembly approved ten resolutions to condemn a century-long tradition of South African apartheid.

Mankind has been seeking the origins of life on this planet for seemingly billions of years. One American astronomer uncovered a very relevant clue to the puzzle. He replicated in a laboratory the creation of a key element found in all living things by exposing water and gases to ultraviolet light, duplicating the sun's life-supporting energy. His experiment yielded that vital life source—amino acids. Born on this day in 1934, Carl Sagan is better known to the public for his highly-acclaimed television series, *Cosmos*, than for his pioneering efforts in the laboratory.

10th.

1483 Martin Luther was born in Eisleben, Germany. (See January 3rd and October 31st entries.)

1775 The U.S. Marine Corps was established.

1871 Henry M. Stanley found David Livingstone.

1926 Hirohito became emperor of Japan. (See April 29th entry.)

Today is the U.S. Marine Corps' birthday. Established by the Continental Congress in 1775, the Marines have seen plenty of action and succeeded in getting many situations "well in hand." But today, you might discover some things that do not fall into that popular category of "Tell it to the Marines." For example, did you know that the expression originated with Sir Walter Scott? A character in his novel *Redgauntlet* said: "Tell that to the marines—the sailors won't believe it."

A momentous meeting took place on this day deep in the African jungle. In 1871, journalist Henry M. Stanley met missionary David Livingstone. Most of us think that when Mr. Stanley said, "Dr. Livingstone, I presume," the good doctor should have answered, "You certainly do presume." You see, Dr. Livingstone was far from being lost or in need of rescue. In fact, he remained in Africa long after Stanley returned to civilization and glory.

11th.

1528 Margaret Hunt revealed the secrets of her medical practice.

1918 Armistice was proclaimed during the First World War.

1922 Kurt Vonnegut, Jr. was born.

1939 "God Bless America" was first sung.

1973 Egypt and Israel signed a cease-fire agreement sponsored by the U.S. and began peace discussions. (See October 27th entry.)

On this day in 1918, the First World War came to an end. The guns fell silent. And the world waited to assess the destruction of the world's first mechanized, bio-chemical, impersonal war. Unfortunately, the silence did not last as long as the world hoped.

Today, "God Bless America" is so well known as a sort of semi-official national anthem, that it may come as a surprise to you to learn that the song was twenty-two years old before it was heard in public. Irving Berlin wrote it during the First World War, but it was not publicly sung until this day, in 1939, when Kate Smith introduced it on a radio broadcast.

In 1528, a "sorceress" by the name of Margaret Hunt revealed the secrets of her medical practice before the bishop of London's commissary. On this day, she explained how she used a combination of natural herbs and prayers to heal the sick—powerful cures she had learned from a wise woman named Mother Elmet. In Margaret Hunt's day, most people couldn't afford to consult a physician when they were ill. Many more trusted in the old ways of folklore cures and traditional medicine. Surprisingly, the bishop didn't condemn Hunt for heresy or witchcraft. He was simply curious about the methods that had gained her a popular reputation among the common folk during a time when doctors were generally mistrusted.

Wouldn't it be fun to travel through time just by thinking? Imagine what you could do if you could see the future in one place; go back to the past somewhere else knowing things turn out fine; and take a quick break in the present on another planet. Obviously, author Kurt Vonnegut, Jr. thought about it, too. Born on this planet, on this calendar coordinate, in the year allocation 1922, Vonnegut described the highs and lows, the joys and sorrows, the adventures and personal moments of a time traveler who did all of the above in his novel *Slaughterhouse Five*.

12th.

1815 Elizabeth Cady Stanton was born.

1929 Grace Kelly was born.

1956 The U.S. Supreme Court ruled that segregation on public buses was unconstitutional. (See December 1st entry.)

1975 The World Health Organization announced that Asia was free of smallpox for the first time in history. (See April 7th entry.)

Elizabeth Cady Stanton, who was born in Johnstown, New York, on this day in 1815, was an early feminist leader and author of the historic "Declaration of Sentiments" which was presented at the first Women's Rights Convention in 1848. Stanton spearheaded the successful efforts to give New York State women joint guardianship of their children, the right to own property, and the right to sue in court. Just listing the rights she fought to win is an indication of how bad things were for women before she came along. She did not live to see women win the right to vote.

How many girls these days dream of becoming royal princesses? It's an old fashioned idea, but it happened once in our own time. Grace Kelly, born on this date in 1929, was a young woman from Philadelphia, Pennsylvania, who became a movie star. That would have made most young women pretty happy. Then she married a monarch named Prince Rainier. As Princess Grace of Monaco, she embarked on a journey that took her a world away from her childhood home.

13th.

1856 Louis Brandeis was born. (See January 28th entry.)

1927 The Holland Tunnel was officially opened.

1969 Vietnam War Moratorium demonstrations occurred nationwide.

On this day in 1927, the Holland Tunnel was officially opened. This major throughway between New York City and New Jersey runs under the Hudson River. Before it was built, the only way to get across in an automobile was by ferry. There was an earlier railroad tunnel, but the Lincoln Tunnel and the modern-day George Washington Bridge were yet to come.

Over a three-day period that began on this day in 1969, hundreds of thousands of Americans participated in nationwide demonstrations. Despite fears of violence, the Vietnam Moratorium demonstrations were peaceful.

14th.

1832   The first streetcar went into operation. (See August 2nd entry.)

1851   *Moby Dick* was published. (See August 1st entry.)

1889   Nellie Bly set out to go around the world in 80 days. (See January 25th entry.)

1922   The British Broadcasting Corporation began broadcast of domestic radio service. (See March 27th entry.)

1972   The Dow Jones Industrial Average closed above the 1,000 level for the first time, cnding the day at 1003.16. (See January 2nd and January 8th entries.)

1986   The Securities and Exchange Commission imposed a record $100 million penalty against Ivan Boesky.

Herman Melville had written five novels before the one which was published on this day in 1861. *Moby Dick* begins with the words, "Call me Ishmael" and goes on to say, "I love to sail forbidden seas, and land on barbarous coasts" before relating the story of Captain Ahab's grim pursuit of the great white whale Moby Dick.

Opportunity is a wonderful thing, but it's also dangerous. It was on this day, in 1986, that the SEC fined Wall Street trader Ivan Boesky a record $100 million for using insider information to make investments. Traders are gamblers. He bet his reputation, his career, and money that he'd earned honestly that he could beat the system. He lost.

15th.

1777 The Articles of Confederation were adopted by Congress. (See January 30th entry.)

1806 Pike's Peak was sighted.

1969 Antiwar protesters gathered in Washington, D.C.

On this day in 1777, the Continental Congress adopted the Articles of Confederation, facing up to the fact that thirteen separate colonies were engaged in a war with England. Copies of this document were distributed two days later for ratification. The thirteen Articles which provided a framework for uniting the colonies were not completely ratified for four years.

A young Army officer named Zebulon Montgomery Pike sighted a high mountain and decided to climb it. Before he got to its base, he was arrested by the Spanish authorities for trespassing on Spanish territory. He didn't climb the mountain. But Pike's Peak in Colorado still bears his name, and this was the day, in 1806, that he first sighted his goal.

Protest demonstrations are usually limited to single-minded special interest groups banded together by a single cause. But on this day in 1969, passionate protesters representing a variety of interests gathered together in Washington, D.C. Under most circumstances, these 250,000 people would not have united in solidarity for a common cause. But this particular issue—American involvement in the Vietnam War—affected many Americans from many different walks of life. Their assembly did not garner an immediate response from the government, but it did enlighten a large portion of the nation. On that day, many Americans learned that not all wars are fought for patriotic reasons; and not all patriotic Americans advocated the Vietnam War.

16th.

1532 The Incan empire fell to Spain. (See July 24th entry.)

1864 General William Sherman made his march to the sea.

1933 The U.S. and U.S.S.R. established diplomatic relations.

Back in 1933, this was the day when the United States and Soviet Russia established diplomatic relations. They finally agreed to talk to each other. It had been an unsettling silence for near a decade that had been preceded by American support for the Bolshevik Revolution. That support turned to denial when America realized that Communism's goals were not the same as democracy's hopes. However, diplomatic communications returned despite a difference in opinion.

A bitter residue was all that was left after General William Tecumseh Sherman marched with his troops from Atlanta to the sea. It began on this day, in 1864, and in its wake a broad scar of ruin and destruction marred the South; and tainted the memories of later generations. That memory only recently seems to be fading.

For want of a nail, a shoe was lost. For want of a shoe, the horse was lost. For want of gold, an empire was lost—all in the name of greed. As explorers arrived in the New World, they heard tales of riches beyond the imagination—stories of golden cities. They were lured by the lust for gold. Spanish explorer Francisco Pizarro was no exception when he landed in South America. He destroyed entire Incan cities which had been built by an advanced civilization that worshipped the sun and treated gold as a gift from their god. On this day, in 1532, the Incan empire fell. Pizarro took the Incan emperor Atahualpa prisoner and demanded a ransom of gold. The Incans paid, but Pizarro murdered his prisoner in the name of Christianity. What Pizarro didn't destroy on that day was a treasure that remained concealed high up in the clouds, protected by the sun god. It was Machu Picchu, the last city of the Incas.

17th.

1534 The Act of Supremacy—which declared King Henry VIII as head of the Church of England—was passed by Parliament. (See February 11th entry.)

1558 Elizabeth I ascended to the British throne after the death of Queen Mary I. (See September 7th entry.)

1734 John Peter Zenger was arrested for libel. (See August 4th entry.)

1969 The SALT talks began in Helsinki, Norway.

1993 The U.S. House of Representatives approved the North American Free Trade Agreement: 238 to 200 votes. (See April 14th entry.)

On this day in 1969, the United States and Soviet Russia began the strategic arms limitation talks. In one sense, SALT proved to be a smashing success: The two nations were still talking eight years later.

18th.

1789   L.J.M. Daguerre was born.

1820   U.S. Navy Captain Nathaniel B. Palmer discovered Antarctica.

1836   W.S. Gilbert was born.

1883   Standard Time was adopted in the U.S.

1928   Mickey Mouse made his debut.

Until this date in 1883, every locality in America set its own time preference. Standard Time was adopted in the United States and the resulting time zone system made life a lot simpler for everyone who would eventually travel from coast to coast by telephone or plane.

Most of us have an ancient photograph or two of ancestors. Most of us own at least one camera. All of this traces back to a man who was born on this day in 1789 in Cormeilles, France. Louis Daguerre gave his name to the daguerreotype—an early type of photograph. It was Daguerre who popularized photography; who first proved that a picture was worth a thousand words.

W.S. Gilbert of Gilbert and Sullivan fame, was born on this day in 1836, in London, England. He viewed life with a sometimes ironically lighthearted view; and wrote satirical operettas with Sir Arthur Sullivan that reflected the not-so-subtly humorous side of Victorian morals and mores. Gilbert once wrote that "when everyone is somebody, then no one's anybody." He also felt that "things are seldom what they seem, skim milk masquerades as cream." And he duly noted that "the Law is the true embodiment of everything that's excellent; it has no kind of fault or flaw, and I, my lords, embody the Law."

Not to bring up a chilly subject, but on this day in 1820, U.S. Navy Captain Nathaniel B. Palmer discovered the last continent: Antarctica. This desolate land of ice and snow may not be fit for man's habitation, but it is still the home to a unique collection of birds and beasts. Elephant seals wallow on the rocky shores; but Antarctica's more famous residents are the penguins. Majestic emperor penguins proudly stand in their colorful suits; eccentric rockhoppers, with their lime-green and shocking pink headdresses leap from boulder to boulder; and king penguins, uniformly stroll in groups to the beach in their trademark tuxedos, and patiently wait for one brave soul to dive into the water before the rest follow in unison. It's a great relief to know that Captain Palmer didn't think Antarctica was a future settlement site. He thought the place was already overrun with enough layabouts, strutting dandies, eccentrics, and meek conformists without adding on humanity's unique species.

One of the most well-known characters of our time is Mickey Mouse. Well, today is his birthday. He was born in the 1928 animated cartoon *Steamboat Willie* which premiered on this date. This was also the first animated movie with properly synchronized sound, and it was an instant hit. But what was this happy rodent's appeal? Walt Disney himself said, ". . . Mickey is so simple and uncomplicated, so easy to understand, that you can't help liking him."

19th.

1620   The *Mayflower* arrived off the coast of Cape Cod. (See July 22nd and November 21st entries.)

1620   Peregrine White was born aboard the *Mayflower*.

1745   Lord Chesterfield wrote about wisdom.

1863   President Abraham Lincoln delivered the Gettysburg Address.

1917   Indira Gandhi was born. (See January 19th and June 6th entries.)

1942   The Alaska Highway was formally opened. (See June 12th entry.)

1993   The U.S. Senate voted 61 to 38 in favor of the North American Free Trade Agreement. (See November 17th entry.)

On this day, in 1620, the *Mayflower* arrived off Cape Cod. Peregrine White, the first English child born in New England, who was born on this day aboard the *Mayflower*, wasn't expected to make such a dramatic debut.

The Earl of Chesterfield was a fountainhead of good advice for his son; and he wrote most of his suggestions in a journal. On this date, in 1745, Lord Chesterfield's advice was this: "Be wiser than other people if you can, but do not tell them so."

On this day in 1863, President Abraham Lincoln dedicated a national cemetery with a few brief remarks. He stood at the site in Gettysburg, Pennsylvania, and delivered an address that he had written on a paper bag during the train trip from Washington. Not all great words are divined by professional writers nor developed from days of toil.

Jawaharlal Nehru, independent India's first prime minister, headed a government caught in a political whirlwind. Freedom from British rule was not followed by peace; extremists representing numerous political and religious sects demanded to be heard—and sometimes violently. Nehru's daughter Indira Gandhi—who was born on this day in 1917—entered an equally unsettled world during her four terms as India's prime minister. During her last term in office, Sikh extremists instigated riots and used terrorist tactics in an attempt to be heard. Gandhi sent armed forces to their holiest shrine—the Golden Temple of Amristar in the Punjab—where reportedly six hundred lives were lost in a violent confrontation. To avenge the death of their compatriots, Gandhi herself was assassinated by Sikh terrorists who took full responsibility.

20th.

1925 Robert F. Kennedy was born.

1945 International War Crimes Tribunal trials began.

1995 The Hubble Space Telescope photographed the Eagle Nebula.

Today is Robert F. Kennedy's birthday. Born in 1925, in Brookline, Massachusetts, Kennedy once said, "Some people see things as they are, and say why. I dream things that never were and say, why not."

An International War Crimes Tribunal was set up to try suspected Nazi war criminals on this day in 1945, in Nuremberg, Germany. The trial process was not endless and the verdicts were prompt; but many decades later, in our own country and elsewhere, war criminals were still being sought, extradited, or simply died while still in hiding.

An awe-inspiring image was sent back to earth on this day in 1995. In its exploration of our universe, the Hubble Space Telescope sighted and photographed the birth of a star. The image of the Eagle Nebula's towering mass expanding and taking shape reminds us how powerful and majestic life truly is.

21st.

1620 The Mayflower Compact was signed. (See July 22nd and November 19th entries.)

1694 Voltaire was born.

1783 The first manned balloon flight took place. (See June 5th entry.)

The first human flight in a free-floating balloon took place on this day. Back in 1783, Joseph and Jacques Montgolfier had already demonstrated their hot-air balloon with a ten-minute flight over Annonay, France. Their project interested the King of France, who decided to approve a manned-flight demonstration. Jean Pilatre de Rozier and the Marquis d'Arlandes thought it would garner some personal notoriety in the history books if they volunteered to fly. They got their wish.

Self-government in America actually began in deep water aboard the *Mayflower* off Cape Cod on this day in 1620. This is when the Pilgrims signed the Mayflower Compact for what they called "a civil body politic," settling matters of responsibility before they embarked on the job of settling in the new land.

François-Marie Arouet was born on this day in 1694, in Paris. This fact becomes a little more meaningful when you note that François-Marie Arouet adopted the pen name Voltaire. Among this playwright and author's observations was his remark that "The way to be a bore is to say everything."

22nd.

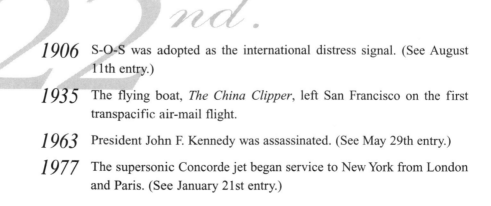

1906 S-O-S was adopted as the international distress signal. (See August 11th entry.)

1935 The flying boat, *The China Clipper*, left San Francisco on the first transpacific air-mail flight.

1963 President John F. Kennedy was assassinated. (See May 29th entry.)

1977 The supersonic Concorde jet began service to New York from London and Paris. (See January 21st entry.)

November Twenty-second is a date that will always be remembered by the generations who lived through it in 1963. It was the fatal day President John F. Kennedy was assassinated. So much of what transpired after that was seen on television throughout the world, vividly engraved in millions of minds. Questions about the incident have persisted ever since. It is the nature of human beings to ask questions, to wonder, to be skeptical. It was President Kennedy's nature to stand back and look at himself—and sometimes to be amused. In this regard he was a typical American; that, while we are serious in our purposes, we don't take ourselves too seriously. As Kennedy said months before he died, ". . . if we cannot end now our differences, at least we can make the world safe for diversity."

It's rough enough when people from different parts of the world attempt to talk to each other. Luckily, there is one universal phrase. Ever since this day, in 1906, the letters S-O-S—spelled out in wireless code—have been used as the international distress signal.

The act of flying over deep waters saw two high points on this day in history. In 1935, Pan-American's flying boat—*The China Clipper*—left San Francisco carrying the first air-mail load across the Pacific Ocean. And in 1977, the supersonic Concorde jet expanded its service across the Atlantic Ocean to New York City from London and Paris. The *China Clipper* was eventually mothballed as faster planes were developed. But neither it nor the Concorde added to the air-crash statistics that have happened with faster and more modern aircraft today.

23rd.

1744　Abigail Smith Adams was born. (See October 30th entry.)

1848　The Female Medical Educational Society was established.

1888　Adolph "Harpo" Marx was born. (See October 2nd entry.)

1903　Opera tenor Enrico Caruso made his American debut. (See February 25th entry.)

1942　The Coast Guard Woman's Auxiliary (SPARS) was authorized. (See August 4th entry.)

When Abigail Smith was born in Weymouth, Massachusetts on this day in 1744, she never dreamed that she would celebrate her fifty-sixth birthday in the new Executive

Mansion as the nation's First Lady. When Abigail Smith married John Adams, she became the wife of one President and the mother of another. She also became one of the first major spokespersons for women's rights in America. After the Declaration of Independence was signed, she wrote to her husband, "In the new code of laws which I now assume will be needed—please give a thought to the ladies and see to it that it is put beyond the power of the vicious and lawless . . . to treat us with cruelty and indignity with impunity. Don't forget that all men would be tyrants if they could."

Today is the anniversary of the founding of the first women's medical society in America, in 1848. The organization was called the Female Medical Educational Society of Boston. It was established in the same year as the all-male American Medical Association; and that the Female Medical Educational Society's officers were all men!

24th.

1874 Barbed wire was patented by Joseph Glidden of DeKalb, Ilinois.

1963 Lee Harvey Oswald was killed. (See November 22nd entry.)

1963 Chief Justice Earl Warren spoke at President Kennedy's memorial service.

1993 The U.S. Congress passed the Brady handgun-control bill.

Probably no homicide has ever been witnessed by more people than the shooting of President Kennedy's accused assassin Lee Harvey Oswald. He was shot by Jack Ruby at the Dallas city jail in front of national television cameras, on this day, in 1963. The whole world saw it happen; but we have yet to fully understand how and why. Ironically, on this same day in 1993, the U.S. Congress passed the Brady handgun-control bill, a long-needed measure that was triggered by the attempted assassination of President Ronald Reagan and the shooting of one of his aides. It often challenges our sense of logic to see how much time goes by before we react to a serious situation. Sadly, it sometimes takes more than a single incident to make us face the truth and move forward. Chief Justice Earl Warren said at President Kennedy's memorial tribute on this day in 1963: "If we really love this country, if we truly love justice and mercy, if we fervently want to make this nation better for those who are to follow us, we can at least abjure the hatred that consumes people, the false accusations that divide us and the bitterness that begets violence."

When our national poet laureate Robert Frost penned the phrase "good fences make good neighbors," he also went to say that walls were only good for tearing down. But on this day in 1874, Joseph Glidden of DeKalb, Illinois, received a patent for barbed wire, which has proved useful in agriculture, security, and defense.

25th.

The feast day of St. Catherine.

1846 Andrew Carnegie was born. (See December 24th entry.)

1846 Carry Nation was born. (See August 29th entry.)

1864 Great Britain's Prime Minister Benjamin Disraeli described his times.

1917 Russia held its last free election for more than half a century.

1952 The world's longest-running play, Agatha Christie's *The Mousetrap*, opened in London, England. (See September 15th entry.)

According to tradition, today is when young Parisian seamstresses are supposed to go out on a carnival manhunt. Why? Because that's how they celebrated the feast of St. Catherine for centuries.

On this day in 1917, there was a free election held in Russia to select a constituent democratic assembly after Czar Nicholas II abdicated. Russian voters chose an assembly in which less than a third of the deputies were Bolshevik Communists. So the Bolsheviks suppressed the assembly when it convened the following January.

Great Britain's Prime Minister Benjamin Disraeli viewed his times with a very critical eye. On this day in 1864, he noted that "the characteristic of the present age is craving credulity." If Disraeli were alive today, he would say the same thing. "Craving credulity"—the ardent eagerness to find things to believe in—is also part of our time.

The world's richest man, Andrew Carnegie, once said, "A man who dies rich, dies in disgrace." On this day in 1835, Carnegie was born into a working-class family in Dunfermline, Scotland. When they emigrated to the United States, the young nation was just emerging as an industrial giant; and Andrew Carnegie's wealth grew right along with it. He built a steel-manufacturing empire which he sold, in 1901, to industrial giant J. Pierpont Morgan for what was at that time $250 million. Today, that same sum would be worth billions. That sale of the Carnegie Steel Company made Carnegie the richest man in the world, allowing him to do whatever he wanted. So he built and stocked hundreds of free public libraries across the United States, Canada, and Great Britain. He established social-assistance programs in Scotland. He founded universities and educational foundations which are still in existence today. Carnegie was still rich when he died, but he certainly did not die in disgrace.

26th.

1716 A lion was first exhibited in America.

1789 The first presidentially-proclaimed Thanksgiving Day was observed. (See October 3rd entry.)

1992 Queen Elizabeth II announced she would start paying taxes on her personal income and take her children off the national payroll. (See April 21th and June 2nd entries.)

Among the more obscure annals of American history is the saga of the first lion ever seen on these shores. The exhibition of this king of beasts was announced in Boston on this day in 1716. Today we've all seen lions, in photographs, on television, and in the movies. But before any of these had been invented, a lion in the flesh would have brought myth and legend to life, much like seeing a unicorn or mermaid today.

27th.

1095 Pope Urban II called for a crusade.

1874 Chaim Weizmann was born.

1901 The Army War College was authorized.

1910 New York City's Pennsylvania Station opened.

On this day, in 1901, the Army War College was authorized. With this act, our nation officially recognized that the art of warfare had become much more complex.

During the First World War, an émigré scientist was director of the British Admiralty laboratories. In 1874, Chaim Weizmann was born on this day in Russian-owned Poland. This brilliant scientist helped synthesize some of the elemental ingredients needed for the manufacture of explosives. He was also an active Zionist. Years later, when Israel became a nation, Weizmann was elected to be its first president; and a great scientific institute bears his name today.

This is the anniversary of the crusades. In 1095, Pope Urban II called for a crusade to free the Holy Land from Islamic occupation. The supreme head of the Catholic Church promised that every soldier who participated in this holy war would be absolved of his sins. Many requests for the defense of the Byzantine empire and the Holy Land had come from lords and ambassadors. But it took Pope Urban's plea to inspire armies to take up the sword for their faith.

By 1910, the nation's railroad system had grown from horse-drawn trains to a gigantic web of locomotives streaming down steel roads from coast to coast. It had taken nearly a half century for this invention to became the backbone of the nation's transportation system. And on this particular day, the world's largest railroad station opened. In its time, New York's Pennsylvania Station soon had more trains, more passengers, and more cargo passing through its maze of tracks and platforms than the world had ever seen. It helped make that city the nation's eastern hub.

28th.

1520 Ferdinand Magellan reached the Pacific Ocean from the Atlantic.

1929 Commander Richard E. Byrd started his flight over the South Pole.

1967 Communist China was turned down for admission to the United Nations.

Down at the tail end of South America is a rough body of water known as the Straits of Magellan. The Straits were discovered by Ferdinand Magellan in 1520, while he was trying to find an eastern route to the Moluccan Islands in the Pacific. On this day, Magellan reached the Pacific Ocean. It is fair to say that he did it the hard way, but he accomplished what he set out to do. When Ferdinand Magellan went through the Straits that now bear his name he must have thought he was at the bottom of the world. But four centuries later, Commander Richard E. Byrd actually hit bottom. On this day in

1929, Byrd took off with copilot Bernt Balchen and a flight crew from their Antarctic base, called Little America, and headed for the South Pole.

On this day in 1967, the United Nations assembly voted on the question of admitting the People's Republic of China into its organization. And for the eighteenth time, that nation was turned down. This sounds like ancient history, now, because the People's Republic of China has been an active United Nations member for quite a few years. But many of the reasons China was excluded for so long remain. Allegations of human rights violations by the government, and piracy by the navy are hard to ignore, but so is one quarter of the planet's population.

29th.

1865	Karl Marx wrote to Abraham Lincoln.
1890	The First Army-Navy football game was played.
1895	Busby Berkeley was born.
1929	Commander Richard E. Byrd flew over the South Pole. (See November 28th entry.)

This day marks the anniversary of a bitter, continuing battle between two major armed forces—the Army and the Navy. The battle began in 1890 and there are still no signs of its ending. What we are talking about, of course, is the annual Army Navy football game.

A letter dated November 29, 1865, was supposedly sent to Abraham Lincoln. The year is obviously wrong, because Lincoln died in April of that year. But if the text of the letter is accurate, it is rather interesting. The letter read, "From the commencement of the titanic struggle in America, the working men of Europe felt instinctively that the Star Spangled Banner carried the destiny of their class." This letter is rather interesting not only because of its content but also because of its author. We are told the letter was sent by Karl Marx.

In the dark days of the Great Depression, many people went to the theater to forget their troubles for an hour or two in front of the flickering silver screen. Thanks to filmmaker Busby Berkeley who was born on this day in 1895, audiences got what they wanted: light comedy and pretty girls; hit songs and pretty girls; tap dancing and pretty girls;

and oh yes, pretty girls. Berkeley nicknamed them and titled many of his films as the *Golddiggers*. Of course, the prettiest, most talented member of Berkeley's star-studded *Golddiggers* cast was his wife Ruby Keeler who, along with costar Dick Powell, tap-danced and sang their way into America's hearts.

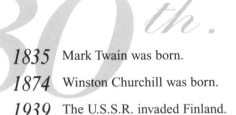

1835   Mark Twain was born.

1874   Winston Churchill was born.

1939   The U.S.S.R. invaded Finland.

On this day, in 1874, Winston Leonard Spencer Churchill was born in Oxfordshire, England. His sometimes adventurous, but always distinguished career as a writer and politician didn't end when he reached retirement age. In fact, he embarked on a new career—at a time when most people would rest on their laurels—as Great Britain's Prime Minister during the Second World War. Churchill's eloquent words rallied a nation bombarded by bombs. And on his eightieth birthday, in 1954, Churchill fudged a bit, for the first time, when he said, "I have never accepted what many people have kindly said, namely that I inspired the nation. It was the nation . . . that had the lion heart. I had the luck to be called upon to give the roar."

Back in 1835, Samuel Langhorne Clemens was born on this day in Florida, Missouri. People didn't think Samuel would amount to very much while he was growing up along the Mississippi River valley. He never held down a job for very long, or put much effort into the ones he held. But Samuel was just a late bloomer. In fact, when he took the pen name of Mark Twain, the whole world opened its doors and its hearts to him. "Thunder is good," he once wrote, "thunder is impressive; but it is lightning that does the work."

In 1938, a lot of people tried to find excuses for Soviet Russia's actions when that nation signed a treaty with Nazi Germany. But excuses were hard to find when, on this day in 1939, Russia invaded Finland. The world cheered when that nation held off the invasion for three months. Ultimately, of course, Russia imposed its own peace on Finland.

December

Christmas comes but once a year, and unluckily the Christmas shopping season lasts longer than that. There was a time when Christmas advertising didn't appear in newspapers, magazines, or on television until the first week of December. Slowly but surely, the kickoff date was moved to the day after Thanksgiving. Nowadays, you'll find Christmas gift-giving ideas and advertising making an appearance just before Halloween. At this accelerated rate, in another century, we'll be Christmas shopping all year long!

1st.

1880 A telephone was first installed in the White House.

1913 The first drive-in gas station was opened in Pittsburgh by the Gulf Refining Company.

1917 Boys Town was founded.

1919 Lady Astor joined the British Parliament.

1922 Skywriting was introduced.

1955 Rosa Parks refused to give up her seat on a city bus. (See November 12th entry.)

1978 President Jimmy Carter placed more than 56 million acres of Alaska's federal lands into the national park system.

In 1917, Father Edward Flanagan founded a unique institution on this day in Omaha, Nebraska. It's called Boys Town. Its basic concept centered on Father Flanagan's firm belief that, in his words, "There is no such thing as a bad boy." Father Flanagan was no starry-eyed dreamer. He defined a serious problem that faced the nation; it wasn't that there were bad boys being born, it was the conditions they lived in that created their problems. Flanagan placed friendless boys into an environment where they could have an opportunity to grow up as good citizens.

We first saw the writing in the sky instead of on the wall, on this day in 1922, when a pilot flew over New York City and released a trail of white smoke that spelled out the friendly word "hello." Since then, skywriters have announced everything from "Eat at Joe's" to "Will You Marry Me?" Certainly the British Parliament saw the writing on wall on this day, in 1919, when Lady Astor was sworn in as their first female member.

This was certainly an historic day, in 1880, when the first telephone was installed in the White House. This invention assured the public, in no small way, that the President of the United States could keep in touch with the needs of the nation. In 1913, those needs had certainly changed. On this day, the nation's first drive-in gas station was opened for business by the Gulf Refining Company in Pittsburgh, Pennsylvania. But the nation's chief executive must always remain mindful of the nation's future needs, not just those in the immediate present. And also on this same day, in 1978, President Jimmy Carter responded to the needs of future generations when he placed more than 56 million acres of Alaska's federal lands into the national park system to protect them from mineral or oil development.

Some people say that one small individual can't make a difference in this huge world. But today marks an anniversary that proves those naysayers are wrong. In 1955, Miss Rosa Parks had finished a long, exhausting day of work. She boarded a city bus in Montgomery, Alabama, but rather than walking to the back and taking a seat, she chose to sit toward the front. This African-American seamstress was arrested when she refused to give up her seat to a white person. It was a crime back then, not only in South Africa, but right here in America. And this was the incident that sparked a citywide boycott; that progressed into a court battle; and eventually ended in a U.S. Supreme Court ruling that decided against the racial segregation of public transportation throughout the nation.

2nd.

1823 President James Monroe declared the Monroe Doctrine. (See April 28th entry.)

1942 The Manhattan Project achieved the first man-made atomic chain-reaction.

1954 Senator McCarthy was censured by the U.S. Senate. (See February 21st entry.)

1960 The Archbishop of Canterbury visited Pope John XXIII.

In 1823, on this day, President James Monroe told the European powers to stay out of the western hemisphere. We may remember that portion of the Monroe Doctrine, but most of us don't recognize the other statement from that document, in which President Monroe declared that "In the wars of the European powers, in matters relating to themselves, we have never taken part, nor does it comport with our policy to do so."

Some years ago, a small plaque was placed on the wall at Stagg Field, the University of Chicago's football stadium. Inscribed on this marker are the following words: "On December 2, 1942, man achieved here the first self-sustaining chain reaction and thereby initiated the controlled release of nuclear energy." In a secret laboratory below the stadium, the Manhattan Project research team created the first man-made atomic chain reaction from uranium ore. Its success exploded into the public's consciousness three years later at the Japanese cities of Hiroshima and Nagasaki; and later still on Bikini Atoll in the South Pacific. One of the Manhattan Project's leaders, J. Robert

Oppenheimer, fought for the peaceful use of atomic power for the rest of his life. Other team members, like Enrico Fermi, sought to build bigger and better weapons from the knowledge gained under the football stadium.

Precedents are often made to be broken. This day marks the anniversary of a long-held precedent that stood on a flimsy foundation for nearly four hundred years. In 1960, The Archbishop of Canterbury visited Pope John XXIII at the Vatican. The two heads of two major Christian religions broke a senseless tradition that had been set back in the 1500s by Great Britain's King Henry VIII and Pope Leo X.

3rd.

1621   Galileo perfected the telescope. (See February 13th and February 15th entries.)

1775   John Paul Jones hoisted the first seagoing American flag.

1948   The first female U.S. Army officer not in the medical corps was sworn in. (See May 14th entry.)

1960   *Camelot* opened on Broadway.

1979   Christie's auctioned a thimble for $18,400.

On this day in 1775, Lieutenant John Paul Jones raised the American flag aboard the flagship of the newly-formed Continental Navy, the Alfred. The banner he proudly flew bore thirteen stripes and the British Union Jack in place of the familiar stars. It was called the Grand Union flag.

The Kennedy era of the early 1960s has frequently been dubbed Camelot: a reference to the impossible happiness that allegedly existed during King Arthur's reign in England. The legendary bliss experienced by Arthur and his court was portrayed in the Broadway musical by the same name that opened on this very day in 1960 at the Majestic Theater.

You might be interested to know that on this day, Christie's auction house in New York City set a record, selling a thimble for $18,400. It was the highest price ever paid for a thimble. Sew what? Could it be, as Ben Franklin said, that "A stitch in time sames nine," or as he also observed, "a fool and his money are soon parted."

4th.

1619   The first Thanksgiving celebration took place in America.

1674   French Jesuit missionary Jacques Marquette erected a mission on the shores of Lake Michigan. (See August 10th entry.)

1783   General George Washington bade farewell to his officers at Fraunces Tavern in New York City. (See February 22nd and July 3rd entries.)

1877   The phonograph was invented.

1942   President Franklin D. Roosevelt ordered the dismantling of the Works Progress Administration (WPA). (See January 30th and November 8th entries.)

When we think of Thanksgiving, visions of the Pilgrims sitting down to a groaning board of food come to mind. But the Pilgrims weren't even at the first American Thanksgiving. That historic event occurred on this day in 1619, at Berkeley Plantation in Virginia—a year before the Pilgrims landed in Massachusetts.

In 1877, on the night of December 4, some of Thomas A. Edison's co-workers sat up until the wee dawn hours in his New Jersey laboratory at Menlo Park. They were playing with a new device that had just been completed—the phonograph. Edison and his assistants weren't really playing; they were recording and testing their presentation for a public demonstration that was held a few days later. However, history does not record how early in the game they had trouble with a needle stuck in a groove.

5th.

1776   Phi Beta Kappa was organized. (See February 6th entry.)

1839   General George Armstrong Custer was born. (See June 25th entry.)

1901   Walt Disney was born.

1906   Otto Preminger was born.

1933   The Twenty-first Amendment, which repealed the Eighteenth Amendment, was passed by the U.S. Congress. (See January 16th entry.)

Today is Walt Disney's birthday. In 1901, the man who introduced Mickey Mouse and Donald Duck and Sneezy and Dopey and Goofy to the world was born in Chicago, Illinois. Disney's contributions went a lot deeper than his talents as an animator. Did you ever hear the song, "Who's Afraid of the Big Bad Wolf?" That came to us courtesy of Walt Disney, who also created a park just south of Los Angeles where parents and children could have fun living out their fantasies of frontier life, exploring fairy tale castles, and touring snow-capped alpine mountains.

Even though today is Otto Preminger's birthday, we should avoid making a spectacle of ourselves. Preminger, who was born in Austria in 1906, was known for making spectacles. His megabudget films such as *Exodus* were not as controversial as his cold, hard studies of very real social problems such as drug addiction which he confronted in *The Man with the Golden Arm*; racism which he attacked in *Hurry Sundown*; and rape which he admonished in *Anatomy of a Murder*. It is sometimes said that movies are larger than life. But in Preminger's case, his films showed us how large and sometimes difficult life really is.

6th.

The feast day of St. Nicholas.

1886 Joyce Kilmer was born.

1973 Gerald R. Ford was appointed Vice President. (See July 14th entry.)

Today is the feast of St. Nicholas, patron saint of children and sailors. In many parts of the world, this day is considered a pleasant prelude to the Christmas season. St. Nicholas was a bishop who lived in Asia Minor during the fourth century; who has become the worldwide personification of kindness and good will. Stories of his legendary deeds grew over the years until he became a sleigh-riding, jolly gentleman named Santa Claus.

"I think that I shall never see / a poem lovely as a tree" was a sentiment written by a poet born on this day in 1886. Joyce Kilmer wrote that immortal contemplation while serving as a soldier during the First World War. Even though his life was cut short by the violence of war, Kilmer's spirit lived on in his simple, yet poignant poem about the joys of nature.

7th.

1787   Delaware became the first state to ratify the U.S. Constitution. (Delaware Day)

1917   The U.S. declared war on Austro-Hungary. (See April 6th entry.)

1941   Japanese air forces attacked the U.S. naval base at Pearl Harbor, Hawaii.

1944   The U.S. formally announced that all six Japanese aircraft carriers involved in the attack on Pearl Harbor were sunk.

Are you aware that today is Delaware Day? Outside of Delaware, that is. On this day in 1787, Delaware became the first state to approve the contents of the U.S. Constitution.

On the morning of this day in 1941, the Japanese Navy launched a sneak attack from the air over the U.S. Naval Base at Pearl Harbor, Hawaii. An oil embargo had been imposed on Japan by numerous nations—including the U.S.—because of their aggressive actions in China and Manchuria. That sanction provoked a conflict; and broke a peaceful trading agreement between the Americans and Japanese. When the war ended, Americans and Japanese worked together to resume their previously close relationship.

For every action, there is a reaction, as a pair of anniversaries which occurred on this day will prove. In 1941, Japanese air forces launched an attack on the U.S. naval base at Pearl Harbor, Hawaii. In 1944, America formally announced that all six Japanese aircraft carriers involved in that raid were sunk.

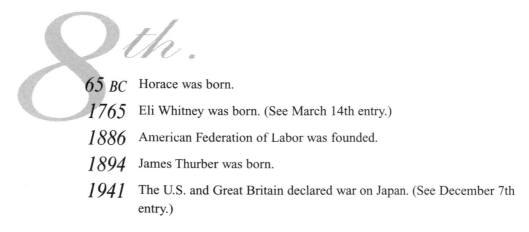

8th.

65 BC   Horace was born.

1765   Eli Whitney was born. (See March 14th entry.)

1886   American Federation of Labor was founded.

1894   James Thurber was born.

1941   The U.S. and Great Britain declared war on Japan. (See December 7th entry.)

On this day in 1886, an assembly of labor union leaders met in Columbus, Ohio, and organized the American Federation of Labor. It wasn't the first collaboration of labor unions, but it proved to be the one that worked for many generations. There has been much dispute about union power. But there is no disputing that, before unionism gained its strength, the lot of the average working person was a good deal harder. History is a sort of pendulum; when it swings too far in one direction, it eventually swings back in the other direction; ultimately it reached its own gentle balance. The AF of L has been part of that delicate balance for a long time.

The great Roman poet Horace was born in Venusia in the Roman Empire on this day in 65 BC. For many generations, Latin students struggled through Horace's writings. There is one Latin phrase that seems most appropriate even in these modern times: "Brevis esse laboro, obscurus fio." Translation: "It is when I am struggling to be brief that I become unintelligible."

Writer and cartoonist James Thurber had a lot in common with his fictional characters like Walter Mitty. Born in 1894, Thurber lived a mild-mannered childhood in Columbus, Ohio, until he lost one eye in a bow-and-arrow accident. This twist of fate kept him from pursuing a life of wild adventure, but it encouraged him to spend more time observing the mechanized, automated, modern world emerging around him. His cynical wit graced the pages of *The New Yorker*. As Thurber once wrote: "Open most heads and you will find nothing shining, not even a mind." He aimed his critical pen at the war between the sexes, the fate of the average man caught in the bureaucratic whirlwind, and the far more intellectual life of dogs.

9th.

1608   John Milton was born.

1621   The first sermon was delivered in New England.

1793   Noah Webster established New York City's first daily newspaper, *The American Minerva*.

1884   Ball-bearing roller skates were patented.

John Milton was born in London on this day in 1608. This great British poet was the author of the lines: "Peace hath her victories, no less renowned than war." He also wrote, "Give me the liberty to know, to utter, and to argue freely according to conscience, above all liberties." Although one should also heed the warnings posted by another event that occurred on this day. In 1621, the first sermon in New England was delivered at Plymouth, Massachusetts. Preacher Robert Cushman's topic for that day, was "The Sin and Danger of Self-Love."

When Noah Webster established Manhattan's first daily newspaper, *The American Minerva*, in 1793, he started a media ball rolling in that city. Newspapers have come and gone, but the news and the media's delivery of it never stop. It's like the U.S. patent which Levant M. Richardson received on this day in 1884. Richardson's invention—ball-bearing roller skates—have rolled through the generations.

10th.

The Nobel Prizes are awarded in Oslo, Norway. (See October 21st entry.)

1719 The first recorded sighting of the Aurora Borealis took place in New England.

1869 Wyoming became the first state to adopt women's suffrage.

1936 Great Britain's Duke of York became King George VI when his brother, Edward VIII, abdicated. (See June 23rd entry.)

1948 The United Nations adopted the Declaration of Human Rights.

Today is United Nations Human Rights Day which commemorates the adoption of the United Nations Declaration of Human Rights in 1948. Among other things, that Declaration says that "All human beings are born free and equal in dignity and rights . . . Everyone has the right to freedom of thought . . . Everyone has the right to freedom of opinion and expression."

On this day in 1869, a great victory was won for western women. The Territory of Wyoming became the first government to adopt women's suffrage, giving both genders the right to vote. Out in the Wild West where men were men, Wyoming was a half century ahead of the rest of the world in giving women equal rights.

On this day in 1936, Great Britain's King Edward VIII abdicated his throne to marry the American divorcée Wallis Warfield Simpson. According to media reports, the marriage appeared to be made of the stuff of fairy tales. The handsome king married the commoner whom he loved and lived happily ever after in the lap of opulent luxury. Because of this unprecedented act, his brother was enthroned as King George VI, the father of Queen Elizabeth II. Romantic fairy tales don't usually happen in real life—they are the stuff of fiction. But it took the world and the media another half century to discover this sad truth when the fairy-tale marriages of Elizabeth's sons, Prince Charles and Prince Andrew, both ended in divorce.

In 1719, an awesome sight appeared in the nighttime skies over New England. This natural wonder regularly occurs throughout the northern hemisphere, but it was on this day that the first New England sighting of the spectacular Aurora Borealis was recorded for posterity. According to ancient legends, the Great Northern Lights are said to be the spirits of gods or ancestors; and children conceived under this brilliant nocturnal display are supposedly blessed with remarkable talents. Modern science has told us that the Aurora Borealis is actually a phenomenon created by light refraction. But that's not as exciting or inspiring as the stories told by the people who have witnessed the dancing lights on dark winter nights.

11th.

1620 One hundred and three Pilgrims land at Plymouth Rock. (See July 22nd and September 6th entries.)

1844 Nitrous oxide was first used in dentistry. (See September 30th entry.)

1888 The French Panama Canal company failed. (See August 15th entry.)

1918 Alexander Solzhenitsyn was born.

1919 A monument to the boll weevil was erected in Enterprise, Alabama.

1929 Plans for a dirigible mooring tower on the Empire State Building were unveiled.

1946 The United Nations International Children's Emergency Fund (UNICEF) was established. (See December 10th entry.)

1996 Shipping tycoon Tung Chee-hwa was elected as the first post-colonial leader of Hong Kong. (See September 19th and December 19th entries.)

Today is Alexander Solzhenitsyn's birthday. Born in 1918 in Rostov, Russia, Solzhenitsyn grew up to become an eloquent author and human rights' advocate in the midst of an inhuman Soviet system. His talents won him government persecution and a place in the Siberian labor camps. But Solzhenitsyn proved that one true voice raised in protest can become a chorus. Words can be a mighty weapon.

In 1929, the Empire State Building was a long way from completion when an announcement was made on this day. The building's sponsors unveiled their plans to top the skyscraper with a mooring tower, because it seemed likely that there would be regular worldwide zeppelin service in the near future. One zeppelin did actually tie up briefly, but the tower's major effect was that it gave the building a good deal more height—and another observation deck.

Trips to the dentist became a lot less painful, and much safer, on this day in 1844, when nitrous oxide—laughing gas—was first used in a dental procedure in Hartford, Connecticut. It gradually replaced more dangerous anesthetics such as ether, and was certainly better than nothing, which was also not uncommon at the time.

It may seem strange to erect a monument to a foe, but one such statue has stood as a curiosity in the middle of Enterprise, Alabama, since it was dedicated on this day in 1919. In the land of cotton, the boll weevil feeds on the farmers' main cash crop, burrowing into the cotton bolls and laying its eggs. There's an old saying: Keep your friends close, but keep your enemies closer.

12th.

1800   Washington, DC, was established as the capital of the United States. (See March 29th entry.)

1899   The golf tee was patented.

1913   The *Mona Lisa* was recovered.

1915   Frank Sinatra was born. (See December 30th entry.)

1953   Chuck Yeager reached Mach 2.43 in a Bell X-1A rocket plane. (See October 14th entry.)

1955   The Ford Foundation contributed $500 million to U.S. colleges and universities.

On this day in 1955, the Ford Foundation gave the largest philanthropic contribution package ever assembled: $500 million in funding for U.S. colleges and universities. Very few can donate so greatly to the human condition and some gifts have come in much smaller packages. There are unsung events in mankind's history, and one such occasion also occurred on this day. In 1899, a patent was issued to George F. Grant of Boston for a wooden golf tee.

What secrets lie behind the *Mona Lisa's* enigmatic smile? Certainly one is whether the real painting has been hanging in France or Italy since 1913. It was on this day that authorities in Florence, Italy, announced that they had recovered the *Mona Lisa*, which had been stolen from the Louvre in Paris in 1911. But at that time another *Mona Lisa* surfaced. It appeared to have been painted around the same time, and the two were virtually indistinguishable from one another. One was possibly painted by a student of Leonardo DaVinci, while the other was undoubtedly the work of the master himself. But which is which?

13th.

1577 Sir Francis Drake set out to sail the world.

1642 Abel Tasman discovered New Zealand.

1769 Dartmouth College was chartered.

1862 Robert E. Lee spoke a few wise words.

1928 George Gershwin's *An American in Paris* was publicly performed for the first time. (See September 26th entry.)

1978 The Susan B. Anthony dollar was issued. (See February 15th entry.)

When Moor's Indian Charity School was rechartered as Dartmouth College at about this time of year in 1769, its founder, Eleazar Wheelock, became the college's founding father. It's a fact duly celebrated in Dartmouth song and legend. Some years ago, there was a brouhaha over the fact that Dartmouth athletic teams were nicknamed the Indians. A few people complained that Dartmouth's teams weren't really Native Americans; and neither was the Dartmouth student body.

Contention and competition often spur the adrenaline and stimulate progress. But there can be a cost, especially when disagreement leads to war. Confederate General Robert E. Lee knew the price was high. And on this day, in 1862, he said, "It is well that war is so terrible, or we should grow too fond of it."

Isn't it fascinating how human beings as a species seem to be born with a nonmigratory wanderlust that's not evident in any other living creature? A few anniversaries that are marked on this day will prove this point. In 1577, the British explorer Sir Francis Drake set out to sail around the world. He was the first Englishman to attempt that daring feat. In 1642, the Dutch navigator Abel Tasman discovered New Zealand in the relatively uncharted waters of the southern hemisphere. In 1928, American composer George Gershwin completed his symphonic narration of his European travel experiences. He gave *An American in Paris* its first public performance on this day.

14th.

1503 Nostradamus was born.

1911 Roald Amundsen reached the South Pole. (See May 9th and January 18th entries.)

Back in 1911, the Norwegian explorer Roald Amundsen became the first human being—as far as we know—to reach the South Pole. It was the ultimate gesture in getting to the bottom of things.

On December 14, 1503, Michel de Notredame was born in the Provence region of France. He became a physician and astrologer, enjoying the financial support of the powerful Medici family. He was personal adviser to Catherine de Medici and her husband King Henry II of France. Nostradamus became well known for his books on medical astrology, but his fame came from a different source. He wrote down hundreds of visions in the form of short poems that came to him about future events. The volume was called *Centuries*. These alleged prophecies are still being analyzed in modern times because many people believe that much of what he dreamt has come true.

15th.

37 AD Nero was born. (See July 18th entry.)

1939 The motion picture *Gone With the Wind* premiered in Atlanta. (See June 30th entry.)

1986 Carnegie Hall reopened.

On any list of bad kings, Nero's name is pretty prominent. The emperor who fiddled while Rome burned was born in Antium on this day in 37 AD. Four years after Rome's slums went up in flames, Nero went down in disgrace and was branded by the Senate as a public enemy. He committed suicide—which may have been the only thing he really did well.

Rome may have gone up in flames in a day with Nero as its emporer. But he shares his birthday with the anniversary of the rebirth of house that every fiddle player—or rather classical musician—aspires to. New York's Carnegie Hall opened in 1891, and quickly became a living monument to music. Carnegie Hall's $50 million renovation, which was completed in 1986, ensured that it will stand proud as it enters another century.

16th.

1770 Ludwig van Beethoven was born.

1773 Boston Tea Party took place.

1899 Noel Coward was born.

1917 Arthur C. Clarke was born.

1944 Battle of the Bulge began.

We meet here today on the anniversary of history's most memorable tea party. In 1773, The Boston Tea Party took place in Boston Harbor. The incident was staged as a protest against British taxation. It was a picturesque demonstration, but we had to do a good bit more to get rid of British taxation in this country.

The real Battle of the Bulge began on this day in 1944, when German forces launched a counterattack against the U.S. 101st Airborne Division lead by Major General Anthony McAuliffe in Bastogne, Belgium. The incident created a dangerous bulge in the battle line. And stubborn courage was the weapon that ultimately stopped the German threat.

German composer Ludwig van Beethoven was probably born on this day, in 1770. It has been said that what Shakespeare was to drama, Beethoven was to music. The composer himself said that "true art is selfish and perverse—it will not submit to the mold of flattery." There is an old tradition that the show must go on. It goes back for many generations. But Noel Coward—who was also born on this day in 1899, in Teddington, England—once wrote a song entitled "Why Must the Show Go On?" He pointed out that if one packed up one's talent, there were plenty more artists to step into the breach. Yet very few have the artistic talent to become true legends as these two composers did within their own lifetimes.

A modern-day visionary was born on this day in 1917. When author Arthur C. Clarke was a child, he made his own telescope so he could observe the stars. His fascination grew, and even though he couldn't afford to get a university education, he was honored with a membership in the British Interplanetary Society—a select group of astronomers who kept their well-trained eyes on the skies. During the Second World War, Clarke joined the R.A.F. so he could get a closer look at the world above us. And in 1945, he wrote his first science-fiction story which predicted in amazing detail the transmittal of television and radio signals via satellite. Readers thought Clarke was a little outlandish in his description. But twenty years later, when the first Early Bird satellites were launched, they realized his ideas weren't so farfetched after all. According to Clarke's Third Law, which was stated in his book *Profiles of the Future: An Inquiry into the Limits of the Possible*: "Any sufficiently advanced technology is indistinguishable from magic." The scientific world began consulting with this teller of tales from our not-so-distant future on other projects like the *Apollo 11*, *Apollo 12*, and *Apollo 15* space missions which Clarke broadcasted with Walter Cronkite.

17th.

1777 France recognized the United States' independence. (See January 27th and March 6th entries.)

1894 Arthur Fiedler was born.

1903 Wilbur and Orville Wright made their first airplane flight.

1929   William Safire was born.

1969   The U.S. Air Force closed Project Blue Book. (See June 24th, July 2nd, and October 26th entries.)

1991   The most lopsided game in NBA history: Cleveland beat Miami 148 to 80.

This is an auspicious day for flights of fancy and for airy promises. That's because today marks the anniversary of the Wright brothers' historic first flight at Kitty Hawk, North Carolina. We first learned on this day, how to take off into the wild blue yonder in a flying machine. Wilbur and Orville Wright's flights were short and not too lofty. But their efforts allowed their successors to reach for the moon.

Today is a great day for communication. This is the birthday of two great communicators. One is William Safire, the renowned columnist and defender of the English language. The other is Arthur Fiedler, the legendary conductor of the Boston Pops who reached millions through his music.

We are faced with such a great opportunity for success today that we should remember a basketball game that took place on this very day in 1991. Cleveland beat Miami 148 to 80. It was one of the most lopsided victories in the history of basketball.

18th.

1890   Edwin Armstrong was born.

1947   Steven Spielberg was born.

1957   The first commercial nuclear power plant in America was placed in operation.

1958   The first communications satellite broadcast was made.

Edwin Armstrong, who was born on this day in 1890, created FM—or frequency modulation—which eliminated radio static. And on this day in 1958, a voice from outer space was heard over radios worldwide. It was a very human voice that had been sent from earth out into space. It was then transmitted back to this planet via a communications satellite. The voice belonged to President Dwight D. Eisenhower, who delivered a Christmas message to every one on the planet.

America's first commercial nuclear power plant began supplying electricity on this day. In 1957, the town of Shippingport, Pennsylvania, got turned on to nuclear-generated electricity. It had taken two years to successfully develop the lessons learned from setting up the first atomic-powered electrical plant in Arco, Idaho, to establishing this form of power-generator as a commercial venture.

The Christmas season seems to bring out the child in all of us—young and old alike. Perhaps that is one of the reasons why we find Steven Spielberg's films so appealing. Born on this day in 1947, Spielberg has generously shared his childhood visions of extraterrestrials, gremlins, and dinosaurs with us on the big screen. He's retold the heroic myths and adventures we read as children with characters like Indiana Jones.

19th.

1547   Great Britain passed a vagabond law.

1776   Thomas Paine published "The American Crisis."

1777   The Continental Army went to their winter quarters at Valley Forge.

1843   *A Christmas Carol* was first published.

1871   Corrugated paper was patented by Albert L. Jones of New York.

1984   Great Britain and China signed an accord to return Hong Kong to China in 1997. (See September 19th entry.)

"These are the times that try men's souls." Thomas Paine published those words on this day in 1776, in the first of his essays on "The American Crisis" which appeared in *The Pennsylvania Journal*. Paine also wrote, "The summer soldier and the sunshine patriot will, in this crisis, shrink from the service of his country; but he that stands it now, deserves the love and thanks of man and woman." And he added, "Those who expect to reap the blessings of freedom, must, like men, undergo the fatigue of supporting it." It was a state which the men who experienced another event that occurred on this day in 1777 knew all too well. That was when General George Washington led the Continental Army into their winter quarters at Valley Forge, Pennsylvania. According to historical records, Valley Forge was not exactly a winter vacation resort. But each of them know that they and their successors would reap the blessings promised by Thomas Paine the year before.

Back in 1547, homeless vagabonds were considered a source of embarrassment which "soiled the nation's social fabric" in the British government's eyes. So to stem this rising tide, Parliament passed a law which decreed that vagabonds who refused to return to their hometowns and find gainful employment would be publicly whipped. Second-count offenders would be whipped and branded with a "V." Third-time offenders would be enslaved for two years. Chronic homelessness was punishable by death before this day, so this new, stringent law seemed lenient to the many dispossessed peasants who had lost their lands in tax foreclosures.

On this day in 1843, a Christmas tradition was born. Tiny Tim and Bob Crachit came to life when Charles Dickens published his delightful tale of miser Ebenezer Scrooge's Christmas epiphany entitled, *A Christmas Carol*. Believe it or not, the story was partially based on personal experience. Dickens didn't encounter the Spirit of Christmas Past, but he did see the poverty, work houses, and child labor. His own father, unable to support eight children, was sent to debtors' prison. But what was Dickens' primary motivation in writing this classic Christmas work? His wife was pregnant, and he needed money. Like many of history's immortals, Dickens clearly thrived under pressure.

It may interest you to know that corrugated paper was patented by Albert L. Jones of New York, on this day in 1871. Corrugated paper, often called cardboard, became packing material, boxes, moulds for pouring concrete, and many other things. Uses are still being discovered. Long used for improvised shelter by the homeless, and play-housing by kids, the United Nations now uses it to construct emergency housing that is light and portable enough to be delivered to disaster areas at a moment's notice. It is also used by designers in the U.S. and Europe to make high-concept—and very expensive—modern furniture.

20th.

1803 New Orleans first flew the American flag.

1880 Electric lights were installed on Broadway.

1892 The pneumatic tire was patented.

1922 The Union of Soviet Socialist Republics was formed. (See December 21st entry.)

This is the day when, back in 1892, the pneumatic tire was patented. It demonstrated that an air-filled hollow surface could provide support for a heavy vehicle. A lot more people appreciated this great invention when we took to the thousands of miles of interstate highways and discovered the joys of a cushioned ride.

In 1880, the electric lights went on throughout Broadway's theater section for the first time on this day. We do a great many more things with electric lights today. Light, we have found, is not simply a source of illumination. It also has a cutting edge and can burn and even obscure. If you shine a light that's very bright, it can have a blinding effect. Many aspiring actors and actresses learned this harsh lesson, trying to make it big in the theater. In fact, it wasn't long after the lights went up on Broadway that a familiar saying was coined: "There's a broken heart for every light on Broadway."

In 1803, on this day, the city of New Orleans flew the American flag for the first time. This simple act signaled a transfer of ownership as the Louisiana Territory was handed over to the United States who had purchased it from France. Another transfer of ownership occurred in 1922, when fourteen eastern European republics merged to form the Union of Soviet Socialist Republics.

21st.

1898 Radium was discovered by Marie and Pierre Curie. (See November 7th entry.)

1923 Nepal gained independence from Great Britain.

1937 *Snow White and the Seven Dwarfs* premiered.

1954 Dr Sam Sheppard's wife Marilyn was murdered.

1991 Eleven Soviet republics proclaimed the birth of the Commonwealth of Independent States, and the end of the U.S.S.R. (See December 20th entry.)

Back in 1937, Walt Disney premiered the animated cartoon feature film, *Snow White and the Seven Dwarfs*. Even thought it was based on the famous fairy tale by the Brothers Grimm, Disney had added some of his own touches to his production. The Brothers Grimm had never given the seven dwarfs individual names, but Disney certainly did. Doc and Happy and Grumpy and Sneezy and Sleepy and Bashful and Dopey were all cartoon profiles of human nature. It's hard to imagine that other names and caricatures were ever considered, but they were. Wheezy, Puffy, Baldy, Jumpy, Gabby, Nifty, Stumpy, Stuffy, and Biggo-Ego, were just a few of the characters that didn't measure up.

If irony is humor, then politics creates the most sublime comedies. On this day in 1923, the ancient nation of Nepal, with a history of independent government and complex culture dating back thousands of years, ceased to be a British protectorate when it was granted independence from England—a far younger country. The real irony, however, is that it took its southern neighbor India another twenty-three years to make the same change.

It's easy to portray history as tightly woven strings of facts. But all too often it is more holes than cloth. This is the anniversary of one of the most celebrated mysteries of the second half of the twentieth century. It was on this day in 1954 that Dr. Sam Sheppard's wife was murdered. You might not recognize his name immediately, but the television series and the movie versions of *The Fugitive* were based on his story. Did he kill his wife, or was the murderer a one armed man as he said? The doctor was tried and convicted. He escaped to search for the killer, but he was recaptured. No one armed man was ever linked to his wife's murder, and the case remains unsolved.

22nd.

Winter solstice.

1775 Esek Hopkins took command of the Continental Navy.

1894 The U.S. Golf Association was founded. (See December 12th entry.)

1944 Germans demanded the surrender of American troops at Bastogne, Belgium.

On this day in 1775, a new naval fighting force came into being as Esek Hopkins took command of the Continental Navy. Esek Hopkins himself turned out to be a controversial figure, and was suspended from command early in 1777. However, when Hopkins took his commission on this day, the military fleet consisted of seven ships.

Brigadier General Anthony C. McAuliffe gave a memorable reply on this date in 1944. The German army, surrounding the American troops defending Bastogne, Belgium, demanded that the Americans surrender. He didn't negotiate. He didn't capitulate. His reply was, "Nuts!" And he went on fighting the Battle of the Bulge. He won in the end.

The winter solstice, which usually occurs on this date marks the shortest day of the year in the northern hemisphere. The further north of the equator you are, the longer your summer days are. In Alaska, the midnight sun makes sleep nearly impossible in late June. But people don't seem to mind. Long days are a perfect time to get everything done and still have time left over for a midnight softball game—without electric lights. The winter solstice is the price we pay for those long summer days. The winter solstice also heralded the beginning of the month-long Saturnalia festivities in ancient Rome— pagan rituals and unrestrained merrymaking honoring Saturn, the father of Jupiter, and god of agriculture. He was said to have ruled the earth during a time of peace, happiness, and virtue before being deposed by his son. Many of these rituals carried over into Christianity to form Christmas.

23rd.

1788   Maryland donated land for the creation of the District of Columbia.

1823   "A Visit from St. Nicholas" was first published.

1947   The transistor was invented.

Today marks the anniversary of the invention of the transistor. On this day in 1947, John Bardeen, Walter H. Brattain, and William Shockley saw the fruition of their research at the Bell Telephone Laboratories in New Jersey. The transistor's inventors won the Nobel Prize for their discovery, which not only made equipment miniaturization possible, it ushered in a tidal wave of electronic miracles including the personal computer.

In 1788, on this day, the state of Maryland gave ten square miles of its territory to the United States for the establishment of a national capital city. The U.S. Congress finally got around to voting on the issue of what to do with this gift in 1790. The pace of government in those days was rather leisurely. But times have changed; government has become just about our largest growth industry. Since government is generally a process of talking things over, talk seems to have become a very large growth industry. One should keep in mind poet James Russell Lowell's advice: "No, never say nothin' without you're compelled tu, / An' then don't say nothin' that you can be held tu."

On this day in 1823, Clement Clarke Moore's "A Visit from St. Nicholas" was first published. For those of you who don't recognize it by its title, it begins: "Twas the night before Christmas / And all through the house . . ." This simple poem, which appeared in the *Troy Sentinel* newspaper reminds us that as we grow and mature we oftentimes forget the exuberance, the innocence, the joy we experienced in childhood. We replace enthusiasm with serious, often harsh logic rather than inspiring ourselves and others to wish and to dream.

24th.

Christmas Eve.

1515 Thomas Wolsey became Chancellor of England.

1902 Andrew Carnegie became the Laird of Pitton Green.

1905 Howard Hughes was born.

A butcher's son became the Chancellor of England on Christmas Eve. In 1515, Thomas Wolsey was appointed by King Henry VIII to this high political position. Wolsey had advanced his station before this date. At fifteen years of age, he was an Oxford graduate, and quickly became the vicar of two parishes. Wolsey's reputation as a hard worker preceded him throughout his life. Within a few years, he was promoted to archbishop of York. Known for putting in twelve hours a day, Wolsey not only impressed his king, he proved that even a poor man's son can rise to greatness if he's willing to work. Persistence pays. An aside about Thomas Wolsey: As archbishop, he built a magnificent palace outside London. He had a great passion for architecture and soon, word spread that his palace was more impressive than the king's. Henry came to see for himself. Apparently he agreed, because shortly after his visit, he moved Wolsey out and moved in himself.

On Christmas Eve in 1905, an enigma was born in Houston, Texas. During his life, Howard Hughes' personal activities and professional practices raised many unanswered questions. Howard Hughes managed to avoid the public throughout most of his life. The tangle that he left as his legacy proved once again that real life has a more complex plot than any fictional work.

As an impoverished child, Andrew Carnegie grew up across the street from the Pitton Estates which had a beautiful park that was open to the neighborhood children and families for their enjoyment on Sunday afternoons. But Carnegie wasn't allowed to enter the park because his uncle, Tom Morrison, had been publicly harassing important local and national politicians including the Laird of Pitton Green. On Christmas Eve in 1902, Andrew Carnegie—the world's richest man—became the Laird of Pitton Green. He purchased the estate and permanently opened the park for the enjoyment of all children.

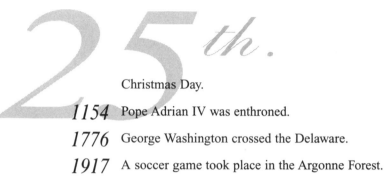

Christmas Day.

1154   Pope Adrian IV was enthroned.

1776   George Washington crossed the Delaware.

1917   A soccer game took place in the Argonne Forest.

Some of you feel Christmas was created by department-store owners and advertising agencies. But the truth is that this gift-giving holiday has been celebrated throughout the world for a long, long time. The early Christians celebrated the first Christmas in Rome back in 336 AD. It was the perfect counter-balance to the week-long pagan celebration of Saturnalia, a Roman festival that was highlighted by merrymaking and gift-giving. The ancient Persians celebrated this very day as the birthday of their mystery god, Mithra, who was also represented as the Sun of Righteousness. During this same time, the Celts and Teutons celebrated their Yule rites by decorating their homes with greenery and lights and sending gifts and greetings to family and friends. Traditions are hard to break.

It was on Christmas night, back in 1776, that George Washington led his troops across the Delaware River to attack the British the next day in New Jersey. Another incident occurred many years later on another battlefield with completely different consequences. On Christmas Day during the First World War, German soldiers from one side and British, Scottish, Canadian, and American soldiers on the other—men who had spent months shooting at each other from muddy trenches—rose from their foxholes in the Argonne Forest. And on this day in 1917, the two sides met each other face to face and played soccer. For that short moment, each person became involved in the spirit of camaraderie under strained circumstances to celebrate a common bond—the bond of Christian fellowship.

An English cardinal made history on Christmas Day. In 1154, Cardinal Nicholas Breakspear of Albano was enthroned as Pope Adrian IV. He was history's only British pope. While the English monarchy continued its long battle with the Vatican over the supremacy of state over church, the accession of this "by-the-book" cardinal seemed a most auspicious decision by the Church. Ironically, it was Pope Adrian IV who officially sanctioned King Henry II's invasion of Ireland five years later.

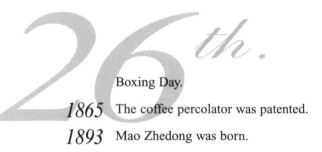

Boxing Day.

1865 The coffee percolator was patented.

1893 Mao Zhedong was born.

Today is Mao Zhedong's birthday. Born in Hunan province of northern China in 1893, Mao became a sort of prophet to his people. Even more than the thoughts of Lenin, the sayings of Chairman Mao—collected in Mao's Little Red Book—have been extensively quoted in the Communist world. Though much of the book is pure Communist manifesto, there are also ideals expressed which echo our own concepts of democracy. Mao wrote: "Our point of departure is to serve the people whole-heartedly and never for a moment divorce ourselves from the masses, to proceed in all cases from the interests of the people and not from one's self-interest . . ."

In Great Britain and Canada, today is known as Boxing Day. The story goes that this is the day when presents are given in boxes to the postal carrier, the gardener, the family doctor, and so forth. Other versions of the story tell a tall tale of neatness. This is the day when all good British throw away their boxes or return gifts. Nevertheless, it is nice to know that the spirit of giving or receiving need not end on Christmas Day. It's also a great idea to have a day devoted to recovering from the Christmas excesses.

This is the anniversary of a true eye opener. Mr. James Nason of Franklin, Massachusetts was granted a patent for his invention—the coffee percolator—on this day in 1865. One can only wonder how many sleepless nights he spent perfecting his creation, until he had sufficient grounds to file for his patent without finding himself in hot water or accused of being just another drip.

27th.

1657 Flushing Remonstrance was issued.

1822 Louis Pasteur was born. (See July 6th entry.)

1903 The song "Sweet Adeline" was first publicly performed.

In 1657, Peter Stuyvesant was the governor of New Amsterdam. And as governor of this fledgling Dutch colony, Stuyvesant ordered the people of Flushing, Long Island, not to extend their hospitality to Quakers. On this day, the people of Flushing sent a petition to the governor known as The Flushing Remonstrance, which stated: "we are bounde by the law of God and men to doe goode until all men and evil to noe one."

Louis Pasteur—who was born on this day in 1822, in Dole, France—discovered that diseases can be produced by various bacteria. This remarkable discovery laid the groundwork for future research in the areas of antisepsis, sterilization, and the prevention of infection. Pasteur also lent his name to the purification process he discovered while trying to make milk safe to drink—pasteurization.

The first public performance of the song "Sweet Adeline" took place on this very day in 1903, in New York City. "Sweet Adeline" has been the flower in the hearts of every barbershop quartet ever since.

28th.

1856 President Woodrow Wilson was born. (See September 26th entry.)

1869 Chewing gum was patented.

1917 H.L. Mencken published the great bathtub hoax. (See September 12th entry.)

Today marks the anniversary of a major addition to the American lifestyle. On this day, in 1869, William F. Semple of Mount Vernon, Ohio, received a patent for chewing gum.

We had various kinds of gums before then, but Mr. Semple's patent covered "the combination of rubber with other articles" for "an acceptable chewing gum."

Back on December 28, 1917, H.L. Mencken published an article in *The New York Evening Mail* describing the origin of the great American bathtub. He narrated how it was first installed in a Cincinati mansion by Adam Thompson, in 1842; and how various cities and states passed laws to regulate or tax it. The article was a pure hoax. Mencken never intended it to be taken seriously, but it was. To this day, you can probably find articles relaying as fact the items of Mencken's imagination.

29th.

1170 Archbishop of Canterbury Thomas á Becket was assassinated in his cathedral.

1800 Charles Goodyear was born. (See January 16th entry.)

1845 Texas became a state.

1890 The Battle of Wounded Knee took place. (See February 27th and May 8th entries.)

1989 Vaclav Havel was elected president of the Czech Republic by the nation's Federal assembly. (See February 21st entry.)

History books tell us that on this day in 1845, Texas joined the United States as its twenty-eighth state. Considering the size, riches, and political wiliness of the Lone Star State, people have reversed the phrase from time to time, and said that the U.S. joined Texas. In any case, the combination proved to be a rewarding and stimulating one.

The Battle of Wounded Knee occurred on this day, in 1890. When it was over, twenty-five U.S. cavalrymen were dead, and so were about one hundred and fifty Native American men, women, and children. It took years for the battle to be more aptly described as a massacre. This was the last major engagement between Native Americans and the U.S. Army. It aroused the conscience of Americans then and even more so years later.

A close friendship ended in murder on this date in history. In 1170, the Archbishop of Canterbury, Thomas á Becket, was murdered in his cathedral during vespers by four barons of King Henry II's court. The king and the archbishop had been close friends until Henry made Becket—who was his chancellor at the time—into an archbishop. Henry had hoped to settle the battle between church and state by stacking the odds in his favor. What Henry hadn't calculated was that Becket would take his new duties very seriously. The questions of jurisdiction over a crime allegedly committed by a priest divided these two friends; and in an emotional outburst, the king vented his anger over dinner with his barons. The rest of the story became the stuff of legend.

Today is the day in 1800, when Charles Goodyear was born. Goodyear developed and patented a process called vulcanization which rendered India rubber less sticky and able to withstand temperature extremes. Despite this revolutionary achievement, he died penniless. Much of his life was spent in poverty, with one failed attempt after another to prevent rubber from melting in summer weather—which made it useless for boots, or most any other purpose. When—by happy accident—a piece of sulphurized rubber came in contact with a hot stove he discovered the answer he'd been seeking. But opportunists descended like vultures on his ideas. He held a pile of patents, and nearly all were infringed upon. At one point he even employed Daniel Webster to represent him in a lawsuit. But Goodyear was an inventor, not a businessman. When he showed his wealthy brother-in-law that rubberized thread could be used to make ruffled-front shirts, which were in fashion at the time, his brother erected two factories. Goodyear could have become a wealthy man, but he pulled out of the business to return to finding new uses for rubber—despite the fact that he was about the only person who wasn't reaping hand-over-fist profits from his work. He was incarcerated in the U.S. and France for his debts. He even received the Cross of the Legion of Honor from Emperor Napoleon III for his inventions, in a Paris debtors' prison. But he wasn't bitter. "Life," Goodyear wrote, "should not be estimated exclusively by the standard of dollars and cents. I am not disposed to complain that I have planted and others have gathered the fruits. A man has cause for regret only when he sows and no one reaps."

30th.

1853 The Gadsden Purchase was signed.

1942 Frank Sinatra began a singing engagement at the Paramount Theatre.

1948 *Kiss Me Kate* opened on Broadway.

On this day in 1853, James Gadsden signed an agreement with the Republic of Mexico to purchase the southern portion of Arizona and New Mexico for ten million dollars.

That was by no means America's biggest land purchase. There was the Louisiana Territory; there would be Alaska; and there would also be the Virgin Islands.

On December 30, 1948, William Shakespeare made it to Broadway with a little help from Cole Porter and Bella and Samuel Spewack. The immortal Shakespearean farce *The Taming of the Shrew* premiered at the New Century Theater under the title *Kiss Me Kate*. In 1948, this essentially antifeminist classic became a smash hit with Cole Porter's music.

Frank Sinatra began a singing engagement at the Paramount Theatre on this day in 1942. The New York City police reserves had to be called in to cope with the swooning, crushing, and enthusiastic screaming of the hordes of teenage girls who flocked to see and hear their idol.

31st.

New Year's Eve.

1879 Thomas Edison first demonstrated his electric incandescent light bulb to the public. (See October 21st entry.)

1946 President Harry S Truman officially proclaimed an end to the Second World War. (See May 2nd, May 8th, September 1st, and September 2nd entries.)

Here's to the brightest of all bright ideas. We've all seen light bulbs used to symbolize ideas, but did you know that Thomas Edison first demonstrated his most famous invention, the light bulb, to the public on this very day in 1879? It may seem miraculous and it may seem simple, but this glass globe with a filament in it took Edison over a thousand attempts before he found the right materials. Someone once asked him if he'd ever considered giving up. Edison replied, "Those were steps on the way. In each attempt I was successful in finding a way not to create a light bulb. I was always eager to learn, even from my mistakes."

For many cultures hostilities, anger, bitterness, and hurt are left behind with the passing year. This is the time to forgive, and to heal, so that the coming year can always be better than the past. In what is perhaps the most universal example of this, President Harry S Truman officially proclaimed an end to the hostilities of the Second World War on this very day in 1946.

Index